Making of

It is a critical commonplace to note sharp cultural differences between Elizabethan and Jacobean England. But how and why did this transition take place? What kinds of decisions and assumptions were involved as writers responded to the new king? How did residual Elizabethan expectations and habits of mind shape the English response to James I, and what were the consequences? How much control did James have over his reception? This study examines these questions in detail by exploring a wide range of texts written during the first decade of his reign in England, from 1603 to 1613. At stake in these questions are some larger issues which have been central to much recent historically oriented work on English Renaissance literature, concerning the relationships between king and culture, literature and authority. Curtis Perry's original study provokes a fresh examination of the contingencies shaping long-familiar notions of what constitutes the Jacobean as a literary period.

THE MAKING OF JACOBEAN CULTURE

THE MAKING OF
JACOBEAN CULTURE

James I and the renegotiation of Elizabethan literary practice

CURTIS PERRY

Arizona State University

CAMBRIDGE
UNIVERSITY PRESS

PUBLISHED BY THE PRESS SYNDICATE OF THE UNIVERSITY OF CAMBRIDGE
The Pitt Building, Trumpington Street, Cambridge CB2 1RP, United Kingdom

CAMBRIDGE UNIVERSITY PRESS
The Edinburgh Building, Cambridge CB2 2RU, United Kingdom
40 West 20th Street, New York, NY 10011–4211, USA
10 Stamford Road, Oakleigh, Melbourne 3166, Australia

First published 1997

Printed in the United Kingdom at the University Press, Cambridge

Typeset in Baskerville no. 2 11/12½ pt

A catalogue record for this book is available from the British Library

Library of Congress cataloguing in publication data

Perry, Curtis.
The making of Jacobean culture: James I and the renegotiation of
Elizabethan literary practice/Curtis Perry.
p.   cm.
Includes index.
ISBN 0 521 57406 4 (hardback)
1. English literature – Early modern, 1500–1700 – History and
criticism. 2. Politics and literature – Great Britain – History – 17th
century. 3. Literature and society – Great Britain – History – 17th
century. 4. James I, King of England, 1566–1625 – Views on
literature. 5. Elizabeth I, Queen of England, 1533–1603 – Views in
literature. 6. James I, King of England, 1566–1625 – In literature.
7. Great Britain – Civilization – 17th century. 8. Power (Social
sciences) in literature. 9. Kings and rulers in literature.
10. Monarchy in literature. I. Title.
PR438.P65P47 1997
820 .003 – DC21   96–49142   CIP

ISBN 0 521 57406 4 hardback

CP

Contents

List of illustrations	ix
Acknowledgments	xi
List of abbreviations	xiii
A note on texts	xiv

Introduction   1

PART ONE NEGOTIATIONS IN GENRE AND DECORUM

1.   Panegyric and the poet-king   15
     "The Stile of *Gods*"?   18
     Panegyric negotiations   25
     "What need hast thou of me? or of my *Muse?*"   36

2.   Arcadia re-formed: pastoral negotiations
     in early Jacobean England   50
     "Elizabethan" and "Jacobean" pastoral   53
     Two versions of pastoral in *The*
       Faithful Shepherdess   59
     Drayton's pastoral revisions and the
       Jacobean idea   67
     Daniel and the reformation of Arcadia   73

PART TWO STAGING JACOBEAN KINGCRAFT

3.   Theatre of counsel: royal vulnerability
     and early Jacobean political drama   83
     Philotas and the Jacobean crisis of counsel   85
     Ruling and dissimulation in *The Fawne*   93
     The crisis and Jonson's counsel: *Sejanus*   98
     "Kings are not safe whom any understand":
       Mustapha's well-meaning tyrant   106
     Tyrants and kings   111

4. Nourish-fathers and pelican daughters:
    kingship, gender, and bounty in _King Lear_
    and _Macbeth_   115
    Bounty, plenty, and the maternality of kingship   115
    King Lear and the failure of bounty   124
    Macbeth's "swelling act"   137
    "Mark, King of Scotland, mark": speculations
        on topical meaning   147

PART THREE STRUCTURES OF FEELING

5. The politics of nostalgia: Queen Elizabeth
    in early Jacobean England   153
    The King James version of Queen Elizabeth   155
    Old Elizabeth and the new royal family   165
    The citizens and their Queen   172
    Making opposition   184

6. Royal style and the civic elite in early
    Jacobean London   188
    London's elite and civic pride   188
    Royal performance and citizen style   191
    The Lord Mayor's pageant and the styles
        of civic pride   199
    Civic pride and social tension   210

Epilogue: warrant and obedience in
        Bartholomew Fair   218

Notes   230
Index   274

Illustrations

1. "Benignita" from Cesare Ripa, *Iconologia* (Rome, 1603). By permission of the Department of Printing and Graphic Arts, the Houghton Library, Harvard University.   117

2. Peter Paul Rubens, *Peace and War*. Reproduced by courtesy of the Trustees, the National Gallery, London.   118

3. "Embleme 31" from H. G., *The Mirrour of Majestie* (1618). By permission of the Department of Printing and Graphic Arts, the Houghton Library, Harvard University.   120

4. "Embleme 2" from H. G., *The Mirrour of Majestie* (1618). By permission of the Department of Printing and Graphic Arts, the Houghton Library, Harvard University.   122

Acknowledgments

This book began under the direction of Barbara Lewalski, who read it in earlier versions and offered countless useful suggestions. Her professionalism and ongoing support kept me convinced that there was a book in this when I might otherwise have despaired. Roland Greene also read earlier versions of these chapters with great care, and offered me encouragement mixed with helpful advice. It is a pleasure to record my debt to these two exemplary scholars, and to others who also read all or part of my manuscript in its various stages of disarray: Cedric Brown, Douglas Bruster, Jonathan Fortescue, David Hillman, Taylor Stoehr, and the members of Harvard University's Renaissance Doctoral Colloquium. Richard Dutton and an anonymous reader for Cambridge University Press not only gave my project the go-ahead, but offered a wealth of advice which helped shore up virtually every chapter of the finished book.

The project was supported, in its earliest stages, by a Mellon Fellowship and by an Arthur Lehman Scholarship awarded by Harvard's Graduate School of Arts and Sciences. The English Department at Arizona State University provided me with funds for a research assistant. And in that capacity, Verne Underwood went over my typescript with impressive care. If I had a nickel for every error Verne caught, I'd have been able to pay him myself!

An earlier, shorter version of Chapter 3 appeared in *Renaissance Drama* 24 (1993): 57–81. And some material from Chapter 5 was first published in *The Journal of Medieval and Renaissance Studies* 23 (1993): 89–111. I am grateful to the editors of these journals – Mary Beth Rose, Annabel Patterson, and Marcel Tetel – for permission to reuse the material here. Patterson was particulary helpful, and the revisions she encouraged me to make have improved this book.

My most important debt is a personal one: not only has my wife Jaya Yodh for years put up with the moodiness and enthusiasms that attend my writing, but she moved with me to Arizona at some personal cost so that we might be together and so that I might have an academic career. The generosity of that choice, and of not regretting it afterwards, continues to astound me. For that, and for a thousand other things, this book is dedicated to her.

Abbreviations

Bacon, *Works*
The Works of Francis Bacon, 14 vols., ed. James Spedding, R. L. Ellis, and D. D. Heath (London, 1861–79)

CSP Ven
Calendar of Letters and State Papers relating to English Affairs, Preserved in Archives and Collections of Venice and in Other Libraries of Northern Italy, 38 vols., ed. Rawdon Brown *et al.* (London, 1864–1947)

Daniel, *Works*
The Complete Works in Verse and Prose of Samuel Daniel, 5 vols., ed. Alexander B. Grosart (London, 1885–96)

Drayton, *Works*
The Works of Michael Drayton, 5 vols., ed. J. William Hebel *et al.* (Oxford: Basil Blackwell, 1931–41)

H&S
Ben Jonson: The Man and His Work, 11 vols., ed. C. H. Herford and Percy and Evelyn Simpson (Oxford: Clarendon Press, 1925–52)

Nichols
John Nichols, ed., *The Progresses, Processions, and Magnificent Festivities of King James the First, His Royal Consort, Family, and Court*, 4 vols. (London, 1828)

Political Works
The Political Works of James I, ed. Charles Howard McIlwain (Cambridge: Harvard University Press, 1918)

A note on texts

In passages quoted from Renaissance texts, I have silently modernized i/j and u/v, and regularized abbreviations requiring special orthography.

My text for Shakespeare's plays throughout is *The Riverside Shakespeare*, G. Blakemore Evans, ed. (Boston: Houghton Mifflin, 1974). In quotations from this edition, I have dropped editorial brackets. Citations from the Bible refer to the King James Version. In a few cases I have regularized quotations by rendering italic type as roman.

Except with those texts whose titles I abbreviate throughout, I give a full citation the first time a book or series appears in each chapter, and short-title citations thereafter. In detailed examinations of primary sources, I give full citation in a note the first time a given text appears, and parenthetical citation thereafter for the remainder of the chapter.

Introduction

Queen Elizabeth ruled in England for more than four decades. When she died in 1603, she left behind her a rich system of conventional behaviors and ideologies, many of which had been naturalized during the course of her long reign. Her successor, James I (James VI of Scotland), inherited subjects accustomed to Elizabethan practices and ideas. As with any new king, his performance was carefully scrutinized, and he brought with him a particularly well-articulated public style, made concrete in his published poetry, treatises on kingship, and other public volumes.[1] His works sold briskly in England, to subjects curious about their new king as well as to courtiers and would-be courtiers anxious to know how to tailor their addresses to him.

It is a critical commonplace to note marked differences between the cultural artifacts surrounding Queen Elizabeth I and those produced under her successor. Recent critics, eager to relocate Elizabethan and Jacobean literature in its social and political contexts, have clarified these differences, and traced them to the contrasting styles and ideologies of the two monarchs and their courts.[2] After all, the contrasts between the two monarchs are particularly sharp. The transition from Elizabeth to James was also the transition from a woman ruler to a man, from a Tudor to a Stuart, from a charismatic performer to a more aloof public personality, from a revered national heroine to a foreigner, and so on.

What remains less clear, even on the heels of a decade of powerful and persuasive historicist criticism, is the process by which a transition like the one from Elizabethan culture to the recognizably Jacobean takes place. For the circulation of the king's public image was at every point mediated by its intersection with the expectations and habits naturalized under Elizabeth, and these in turn brought with them assumptions about courtly performance, literary decorum, and the behavior of kings. The dissemination of James's influence on English

culture during the early years of his reign necessarily involved a series
of negotiations – conscious or otherwise – between Elizabethan expectation and Jacobean reality.

This study examines the role of these negotiations in the formation
of a recognizably Jacobean culture, paying careful attention to ways in
which various writers reshaped, reused, and rejected old ideas and
conventions in response to the influence of the new king and his
government. Since these negotiations are always mediated by more
localized, idiosyncratic factors – specific authorial agendas, different
milieux, or the formal demands of various literary genres – the book is
organized as a series of case-studies designed to highlight and isolate
specific strands within the larger transition from the Elizabethan to the
Jacobean. Cumulatively, they are designed to provide an overview of
the contingencies and mechanisms by which such change takes place,
of the kinds of influence a king or queen has on a country's literary
production, and of the limitations of totalizing models of culture.

These studies focus generally on the first decade of James's reign in
England, though many of the paradigms I set up here have extended
repercussions, and although to some degree the material in each chapter has dictated the time frame discussed. This is because a number of
events crucial to English perceptions of James and the monarchy
coalesce around 1612-14, with the result that attitudes toward James
and the crown become increasingly rigid after this first decade. First,
the death of James's eldest son, Henry, Prince of Wales, in November
1612 deprived England of its fondest hopes. Henry, in his brief life, had
been widely idealized. The prospect of his eventual succession
promised – to those unhappy with James's policies and behavior – to
restore England to its destiny as Protestantism's international champion.
Strong opposition to James's government, which had been kept uneasily
in check by the hope of better things to come, was released with
Henry's death.

Second, 1614 saw a marked downturn in James's ability to deal with
parliament: he convened and then dissolved the so-called "addled
parliament" within a few months, failing to obtain the desired financial
help. And then, in an effort to generate new revenue, James's endorsed
the so-called Cockayne project, which aimed to increase profits (and
thus revenue to the crown) from English cloth by establishing a native
dyeing industry and forbidding the export of undyed cloth. The wealthy
London alderman William Cockayne was given sole control over the
trade, but without adequate financial backing he was simply unable to

buy the volume of cloth coming to London from the countryside. The plan collapsed within two years, but by then damage had been done both to the cloth trade and to the relationship between the crown and England's most important industry. The resulting constriction of the cloth trade helped put an end to a decade of mercantile expansion.[3]

Finally, 1613 saw the divorce of Lady Frances Howard from her husband, the Earl of Essex, and Lady Frances's hasty remarriage to James's favorite, Robert Carr, Earl of Somerset. The divorce itself was a scandal, as was James's encouragement of the marriage. In 1615, lurid revelations about the poisoning of Sir Thomas Overbury – a follower of Somerset opposed to the marriage – capped a distasteful series of events which generally damaged the reputation of James's court. The favorite Somerset and his new wife were tried for the murder and convicted, though James stepped in to commute the death sentence. The enormous attention focused on the scandal from start to finish helped make the corruption of the court notorious. Generally speaking, these events contributed to a change in English attitudes towards James, as responses to him and his court became more clearly polarized.

Focusing my study in this way has placed it at the intersection of a number of the crucial methodological issues which have surfaced along with recent interest in historicism. Many of these, in turn, hinge on the influence in Renaissance studies of a Foucauldian notion of power as being "everywhere; not because it embraces everything, but because it comes from everywhere."[4] As Jeffrey Weeks explains it, this means that power, for Foucault, "is not something that can be held or transmitted, it is not the possession of one class (or of one gender) over another, it is not embodied in the state or any single institution."[5] Rather, it inheres in what Foucault calls "the fundamental codes of a culture," the discursive systems which govern language, "schemas of perception," values, and "the hierarchy of . . . practices."[6]

More importantly, this notion of power has only a tangential relation to the coercive and persuasive powers of government, though these latter are certainly among the formations determined within a culture's "fundamental codes":

relations of power, and hence the analysis that must be made of them, necessarily extend beyond the limits of the State. In two senses: first of all because the State, for all the omnipotence of its apparatuses, is far from being able to occupy the whole field of actual power relations, and further because the State can only operate on the basis of other, already existing power relations.

The State is superstructural in relation to a whole series of power networks that invest the body, sexuality, the family, kinship, knowledge, technology and so forth.[7]

A king speaks and acts from a position of unique privilege, but for Foucault that privilege is itself constructed by and within these networks of power.

Within Foucault's model of discursive networks, "power and knowledge directly imply one another . . . there is no power relation without the correlative constitution of a field of knowledge, nor any knowledge that does not presuppose and constitute at the same time power relations."[8] This important observation – that power relations involve the creation of fields and subjects of knowledge – has authorized much of the most exciting work done by the so-called new historicism, encouraging critics to unearth analogies between seemingly disparate discursive fields (governmental, sexual, legal, psychological, literary), and to see these analogies as the skeletons of Foucauldian networks. Foucault, however, is always evasive about the relationship between power / knowledge and more conventional notions of social domination. To a considerable degree, this is the result of his understanding of power as "both intentional and nonsubjective" – calculated but not the result of any individual's strategic decisions – a description bound to baffle any old-fashioned discussion of the give-and-take of government.[9] Critics attempting to use Foucauldian methods while retaining an interest in the state have frequently had difficulty with the relationship as well.

The most important example for me here – both because it pioneered the use of Foucault in Renaissance studies and because it is still the most influential contemporary study of Jacobean literature – is Jonathan Goldberg's *James I and the Politics of Literature*. When Goldberg discusses King James's "means to articulate power" he combines the political centrality which comes with being a king with the systemic discursive power subtending all manner of relations and practices in Foucault's analyses.[10] The result of this conflation is a King James whose royal articulations, rather than being seen as superstructural to power networks, are instead taken to be fundamentally constitutive of them. Small wonder then that in Goldberg's book "the world of absolutism begins to seem disquietingly analogous to the universe of discourse."[11] Authorized by this slippage within the concept of power, Goldberg's landmark study describes paradigmatic strategies and contradictions in the articulations of Jacobean power, and then attempts to trace reproductions of these strategies and contradictions through a wide range of artistic production. Since the reach of James's power is taken to be coterminous with the field of discourse, these juxtapositions can proceed without respect for the conventional organizing categories of genre, medium, or historical narrative, a freedom which in fact gives Goldberg's work its considerable clarity of focus.

The Foucauldian model of culture, as used by Goldberg and others, occludes crucial historiographical and sociological questions. And since the present study attempts to give a very different model of cultural production and transmission, it seems worth taking up these questions here in some detail. As a starting-point, I have found E. P. Thompson's remarks about "The Poverty of Theory" to be as relevant to Foucauldian cultural analysis as they were to the Althusserian structuralism which they were intended to counteract. For the Foucauldian notion of power as "intentional and nonsubjective" also offers us what Thompson has called a "pseudo-choice: either we must say that there are no rules but only a swarm of 'individuals', or we must say that the rules *game* the players."[12] And this in turn means that a social science based on Foucault's discursive networks can have "no category (or way of handling) 'Experience,'" and consequently "no adequate categories to explain . . . change."[13]

Foucault's own work, as Hayden White points out, avoids this problem by eschewing narrative line altogether and representing historical change as a series of abrupt, inexplicable, catastrophic shifts.[14] By the same token, Goldberg's study of Jacobean art focuses on relations of similitude within a synchronic cultural moment rather than on diachronically conceived historical developments. That is to say, his study treats James's long reign as a more or less homogeneous cultural moment.

This historiographical move characterizes many of the familiar new historicist essays. Louis Adrian Montrose describes it as a basic tenet of new historicist methodology, arguing that its project is to revise traditional literary history by reorienting "the axis of inter-textuality, substituting for the diachronic text of an autonomous literary history the synchronic text of a cultural system."[15] Enabled by the Foucauldian model of culture traduced by networks of power / knowledge, the critics Montrose describes have traced compelling and unexpected connections within a "cultural system" that includes literature. A major cost of this reorientation, however, has been the substitution of analogy and similitude for cause and effect as the structuring principle of argument. The result, it seems to me, is a body of scholarship which has generally been reluctant to describe either the material transmissions and causalities involved in its similitudes, or historical significance of the sort distributed and argued for in old historical narratives.

I see this book as part of an ongoing movement in Renaissance studies towards the reconsolidation of the considerable advances of new historicism with old historical narratives of individual agency (Thompson's "experience"), and cause and effect. This trend follows naturally on the heels of early new historicist polemics, and in some cases has even been the work of the same critics.[16] In keeping with this program, there has been a renewed emphasis in a great many recent studies on the material circulation of texts, on the specific strategies used by different writers, and on the causal significance of the social work done by literature, either as propaganda or by contributing to cultural ideals, stereotypes, and fantasies. All of these emphases serve to move the study of culture away from the impersonal Foucauldian notion of "intentional and nonsubjective" structures, and to put historicist literary criticism back into dialogue with traditional historical narrative.

Turning from the historiographical to the sociological implications of the Foucauldian model of culture, we find a closely related series of problems: we might call them the problems of top-down analysis. Here too *James I and the Politics of Literature* is representative, for critics of Goldberg's book have argued that its analysis of royal discursive power implies a reductive model of culture, focusing narrowly on "a dominant social order that reproduces itself by producing and containing its own controlled subversion."[17] This understanding of the functioning of the dominant culture elides any useful understanding of individual agency and intention, explaining literary production as a function of the discursive matrices put into play by the social elite or the king himself.[18] One deficit of this often reproduced model of cultural production is that it has difficulty allowing for the possibility of genuine opposition to the dominant social order.[19]

In place of Goldberg's functionally absolute king, this study offers a version of James caught up within structures of discourse, ideology, and sentimental association over which he often had little control, structures which in turn influenced the dissemination and reception of his words in his new realm. Though James was a centrally important figure in the period that bears his name, his influence on literature and culture was manifold, mediated in practice by a wide variety of local agendas and contingencies: he was a figure to be commented on, flattered, ignored, copied, feared, courted, revered, advised, and mocked.

In fact, he was even a figure to be spoken for, ventriloquized, manipulated: it has been recognized that some of James's early initiatives were shaped and guided by Cecil, Henry Howard, and their followers.[20] More strikingly, R. C. Munden has suggested that the speech delivered by James to the House of Commons following the dispute over the election of Sir Francis Goodwin in 1604 was written for him to serve the interests of Cecil and Lord Chief Justice Popham. This, Munden argues, has been the cause of some misunderstanding since the speech is written in the style of James: "On the face of it, the main body of the speech might have been written for [James's] critics. It is pompous, didactic, and even contains the customary biblical allusion."[21] Elsewhere, the same speech has been described as "the king at his worst."[22] This ventriloquization, using the king's voice against his own better interests, seems strikingly emblematic of a point I want to insist on: James did not have – could not have had – full control over the received meanings of his own public image.

These chapters, insofar as they are attentive to such mediating acts of circulation, offer an approach to royal influence which recognizes and describes the king's centrality without relying on a reductive model of his relation to his various subjects. Literary studies which take the influence of monarchs into account often oversimplify the relationship between royal orthodoxies and the expression of subjects, either by overemphasizing the monarch's interest in intervention or by overstating his or her power of imposition. As to the latter, it is important to remember that many writers imagined audiences for their writings (various patrons, theatre audiences, coteries, book-buyers, and so on) whose interests were different than the crown's. As to the former, Leeds Barroll has recently overturned generations of topical readings of Shakespeare's Jacobean plays by arguing persuasively that James himself probably did not care much about the contents of Shakespearean drama.[23] His argument could be extended as a challenge to political readings of a range of non-Shakespearean literary production as well.

In order to allow for the variety of kinds of circulation and dissonance found everywhere in cultural production, critics have increasingly turned toward different models of social interaction based on ideas of negotiation.[24] This has been a keyword in Renaissance studies at least since the publication of Stephen Greenblatt's *Shakespearean Negotiations* in 1988.[25] For Greenblatt, negotiation names the range of exchanges (of money and of cultural capital), appropriations, exclusions, and influences which make up the cultural field within which both subjects and their artifacts are constituted. The advantage of using negotiation as a model for these interactions is that it presumes some agency (however attenuated by Greenblatt's poststructuralist critique of individualism) for all parties involved – instead of only for the dominant culture or the king – and consequently allows Greenblatt's analyses to move beyond the totalizing impulses of a subversion-containment model of social interactions. Subsequent critics have recognized the usefulness of this model, but have attempted to revise it, to politicize it, to make it less abstract. Ann Rosalind Jones, for example, argues that a model of cultural interaction based on negotiation, rather than emphasizing impersonal circulation, should be "the basis for an analysis of deliberate strategies that human agents direct against repressive cultural systems."[26]

I want to retain both senses of the word here, for it has become clear that the processes which made England Jacobean are themselves made up of a variety of kinds of response, both deliberately strategic and otherwise. Indeed, one of the goals of this project has been to describe how these two kinds of negotiation – individually strategic and impersonally cultural – interact with each other. For this book attempts throughout to locate the individual representational choices of canonical and non-canonical writers with a wide variety of backgrounds, interests, and agendas within and against larger cultural paradigms and trajectories.

The six chapters that follow are divided into three pairs, each of which isolates a different approach to the problem of England's negotiated response to James. The first pair examines ways that James's public pronouncements and literary performances influenced literary genres and fashions, as cues taken from the king himself interfered with Elizabethan assumptions about the function and purpose of various genres and modes of address. These studies presuppose a court culture in which writers negotiate self-conscious solutions to representational problems and cues, taking into account notions of decorum, a sense of what is current, and the extant resources of genre and mode in order to create literary artifacts responsive to James's ideas, interests, and public style. At the same time, these productions have an influence on literary fashions which extends well beyond those texts produced specifically for James or for his important courtiers, which means that sophisticated literary responses to court decorum must be seen as part of a larger process of cultural negotiation in which less self-consciously courtly – and occasionally even subversive – texts also participate.

The first chapter takes as its subject the phenomenon of the poet-king. Within the patronage system, many characteristic gestures of poetic self-presentation are directed at and formed in relation to the authority of their potential patron. Supplication and apology, to give two examples, are conventional gestures of the occasional courtly poet which formally encode the poet's offer of service to his patron-reader. James's volumes of poetry, because they consciously follow conventions of poetic self-presentation, reproduce these gestures of service despite the fact that they are at best paradoxical and at worst indecorous in a king. At the same time, James's poems encode their author's power in a variety of ways, with the result that his poems fit only uneasily within conventional lyric forms: James tries to establish a parallel between poet and king, but the performative norms of the two roles interfere with each other. The poet-king is forced to invoke his privileged royal insight in order to avoid the disempowered stances built into poetic performance.

If James found the poet's stances difficult to reconcile with his authority, occasional poets in England found the figure of the poet-king equally difficult to address. The poet under the poet-king was in danger of seeming either redundant (Drayton writes: "thine owne glory from thy selfe doth spring") or presumptuous (by aligning oneself with the king's voice).[27] The many panegyrics written to celebrate James's accession generate a variety of strategic responses to this difficulty. Moreover, I argue that this problem of royal address influences epideictic style even in occasional verse not directed to the king. Sophisticated, courtly verse addressed to a variety of early Jacobean subjects by Donne and Jonson demonstrates their mastery of court fashion by reflecting the epideictic maneuvers developed to praise the king. Put briefly, Donne obsessively interrogates the coupling of subservience and authority in the person of the poet, while Jonson's occasional lyrics repeatedly ask "What need hast thou of me? or of my *Muse*?"[28]

The second chapter looks at early Jacobean pastoral literature, with an eye towards broader questions of generic continuity. Because pastoral was a specially privileged mode for Elizabethan courtly expression, its formal conventions were shaped by demonstrably Elizabethan exigencies. Early Jacobean writers, responding both to the mode's residual prestige and to Jacobean courtly fashions, produced texts characterized by gaps and equivocations which mark subtle incompatibilities between received generic conventions and Jacobean innovation.

These discontinuities, in turn, illuminate differences between Elizabethan and Jacobean court ideologies: more specifically, I argue that these local generic disjunctions reflect differing formulations – within the genre – of the subject's position in relation to larger communities and authorities. Exemplary here are Drayton's 1606 revision of his *Idea, The Shepheardes Garland* (1593), Daniel's *Queenes Arcadia* (1605), and Fletcher's *The Faithful Shepherdess* (1609), as well as a number of less familiar texts by a variety of early Jacobean writers.

The second pair of chapters shifts my focus from questions of generic renegotiation to the ways that early Jacobean drama staged and commented on key issues of the new reign. Though scrutinized by the censor, plays produced for public performance are on the whole less closely tied to interests of king and court, since "the better playwrights had just enough economic independence to earn a living without regard to the whims or special tastes of anyone beyond their immediate audience."[29] Of course, even if comparatively free from the strictures and rewards of courtly literature, many early Jacobean plays are nevertheless powerfully motivated by their observation of and interest in issues of public government. Here I have found useful David Bevington's discussion of topical meaning in Tudor drama, and in particular his observation that political drama often handles "ideas and platforms rather than personalities."[30] Though early Jacobean drama has its share of *roman à clef*, its most interesting responses to James lie in its stagings of the crux issues of Jacobean kingship.

The exploration of the ideals of kingship undertaken in these plays has been seen as a contribution to the development of radical thought in England.[31] But to see early Jacobean political drama in this way is to assimilate it to a familiar literary history in which its radicalism is seen as an early indicator of political trouble to come. Raymond Williams, for example, writes that

the Jacobean [dramatic] form enacted the condition of the 'war of all against all' which, in the next generation, was to be taken by Hobbes as the starting point for a new political philosophy which 'answered' the dramatically unanswered questions, in its justification of an absolute safeguarding power.[32]

If these plays participate in the larger intellectual and ideological trajectories, however, the political situations dramatized by early Jacobean playwrights are informed by observations of, speculations about, and relations to the specific, concrete governmental practices of their day. Their interest in the state, in other words, is not necessarily animated either by general radicalism or by dislike for the monarch.

Chapter 3 is a study of the relationship between counsel and king in a number of early Jacobean plays. In it, I argue that dramatic representations emphasizing the inability of the vain autocrat to see beyond the reflection of himself offered by his flatterers provided a formula with which writers responded to and commented on a perceived Jacobean crisis of counsel. The perception of this crisis was in turn the result of inherited Elizabethan anxieties, of James's self-styling, and of the makeup of his court.

These tragedies – plays like *Sejanus* (1603), *Philotas* (1605), and *Mustapha* (1607-10) – effectively retheorize the relationship between royal vanity and tyrannic autocracy in a way that destabilizes the traditional rhetoric used to describe the tyrant. Insofar as the rhetoric surrounding the legitimate monarch constituted itself against the figure of the tyrant, this destabilization weakened the conventional rhetoric of royalty as well. Consequently, though many of these plays voice deeply conservative political positions, their cumulative contribution to the rhetoric of kingship is decidedly radical. As a group, the dramatizations of counsel in early Jacobean England arise out of a specifically topical concern with James's new court, but wind up pointing toward positions which challenge basic assumptions about the majesty of the king.

Chapter 4 looks closely at *King Lear* and *Macbeth*, arguing that these two early Jacobean tragedies respond to the accession of a male ruler after Elizabeth by exploring the gendered language implicit in conventional rhetoric of kingship. Drawing on English and Continental representations of royal bounty as maternal, this chapter argues that the notion of the ideal king – at once an autonomous patriarch and a well-spring of nurturant generosity – is interrogated in these plays. Though Shakespeare's handling of this material is characteristically abstract and equivocal, the concerns at stake in these plays are also the concerns of the state: James's own prodigal generosity had begun to provoke comment by the time these plays were performed.

The final two chapters of this study attempt to address more interdisciplinary questions, looking at ways in which literary representation shapes and is shaped by political history. These chapters draw on a range of genres and styles of printed matter, trying to trace James's impact on what Raymond Williams calls "structures of feeling": related sets of "meanings and values as they are actively lived and felt."[33] Chapter 5 examines the reproduction of Queen Elizabeth's legacy in early Jacobean England, focusing on its different emphases within different sites – particularly James's court, Prince Henry's circle, and

London. Each of these milieux produced versions of the late queen's famous memory motivated by impulses ranging from sheer nostalgia to propaganda mongering, and these various Jacobean appropriations of Elizabeth alternatively reinforced or conflicted with one another. Since these depictions of the late queen contributed to the production of idealized notions of royal behavior against which James and his government were judged, the stakes in this contested re-evaluation of Elizabeth's memory were quite high.

Though the legacy of Elizabeth was subject to various interpretations during the first decade of James's reign in England, praise for Elizabeth became in time a conventional code for the expression of dissatisfaction. This chapter describes how the interplay of various versions of Elizabeth in Jacobean England prepared the way for the generally oppositional version that subsequently prevailed.[34]

The sixth and final chapter examines stylistic and thematic changes in the expression of civic pride in London. The civic pride of Elizabethan London co-existed, albeit at times uneasily, with a strain of nationalist patriotism encouraged by the crown. Though these two systems of affective loyalty are potentially in competition with one another, their co-existence was in large part related to the queen's active cultivation of a loving public persona in her capital. For Elizabeth's public demonstrations of gracious affection for her London citizenry clinched a powerful bond of sentimental reciprocity between queen and citizen. James also attempted to cultivate the city by participating in pageants (1604), and by dining first with the Merchant Taylors Company, and then with the Lord Mayor (1607). Despite James's best efforts, however, his departure from Elizabeth's civic persona released London from the affective bond of these mutual obligations and consequently contributed to a revisionary process within civic self-fashioning during the first decade of his reign in England. As a result, civic pride (as expressed in pamphlets, in the annual Lord Mayor's pageant, and elsewhere) refashions itself along less socially conservative lines.

Implicit in this project's attention to the various local and generic agendas which mediate England's response to James is a model of royal influence which challenges the hypostatizations of power so common in recent historicist criticism. I make this common argumentative thread explicit in an epilogue on Ben Jonson's *Bartholomew Fair* (1614), a play dedicated to James which is deeply concerned with the gap between ideas of authority and its practical limitations and circulations.

PART ONE

Negotiations in genre and decorum

CHAPTER ONE

Panegyric and the poet-king

The obvious place to begin a study of royal influence is at court, that "undefinable conglomerate of thousands of individuals all centring ultimately around the person of the King."[1] As both the symbolic center of court life and an important source of power and bounty, the reigning monarch had of necessity an enormous influence on a range of courtly fashions and practices.[2] Perhaps the most forceful theoretical statement we have of the influence King James exerted over the conventions with which writers in the Jacobean court worked is Jonathan Goldberg's *James I and the Politics of Literature*, a study which describes King James as the "articulate and visible center of society" whose characteristic discursive strategies are inevitably reproduced in the writings of his subjects.[3]

Attention to the kinds of transaction through which royal influence is disseminated, and to the wide range of canonical and non-canonical courtly letters in which it can be traced, however, makes it clear that this account needs to be revised. For one thing, even if kings and queens are in many ways at the center of court culture, the practical conventions of courtly address are shaped by a wide variety of patron-client relationships: the poet angling for a position in the employment of a prominent courtier has an interest in the style and taste of the monarch – insofar as he needs to demonstrate a mastery of current styles – but it would be misleading to imagine this transaction as a direct and unmediated response to royal taste. If the influence of the monarch is wide-ranging, it is never monolithic.

Early English responses to James himself suggest that for many courtly and would-be courtly writers the reproduction of Jacobean orthodoxy required a complicated, *ad hoc* negotiation between Elizabethan writerly strategies and the implications of James's public writing. Jacobean styles of courtly address, rather than being inescapably imposed from above, are the product of numerous writers struggling to respond to a new king whose image fits uneasily with received notions of what a monarch was, what a monarch did, and consequently how a monarch should be addressed.

As a case-study in the complexities of royal influence, this chapter takes as its subject the relationship between King James's literary affectations and the formation of recognizably Jacobean panegyric stances in England, as courtly and would-be courtly makers accustomed to Elizabethan practices tried to adapt to the cues of the new king. It traces the often awkward responses to the new king's self-presentation as both author and authority, noting as its starting-point that the extensive literary production of King James amounts to an ongoing self-fashioning performance of a sort expected perhaps in a courtier but unprecedented in a monarch.[4] The influence of this royal self-presentation on the writing of early Jacobean courtly makers is far-reaching, not only because such writers have a stake in following royal cues, but also because James's peculiar brand of authority violated the categories within which the relationship between writer and monarch had come to be understood in the Elizabethan court.

George Puttenham, in the opening chapter of his late Elizabethan handbook on *The Arte Of English Poesie* (1589), offers an elaborate justification for his boldness in directly addressing the queen:

if I should seeme to offer you this my devise for a discipline and not a delight, I might well be reputed, of all others the most arrogant and injurious: your selfe being alreadie, of any that I know in our time, the most excellent Poet. Forsooth by your Princely purse favours and countenance, making in maner what ye list, the poore man rich, the lewd well learned, the coward couragious, and vile both noble and valiant. Then for imitation no lesse, your person as a most cunning counterfaitor lively representing *Venus* in countenance, in life *Diana*, *Pallas* for governement, and *Iuno* in all honour and regall magnificence.[5]

Elizabeth is a poet or maker in that she represents all worthiness in her own person, and in that she can create worth in others. Royal patronage – the favor of the "Princely purse" – is in Puttenham's compliment an act of poetic creation: it fashions a worthy fashioner. Samuel Daniel, in Book 5 of his *Civile Wars*, ascribes to "great Eliza" an equivalently creative power, describing her as a queen "in whose all directing eye is plac't / A powre, the highest powers of wit to guide."[6]

If Elizabeth's gaze has shaping or guiding power, she herself is frequently the spectacle gazed upon by the best wits of her court. Elizabethan court poets, by creating and embellishing the so-called cult of Elizabeth, also created a set of images for their monarch. Consciousness of this reciprocity has been found preeminently in the "Aprill" eclogue of *The Shepheardes Calender* (1579), where "*Eliza*, Queene of shepheardes" is made the descendant of Syrinx and Pan. According to Spenser's Ovidean source – as explained in E. K.'s gloss – Syrinx

is the name of a Nymphe of Arcadie, whom when Pan being in love pursued, she flying from him, of the Gods was turned into a reede. So that Pan catching at the Reedes in stead of the Damosell, and puffing hard (for he was almost out if wind) with hys breath made the Reedes to pype.[7]

The union of Syrinx and Pan produces pastoral music of the sort that here celebrates Eliza. As the descendant of the same pair, Eliza is effectively equated with the very song in which she is celebrated. As Louis Adrian Montrose points out, the association of Eliza with the music of her praise in this eclogue "works to suggest that in fact the ruler and the ruled are mutually defining, reciprocally constituted."[8]

If the queen – by her judgment and by the favor of her "princely purse" – makes the poet, her poets in turn are aware of their role as fashioners of a courtly system within which the image of the queen is rendered effective. Courtly discourse is continually reproduced by this endlessly generative dialectical relationship, and the poet is given an important role without impinging upon the authority of the monarch. Henry Chettle, in an elegy occasioned by Elizabeth's death, has his speaker call on his hearers to join him in praising the late queen, since "to reckon all, were *Opus infinitum*, a labour without end."[9] This describes the structure of Elizabethan panegyric, both in its call for praise and in its assertion that the praise is necessarily endless.[10] One might say that the reciprocal relationship between poet on the one hand and queen on the other ensured a healthy circulation of symbolic capital.[11]

The popular image of James-as-writer violates this reciprocity, which in turn makes it increasingly difficult for his panegyrists to justify their addresses to him. Forced to resituate themselves in relation to the new king, these writers have recourse to seemingly contradictory rhetorical gestures: they alternatively ally themselves with the king's authorial power, and express their unworthiness or inability to do so. The strain of this awkwardly contradictory encomiastic stance manifests itself in a number of the panegyrics addressed to James I upon his accession to the English throne, poems which for the most part fail to reconcile these opposing impulses.

Before turning to these poems, it will be useful to look in some detail

at James's own published verse, which in many cases highlights conflicts I have alluded to between the conventional stance of the poet and
the authority of the king. Since these poems crystallize the category
violations inherent in the figure of the poet-king, they anticipate some
of the difficulties manifested in early Jacobean panegyric. We will then
turn to the poems written in celebration of James's accession in
England, paying close attention to the often contradictory ways that
they position themselves relative to the discursive authority of the king.
Finally, we will look at poems written by Jonson and Donne to non-
royal patrons during the first decade of James's reign in England, with
an eye towards describing their participation in the dilemmas of
Jacobean epideictic verse.

"THE STILE OF *GODS*"?

Even in his poetry, James lays claim to an explicitly royal authority.
The best-known example here is the sonnet that supplies the argument
to *Basilikon Doron* – the work most responsible for introducing James to
his new English subjects. This sonnet, as has often been recognized,
offers a formulation of James's power which tacitly links authorial
prowess to royal authority: "God gives not Kings the stile of *Gods* in
vaine."[12] The primary meaning of the word "stile" in James's poem
would seem to be the eighteenth listed in the *OED*: "legal, official or
honorific title." Other contemporary meanings, however, deepen the
implications of James's poem: "stile" could mean "stylus," fixed point-
er, or writing implement; it could mean literary manner or, in Scottish
terminology, it could refer to the authorized form of a legal document.
The phrase "stile of *Gods*," then, not only authorizes James, it theorizes
his power as discursive, coming from the pen of a higher authority.

   The poems in James's two published volumes of verse also manifest
their author's sense of royal discursive power. James's poetic debut, at
the beginning *The Essayes of a Prentise, in the Divine Art of Poesie* (1584),
consists of a series of invocatory sonnets asking Jove and Apollo to
bestow upon his poems the power literally to entrap their audiences
within their fictions:

> First *Jove*, as greatest God above the rest,
> Graunt thou to me a pairt of my desyre:
> That when in verse of thee I wryte my best,
> This onely thing I earnestly requyre,
> That thou my veine Poetique so inspyre,

As they may suirlie think, all that it reid,
When I descryve thy might and thundring fyre,
That they do see thyself in verie deid
From heaven thy greatest *Thunders* for to leid,
And syne upon the *Gyants* heads to fall.[13]

In the sonnets that follow, James asks that his other descriptions have similar effects: "let them think, in verie deid they feill, / When as I do the *Winters* stormes unfolde, / The bitter frosts" (1: 11, lines 1–3). These sonnets lay claim to a sort of dictatorial power over the reader, and thus can be read as part of James's ongoing concern with what Goldberg calls his power of "discursive imposition."[14]

But despite James's overt interest in his own authorial power, the voicing of that power in his published work might have seemed somewhat equivocal to English readers. For as James's volumes frequently obey conventions of presentation regularized by less privileged poets, they often find themselves in positions of supplication or apology. Thus, the epistle "To The Reader" at the beginning of the *Poeticall Exercises* contains an apology of the kind one finds again and again in volumes of the period:

in case thou finde ... many incorrect errours, both in the dytement[15] and orthography, I must pray thee to accept this my reasonable excuse, which is this. Thou considers, I doubt not, that upon the one part, I composed these things in my verie young and tender yeares: wherein nature, (except shee were a monster) can admit no perfection. And nowe on the other parte, being of riper years, my burden is so great and continuall, without anie intermission, that when my ingyne and age could, my affaires and fasherie [harassments] will not permit mee, to re-mark the wrong orthography committed by the copiars of my unlegible and ragged hand, far les to amend my proper errours: Yea scarslie but at stollen moments, have I the leasure to blenk upon any paper, and yet not that with free and unvexed spirit. Alwaies, rough and unpolished as they are, I offer them unto thee. (1: 98–100)

The Essayes of a Prentise also begins with a conventional apology for youthful inability. In fact, most of James's published work makes use of similarly commonplace apologies. In the introductory epistle to *Basilikon Doron*, for instance, James explains that he was moved to publish only in order to correct the errors of an unauthorized edition circulated widely against his wishes.

As Richard Helgerson has demonstrated, these apologies and disclaimers functioned as legible signs in the "Elizabethan system of literary careers": amateur court poets aspiring to serve the state as civil servants "rarely began without an apology or ended without a palinode.

They thus enclosed and rejected the self-as-poet in order to reveal the dutiful and employable self-as-civil-servant."[16] Understood in contrast to these amateurs were those poets whose career aspirations were more laureate (preeminently Spenser): "Like the amateur, the laureate presents himself as having been betrayed into verse by youthful passion and exposed in print by a piratical publisher. But, like the amateur's, his private and licentious poems plead indulgence, for they too give promise of more respectable future accomplishment."[17] The private poems of youth promise important public verse to come.

Though James's youthful poems are anything but licentious, his apologies locate him within a system of careers like the one Helgerson describes. In fact, the final poem of James's first book explicitly urges the reader to take his youthful poetry as an earnest of better things to come:

> The facound Greke, *Demosthenes* by name,
> His toung was ones into his youth so slow,
> As evin that airt, which floorish made his fame,
> He scarce could name it for a tyme, ze know.
> So of small seidis the *Liban* Cedres grow:
> So of an Egg the *Egle* doeth proceid:
> From fountains small great *Nilus* flood doeth flow:
> Evin so of rawnis [fish roes] do mightie fishes breid.
> Therefore, good Reader, when as thow dois reid
> These my first fruictis, dispyse them not at all.
> Who watts, bot these may able be indeid
> Of fyner Poemis the beginning small.
> 　　Then, rather loave my meaning and my panis,
> 　　Then lak my dull ingyne and blunted branis.
> 　　　　　　　　　　　　(I: 94)

To Elizabethan readers, this boastful apology would have seemed commonplace.

These apologies, promises, and disclaimers are the conventions of court poets looking for favor; James, by using them, styles himself as a fledgling poet offering his youthful "essayes" to the judgment of the world. Implicitly, this makes the king a supplicant and gives his audience the power of judgment, which means in turn that the literary conventions James makes use of reverse the economy of discursive power suggested by the phrase "the stile of *Gods*." The king's strong formulation of the power of his own authorial voice is in tension with the expectations of a reader of courtly verse for, since conventional courtly performances are subject to the judgment of their audiences, the king's works tend to undermine their own formulations of dictatorial power.

James the poet is able to retain some degree of special authority only by distinguishing within the poems themselves between the inevitable success of his "meaning" and the possible failure of his verse: "rather loave my meaning and my panis, / Then lak my dull ingyne and blunted branis." In response to a potential conflict between his conventional poetic stance and his uniquely empowered position, James acts to separate the performative aspect of the text (the work of the "dull ingyne") from its author's access to higher truth. Faced with the indecorum of presenting himself as a hopeful novice, James retreats to what Goldberg calls "an art of translation": as poet he merely sets down the truths to which as king he has access.[18]

It is also worth noting here that while legibly inscribed within the system of literary gestures described by Helgerson, the sonnet quoted above gives conflicting signals: it seems to be at once the work of an amateur, of a laureate, and of a king. The comparison to Demosthenes would seem to promise a career as a great statesman: this is the promise of an amateur poet looking to demonstrate aptitude for a career as a civil servant. And James's sonnet is clearly a laureate claim, for he presents his work as a promise of "fyner Poemis" to come. Finally, "*Liban* Cedres" and "the *Egle*" both invoke imperial themes, and seem to promise that the poet will become another Solomon, or a mighty emperor. If the poem is offered as a hint at greater things to come, it is not clear what those achievements will be. Certainly, the distinction between laureate poetry and statecraft, around which Helgerson's system of literary careers is organized, is violated in James's otherwise conventional sonnet. He claims for his monarchic voice the strengths of each of the recognized career trajectories, thereby violating the categories of the system itself.

James's love poetry also hinges on peculiar voicings of its author's discursive power.[19] In these poems, James makes use of Petrarchan commonplaces learned or copied mostly from French models, and consequently finds himself wrestling with a central indecorum: Petrarchan supplication ill befits the majesty of a king.[20] As a result, the king's voice inhabits love conventions uneasily and keeps having to find a way to escape from them at the end of each poem.

A good example of this is the brief sonnet sequence (no. 5 in Craigie) that begins "the Cheviott hills doe with my state agree." The first five of these six sonnets are conventional in their Petrarchan situation. The poet, burning with the fires of love, is tormented by the "crewell Dame" (II: 71, line 25) who refuses to acknowledge her lover. The resulting subjugation of the poet reaches its clearest formulation in the third sonnet: "yow Madame have by your beauties might / Bereft, and brookes my hart your humble slave" (II: 71, lines 39–40). Clearly, a king's authority and a lover's abject plea fit poorly together.

And James is either unable or unwilling to let his love fiction compromise his authoritative dignity, as the sequence's final poem demonstrates:

> O womans witt that wavers with the winde
> When none so well may warie [curse] now as I
> As weathercocke thy stablenes I finde
> And as the sea that still can never lie
> Bot since that tyme the trueth hath made me trie
> That in inconstance thou art constant still
> My courage sayes on Cupide ceasse to crie
> That are rewarded thus for thy goodwill
> For thogh Madame I failde not to fullfill
> All sort of service to a Mistres dewe
> Yett absence thogh bot for a space did spill
> The thankes deserved of all my service trewe
>   What shall I saye, I never thought to see
>   That out of sight, should out of langour be.
>
>   (II: 72–73)

As if by fiat, James overturns the Petrarchan lover's endless, unchangeable stance of supplication. In effect, the king reinstates his own privileged, authorial access to the "trueth" in place of the conventional Petrarchan response to cruelty. As in the separation of "meaning" from performance effected in the final sonnet of the *Essayes of a Prentise*, James here uses his claimed access to higher knowledge to escape the felt indecorum of a disempowered stance.

Also interesting in this regard is James's long poem entitled "A Dier at her M:ties desyer." The first fifty-eight lines of this piece are taken up with the familiar complaints of a constant lover: he loves faithfully and is never rewarded; he has little to look forward to save death. Finally, however, a note written in the king's hand calls attention to a missing sonnet which "interprettis all the matter" of the love poem:

> My Muse hath made a willfull lye I grante,
> I sung of sorrows never felt by me;
> I have as great occasion for to wante,
> My love begunne my blessing for to be.

How can I then excuse so lowd a lye?
O yes, I did it even at her desire,
Who made me such successe in love to see,
How soone her flames hade sett my hart on fire.
Since for her sake I presse for to aspire,
To preache of passions which I never prov'd;
What should yee doe who have for haplesse hire
The lucklesse lott, to love and not be lov'd.
    Your plaints I thinke should pierce the starrie skies
    And deave [deafen] the Gods with shrill and cairfull cries.

                         (II: 78)

Again, the king follows up a Petrarchan performance by repudiating it. Here he denies the experience altogether, claims for himself the success that an empowered lover should have, and redefines the poem as a sort of blueprint for those less fortunate.[21] James in effect agrees with Shakespeare's Duke Vincentio who, in *Measure For Measure*, declares, "Believe not that the dribbling dart of Love / Can pierce a complete bosom" (1.3.2–3).

James's poetry is indicative both of his desire to monopolize what we have called symbolic capital, and also of the uneasiness implicit in his attempts to collapse together the paired roles of king and poet. Though James's poetry tries to establish a parallelism between the two roles, their performative norms interfere with one another. The poet-king is forced, time and again, to invoke his privileged royal insight in order to avoid the disempowered stances built into poetic performance.

Poets in England writing panegyrics to James recapitulate these problems since, on the one hand, they are more truly petitionary than James and, on the other, they frequently wish to ally themselves with the prestige and authority of the royal poet. Consequently, the peculiarities of voice which we have been tracing in James's own poetry are also symptomatic of a central rhetorical difficulty facing English poets eager to address the new king.

This is true not necessarily because James's poems were widely read, but because the idea of James as a royal author was itself widely circulated.[22] In fact, James's status as a royal poet was felt in England to lend dignity to poetry even before his accession. The epistle "To the Reader" in John Bodenham's verse miscellany *Bel-Vedére* (1600), for example, makes much of the fact that the volume contains the works of "that learned and right royall king and Poet, JAMES king of Scotland."[23] Similarly, the publication of James's *Essayes of a Prentise* has been described as a watershed publishing event, setting a precedent for gentlemen-writers and responsible in part for diminishing the so-called "stigma of print."[24] And James-as-author was unavoidable in 1603–04. A number of James's books – *Basilikon Doron*, *The Trew Law Of Free Monarchies*, and *Daemonologie* – were reissued and went through numerous English editions. His poetry was not reissued, but there is evidence that it was at least fairly well known in England: it is remarked upon by a number of contemporaries and is excerpted in two of the many late Elizabethan miscellanies.[25]

This widespread dissemination of the king's works – and of the image of the king as author – changed the way English writers of verse, scholarship, and religious controversy constructed their own authorship. From 1598–1603 there were, on average, about five books produced with dedications to Queen Elizabeth each year. By contrast, during each of the first five years of James's reign we find between fifteen and thirty-five dedications to the new king.[26] The increase in dedications shows not that James had more of an effect on English letters than Elizabeth, but rather that James's self-styling made direct authorial address seem appropriate to English writers. Implicit in this change is a subtle but important assumption about the relationship between authors and the king's authority: scholarly, artistic, or controversial books dedicated to the king tacitly align their own claims with the authoritative intellect of the king.

Among the earliest of these publications addressed to James we find an outpouring of verse panegyrics celebrating the new king's accession, an outpouring occasioned partly by the sense that poetry might be specially appreciated by a king who had styled himself an apprentice in the art.[27] Each of these panegyrics, as it recommends its author for some sort of royal favor, either tacitly relies on or consciously retheorizes assumptions about the poet's usefulness to the king. Often, however, assumptions about poetry's usefulness which are put forward are retracted or contradicted within the same poem. As in James's own poetry the voice of authority tends to undermine or unravel a given poem's adopted poetic stance, so in panegyrics addressed to James the king's "trueth" becomes doubly problematic: the court poet has no such authority, and to claim it is either redundant (to repeat the king) or presumptuous (to set oneself up as an alternative source of "trueth"). Attempts to maintain some claim for the usefulness of poetry (and therefore of the poet) while at the same time adjusting to James's authorial self-representation characterize the rhetorical purpose behind these panegyrics.

PANEGYRIC NEGOTIATIONS

Among the king's early panegyrists, Samuel Daniel is unique in that he refuses to reformulate his conception of the role of the poet. Fashioning himself a spokesman of the old court, Daniel uses his status as a leftover Elizabethan writer – one "whom she did grace" – as his main credential.[28] In his *Panegyrike Congratulatorie*, the Elizabethan poet-advisor and author of the *Civile Wars* takes up the tone of a hopeful but stern advisor to the new king:

> Thou wilt not alter the foundation
> Thy Ancestors have laid of this Estate,
> Nor grieve thy land with innovation.
> (stanza 30)

The title page of Daniel's 1603 edition of the *Panegyrike* features Elizabeth's motto "semper eadem" ("always the same"), and in the context of Daniel's conservative poem this tribute to Elizabeth doubles as a recommendation to her successor to avoid "innovation."

This admonitory tone is in keeping with contemporary epideictic theory, which held that the poetry of praise should be didactic, encouraging its subject to live up to the terms of his or her praise.[29] Implicit in this theory – and throughout Daniel's poem – is the humanist assumption that a poet should be a kind of counsellor, that he should have some insight to offer to his subject. In James, however, Daniel had an addressee who claimed for himself a kind of completeness, an ability to be both author and authority. Why would a poet-king need a poet's counsel?[30]

The discrepancy between Daniel's conception of epideictic duty and James's self-styling comes to the fore when Daniel writes,

> It is the greatest glory upon earth
> To be a King, but yet much more to give
> The institution with the happy birth
> Unto a King, and teach him how to live.
> (stanza 21)

The occasion for this remark within the poem is James's *Basilikon Doron*, a book designed to teach Prince Henry how to be a king. At the same time, this passage encapsulates the humanist agenda which lies behind Daniel's epideictic theory itself. If it is the greatest glory to instruct a king, Daniel shows little hesitation in claiming that glory for himself. In fact, the strident forcefulness of the poem's advice to

James suggests that Daniel saw himself as the more qualified advisor, and as the rightful recipient of the "glory" which James's treatise appropriates.

Daniel here assumes a reciprocity between king ("the greatest glory upon earth") and the poet who helps to "teach him how to live." The king's claim to authorial prowess violates this traditional reciprocity, accumulating both roles for the king himself. This violation, in Daniel's almost antagonistic poem, sets the poet's function against the king's self-sufficiency. The tension within the epideictic scheme of Daniel's poem points out, however awkwardly, that James's self-styling encroaches on the traditional authorizing stance of the poet.

The problem manifests itself differently in the poems of less polemically retrograde writers. Thomas Greene's *A Poets Vision, and a Princes Glorie* (1603) is typical here, in that it takes as its theme both the glory of the poet-king and the resulting elevation of the poet.[31] The poem is a dream vision: the speaker, falling asleep on a hillock by a brook under a shade-tree, is visited by Calliope, who complains that the muses have fallen into poverty. However, as Calliope explains, the accession of a poet-king signals an end to the muses' disgrace:

> But now, O ever blest, eternall sweete!
> The Lawrell and a triple Crowne doth meete.
> Now commeth in our long-detained Spring,
> Reduced back by a victorious King,
> Whose triple Crowne, to adde more glorious praise,
> Is triply Crowned with a triple Bayes,
> Which is the richest Crowne a King can have,
> It keeps him from oblivion of the grave;
> Where, after some expence of running time,
> Upon whose backe doth dissolution clime,
> His other Crowne, that guilded but the eye,
> Will quickly fade, when fadeth majestie.
> But this so long as Heaven lends a breath,
> Shall freshly spring in spite of Fate and death.
> To be a Prince it is an honour'd thing,
> Yet ev'ry Poet to himselfe's a King.
> But where in one they both commixed be,
> He then is equall with a Dietie.
>
> (210–27)

Inspired by the accession of such a "dietie," Calliope explains that she and her sisters plan to erect a second Helicon in England. The fiction of the poem is that Calliope herself has "stolne away" (240) from her sisters in order to urge Greene to avail himself of this new source of inspiration:

> That if thou covetst to have thy name nere die,
> But wrap thy memorie in eternitie,
> Past deprivation of corrupting dust,
> When thou into thy latest bed art thrust,
> This place can yeeld thee such *Promethean* fires,
> As shall give answere to thy blest desires.
> Therefor no longer hide thy Muse from light
> But pray thee, pray thee, take thy pen and write.
>
> (244–51)

Curiously, the glory of the poet-king, here figured as the ability to eternize himself, makes a similar eternization possible for other poets in his realm. The king's authorizing example, Calliope suggests, lends authority to poetry in general, and to those poets in particular who take advantage of the occasion and compose public celebrations of the new king.

Greene's elaborate fiction – that the "commixed" triumphs of the poet-king can transform English poets into inspired laureates – doubles as a fairly transparent bid for the king's financial generosity. In a gesture so direct as to border on rudeness, Greene has Calliope promise him a share of the king's bounty, predicting that "thy Muse may once be blest, / And gently fost'red in a Kingly brest" (308–09). Moreover, Greene's confidence in the new prestige of poetry is revealed by the attribution of the volume on the title page to "THOMAS GREENE, gentleman." Greene was not a gentleman, he was a professional comic actor in London, and his proclaimed title amounts to a newly elevated self-construction commensurate with his poem's description of the increased status of authorship. *A Poet's Vision, and a Princes Glorie* can be seen as an attempt both to test and to take advantage of what Greene perceived as a new dignity bestowed upon poetry by the accession of the poet-king.

Greene's fiction can also be seen as an attempt to adapt the kind of address Puttenham made to Elizabeth ("Forsooth by your Princely purse favours and countenance, making in maner what ye list") to the exigencies of Jacobean praise. However, it is one thing to say to Elizabeth, "your purse and visage make poets of men" and quite another to say to James, "your poetry makes laureates of men": the former keeps the dialectically defined distance between poet and queen intact; the latter implies a kind of encroachment by the poet, a diminution of the distance between poet and king. The phrase "ev'ry Poet to himselfe's a King" – so reminiscent of Jonson's more self-conscious explorations of the relationship between authorship and authority – suggests darkly that Greene's claim to Calliope's attention is potentially a kind of usurpation, an appropriation of the dignity and authority of royal poetic style. Greene's poem, then, inadvertently underscores a rhetorical difficulty which we might describe as the flip-side to the equivocations and gaps characteristic of James's own verse: where James's poems frequently have difficulty reconciling royal authority with the disempowered stances built into conventional poetic tropes of supplication and apology, Greene's poem seems inappropriately to claim a kind of royal authority for his own marginal, supplicatory poem.

Verse celebrations like Greene's, which hoped to capitalize on the king's participation in "the divine arte of poesie," were treated with scorn by courtiers who recognized the indecorum implicit in such direct address. John Chamberlain, for example, complains about the presumption of common poets in a letter dated April 12, 1603: "These bountiful beginnings raise all men's spirits, and put them in great hopes, insomuch that ... the very Poets, with their idle pamphlets, promise themselves great part in his favour."[32] The prestige accorded to poetry by James's apprenticeship would have made the efforts of Greene and other "idle" poets appear all the more inappropriate: Greene's understanding of the relationship between the poet-king and his subjects seems, in retrospect, to have been rather naive.

A second rhetorical trap, which is even more prevalent in early Jacobean panegyric, is the threat of redundancy: James's "commixed" skills, after all, mean that he has no real need for panegyrists. The problem of James's literary self-sufficiency – of the poet-king's threatened monopoly of symbolic capital – is wittily encapsulated in the sonnet Michael Drayton wrote to celebrate the Scottish poet-king in 1600:

> Not thy grave Counsells, nor thy Subjects love,
> Nor all that famous Scottish royaltie,
> Or what thy soveraigne greatnes may approve,
> Others in vaine doe but historifie,
> When thine owne glory from thy selfe doth spring,
> As though thou did'st, all meaner prayses scorne:
> Of Kings a Poet, and the Poets King,
> They Princes, but thou Prophets do'st adorne;
> Whilst others by their Empires are renown'd,
> Thou do'st enrich thy Scotland with renowne,
> And Kings can but with Diadems be crown'd,

> But with thy Laurell, thou doo'st crowne thy Crowne;
>> That they whose pens, (even) life to Kings doe give,
>> In thee a King, shall seeke them selves to live.[33]

For Greene, the twin crowns of the poet-king, together with his judgment, promise artistic and financial advances for English poets. Drayton, however, playfully suggests that since the king collapses in himself the dialectically paired roles of poet and monarch, all other courtly panegyric may be useless: "thine owne glory from thy selfe doth spring." The king's ability to eternize himself, rather than signalling parallel advances in glory for the gentleman-poet, here threatens to make court poetry obsolete.

Drayton's sonnet, written at a time when James was only the most likely of a number of possible successors to Elizabeth, raises an issue which would become more pressing to writers in the years after James's accession in 1603. Phineas Fletcher, for instance, in a brief 1603 tribute to Elizabeth and James asks of the latter "who better sings / Of thee, then thine owne oft-tride Muse" (63–64)? The answer, of course, is nobody, and Fletcher opts to leave the job of royal glorification to the new poet-king: "thou thy selfe, thy selfe historifie" (73).[34] Perhaps even more striking is the formulation of the poet-king's glory in William Harbert's *Prophesie of Cadwallader* (1604), which invokes a litany of great poets – including Chaucer, Lydgate, Gower, Sidney, and Spenser – merely in order to point out that none of them would be equal to the task of celebrating James. Of Sidney, for example, Harbert writes, "if thou couldst live, and purchase Orpheus' quill, / Our monarch's merits would exceed thy skill."[35] The only poet capable of celebrating these merits is James himself, a point which Harbert makes unusually explicit: "None but thy selfe – great king – can sing of thee" (1: 250).

This recurring panegyric gesture is a special form of what Ernst Robert Curtius named "the inexpressibility topos," and there is, of course, also a rich tradition of sacred praise of God which insists both that its subject is its source and that its speaker is insufficient.[36] But though the panegyric strategies which these Jacobean writers adopt are in some ways traditional, the poems themselves make it clear that the special problems of address presented by the figure of the poet-king put the court author in a uniquely awkward position.

Perhaps the most suggestive example of the resulting rhetorical strain occurs not in verse panegyric but in the dedicatory introduction to Bacon's two-book 1605 *Advancement of Learning*. The subject-matter of the text, as Bacon makes clear, is intended to reflect James's own demonstrated scholarly tastes. Indeed, Bacon describes his treatise as an "oblation" to the new, scholarly monarch. However, he is forced into a wonderfully twisted construction when he tries to theorize the usefulness of his work to a monarch who in theory should be capable of scholarly writing himself:

> though I cannot positively or affirmatively advise your Majesty, or propound unto you framed particulars, yet I may excite your princely cogitations to visit the excellent treasure of your own mind, and thence to extract particulars for this purpose agreeable to your magnanimity and wisdom.[37]

Bacon acknowledges the redundancy of his own endeavors, saying in effect: "I cannot do anything that you cannot do yourself, I can only turn you inward to gaze upon your own perfection." Since James – according to his own construction – is totally self-sufficient, the author wishing to make an oblation can do no more than reflect his own achievements back to him. To promise more would verge on Greene's impertinence; to promise less would verge on irrelevancy.

Sir John Davies's verse celebration of James's accession also makes manifest the rhetorical difficulties implicit in Jacobean panegyric.[38] Davies is more sensitive to the problematic decorum of his address than is Greene, which is not surprising since his poem – "The Kinges Welcome" – is the performance of an accomplished Elizabethan panegyrist. "The Kinges Welcome" takes the form of an invocation to the muse, who is to fly to meet the king on his journey to London. And Davies begins by distinguishing between the throng of celebrants and his own muse. Only the latter will be able to perceive the true inner virtues of the approaching king:

> knowe him too thow shalt at first survaye,
> By proper notes, and by distinctions plaine.
>
> By his faire outward formes and princely port,
> By honors done to him with capp and knee,
> He is decyphred by the vulgar sorte,
> But truer caracters will rise to thee.
>
> (11–16)

Described in this way, Davies's muse is aligned with the intellectual virtues claimed by the king himself. For the ability to make "plaine" judgments based on "truer caracters" parallels a claim to special insight commonly made by and for James in the early part of his reign. Thus, for example, the author of the 1603 tract *The True Narration of the Entertainment of his Royal Majestie* warns dissemblers of the king's powers of perception: "this is one especiall note in his Majestie; any man that hath ought with him, let him be sure he have a just cause, for he beholdes all men's faces with stedfastnesse, and commonly the looke is the window for the heart."[39] This, of course, should remind us of the rhetoric of James himself when he distinguishes between his true "meaning" and his flawed verse in the sonnet that concludes the *Essayes of a Prentise*. Indeed, following royal cues, Davies praises the king for this same plain-style wisdom: the muse, flying northward, is told to recognize the king by finding he who is "more than other clearly wise, / Or wisely just … " (33–34). Davies implies that his muse and the king are kindred intellects, since both have the insight needed to make plain distinctions based on privileged judgments beyond the perception of the "vulgar sorte."

Implicit here is a model of the relationship between monarch and panegyrist: each partakes of a shared intellectual superiority which allows the poet to recognize the hidden virtues of the monarch, and vice versa. Davies's poem, then, announces itself as Jacobean in much the same manner as Greene's vision: it begins by re-enacting James's conflation of the dialectically paired roles of poet and monarch, and by making the two roles parallel. "Ev'ry Poet to himselfe's a King."

Apparently, the claims Davies makes for his muse in the opening stanzas were felt to be too bold: his muse does not remain in its privileged position. Instead, the king's glory abruptly becomes too great for Davies's muse to look upon directly: "But soft, thine Eglets eye will soone be dym, / If thou this rising sunne directly viewe" (37–38). Accordingly, the poem relocates its poetic welcome, placing it among the prayers of the "vulgar" multitude:

> Thousandes while they possesse and fill the waies,
> Doth both desire, and hinder his repaire;
> They fill the emptie heaven with praier and praise,
> Which he requites with demonstrations faire.
>
> Then what hast thowe to doe, and what remaines?
> Praie as the people doth, and add but this,
> This litle wish: that whiles he lives and raignes,
> He maye be still the same, that nowe he is.
>
> (65–72)

In effect Davies is forced, for the sake of decorum, to reinstate the dialectical relationship between poet and monarch which the poem's earlier addresses have violated. This abrupt change marks an ambiva-

lence in "The Kinges Welcome" which, in turn, reveals Davies's difficulty in finding an appropriate panegyric voice with which to celebrate
the poet-king.

Not only does the parallel established in Davies's opening stanzas
between poet and king come to seem indecorous, it also makes the
poet's skill redundant. Here, Davies seems to have found – like
Drayton, Bacon, Fletcher, and Harbert – that the Jacobean violation
of the reciprocal relationship between poet and king leaves the court
poet without a clearly defined purpose. Davies's poem is impressively
sensitive to the rhetorical demands of Jacobean panegyric, but it is also
fractured, unable to resolve an internal contradiction between the
assumption of poetic privilege on the one hand, and the problem of
poetic irrelevancy on the other.

This should in turn point towards an alternative to Goldberg's
largely Foucauldian model of royal influence: though James's "articulate power" had a pervasive effect on the verse produced to honor him,
his influence is neither evidence of nor necessarily helpful in sustaining
the kind of effective discursive power Goldberg describes. Rather than
entangling subjects straining towards subversive expression, James's
literary cues puzzled courtiers like Greene, Davies, and even Daniel,
who were attempting to find appropriate and flattering modes of
address. This account of the influence of James's "stile" reverses
Goldberg's, seeing it instead as a practical impediment to the production of effective royal propaganda. Where Goldberg's account stresses
the inability of Jacobean writers to escape the terms of James's discourse, this reading emphasizes the inability of poets to negotiate for
themselves a satisfying position within the world of discourse imagined
by James's writings. By looking at relatively unfamiliar poems by writers like Greene and Davies one can see that even in panegyrics
addressed directly to James (and presumably these poems as a group
respond unusually immediately to James's taste and "stile") there is a
good deal of dissonance between royal cues and poetic response.

Goldberg's study, which emphasizes the inevitable transmission of
James's "articulate power," takes Ben Jonson to be "perhaps the representative voice" of Jacobean culture – "the voice that most fully
reproduces his society."[40] Certainly, Jonson is the most successful of
James's early panegyrists in his handling of the kinds of tension we
have been tracing – and if one is looking for a voice that responds fully
and effectively to the formulas and tensions of James's writings and
tastes, Jonson might well seem exemplary. However, since the grace

with which a poem like Jonson's "Panegyre on the Happie Entrance of James" responds to James's difficult cues is unmatched, it hardly seems representative of even courtly discourse. A poem like Davies's "The Kinges Welcome," which fails to gloss over tell-tale dissonances, is probably more typical of the range of expression responding to the new king. That said, the strategic epideictic scheme of Jonson's "Panegyre" becomes fully legible only in terms of the tensions we have been tracing. For the poem responds to precisely the same problem manifested in Bacon's peculiar formulation or Davies's self-abnegating conclusion, effectively balancing self-promotion against royal self-sufficiency.[41]

Written to celebrate the occasion of James's first parliamentary session, the poem describes a visitation by Themis – goddess of justice and of social order – during a public celebration of the new king's entry into parliament. Themis has a double role. First, she "drawes aside / The Kings obeying will" (73–74) and instructs him in both the duties of a good king and the history of his new crown (77–106). Second, she tells the people "How deare a father" they now enjoy (137). In other words, Themis takes upon herself the two roles that a king's poet might be expected to perform: advisor and propagandist.

Like most everything in this poem, the substitution of Themis for the poet is double-edged. On the one hand, it turns James's reliance on his spokeswoman into a compliment: Themis, after all, is a goddess. On the other hand, it dignifies the role Jonson covets for himself, transmuting the poet into a figure either parallel or superior (the distinction is problematic in the poem) to the king himself.

As a propagandist, Themis proves useful. Early in the poem the people lining the streets, though smitten by the king's glory, are presented as at once inarticulate, rowdy, and ravenous:

> Upon his face all threw their covetous eyes,
> As on a wonder: some amazed stood,
> As if they felt, but had not knowne their good:
> Others would fain have shew'ne it in their words:
> But, when their speech so poore a helpe affords
> Unto their zeales expression; they are mute:
> And only with red silence him salute.
> Some cry from tops of houses; thinking noise
> The fittest herald to proclaime true joyes:
> Others on ground runne gazing by his side,
> All, as unwearied, as unsatisfied
>
> (34–44)

Jonson is presumably alluding here to James's notorious unwillingness to satisfy the throng with public performances during his triumphal entry into the city of London. Indeed, comparison between James's distaste for crowds and his predecessor Elizabeth's flair for public performance was a commonplace in contemporary accounts of James's entry into London, and has survived as a historiographical trope to this day.[42]

After Themis praises the king to them, the people respond with a new, joyous unanimity:

> And this confession flew from every voyce:
> *Never had land more reason to rejoyce.*
> *Nor to her blisse, could ought now added bee,*
> *Save, that shee might the same perpetuall see.*
>
> (155–58)

The suggestion, however covert, is that James's public demeanor leaves something to be desired, and that a spokesman might help to satisfy the population. Even as he makes this suggestion, however, Jonson is careful to insist on royal self-sufficiency:

> She blest the people, that in shoales did swim
> To heare her speech; which still began in him
> And ceas'd in them.
>
> (133–35)

The mediator, we are told, does not embellish or otherwise alter the basic rapport between king and subjects. The king's own words (his "trueth") are enough, Themis simply carries them to the hungry crowd.

In her other role, Themis the advisor offers the king a lesson in English history, together with a lesson in statecraft drawn directly from James's *Basilikon Doron.*[43] On the one hand, there is a practical suggestion buried in Themis's speech: James as a foreigner might in fact need to be taught about English custom and about the "kings, praeceding him in that high court; / Their lawes, their endes" (91–92). On the other hand, by couching his suggestion in a speech dominated by James's own published views, Jonson balances it with still more evidence of the king's self-sufficiency. As if that were not enough, Jonson shows us that the king is instantly ready to interpret the history that Themis discloses. She tells him of the bad kings in England's past, and he recognizes them as such:

> Nor did he seeme their vices so to love,
> As once defend, what THEMIS did reprove.

> For though by right, and benefite of Times,
> He ownde their crownes, he would not so their crimes.
>
> (109–12)

Like the reiterations of James's own maxims, this dramatization of the king's total and immediate agreement with Themis balances the poem's suggestion that the king needs instruction.

The "Panegyre," then, is a delicately equivocal piece. On the one hand, it demonstrates the usefulness not only of a panegyrist but also of a poet-advisor. It identifies the poet, as well as the king, with the goddess of justice and order. On the other hand, the poem counters these strong claims by demonstrating royal self-sufficiency even as it demonstrates the poet's usefulness. The poem hedges its bets, theorizing the usefulness of a laureate poet while insisting that one is not really needed. This explains why this poem, which otherwise has little to do with poets or poetry, should have as its concluding motto the line "*Solus Rex, & Poeta non quotannis nascitur.*" We might see Jonson's poem as a balancing act, in which the poet himself remains poised between Greene's "ev'ry Poet to himselfe's a King" and Davies's "what hast thowe to doe, and what remaines?"

Also exemplary in its subtle handling of Jacobean panegyric decorum is Jonson's epigram "To King James." Here Jonson – like so many other panegyrists – praises the king for excelling in both poetry and statecraft:

> How, best of Kings, do'st thou a scepter beare!
> How, best of *Poets*, do'st thou laurell weare!
> But two things, rare, the FATES had in their store,
> And gave thee both, to shew they could no more.
> For such a *Poet*, while thy dayes were greene,
> Thou wert, as chiefe of them are said t'have beene.
> And such a Prince thou art, wee daily see,
> As chief of those still promise they will bee.
> Whom should my *Muse* then flie to but the best
> Of Kings for grace; of *Poets* for my test?[44]

Jonson mobilizes a number of strategies here in order to fashion a workable response to the twin Jacobean problems of indecorum and redundancy. First, he draws a clear temporal distinction between James's days as a poet and his days as king.[45] James is not, Jonson's epigram points out, an active poet; consequently, there is room for another. Second, by calling the king's hoped-for bounty "grace," Jonson makes it clear that James, like God, has no need of praise.

Third, unlike his competitors, Jonson focuses on his own need for the king, rather than worrying about the king's need of a poet: "Whom should my *Muse* then flie to ..." These strategic moves enable Jonson to establish the sort of parallelism felt to be indecorous in Davies's panegyric welcome. The poem might be paraphrased as follows: As a poet, you could have done this better; now I rely on your judgment as a poet-king to recognize me as an excellent poet and, though you do not need me, to support me as such.

Strikingly, this brief panegyric is followed in the 1616 text of the *Epigrammes* by a brief poem, "On the Union," which picks up a metaphor from James's first speech in parliament and nicely encapsulates it. This sort of propaganda is one of the things a poet can do for his monarch, and it seems likely that the placement of the poem in Jonson's collection tacitly suggests that the "grace" of the king might not really be entirely disinterested.[46]

If James's self-sufficiency forces his early panegyrists to re-examine shared Elizabethan assumptions about the usefulness of courtly praise, then Jonson makes a virtue of necessity: by stressing both James's self-sufficiency and the parallels between himself and the king, Jonson is able to effectively write himself into an elite community of poets. In Epigram 36 ("To the Ghost of Martial") Jonson writes:

> MARTIAL, thou gav'st farre nobler Epigrammes
> To thy DOMITIAN, than I can my JAMES:
> But in my royall subject I passe thee,
> Thou flatterd'st thine, mine cannot flatter'd bee.
> (8:38)

Typically, the self-sufficient and obvious excellence of James at once renders Jonson's praises useless and also allows him to surpass his classical model. Jonson turns the threatening possibility that his panegyric may be useless into a sort of poetic boast, building a laureate self-image upon the rhetoric of uselessness in his own poems.

"WHAT NEED HAST THOU OF ME? OR OF MY *MUSE*?"

Helgerson argues that because Spenser, and to a lesser degree Sidney, had exhausted old laureate modes – pastoral, the sonnet sequence, romance, national epic – Jonson and his contemporaries had to find fresh forms within which to construct voices for themselves.[47] This can be only partly accurate, for Spenserian laureate modes of performance were created within the Elizabethan court, and only make sense there.

Sir John Harington, in an epigram written to celebrate the accession of the new king, makes this explicit, suggesting that James's court will require a change in style of poetic performance. Bidding adieu to the "Sweet wanton Muse" of his earlier verse, Harington declares: "Now to more serious thoughts my soule aspyers, / This age, this minde, a Muse awstere requires."[48] Harington's epigram describes a change in literary fashion which is, in itself, familiar enough to literary historians: Jacobean plain style replaces the elaborate, aureate fictions of the Elizabethan court.

The promised austerity of Harington's new muse intentionally mirrors the dignity of James's own authorial style. By aligning his plain-style verse with the austere dignity of royal authority, Harington promises that his poetry, like the king's, will reproduce nothing but "trueth." This austerity, consequently, curtails the scope of the poet's creativity, refiguring invention as wantonness: it is difficult to imagine a laureate self-fashioning constructed around this radically limited version of poetic invention: Davies's question – "what hast thowe to doe, and what remaines?" – describes a dilemma faced generally by the comparatively "awstere" Jacobean muse.

Davies's aporetic question persists as a central concern not only in Jonson's celebrations of James, but throughout his occasional panegyric verse. Consider, for example, the epigram (no. 43) which Jonson wrote to Cecil shortly after the latter became Earl of Salisbury in 1605:

> What need hast thou of me? or of my *Muse*?
>   Whose actions so themselves doe celebrate;
> Which should thy countries love to speake refuse,
>   Her foes enough would fame thee, in their hate.
> 'Tofore, great men were glad of *Poets*: Now,
>   I, not the worst, am covetous of thee.
> Yet dare not, to my thought, lest hope allow
>   Of adding to thy fame; thine may to me,
> When, in my booke, men reade but CECILL's name,
>   And what I write thereof find farre, and free
> From servile flatterie (common *Poets* shame)
>   As thou stand'st cleere of the necessitie.

This epigram makes a number of the moves that we have found in the work of James's panegyrists: like the final couplet of Drayton's sonnet on the poet-king ("They whose pens, (even) life to Kings doe give / In thee a King shall seeke them selves to live") it reverses the expected economy of glorification, suggesting that the subject glorifies the poem; like Jonson's own epigram to Martial, this poem suggests that its subject's perfection makes flattery impossible and consequently distinguishes Jonson from "common Poets."

Moreover, like "A Panegyre," this epigram contains underhanded hints about the poet's real usefulness even as it celebrates Cecil's self-sufficiency. The suggestion of a refusal on the part of his own country to celebrate Cecil, as well as the invocation of his and his country's enemies, effectively reminds Cecil of the resentment aroused by his preeminence. The epigram hints that Cecil, surrounded by enemies, actually needs all the prestige he can muster.[49]

More generally, Stanley Fish finds throughout Jonson's poetry of praise a recurring gesture which we are now in a position to recognize:

Jonson's poems of praise … present the objects of praise to themselves; they say in effect, "Sir or Madame So and So, meet Sir or Madam So and So, whom, of course you already know." Once this is said, the poem is to all intents and purposes over, although the result paradoxically is that it often has a great deal of difficulty getting started since it is, in effect, all dressed up with nowhere to go.[50]

Jonson constantly uses his "difficulty getting started" as a gesture which, by demonstrating the uselessness of his poetic compliment, praises his subject as self-sufficiently virtuous. The subject needs no praise, so all the poem can do is reflect his or her self-evident virtue. Indeed, Jonson's idealization of what Thomas Greene has called the "centered self" can in general be seen as a part of the strategy Fish singles out.[51] It should be clear, by now, that this is a move uniquely well suited to the rhetorical demands of Jacobean epideictic verse: Jonson's strategy of mere reflection – so tortuously articulated by Bacon in the opening of the *Advancement Of Learning* – is also a familiar response to James's self-sufficiency.

We might say, then, that time and again in his occasional verse Jonson deploys a translational plain style of the kind encouraged by James's authoritative "trueth." This "awstere" encomiastic stance, in turn, implies a specific relationship between the poet – who claims merely to reflect his subject's "trueth" – and the subject – who therefore must be praised as a source of stable meaning. The fact that this particular relationship informs Jonson's addresses to a range of different subjects is indicative of the kind of widespread effect James's self-styling had on early Jacobean epideictic fashion.

This dispersed influence should not in itself be surprising. First, the Jacobean court world was, relatively speaking, small and interconnected, which would allow fashion to move swiftly and be widely legible to those who mattered.[52] Second, given the courtly emphasis on what Frank Whigham has called the "rhetorical imperative of performance," emergent styles and conventions were quickly codified, appropriated, and circulated among whichever circles fashioned themselves literate.[53] Third, a courtly writer of occasional verse angling for some form of patronage will attempt, among other things, to demonstrate his mastery over a sophisticated system of often subtly politicized modes of discourse. Accordingly, Jonson's poem to Cecil might be more concerned to show off its author's familiarity with a sophisticated trope of praise than to attribute self-sufficiency to Cecil himself.[54]

Jonson's repeated deployment of this encomiastic stance may have to do with discursive fashions stemming from James's authorial self-styling, but in practice Jonson's poems subtly contradict the king's claim to a discursive monopoly. For this encomiastic stance, when applied to other patrons, sets them up as independent – kingly – sources of "trueth." In the world of Jonson's *Epigrammes*, then, we find many patrons and friends praised for their absolute self-sufficiency; praise for John Donne – which dwells on the poet's self-sufficient creativity – might have been addressed to James himself:

> Who shall doubt, DONNE, where I a Poet bee,
>   When I dare send my *Epigrammes* to thee?
> That so alone canst judge, so'alone dost make:
>   And, in thy censures, evenly, dost take
> As free simplicitie, to dis-avow,
> As thou hast best authoritie, t[o]'allow.
>   (no. 96, 1–6)

It is surely ironic that a form of address designed to respond to the king's unique monopoly over symbolic capital should lead Jonson to attribute king-like "authoritie" to others. The important point here is not that Jonson's mode of praise in the *Epigrammes* is in any real way subversive of the king's authority, but rather that the king's authoritative "stile" functions within the larger world of courtly writing in ways that are beyond his own control and at cross-purposes with his own discursive strategies.

Donne, like Jonson, is sensitive to the problematic decorum of praise occasioned by James's "stile." In fact, Donne's stance has been described as being generally self-abnegating. Thus, Goldberg has described a Donne whose voice is always constituted by its total reliance on the discursive authority of others: "given identity and robbed of self-determination at once; this is like the condition Donne imagines for himself ... totally submissive so that he may gain a place in the world."[55] This might be seen as an extreme version of the trans-lational decorum implied by Harington's turn toward "a Muse awstere." Goldberg's Donne gains a voice only by reproducing the authoritative "trueth" of others.

Goldberg's description of Donne as a poet whose "self-constitution is absolutist" has been challenged recently by critics suggesting that it fails to account for the tonal variety of Donne's writing, and for his obvious ambivalence about an absolutism that excluded him from its charmed circle.[56] Annabel Patterson, for example, argues that "it is impossible to produce a single-minded person, let alone a coherent pattern of behaviours. The story of Donne in the reign of James is a story of self-division and self-contradiction."[57] The Donne that emerges from this reconsideration is characterized by an overriding ambivalence about the relationship between verbal power and authori-ty, an ambivalence which in turn replicates the problematics of Jacobean praise with which we have been concerned.

The dedication to King James from Donne's *Pseudo-Martyr* (1610) powerfully articulates Donne's ambivalence about the king's "trueth":

The influence of those your Majesties Bookes, as the Sunne, which penetrates all corners, hath wrought upon me, and drawen up, and exhaled from my poore Meditations, these discourses: Which, with all reverence and devotion, I present to your Majestie, who in this also have the power and office of the Sunne, that those things which you exhale, you may at your pleasure dissipate, and annull; or suffer them to fall downe againe, as a wholesome and fruitfull dew, upon your Church & Commonwealth. Of my boldnesse in this addresse, I most humbly beseech your Majestie, to admit this excuse, that having observed, how much your Majestie had vouchsafed to descend to a conversa-tion with your Subjects, by way of your Bookes, I also conceiv'd an ambition, of ascending to your presence, by the same way, and of participating, by this meanes, their happinesse, of whome, that saying of the Queene of *Sheba*, may bee usurp'd: Happie are thy men, and happie are those thy Servants, which stand before thee alwayes, and heare thy wisedome. For, in this, I make account, that I have performed a duetie, by expressing in an exterior, and (by your Majesties permission) a publicke Act, the same desire, which God heares in my daily prayers, That your Majestie may very long governe us in your Person, and ever, in your Race and Progenie.[58]

The conceit with which this passage begins, of course, exemplifies the kind of self-constitutive passivity which is central to Goldberg's Donne. It also recapitulates the problems of Jacobean address with which we have been concerned: it might, for example, remind us of the elaborately self-abnegating dedication to James from Bacon's *Advancement of Learning*.

At the same time, the detailed hyperbole which Donne brings to bear in this conventional conceit makes it feel strained, and rather grotesque. It is I think possible to detect, in the almost lurid pleasure Donne takes in the extension of his conceit, the kind of exertion of verbal power which is often described as a hallmark of Donne's poetry, and which Fish diagnoses as "the need first to create a world and then endlessly to manipulate those who are made to inhabit it."[59] Arthur Marotti describes the same characteristic need in political terms: "Donne characteristically called such attention to himself as a thinking subject and laid out arguments of such metaphoric and intellectual complexity that he seems to have been competing with, rather than self-effacingly paying tribute to, his addressee, forcing his primary audience to submit to his intellectual and literary authority."[60] Following this logic, one might detect more than a little irony in Donne's elaborate insistence on his own powerlessness before James's influence. After the exaggerated meekness of the solar conceit, Donne's apology for his "boldnesse" comes as something of a jolt, and perhaps cues us into the fact that it is bold partly because of its ironies.

Bolder still – and more germane to the difficulties we have been tracing – is the assertion that James's books constitute a kind of condescension which authorizes a rising "ambition" on Donne's part. By describing quotation as usurpation, Donne underscores the difficulties of decorum involved in the kind of ambition authorized by the king's descent into print. The implied meaning may be paraphrased as follows: James's publications enter him into a conversation with his subjects; this gesture encourages other authors to associate their writings with the royal "stile"; this in turn allows subjects to appropriate royal "trueth," and therefore to usurp royal dictatorial powers.

As with Jonson, Donne's sensitivity to the implications of James's "stile" led him to adopt an encomiastic stance organized around the God-like "trueth" of his subject. Barbara Lewalski's influential study of Donne's modes of compliment, for example, suggests that his encomiastic stance – he "undertakes to explore religious or philosophical truth by writing the praises of an individual" – "permits Donne consistently to apply to any individual those extreme formulations of the conventional *topoi* most contemporary poets invoked ... only for praises of royalty."[61] Lewalski's paradigm can be politicized by adding that Donne's use of this stance in his poems of praise for non-royal subjects

leads him to challenge the king's monopoly of absolute "trueth" much
more overtly than did Jonson.

It is difficult to date many of Donne's lyrics, but his verse epistles,
particularly those written to the Countess of Bedford (1608–14), provide us with a body of Donne's early Jacobean occasional panegyric.
In fact, the Horatian verse epistle is an ideal site to examine Donne's
negotiations of conventions of praise since, as Margaret Maurer and
others have suggested, it was used by early modern writers to explore
problems of decorum, foregrounding the specific conditions and
rhetorical demands of panegyric address.[62]

The epistle in which Donne most explicitly addresses the problem of
his poem's usefulness is the second written to the Countess of Bedford,
a poem which begins as follows:

> You have refin'd mee, and to worthyest things
>   (Vertue, Art, Beauty, Fortune,) now I see
> Rareness, or use, not nature value brings;
>   And such, as they are circumstanc'd, they bee.
>   Two ills can ne're perplexe us, sinne to'excuse;
>   But of two good things, we may leave and chuse.
>
> Therefor at Court, which is not vertues clime,
>   (Where a transcendent height, (as, lownesse mee)
> Makes her not be, or not show) all my rime
>   Your vertues challenge, which there rarest bee;
>   For, as darke texts need notes: there some must bee
>   To usher vertue, and say, *This is shee*.[63]

As David Aers and Gunther Kress have made abundantly clear, these
twelve lines are themselves a dark text in need of notes.[64] The countess
– presented as an alchemist – has re-made the poet in such a way that
he is now able to see relativity of value where he once saw only a naturalized hierarchy of "worthyest things." These two conceptions of
value lie side by side: on the one hand, the countess has "vertue"
which the poem, here and later, treats as a thing good in itself; on the
other hand, the suggestion is that since virtue is rare at court it will be
treasured there as something scarce.

The density of the conceit complicates what at first glance seems to
be a fairly clear formulation of the usefulness of the panegyrist.
Though it is clear that Donne proposes to annotate the text of the
countess's virtue, it is not really clear what this amounts to. Confronted
with the line "darke texts need notes" we might join Aers and Kress in
asking whose need this is.[65] It could be the countess's, or it could be the

courtiers', but either answer poses problems. Why, following the logic of the poem, does the exalted countess need to be celebrated in court if it is so far below her? Moreover, the poem's conceit does not really explain why the degraded climes of court should value virtue at all. Intuitively, the opposite would be true. In fact, the only clearly accept-able answer is the one not supplied by the logic of the poem: it is Donne's need. In the contingent world of relative values, the poet him-self is so low as to seem like nothing, and when this poem was written Donne – long out of favor – was actively seeking to find some new position at court. "Lownesse" names Donne's real social position.

The poem encodes a request for patronage and a promise of service: in it, Donne asks the countess to help return him to court, while at the same time promising to use his literary skills to praise her. At the same time, the poem's fiction also insists on the countess's "transcen-dent height," likening the relationship between poet and subject to the relationship between petitioner and God:

> Yet to that Deity which dwels in you,
>   Your vertuous Soule, I now not sacrifice;
> These are *Petitions*, and not *Hymnes*; they sue
> But that I may survay the edifice.
>
> (31–34)

Within the conceit that organizes the poem, the countess – not only God-like but also the originator (or refiner) of insight in the poet – evidently would have no need of the poet's services.

Like Jonson's encomiastic verse, Donne's epistle insists that it can do no more than announce (or usher) its subject's perfection: "*This is shee.*" However, the conceit of the two different kinds of value allows Donne to separate his subject's self-sufficiency from his own proposed sphere of agency. By positing two kinds of value, Donne is able to adopt the Jacobean encomiastic stance – poet disempowered, subject complete – and still imagine a role for the poet that is neither redun-dant nor insubordinate. The question "What need hast thou of me? or of my *Muse*?" lurks behind the poem, but is effectively finessed by the poem's elaborately developed logic of value.

It is important to be clear about the interplay between the poem's fiction and the real exchange between suitor and patron. Marotti describes the relationship between Donne and the countess as follows: "In need of social access to a courtly world in which he sought new employment, Donne looked to Lady Bedford for social and political, rather than for simply monetary, assistance, hoping to use her offices as

a courtly mediator or broker to win preferment."[66] Stripped of its elaborate fictional trappings, Donne's poem expresses this basic agenda: it
asks the countess to get him court employment.

The fiction of Donne's poem, then, makes sense only as part of "a
ritual transaction whose formality the participants maintained and
whose stylized hyperboles, euphemisms, and abstractions they understood in relation to an immediate social context."[67] What I am suggesting is that the encomiastic currency of this particular transaction is
specific to an early Jacobean moment: the exaggerated dependence –
even uselessness – of the poet, as well as the God-like self-sufficiency
attributed to the addressee, are the hallmarks of a panegyric gesture
formed in response to James's "stile" of authority. "You have refin'd
mee" is a virtuosic deployment of what I have called the Jacobean
encomiastic stance, directed here to the Countess of Bedford because
virtuosity is precisely the commodity that Donne has to offer.

As in the case of Jonson's *Epigrammes*, it is ironic that Donne should
use a form of address encouraged by James's "stile" to claim absolute,
transcendent authority for another. In Donne's epistle, characteristically, the irony is driven home by his satiric reference to "Court, which is
not vertues clime," which tacitly implies that, unlike the Countess,
James has been unable to refine those in his care. Constructed on the
model of James, the Countess of Bedford becomes an alternative to
him. The hidden logic of this comparison becomes explicit later in the
poem, and the Countess's estate at Twickenham becomes a kind of
alternate court in which she exercises what, in the dedication of *Pseudo-
Martyr*, Donne called the "power and office of the Sunne": "Since a
new world doth rise here from your light, / We your new creatures, by
new recknings goe" (21–22).

Suggested no doubt by the name Lucy, the countess's solar offices
become the center of the poem; Donne's celebration of Lucy is
reminiscent of his hyperbolic celebration of James in the *Pseudo-Martyr*
dedication:

> to this place
> You are the season (Madame) you the day,
> 'Tis but a grave of spices, till your face
> Exhale them, and a thick close bud display.
> (13–16)

This conceit is elaborated with increasing audacity, until stanza 5
makes the comparison between Twickenham and the court – Lucy
and James – perilously explicit:

> In this you'have made the Court th'Antipodes,
>   And will'd your Delegate, the vulgar Sunne,
> To doe profane autumnall offices,
> Whilst here to you, wee sacrificers runne;
> And whether Priests, or Organs, you wee'obey,
> We sound your influence, and your Dictates say.
>
> (25–30)

No longer a pastoral country seat ("in the county'is beauty" [13]), Twickenham has become a political and religious center, a place of hurried activity ("wee sacrificers runne"), a site of worldly authority replete with delegates, offices, dictates. Lucy's light is transformed into an alternative to James's, a light that governs as James's only seems to.

As the poem would have it, the effectiveness of Lucy's government is demonstrated by the obedience of her mouthpieces. When he says "We sound your influence, and your Dictates say," Donne in effect promises perfect replication of Lucy's "trueth." Of course, Donne's epistle itself is evidence that James does not enjoy such obedience. Instead, the poem takes advantage of the perception hinted at in Donne's dedication to James from *Pseudo-Martyr*, recognizing that once published the king's "stile" can be appropriated, and that this in itself constitutes a challenge to his discursive authority. In that dedication, Donne hinted that this appropriation was itself a kind of usurpation; here, by replacing James with Lucy, Donne makes good on his suggestion.

We might be reminded also of "The Sunne Rising," a more familiar example of Donne's early Jacobean verse, and one which also centers on usurpation and on the "power and office of the Sunne."[68] This poem has become something of a touchstone for analysis of Donne's relation to James's authority, and has been repeatedly taken as evidence of the degree to which public, royalist ideologies dominated Donne's consciousness during the years of his exile from court. John Carey, for example, writes, "what the real court and the real king may be doing stays at the back of his mind, and as if to counteract this the poem evolves its announcement of personal kingship."[69] More recently, David Norbrook has attempted to counterbalance this reading of the poem by suggesting, among other things, that "by parodically appropriating a Christ-like or monarchical status to himself, Donne undermines the claims of such discourses to transcendent status."[70]

In the poem's first stanza, the penetrating gaze of the "unruly Sunne" is aligned with – and rejected as representing – the demands made upon the lovers by time, place, and the social world. By the end of the poem, of course, the lovers have taken the place of the social world, installed themselves at its center. The poem's second stanza begins by restating the desire to exclude the sun (and, consequently, the world) as a boast:

> Thy beames, so reverend, and strong
> Why shouldst thou thinke?
> I could eclipse and cloud them with a winke
> But that I would not lose her sight so long.
> (11–14)

At this point, the poem shifts direction, and the remainder of the second stanza rewrites the first, as the speaker invests his lover with all of what had previously been excluded from the room. First, we see her as an alternative to the opening stanza's "unruly Sunne" ("If her eyes have not blinded thine" [15]). Second, where the first stanza included commerce among the worldly concerns to be exiled ("Call countrey ants to harvest offices" [8]), the second describes the lover as the source of exotic commodity: "both the'India's of spice and Myne / ... lie here with mee" (17–18). Finally, where the first stanza exiled king and court, the second finds "those Kings whom thou saw'st yesterday, / ... All here in one bed" (19–20).

The third and final stanza, which I quote in full, provides the crux for readings of Donne's politics:

> She'is all States, and all Princes, I,
> Nothing else is.
> Princes doe but play us; compar'd to this,
> All honor's mimique; All wealth alchimie.
> Thou sunne art halfe as happy'as wee,
> In that the world's contracted thus;
> Thine age askes ease, and since thy duties bee
> To warme the world, that's done in warming us.
> Shine here to us, and thou art every where;
> This bed thy center is, these walls, thy spheare.

This is where the speaker capitalizes on the claims he has made for his lover, using her omnibus richness to locate himself at the center of the world. Seen in this way, the compliment masks a kind of ambition: Donne's speaker moves from his manifestly unsatisfactory exclusionary boast towards a mode of compliment that locates him at the center of a fully political world.

We might say, then, that "The Sunne Rising" miniaturizes the complimentary strategy which Donne uses in his verse epistle to the

Countess of Bedford. In that poem, Donne praised the countess as an alternate source of royal "trueth" in order to locate himself within the new court which that gesture allowed him to imagine. In "The Sunne Rising," too, Donne appropriates that which he is excluded from, centers it on his praise's subject, and is subsequently able to imagine a "new world" in which he occupies a more central position. It is easy, I think, to see "The Sunne Rising" as expressive of Donne's own deep-seated ambivalence about the Jacobean court, to see it as at once a reinscription and a usurpation of its central authority. It is also possible, however, to see the poem's mannered and elaborate system of substitutions as an exposé of the way that encomiastic gestures can be self-serving, and of the way that responses to the king's "stile" can be appropriated or ventriloquized.

Donne offers his most explicit theoretical account of the exchange-ability of topoi of praise in a verse epistle written to Lady Catherine Howard, Countess of Salisbury in 1614. After praising the Countess as the highest example of "What Heaven can doe" (2), Donne's epistle dwells on the problematics of absolute praise.[71] In particular, Donne acknowledges that he has praised other subjects in similarly absolute terms, but argues "if things like these, have been said by mee / Of others, call not that Idolotrie" (37–38). His elaboration is suggestive:

> I adore
> The same things now, which I ador'd before,
> The subject chang'd, and measure; the same thing
> In a low constable, and in the King
> I reverence; his power to worke on mee.
>
> (57–61)

Even in this idealized formulation, Donne makes it clear that the king's virtues are found elsewhere, and that modes of praise are applicable to a range of subjects. This in itself, as we have seen, constitutes a muted challenge to the king's unique monopoly on "trueth."

The suggestion that the poet's reverence is doled out in proportion to subject's "power to worke" on him is also vulnerable to a less idealizing reading: namely, that praise will be apportioned in exchange for something and according to the poet's self-interested agenda. Read this way, Donne's formulation amounts to a double violation of the claims implicit in James's self-styling. First, Donne tacitly suggests that panegyrics are part of an exchange between poet and subject in which both parties stand to gain something. This in turn implies that poets have something to offer, that they create symbolic capital, that they are

not limited to reproducing the king's "trueth." Second, Donne's suggestion that praises for a king can be, at the poet's discretion, offered to
a constable underscores a point I have been concerned with all along:
encomiastic stances fashioned in response to James's putative unique-
ness become codified gestures vulnerable to what Donne himself might
call usurpation.

We might say, then, that Jonson and Donne develop distinctly
different responses to the problematics of early Jacobean courtly panegyric. Jonson tends generally to deploy an elaborately disempowered
encomiastic stance while simultaneously allying his own voice with that
of the king: "*Solus Rex & Poeta non quotannis nascitur.*" Though he
addresses similar panegyrics to other subjects, Jonson does not call
attention to the ways in which this self-quotation challenges James's
unique discursive authority. Donne, by contrast, is eager to theorize
problems which remain more submerged in Jonson's verse, calling
explicit attention to the subtle usurpations and transgressions available
within – and by means of – the Jacobean panegyrist's disempowered
stance. Jonson's delicate manipulation of the rhetorical demands of
Jacobean encomium is the performance of a skilled insider. Donne's
edgier relation to the same demands – the result, one imagines, both of
temperament and of disappointment – makes his poetry reflect more
fully the limits of James's authorial power.

Commentators on James and his court have frequently relied on
models of royal influence which oversimplify the transmission of the
Jacobean "stile," describing the king's influence by tracing a stable
menu of tropes and strategies, and finding these either reproduced (by
flatterers) or rejected (in disdain) by courtly writers. This model has it
that James, in his political ineptitude, created an official ideology
which failed to capture the hearts of Englishmen and which consequently became little more than a tool for flatterers, and for the archi-
tects of public occasions like masques or pageants. Goldberg's study, of
course, inverts the traditionally hostile historiography of James's reign,
treating James's "stile" not as a series of tropes endorsed by the foolish
king and manipulated by courtly writers, but rather as a series of
central and inescapably effective discursive strategies. Goldberg's book
neatly reverses the economy of discursive power assumed by critics
who see James as the wisest fool in Christendom – wresting agency
from the poet and giving it to the king – but he preserves from this
older tradition the assumption of a stable relationship between royal
"stile" and court discourse: James originates it, others reproduce it.

This chapter began by asking how we might understand the influence of a king on the literary styles of his court. As a case study, it has been concerned to show that this influence can be traced through a range of occasional literature produced in the early Jacobean court milieu. More important, I have tried to show that in order to understand this widespread royal influence it is necessary to conceive of court discourse as being constituted not by the handing down of an official ideology, or by the dissemination of a series of royal strategies, but by a series of exchanges and appropriations within which the king is only one specially key player. The royal "stile" is hugely privileged and centrally visible, but its interplay with the literature produced by other courtiers – rather than being merely a series of acceptances and rejections – is characterized by rhetorical dilemmas, shot through with vulnerabilities and internal inconsistencies, and mediated by a series of ventriloquizations and local appropriations.

In fact, the irony of James's "stile" – and perhaps one reason for its failure to contribute to the making of a national cult like the one that surrounded Elizabeth – is that it is simply so difficult to fashion a response to it. Skilled poets like Davies, Jonson, and Donne respond to James's claimed discursive monopoly in a variety of ways, but even the most fully successful response – Jonson's – encodes an implicit challenge to James's dictatorial power. The point, in other words, is neither that courtiers rejected the king's heavy-handed claims, nor that they were entrapped by them, but rather that unlike Elizabeth – who became a magnet for a wide variety of literary and iconographic adornments – James made it difficult for poets to make the kinds of self-advertising claims implicit in court panegyric without impinging on the claims promulgated by the king: praise of James is either redundant or impertinent, while the adaptation of fashionable Jacobean encomiastic stances towards others borders on a kind of usurpation of royal power. We might now return to a formulation which, as we have seen, was originally intended to praise the king. We are now in a position to see that it also adumbrates an important strategic dilemma embedded within James's "stile of *Gods*": "None but thy selfe – great king – can sing of thee."

CHAPTER TWO

Arcadia re-formed
Pastoral negotiations in early Jacobean England

Pierre Macherey warns critics against what he calls the "natural fallacy of empiricism," the tendency to treat a text as given, theorizing its consumption without asking after the conditions of its production.[1] Since the received materials out of which a text is made "are not neutral transparent components," they "retain a certain autonomy ... their real inscription in a history of forms means that they cannot be defined exclusively by their immediate function in a specific work."[2] Consequently, in Macherey's analysis a text is always both "furrowed by the allusive presences of those other books against which it is elaborated" and "generated from the incompatibility of several meanings."[3] These furrows, silences which are forced on the text by its embedded incompatibilities, reveal to the careful critic the suppressed ideology of the text's production. They constitute the "unconscious of the work": they are the sites of "the irruption of the real," places where the text reveals its ideological secrets regardless of the author's intent.[4]

The texts with which Macherey illustrates his theory are drawn exclusively from the nineteenth-century novel, prompting his translator to wonder if the theory applies equally well to other genres and to works from other periods.[5] Surely some of Macherey's polemic loses its force when applied to Renaissance texts, which were often understood to be immediately engaged with ideological questions, and whose conditions of production are so often made explicit in dedications and topical allusions. Moreover, since in Renaissance texts the connections between genre and ideology are so often overt, formal dissonance of the kind Macherey describes can often be treated as authorial exploration rather than as the product of suppressed social conditions.

Taken as a whole, the pastoral literature produced during the formative first decade of King James's reign in England provides a uniquely appropriate example both of the utility of the sort of analysis

Macherey recommends and of the re-adjustments necessitated by Renaissance conditions of literary production. The mode's Elizabethan prestige lingered after the queen's death, prompting ambitious early Jacobean writers to produce a fair amount of pastoral themselves. However, efforts to adapt Elizabethan generic expectations of pastoral to the discursive prompting of the new king resulted in a body of work scarred by precisely the sorts of equivocations, gaps, and uneasy resolutions which in Macherey's analysis are most revelatory. Pastoral, moreover, is a literary kind which tends to be explicitly concerned with "the allusive presences" of its predecessors; the sheer artifice and conventionality of pastoral attitudes and settings underscores the allusive as well as the innovative elements in each individual text.[6] Consequently, unlike Macherey's novelists who effectively deny their reliance on pre-existing cultural material, the Renaissance pastoralist tends both to proclaim and theorize it.

As with the changes in panegyric convention traced in the previous chapter, the dramatic contrast between Elizabeth's public style and that of James led to wholesale changes in the system of courtly modes and fashions, as courtiers and would-be courtiers scrambled to adjust to emerging Jacobean styles. In the specific case of pastoral, this process of adaptation was shaped not only by the passing of Elizabeth – and consequently of the logic behind the court discourse in which pastoral had become naturalized – but also by a specific appropriation of pastoral to the rhetoric of Jacobean power. Early Jacobean writers, in other words, responded not only to the fact that Elizabethan pastoral conventions became passé, but also to a new and recognizably Jacobean vision of government and community promulgated authoritatively and often translated into the pastoral mode.

The authority of the Jacobean pastoral line is made explicit in a lyric written by James himself towards the end of his reign, on the occasion of Prince Charles's ill-advised trip to Spain in 1623. In reference to the false names which the prince and Buckingham adopted while leaving London, James figures the two men as "Jack" and "Tom" respectively:

> Kinde Sheppeherdes that have loved them longe
> bee not soe rashe in censuringe wronge
> Correct *your* ffeares, leave off to murne
> the Heavens will favour there returne,
>   Remitt the Care, to Royall Pan
>   Of Jacke his Sonne, and Tom, his Man.[7]

In contrast with the more performative style of many of Elizabeth's pastoral incarnations, James here imagines himself as a controlling overseer for a pastoral community as big as England. Moreover, as the admonitory tone of his poem suggests, James's pastoral self-styling implies a conception of the pastoral community as itself always ordered by, and opened up to, the knowledge of "Royall Pan." Though written after the period I am concerned with here, these assumptions and assertions are typical of James's public stances, and could easily have been extrapolated from his earlier publications. In fact, James was figured as "Pan" as early as 1603, in Jonson's *Althorpe Entertainment*, and in a speech before his first parliament in 1604, James explained his relation to his undivided realm by declaring "I am the Shepherd, and it is my Flocke."[8]

This pastoral line – England united under the protective care of James – recurs often enough in Jacobean panegyric to seem paradigmatic. For instance Sir John Harington, in a sonnet welcoming the new king, exhorts England to "Be all one flock, by one great sheppard guided: / No forren wolf can force a fould so fenced."[9] Among other things, I will be concerned to show that a model of community cognate with the implications of this pastoral line figures prominently in the literature produced during the first decade of James's reign in England.

Early Jacobean pastoral exemplifies the monarch's central, mediating role in the transmission of literary convention. But these texts are also indicative of the vulnerabilities and ellipses of that process. For early Jacobean writers who took Elizabethan conventions of pastoral seriously produced texts scarred by the kinds of equivocation Macherey writes about, which suggests that they themselves found the process of generic renegotiation to be a difficult one. Implicit in this argument is a model of cultural production which differs significantly from that of Jonathan Goldberg's influential study of Jacobean literature: rather than describing a discursive field always already dominated by the king's absolutist strategies, I attempt to place both the king and his subjects within a larger, diachronic field that includes what Raymond Williams would call "residual" Elizabethan elements.[10] Thus, while producers of early Jacobean pastoral do appropriate the king's representational strategies and discursive stances, they also continue to respond to strategies and stances naturalized under his predecessor; local disjunctions in each of these pastoral texts are symptomatic of larger disjunctions between Jacobean orthodoxy and inherited Elizabethan ideologies and practices.

In particular, the Jacobean vision of pastoral community – ordered and overseen from above – implies a simultaneous redefinition of the pastoral subject as fully available for official scrutiny. The thematic and formal conventions of Elizabethan pastoral define the subject differently, and these received conventions are part of the cultural material with which early Jacobean writers make pastoral texts. As a result, within these early Jacobean pastorals the representation of the individual subject is frequently the site of abrupt disjunctions and telling equivocations.

"ELIZABETHAN" AND "JACOBEAN" PASTORAL

The late Elizabethan appetite for pastoral was fed with numerous entertainments, romances, eclogue books, miscellanies, and a "dauntingly large and various body" of uncollected pastoral lyrics.[11] A number of factors contributed to this proliferation of pastoral: the example of Spenser's *Shepheardes Calender* (1579); the achievement of Sir Philip Sidney, whose first *Arcadia* was most likely completed in 1580; the development of pastoral as a courtly mode in Italy; the prestige of the Virgilian model. Moreover, thanks largely to the ground-breaking work of Louis Adrian Montrose and Annabel Patterson, it has become impossible to ignore the fact that Elizabethan pastoral provided an arena for the negotiation of many of the larger cultural concerns within which it was itself embedded.[12]

I want to focus here on the representational use of the individual shepherd or shepherdess. For where they are addressed in Elizabethan pastoral, questions about the relationship between subject and society tend to be approached by exploring only the emotions and experiences of a particular individual. I call this emphasis the characterological dimension of Elizabethan pastoral in order to distinguish it from a more conventional notion of inwardness as the telling of "what is in the heart."[13] What is at issue in my formulation is not sincerity but simply the use of an individual as a representational site: conventional lyric representations of inward experience would be included under this rubric, as would, for example, the amatory addresses to Elizabeth which frequently use highly conventional language of love in order to allude to more public concerns and desires. Along with, and often mixed into, privileged courtly modes such as the romance and the love lyric, pastoral participates in the development of late Elizabethan characterological focus.

Thus, the Spenserian pastoral eclogue, which, as Paul Alpers has demonstrated, greatly expanded the generic potential of Elizabethan lyric while locating its speaker within and against a community of shepherds, focuses on Colin's emotional state even as it demonstrates his importance to the rest of the pastoral community.[14] A similar example of the Elizabethan characterological focus is the recurrent use, in pastoral romance and elsewhere, of what Richard Helgerson has called "patterns of prodigality": the individual's departure from and subsequent chastened return to social standards of behavior. This plot convention emphasizes the trajectory of the moral life of an individual character rather than focusing either on the standards themselves, or on the structure of the community that produces and is produced by them.[15] Even Sidney's *Old Arcadia*, the most developed social critique among Elizabethan pastorals, explores the problems of Arcadian society primarily by focusing on the characterological vicissitudes of its major characters.

Some of the uses of this characterological emphasis can be singled out, though in practice they tend to be interrelated. First, the language of character helped to mystify the power of the queen. Explicit tributes to Elizabeth under more-or-less transparent pastoral names – Spenser's "Eliza," or Sidney's "Mira" – made her at once a goddess and a chaste shepherdess, using the image of the queen to authorize a given ethos while suggesting that character, rather than rank, was the source of her power. Praise for shepherdesses not explicitly supposed to stand for the queen helped embellish norms of praise for conventional Elizabethan virtues: by linking virtue to beauty and endowing the two with an active civilizing effect, pastorals not explicitly about the queen often reinforced the Elizabethan equation of power and virtue.[16] As a corollary, pastoralism, like Petrarchism, provided the courtier with a useful language of service, an approved stance to take *vis-à-vis* the evocative virtue and beauty of the queen. As in Petrarchan lyric, the Elizabethan pastoral love object is at once wonderfully chaste and powerfully desirable.[17]

Second, the characterological focus of Elizabethan pastoral contributed to the domestication of social criticism, eliding its most telling and potentially subversive questions.[18] Attention to the prodigality, lovesickness, or simply private depths of an individual character deflects attention away from the production of social problems. In privileged modes of the late Elizabethan court, formal conventions of characterological presentation tended to limit the type of critique that could be made.

This attention to and embellishment of private character locates the burden of government squarely with the individual. Given the disproportion between aspirations and actual patronage in the latter years of Elizabeth's court – Wallace MacCaffrey has suggested that as many as 2,500 politically active suitors vied for the 1,200 or so positions "worth a gentleman's having," and Elizabeth was of necessity stingy with gifts – there was always the potential for a great deal of ill-will.[19]

The Elizabethan focus on the individual, in pastoral and in other privileged Elizabethan modes, helped to control this seemingly explosive situation by casting dissatisfaction as a characterological rather than a political phenomenon. Dissatisfaction is often recast as love-sickness, thereby providing an acceptable language in which to express frustration without actually articulating detailed criticism of the queen or her government. The courtly persona defined by love for the queen of shepherds is essentially a self-governing one. This does not mean that the political frustrations expressed were any less urgent, but by limiting explicit criticism and channeling the expression of dissatisfaction into the sustaining fictions of the cult of Elizabeth, the characterological focus of late Elizabethan literature helped to minimize the failure of morale caused by Elizabeth's frugality.

It is by now a cliché to say, with Puttenham, that pastoral provided a site within which it was possible "under the vaile of homely persons, and in rude speeches to insinuate and glaunce at greater matters, and such as perchance had not bene safe to have beene disclosed in any other sort."[20] It is possible, however, that the safety of pastoralism in the Elizabethan court may have had less to do with the "vaile of homely persons" than with the development and exploitation of a rhetoric of inwardness which provided discursive space within which it was possible to domesticate potentially subversive content.

In his first approach to England's new royal family in 1603, Jonson displays his characteristic sensitivity to the complexities and ambiguities of occasion. His *Althorpe Entertainment* – presented to Queen Anne and Prince Henry as they journeyed south from Scotland into their new realm – is a pastoral entertainment. But it is structured around the perception that the characterological emphasis so prevalent in Elizabethan pastoral fictions fits uneasily with the all-encompassing rhetoric of James.

Briefly, the entertainment is dominated by a "bevy of Faeries, attending on Mab their Queen" (26), on the one hand, and a satyr, on the other. The former group are given as Elizabethan, both because of the general familiarity of the motif, and also because they immediately "dance a round" in an "artificial ring" (27) in what might be described as a visual quotation of the dance of the graces observed by Calidore in book 6 of Spenser's *Faerie Queene* (6.10.5–17). The function of these faeries in Jonson's conceit is to deliver a valuable jewel to Queen Anne, and they explain the gift by means of a peculiar fiction: a faerie explains that they are worried lest the courtesy of the queen's host (Sir Robert Spencer, in actuality) fail him:

> 'Tis done only to supply,
> His suspected courtesie,
> Who (since THAMYRA did dye)
> Hath not brookt a ladies eye,
>
> Nor allow'd about his place,
> Any of the female race.
> Only we are free to trace
> All his grounds, as he to chase.
>   (130–37)

One recognizes this as a gesture towards the characterological: it handles this manifestly public, social occasion by casting it in terms of a putatively private love experience. In fact, the faerie explicitly forbids the publicization of their gift: "Utter not; we you implore, / Who did give it, nor wherefore" (146–47). Consequently, one expects that whatever point the entertainment will go on to make – about Spencer's loyalty to the new king, for example, or about his admiration for Anne – will be made in terms of this characterological plot.

Instead the satyr, who has been watching the faeries all along from behind a tree, steps forward and overturns everything that has hitherto taken place. First he dismisses the faeries' pretence of secrecy ("Not tell? Ha, ha" [155]), then he dismisses their fledgling love plot altogether:

> Say, that here he like the groves,
> And pursue no forraine loves:
> Is he therefore to be deemed
> Rude, or savage? or esteemed,
> But a sorry entertayner,
> 'Cause he is no common strayner
> After painted Nymphs for favours,
> Or that in his garbe he savours
> Little of that nicety,
> In the sprucer courtiery[?]
>   (159–68)

The love conceit put forward by the faeries is treated by the satyr as trifling courtly affectation. He then proposes that this kind of posturing will be replaced by plain honesty in the new king's court, so that Spencer will be able to flourish there despite lacking "sprucer courtiery":

> Now he hopes he shall resort there,
> Safer, and with more allowance;
> Since a hand hath governance,
> That hath given those customes chase,
> And hath brought his owne in place.
>
> (182–86)

Literally, the satyr's speech declares that the characterological language of love will be replaced by a plainer, more transparent courtly style. At the same time, the satyr literally gives the entertainment's Elizabethan pastoral plot chase, replacing it with a new style of entertainment. The last lines of the first night's entertainment call for the fiction to dissolve into sport:

> *Satyres* let the woods resound,
> They shall have their welcome crown'd,
> With a brace of bucks to ground.
>
> (225–27)

With that, "the whole wood and place resounded with the noyse of cornets, hornes, and other hunting musique" (228–29).

Jonson's entertainment replaces an Elizabethan love plot with a call to communal sport. This is doubly appropriate: it replaces an Elizabethan, characterological pastoral fiction with a more Jacobean call to transparent plainness and unanimity even as it explicitly praises the new monarch for giving chase to old discursive "customes" and replacing them with "his owne." The text of the entertainment – interrupted and in effect revised by the satyr's intrusion – is marked by a formal division of the sort Macherey might call our attention to, but, since the break in form reinforces the show's encomiastic message, I am inclined to see the fracture in this particular text as entirely self-conscious.[21]

In order to understand Jonson's conceit, it is necessary to see the communal sport with which the entertainment closes as a distinctly Jacobean vision of society. Leah Marcus points out that even before coming to England "James was prone to identify the exercise of his royal autonomy with the promotion of traditional pastimes."[22] James himself discusses the usefulness of such sports, stressing the fact that they foster ritual communality among the people: the festivals will "allure them to a common amitie among themselves," he writes, and are useful for "conveening of neighbours, for entertaining friendship and heartlinesse."[23] If pastoral and other privileged Elizabethan literary modes tend to emphasize private characterological development, James's support for ritual communality reverses this Elizabethan strategy, encouraging a redefinition of his subjects in terms of public, social relations.

In Marcus's analysis, James's investment in rural festival has to do with a "paradox of state" (7) – by including mild misrule under the *aegis* of royal license the central authority exerts some control over potentially subversive energies. The irony here is that the characterological dimension in Elizabethan discourse can itself be described as a "paradox of state" in Marcus's terms: as I have described it, the characterological emphasis provided "a form of social control that erased its own actions and its links to a central authority, a form of control that looked and felt like liberty."[24] James's strategic emphasis on festival sport, even as it allows for a kind of limited carnival play, fails to allow space for independent expression. This problem is registered in Marcus's study by the observation that even court artists writing in praise of public sport "developed strategies . . . for saving their art from engulfment in the ethos of the court."[25]

Festival communality is linked with a Jacobean vision of absolutism in a number of the minor pastoral celebrations of James's young reign. Phineas Fletcher, in a pastoral written for the Cambridge University anthology "Sorrowes Joy" (1603), signals the new ascendancy of festive sport over private song by imagining the Muses themselves fleeing their wonted habitats to join in the general festivities, dancing to James's own singing:

> And sacred Muses leaving their woont use
> Of carroling, flying their loathed cell,
>   Run to thy silver sound,
>   And lively dauncen round:
> What caren they for *Helicon*, or their *Pegasean* well?[26]

Similarly, Henry Chettle's "Spring-Song" for James is a good example of the call to festival communality and of its relationship to James's absolutist discourse, especially when compared to the pastoral elegy for Elizabeth to which it is appended: *Englandes Mourning Garment* (1603). The elegy takes the form of an eclogue in which Thenot inquires after the cause of Collin's misery. Although the pastoral façade quickly gives way to the extended prose exploration of the glory of Elizabeth and of Elizabethan England for which Chettle is chiefly remembered today, it begins with a gesture towards the voice of the private lovelorn swain of Elizabethan pastoral:

> I answere thee with woe and welaway,
> I am in sable clad, sith she cannot be had
> That me and mine did glad;
> > there's all I'le say.[27]

By contrast the "Spring-Song," though putatively spoken by the same Collin, has no private characterological elements and is instead a call to the community of shepherds to join in festival celebrations of the new king: "Shepheardes, Ile not be tedious in my Song; / For that I see you bent to active sport" (sig. GI). Active sport, in Chettle's "Spring-Song," takes the place of private emotion, linking the whole community of shepherds together in public harmony under the protection of the absolutist monarch himself:

> Showt joyfully, ye Nymphs, and rurall Swaines,
> Your maister *Pan* will now protect your foldes,
> Your Cottages will be as safe as Holdes,
> Feare neither Wolves nor subtill Foxes traines,
> > A Royall King will of your weale take keepe,
> > Hee'le be your Shepheard, you shalbe his sheepe.
> > > (sig. GI)

Jacobean festival communality ("active sport") defines its participants in terms of the community's structure; it participates in the Jacobean pastoral line insofar as it imagines the individual as being completely subjected and exposed to the panoptic control of the king.[28] A composite picture emerges of a coherent Jacobean pastoral strategy: in the place of the bifurcated praise of Eliza as at once shepherdess and goddess, James appears as Pan or the shepherd king, overseeing the clockwork of society below; the individuals that make up the clockwork are seen in terms of its structure, so there is a characteristic flattening out of the rhetoric of inwardness.[29]

TWO VERSIONS OF PASTORAL IN *THE FAITHFUL SHEPHERDESS*

Jonson, of course, came to be the preeminently articulate voice of the Jacobean line, and his early pastoral entertainment is a harbinger of later court success. Other early Jacobean writers – those who took the essentially Elizabethan generic conventions of pastoral more seriously, or those less eager to celebrate the new king – also wrestle with the two kinds of pastoral I have described, but find themselves variously unable

to reconcile the conflicting demands of the two representational
modes. These cases seem to me to be the most interesting, for they suggest just how fitful the kind of discursive reorganization announced in
Jonson's entertainment ("a hand hath governance / That hath given
those customes chase / And hath brought his owne in place") is in
practice. Since Elizabethan pastoral "customes" linger even as new
styles are brought into place, early Jacobean writers of pastoral find
themselves working with material that is already shot through with
potential dissonances, at once formal and ideological.

An ideal place to begin to tease out the manifestations of these problems is John Fletcher's *The Faithful Shepherdess*, performed around
1608–09, probably at Blackfriars.[30] Although the play seems to have
been a failure on stage, Fletcher's published edition (1609–10) presents
itself as a masterpiece. Packaged with commendatory verses by Jonson,
Chapman, Beaumont, and Nathaniel Fields, Fletcher's volume presents the play as a carefully constructed generic innovation in step with
the latest continental fashions but scorned by the vulgar ignorant. The
commendatory poems insist on this, and Fletcher reiterates it in his
own prickly epistle to the reader:

If you be not reasonably assurde of your knowledge in this kinde of Poeme,
lay downe the booke or read this, which I would wish had been the prologue.
It is a pastoral Tragie-comedie, which the people seeing when it was plaid,
having ever had a singular guift in defining, concluded to be a play of country
hired Shepheardes, in gray cloakes, with curtaild dogs in strings, sometimes
laughing together, and sometimes killing one another: And missing whitsun
ales, creame, wassel and morris-dances, began to be angry. In their error I
would not have you fall, least you incurre their censure. (p.15)

By distancing his play from a rough, popular tradition, Fletcher presents *The Faithful Shepherdess* as a scholarly work produced in accordance with subtle distinctions in generic decorums, and intended for
an elite, courtly audience. My reading of Fletcher's play corroborates
his own appraisal of it: the play self-consciously responds to the kind
of internally contradictory generic material thematically and formally
evoked in the *Althorpe Entertainment*. And, like Jonson, Fletcher seems at
all times to be in control of the contradictions between characteristic
Elizabethan and Jacobean pastoral strategies, though *The Faithful
Shepherdess* is certainly less politically programmatic than Jonson's
entertainment. Fletcher's play in effect theorizes the kinds of rupture
Macherey discusses; it evokes and endorses both versions of pastoral,
laying them next to each other without further comment.

The faithful shepherdess around whom the plot revolves is Clorin. Having buried her love in the play's first scene, she inhabits the arbor in which he is buried and remains untouched by the turmoil of the rest of the play's characters. In the elegy for her lost love with which the play begins Clorin tells us that she can cure both physical and psychic wounds since "such secret vertue lies / In herbes applyed by a virgins hand" (1.1.39–40). Her role in the play is essentially limited to the administration of these cures.

As James Yoch has pointed out, the association between healing power and chastity here evokes a typical pattern of praise for Elizabeth.[31] Nor is this power Clorin's only Elizabethan virtue. In the play's first scene the very sight of Clorin calls forth an enraptured offer of service from a satyr, causing Clorin herself to wonder at the power of her virginity:

> Sure there is a power
> In that great name of virgin, that bindes fast
> All rude uncivill bloods, all appetites
> That breake their confines: then, strong chastity,
> Be thou my strongest guarde, for heere Il'e dwell
> In opposition against Fate and Hell.
>
> (1.1.124–29)

In Clorin's formulation, virginity is given an essentially governmental power: it can "bind fast" the "uncivill," restore order to the torrential, civilize. This same "strong chastity," was commonly attributed to Elizabeth, and had the effect of attributing her power to her character rather than to her rank.[32]

Clorin also shares with many Elizabethan heroines an ability to read the normative expectations of other characters and to improvise strategies for manipulating them. This ability characterizes in particular a number of Shakespeare's late Elizabethan heroines, who frequently improvise roles for themselves – often, though not always, male roles – in order to effect happy solutions to otherwise insoluble problems. As Marcus has argued, these improvisational heroines are part of the discursive complex surrounding the Virgin Queen.[33] Here Clorin is powerfully associated with that complex as well. That the play's Elizabethanism is concentrated in a character mourning for her lost love, Yoch suggests, might be "a young writer's attempt to place the venerable past within the new perspectives of the present."[34]

The bulk of the play's other characters are involved in a tangled series of love plots. Perigot and Amoret, two hitherto blameless lovers, agree to meet in the woods at night for the enjoyment of "chaste desires" (1.2.122). Amarillis loves Perigot, but is spurned by him. Meeting Sullen, an unredeemably base shepherd, Amarillis makes a deal: she promises to let Sullen have his way with her if he is willing to help her interpose herself between Perigot and Amoret. What's more, Amarillis reveals that she knows a spell which will allow her, with Sullen's help, to make herself look exactly like Amoret. They work the magic, and Amarillis intercepts Perigot before he meets his real love.[35] At the same time another Shepherdess named Cloe is trying to lose her virginity ("It is Impossible to Ravish mee / I am soe willing" [3.1.212–13]), so she promises to meet in the woods with two different shepherds: Alexis and Daphnis. The former is a lusty shepherd, the latter a chaste youth brought along as a back-up. At this point, with all the shepherds and shepherdesses gathered in the woods, confusion takes over. Perigot meets the transformed Amarillis, mistakes her for Amoret, and is outraged when she expresses her less-than-chaste desires. In his anger he vows to kill her, chases her, finds the real Amoret and wounds her. Left for dead, Amoret's body is thrown into a stream where the God of the river – in a masque-like sequence – recognizes her virtue, revives her, proposes, and has his offer of marriage declined. Perigot finds her again, wounds her again, and her body is brought to Clorin to be healed. Meanwhile Cloe and Alexis are interrupted by Sullen, who wounds Alexis hoping to take his place and is in turn chased away by the civilized Satyr, who carries Alexis's wounded body to Clorin's arbor as well. Left a reluctant virgin, Cloe tries to seduce Daphnis, but his comically rendered chastity cannot be swayed. Perigot finds himself unable to wash Amoret's blood from his hands, and he too finds his way to Clorin's arbor hoping for a cure. Thanks to the ministrations of Clorin, Amoret and Perigot are finally reconciled, while Alexis, Cloe, and Amarillis are purified and reformed.

As this breathless summary may suggest, Fletcher's play is concerned above all with the interrogation and exposure of excessive, intemperate passions. The uncontrolled rage of Perigot and the childish, posturing chastity of Daphnis are exposed as surely as is the appetitive lust of Amarillis, Cloe, and Alexis. Clorin ministers to "all appetites / That breake their confines," and that includes Perigot's appetite for revenge and Daphnis's self-importance. Moreover, the intemperance of individuals is shown to have disrupted the community as a whole. At the beginning of Act 5, an old shepherd and the Priest of Pan call on the community to wake up and set about their allotted tasks, but find nobody at home. As Clorin's ministrations govern individual passions, they help to cure the body politic. One might argue, then, that the play reproduces the Elizabethan pastoral scheme with which we have been concerned: it addresses social concerns by means of an interrogation of individual experience, and locates governing power in chastity and virtue rather than in rank or authority.

At the same time, it has been suggested that Pan – whose actions are reported by the Satyr and whose will is enforced by his priest – is used in the play as a figure for James. For Pan, as Yoch points out, is described by the mythographer Natalis Comes as the "governor and moderator of all things," and in this role he is of course a common symbolic analogue for the king: we have already encountered the association.[36] Indeed, the Pan in Fletcher's play seems more like a king than a god, for the Satyr gives us a few glimpses of Pan's activities, and they sound like pastoral court entertainments:[37]

> great *Pan* commaunded me
> To walke this grove about, whilst he
> In a corner of the wood,
> Where never mortall foote hath stood,
> Keepes dancing, musicke and a feast,
> To intertaine a lovely guest.
> (3.1.170–75)

But to see Pan as a figure for James raises a host of interpretive problems. For when seen in terms of the values and assumptions upon which much of the play rests, the representation of Pan seems relentlessly equivocal.

First, though the play is centrally concerned with chastity as a virtue, whenever we get a glimpse of Pan he is busy romancing "His Paramoure, the Syrinx bright" (1.1.56). Pan clearly does not live up to the behavioral standard set by Clorin. Moreover, as Clifford Leech has pointed out, Pan is invoked by the play's characters both as the protector of chastity ("Thou that keepest us chaste and free" [1.2.38]), and as an aide to Cloe's amorous adventure with Alexis ("Great Pan for Sirinx sake bid speed our plow" [2.4.108]).[38]

For Philip Finkelpearl, the discrepancy between Clorin's chastity and Pan's reported behavior reveals Fletcher's play to be a criticism of the sexual mores of James's court and a "plea ... for England's moral regeneration."[39] But though the case can be made, difficulties arise. Most tellingly, Pan's amours are reported without criticism by the Satyr, whose service to Clorin makes him one of the play's moral authorities. In fact, the same Satyr who polices the woods for any moral transgression happily gathers fruit for Pan's dalliances. Fletcher's play, in other words, not only stops short of condemning Pan's erotic adventures, it endorses them. Pan seems to be exempt from the values invoked and evoked by Clorin and Amoret.

The discrepancy between the behavior of Pan and the example of Clorin – rather than being an indictment of James – arises from Fletcher's desire to endorse a Jacobean conception of the power of Pan within an essentially Elizabethan plot. In order to hold on to both, Fletcher separates them: different standards apply at different moments in *The Faithful Shepherdess* because of the incompatibilities between two competing discursive systems. Fletcher eschews the Elizabethan emphasis on personal chastity when concerned with Pan's actions, choosing instead a description more in keeping with Jacobean decorums of kingship: Pan's entertainments, rather than indicting his moral character, are used within the play as an index to his magnificence.

In fact, the play's benign attitude towards Pan's entertainments agrees with James's own account of royal recreation, in which time spent at play provides a necessary antidote to the tribulations of kingship. Accordingly, James represented his own prolonged absences from court as necessary correctives to the stress of duty. Something of this justification is preserved in one of John Chamberlain's letters of 1605:

The Kinge went to Roiston two dayes after Twelfetide, where and thereabout he hath continued ever since, and findes such felicitie in that hunting life, that he hath written to the counsaile, that yt is the only meanes to maintain his health, (which being the health and welfare of us all) he desires them to undertake the charge and burden of affaires.[40]

The case of the king is exceptional. He deserves his recreation because he carries the weight of the nation on his shoulders. Though Pan's entertainment clashes with the decorum of Clorin's Elizabethan pastoral, it is evidently in keeping with the decorum of Jacobean kingship.

Second, despite Clorin's Elizabethan ministrations, Pan's Priest governs throughout Fletcher's play in accordance with a Jacobean vision of public identity and ritually defined pastoral community. Thus, for example, Scene 2 begins with the Priest announcing to one and all that it is time to go to bed, and reminding them that concurrence with this curfew is required by Pan:

> So you shall good Shepheardes prove,
> And for ever hold the love
> Of our great God.
>
> (2.1.29–31)

To be a good shepherd is to take part in the community-wide rhythm of work and sleep. The shepherd-subject is imagined only in terms of communal order, and government of the Priest of Pan assumes no space for private actions or concerns. The involved and violent amatory adventures that take place during the night violate the Priest's governmental assumptions; one could argue that they dramatize the limitations of the Jacobean governmental model, and celebrate instead the effectiveness of Clorin's more Elizabethan form of influence.

But the play finally reinstates both the government of the Priest and the public unanimity upon which it is based. After purifying the errant shepherds and shepherdesses, Clorin delivers them over to the Priest once again:

> Now, holy man, I offer up againe
> These patients full of health, and free from paine:
> Keepe them, from after ills, be ever neere
> Unto their accions.
>
> (5.5.164–67)

It is as if the turbulence of the evening has been merely an anomaly. From now on they will be supervised by the Priest and Pan.

One of Fletcher's models for the structure of *The Faithful Shepherdess* is *A Midsummer Night's Dream*. Both plays begin with a social crisis, move to a series of disturbing amatory adventures in the woods and finally return to society with the crisis resolved. In Shakespeare's play, events in the woodland realm of Oberon and Titania lead to the successful reintegration of the lovers into Athenian society, but the suggestion that the misrule in the woods is in fact structurally related to the orderliness of Athenian society itself raises lingering questions about the nature of Theseus's Athenian reign. By contrast, the final scene of civic harmony in Fletcher's play is presented almost naively. Clorin offers the prodigals to the Priest, and the communal order is restored. Where Shakespeare's play hints finally at the interpenetration of Athens and the woods, Fletcher's struggles to separate the romance world inhabited by Clorin from the community overseen by the Priest of Pan. The end of Fletcher's play ratifies Jacobean governmental fantasy, and the Priest's final speech is a paradigmatic statement of the Jacobean pastoral vision:

Kneele, every Shepheard, whilst with powerful hand,
I blesse your after labours, and the land,
You feede your flocks upon. Great *Pan* defend you,
From misfortune and amend you,
Keepe you from those dangers still,
That are followed by your will.

(5.5.192–97)

A solution to the foibles of the will is still found in the panoptic protection of Pan. On the heels of the Priest's blessing, the assembled
shepherds and shepherdesses sing a unanimous hymn to Pan before
leaving the stage: with the exception of Clorin and the Satyr, who are
not properly part of the communal order and who remain on stage for
one final exchange, individual voices are silenced in favor of public
song. Of course, since it was Clorin's civilizing power which made
communal harmony possible in the first place, it could be argued that
the play dramatizes precisely the reliance of Pan's government on the
Elizabethan heroine. But Fletcher celebrates the Priest's pastoral community without in any way hinting toward its instability or toward
Pan's ineffectiveness. Though Clorin's characterological influence has
been instrumental in establishing the public, social order with which
the play ends, the text does not imply that her ministrations will prove
necessary for its maintenance. In effect, a Jacobean pastoral panegyric
is given as the conclusion to what is essentially an Elizabethan plot.

The Faithful Shepherdess, then, has a confusing attitude towards the
Jacobean government of the Priest of Pan: first it dramatizes the failure
of the Priest's government, then it turns around and celebrates its rein-
stallation. In fact, readers of Fletcher's play have frequently been put
off by the disjunction between the Clorin plot and the final celebration
under the Priest's auspices. Thus, Lee Bliss dismisses the Priest of Pan
as "a peripheral figure in moral as well as structural terms," while
Yoch has described the final scene as "token flattery of King James I"
tacked onto the play as an afterthought.[41] Rather, it seems to me that
the disjunction between the play's two governmental models is Fletcher's
strategic response to the incompatibility between Elizabethan pastoral
and the Jacobean pastoral line. As with the play's conflicting attitudes
towards chastity, different governmental models apply at different
moments in *The Faithful Shepherdess*. Fletcher is able, in effect, to modu-
larize the visions of Elizabethan and Jacobean pastoral, deploying each
locally and choosing to ignore the troubling contradictions which have
subsequently bothered the play's critics.

Bliss has demonstrated convincingly that "allusion, even downright pilfering, is an important component of Fletcher's art," and has attributed to him a Sidnean sense of the resources and potentials of genre and mode.[42] Indeed, in *The Faithful Shepherdess* Fletcher skillfully cobbles together elements from a wide range of sources – a partial list would include Guarini, Shakespeare, Daniel, Spenser, and the early Jacobean masque. The fact that Fletcher is able locally to endorse both Elizabethan and Jacobean elements without letting them undercut each other is a tribute to his mastery of his cultural materials. One might argue that Fletcher's play takes as its formal challenge the handling of the kind of built-in incompatibilities which for Macherey define literary language as such.

DRAYTON'S PASTORAL REVISIONS AND THE JACOBEAN IDEA

To this point we have been concerned primarily with texts that fit uneasily within the terms of Macherey's discussion of formal fragmentation. The *Althorpe Entertainment* and *The Faithful Shepherdess* both seem to handle the process of generic negotiation masterfully; in neither case does it seem appropriate to describe these generic ruptures as their "unconscious." There are, however, early Jacobean pastorals for which Macherey's approach seems quite germane, texts in which the incompatibilities theorized in Jonson and Fletcher seem to manifest themselves more uncontrollably. In particular, I will turn now to early Jacobean pastorals produced by Michael Drayton and Samuel Daniel. Each of these writers remains engaged with Elizabethan literary conventions, and yet in the work of each we can detect an impulse toward the Jacobean pastoral line.

In his *Poemes Lyrick and pastorall* (1606), Drayton published a heavily revised version of his Elizabethan eclogue book, *Idea, The Shepheardes Garland* (1593).[43] The Elizabethan version of these poems is essentially a response to Spenser's *Shepheardes Calender*: it copies the structure of Spenser's book, and often echoes its poetry.[44] By the time Drayton published the 1606 version, however, all but one of the eclogues had undergone revision, making the whole markedly less Spenserian: the order of the eclogues is changed, a new eclogue is added, and most of the speeches are rewritten.[45] Drayton's revisions are telling, the more so because the new eclogues are characterized by demonstrably Jacobean modalities despite their author's growing antipathy to James and nostalgia for Elizabeth.

The fifth eclogue of the 1593 eclogue book has, as its centerpiece, Rowland's song of praise for Idea. Although Drayton's heroine is supposed to stand for the spirit of poesy, the terms in which she is praised are clearly part of the complex of tropes with which Elizabeth was praised in pastoral. Rowland's song praises Idea as both a temple consecrated to the "Queene of Chastitie" (100), and as erotically desirable: "thy lips those lips which *Cupid* joyes to kisse" (91). She is also both a goddess and a shepherdess, and we find in Rowland's song the characteristic Elizabethan linkage between beauty and virtue: "Thy cheekes the bankes of Beauties usurie, / Thy heart the myne, where goodnes gotten is" (89–90). In other words, Idea not only stands for the spirit of Elizabethan pastoral poetry, she is intentionally created along the lines of one of its conventional figures. Drayton's poem of praise for the personification of late Elizabethan poetry is itself a self-consciously constructed specimen of it.

In its 1606 version the praise for Idea takes a different shape. Rowland praises Idea's beauty for twenty-five lines and then declares that physical beauty is irrelevant:

> Although surpassing, yet let I them passe,
> Nor in this kind her excellence is shown,
> To sing of these not my intent it was.
>   Our muse must undergoe a waightier masse,
> And be directed by a straighter lyne,
>   Which me must unto hyer regions guide,
> That I her vertues rightly may define.
>
> (92–98)

There follows a long discourse on Idea's virtues which retains the skeleton of the equivalent passage in the 1593 version but revises the emphasis. Both passages describe Idea as first a stage on which all virtues appear and then a book containing them, but while the 1593 version emphasizes an Elizabethan melange of beauty and morality, pleasure and instruction, the revised version stresses only her wisdom and virtue. Thus, the following lines from the 1593 edition

> Read in her eyes a Romant of delights,
>   Read in her words the proverbs of the wise,
> Read in her life the holy vestall rites,
>   Which love and vertue sweetly moralize:
> And she the *Academ* of vertues excercise
>
> (127–31)

appear in the revised edition as

> Who unto goodnes can she not excite,
>   and in the same not teacheth to be wise
> and deeply seen in each obsequious rite
>   wherein of that sum mystery there lyes
>   which her sole study is and only excercise.
>
>   (106–10)

The new spirit of poetry evidently has no place for romances, and is not as concerned to please while instructing.

If the Idea of the 1593 eclogues both stands for and exemplifies the poetry of its age, the same might be said for the new Idea of the 1606 version. Rowland – with his new emphasis on the "waightier masse" and "straighter lyne" of his muse and the "hyer regions" of his subject, as well as his new emphasis on right definition – seems himself to have a Jacobean "Idea" in mind. Moreover, this new didactic plain style Idea is easily linked to the tastes of James himself, whose scholarly publications and public addresses tended to manifest "waightier" learning and didactic intent as well as some vanity about them. Indeed, a great deal of Rowland's description of Idea's wisdom, insight, and virtue is reminiscent of contemporary panegyric intended to flatter James himself.[46]

By revising his fifth eclogue in accordance with this new "Idea" of poetry, Drayton produced an eclogue recognizably scarred by the kind of formal disjunction central to Macherey's analysis of literary texts: it combines identifiably Jacobean attitudes with the skeletal form of a recognizably Elizabethan eclogue. For example, the praises for Idea's beauty – interspersed in 1593 – are preserved in the 1606 edition but lumped together in one long passage and then dismissed as unimportant. The Jacobean "Idea," in other words, is surrounded by vestiges of her old self, and consequently by the allusive presence of Elizabethan pastoral.

The awkward splicing of this eclogue results in gaps and ellipses which in turn manifest important disjunctions between Elizabethan pastoral and emergent Jacobean literary style. By severing the association of beauty, virtue, and power Drayton's eclogue suggests not only that conventions of praise for the two monarchs are different, but that the characteristic Elizabethan uses of love are no longer viable. Rowland is still in love with Idea in the 1606 version – "Go gentle winds and whisper in her eare, / and tell *Idea* how much I adore her" (131–32) – but the new emphasis on only her virtues eliminates the conventional language of desire around which so much of the rhetoric of inwardness is built in Elizabethan pastoral. Eliminating the narrative framework once provided by desire means eliminating the private sphere. Where Rowland's desire for Idea was in 1593 a private response to public virtue, his more rationally based admiration for her in the revised version should be universally shared. This change is consistent with the eclogue's new emphasis on correct definition and didactic insight, on objectivity over subjectivity. Other eclogues in Drayton's revised collection also respond to a Jacobean idea of pastoral, replacing the characterological focus of the Elizabethan volume with more current representational gambits.

One of the generic expectations of pastoral – an expectation bolstered by classical, continental, and Elizabethan precedent – is that it is a mode used to comment obliquely on dangerous political material.[47] Both versions of Drayton's collection participate in this long-standing tradition. However, in Drayton's revised eclogue the abandonment of the Elizabethan inwardness is frequently accompanied by a new stridency in the social commentary. The excision of the characterological makes Drayton's political commentary more explicit, as his revisions turn simultaneously away from the characterological and toward criticism of James and his government. If the use of inwardness as a site for pastoral representation has a mollifying effect on social criticism, Drayton's Jacobean revisions do away with it.

Thus, the first eclogue of the 1593 version finds Rowland, "O'r growne with age, forlorne with woe" (24) crying out to "blessed *Pan*" (25):[48]

> My sorowes waxe, my joyes are in the wayning,
> My hope decayes, and my despayre is springing
> My love hath losse, and my disgrace hath gayning,
> Wrong rules, desert with teares her hands sits wringing.
>
> (55–58)

The reference to "desert" hints that part of Drayton's concern in this eclogue is to ask for patronage and to suggest that he has been unjustly slighted heretofore. Most of Rowland's outburst, however, makes it clear that his despair is his own fault: "Let smokie sighes be pledges of contrition, / For follies past to make my soules submission" (47–48). Drayton's eclogue expresses his desire for patronage and allows him to voice a mild complaint, but since the focus of the eclogue is on the prodigality of the speaker the complaint is blunted. The sentiments here are commonplace, as is the strategic expression of them.

By contrast, the 1606 version of the first eclogue is quite explicit about the injustice behind Rowland's lament, and Rowland himself is not prepared to take the blame. The new version of the eclogue insists that the poor judgment of a decadent society is to blame for Rowland's woes:

> My hopes are fruitles, and my fayth is vaine,
> and but meere showes disposed me to mock
> such are exalted basely that can faine,
> and none regards just *Rowland of the rock*.
> (49–52)

The revisionary thrust of Drayton's rewriting is two-fold: he erases the private love drama, and he includes in its place an analysis of his frustration which blames public society.[49] It is important to recognize that the sentiments behind these two versions of the first eclogue might be substantially the same. The revised version of the eclogue expresses its criticisms much more forcefully, to be sure, but instead of explaining this new directness by positing an increase in Drayton's level of dissatisfaction, it is possible to see instead a change in conventional modes of expression. As the Elizabethan fictions of private love and desire are replaced, dissatisfaction is expressed more explicitly.

The same revisionary thrust recurs throughout Drayton's eclogue book: private sadness is replaced by pointed social criticism. The tenth and final eclogue, like the first, is changed from a love lament to a bitter complaint about the poet's obscurity, which dwells on his record of virtue and dedicated service. The fourth eclogue in the 1593 version has as its centerpiece a pastoral elegy for Sidney (under the name "Elphin"), and focuses on the personal grief of its main speaker, Wynken. Revised as the sixth eclogue of the 1606 edition, the elegy becomes a scathing and explicit satire of contemporary *mores* and politics, hearkening back to the days of Elphin as a golden age gone by.[50] We might describe Drayton's new directness as the result of mixing an Elizabethan sense of the political function of pastoral with a Jacobean representational style.

Drayton wrote one new eclogue for the revised version of his volume, and this new eclogue – the ninth – reproduces Jacobean pastoral's characteristic emphasis on "active sport" rather than characterological exploration. It is set at a sheep-shearing festival in Cotswold, and is the only eclogue setting in the book without a Spenserian precedent. Once again Rowland is central, though here we are further

removed from any description of his own individual experiences. He is
chosen to preside over a rural feast since, as we learn,

> by the auncient statutes of the field,
> He that his flocks the earliest lamb should bring
> (as it fell out now *Rowlands* charge to yeeld)
> Alwayes for that yeare was the Shepherds king.
>
> (37–40)

After a brief description of the rural sport and a few roundelays
composed at the request of Rowland – "at whose commaund they all
obedient were" (74) – it falls to him as the festival's "clownish king"
(172) to sing a roundelay and conclude the festivities. Just as he is about
to begin, Idea makes her appearance:

> she (whom then they little did expect,
> The dearest nimphe that ever kept in field)
> *Idea*, did her sober pace direct
> Towards them.
>
> (176–79)

She comes towards them replete with proof of the civilizing effects of
her beauty and virtue:

> And whereas other drave their carefull keepe,
> Hers did her follow, duly at her will,
> For through her patience she had learnt her sheep
> Where ere she went to wait upon her still.
>
> A Milkwhite Dove upon her hand she brought,
> So tame, t'would go, returning at her call.
>
> (180–85)

As the reader recognizes this characteristic Elizabethan link of beauty,
virtue, and command, Rowland begins his roundelay, praising Idea in
unabashedly Elizabethan terms: she is "the shepherds Queen" (195)
and "the goddesse of these medes" (197); her eyes are like "Cynthia's
light" (226). Finally, the roundelay ends with a reference to Idea's
eventual death, promising to worship her forever and thus perhaps
commenting on the Elizabethan nostalgia of the eclogue itself:

> [ROWLAND]: Above where heavens hie glorious are,
> [CHORUS]: When as she shall be placed in the skies,
> [ROWLAND]: She shall be calld the shepherds starre,
> [CHORUS]: And evermore
>   We shepherds will adore,
>   Her setting and her rise.[51]
>
> (230–35)

With its reference to the "auncient statutes of the field," and its unabashed Elizabethanism, it is easy to see that this eclogue was not written with James's tastes in mind. In fact, its rural nationalism and nostalgia seem to anticipate some of the elements of Drayton's late anti-courtly pastorals.

Though not explicitly satirical or critical of James's government, Drayton's use of the Jacobean pastoral of "active sport" makes it easier to see his Elizabethanism as commentary on English society as a whole. For the eclogue focuses not on the emotional life of one shepherd but rather on the nostalgia of a whole community. As with his revised eclogues, Drayton's new effort underscores the manner in which emergent representational fashion accentuated the volatile political content traditionally muted behind pastoral's "vaile of homely persons." Describing precisely this change in Drayton's writing, Bernard Newdigate has suggested that Drayton became "less subjective and more vehement" after the accession of James.[52] To this I would only add that the change was at least partly due to the ascendancy of newly fashionable discursive stances. To be sure, Drayton was by 1606 considerably more frustrated than he had been in 1593, but the production of this newly direct criticism must also be related to the absence of Elizabethan languages of private love and characterological exploration.

Given Drayton's dissatisfaction with James and his court, it is perhaps hard to know what to make of the Jacobean flavor of his eclogue revisions.[53] It seems to me that Drayton's engagement with the representational norms of what I have called the Jacobean pastoral line has more to do with literary craftsmanship – the desire not to seem out of date – than with a specific desire to appeal to the court or to appropriate its language. Instead, it seems more plausible to argue that Drayton's revisions respond to perceived changes in literary fashion brought about in part by the accession by James and the Jacobean appropriation of pastoral. If so, then it is important to recognize as well that the effects of this change in fashion go well beyond flattery. In fact, Drayton's revisions suggest ways in which, broadly speaking, James's self-styling may have contributed to the creation of new discursive strategies and assumptions which in turn enabled the development of a newly strident oppositional literature.

DANIEL AND THE REFORMATION OF ARCADIA

Like the *Althorpe Entertainment*, Samuel Daniel's *Queenes Arcadia* was performed before Queen Anne in the absence of her husband (at Oxford

in 1605, under the title "Arcadia Reformed"). Unlike Jonson, Daniel
seems to have considered Anne to be its most important audience,
prefacing the published version with a dedication to her and renaming
it accordingly. In choosing the pastoral mode, Daniel may even have
intended to compliment Anne. For in the work of contemporaries, flattering comparisons between the new queen and the old were often
couched in the characteristic pastoral tropes and settings of Elizabethan
pastoral. Henry Godyere's *Mirrour of Majestie*, for instance, associates
Anne with a pastoral Elizabeth figured as "She whose faire Memories,
by *Thespian* swaines / Are sung, on *Rheins* greene banks, and flowerie
plaines."[54]

   In addition to constructing her as his audience, Daniel's dedicatory
poem makes it clear that he counted on Anne's protection. For while
the play goes out of its way to include overt flattery for James (a
counterblast to tobacco for instance, echoing James's publication on the
subject), its politics, in keeping with Daniel's own, are anti-absolutist.
The play's Arcadia is governed by its elders, in accordance with long-
standing customary liberty:[55]

> You gentle Shepherds and Inhabitors
> Of these remote, and solitary parts
> Of montaynous *Arcadia*, shut up here
> Within these Rockes, these unfrequented Clifts, –
> The walles and bulwarkes of our libertie, –
> From out the noyse and tumolt, and the throng
> Of sweating toyle, ratling concurrencie;
> And have continued stil the same and one
> In all successions from antiquitie.
>
>   (2,200–08)

Daniel's vision of Arcadian utopia depends on the topoi of what J. G.
A. Pocock has named "the common-law mind."[56] Since the quasi-par-
liamentary government of elders and the belief in customary liberty
form the political core of the play, one imagines that despite the attack
on tobacco it was not constructed to reflect James's tastes.[57] Nevertheless I will argue that this play, like Drayton's 1606 "eglogs," revises
a conventional setting in accordance with the emergent Jacobean
pastoral line.

   Daniel's dedicatory poem to Queen Anne simultaneously announces
the text's subservience to James and its retention of Elizabethan pastoral
politics. On the one hand, Daniel says that he

dare not enterprise to show
In lowder stile the hidden mysteries,
And arts of Thrones; which none that are below
The Sphere of action and the exercise
Of power can truly shew.

(21–25)

Here, and more explicitly elsewhere in the dedicatory poem, Daniel reproduces James's published opinion that matters of state are "to grave materis for a Poet to mell in."[58] This disclaimer is somewhat disingenuous, to be sure, but it signals the author's recognition of James's prohibition. At the same time, even as he seems to be saying that matters of state are entirely beyond his ken, Daniel reproduces the familiar defense of the Elizabethan pastoralist, insisting on the humble voice of pastoral, and criticizing those who meddle in politics "in lowder stile." In other words, Daniel's dedication is reminiscent both of James's instruction to poets to avoid grave matters altogether, and of Puttenham's description of pastoral as a mode in which grave matters may be discreetly hinted at with impunity.

Disclaimer notwithstanding, *The Queenes Arcadia* takes as its focus social decline. Like Drayton's eclogue book, it maintains pastoral's traditional engagement with social issues. In the first scene we find Melibaeus and Ergastus – "two ancient *Arcadians*," as they are described in the list of characters – lamenting a recent decline in Arcadian *mores*. The opening lines set the dramatic situation:

How is it *Melibaeus* that we find
Our country, faire Arcadia, so much chang'd
From what it was; that was thou knowst of late,
The gentle region of plaine honesty,
The modest seat of undisguised truth,
Inhabited with simple innocence:
And now, I know not how, as if it were
Unhallowed, and divested of that grace,
Hath put off that faire nature which it had,
And growes like ruder countries, or more bad.

(1–10)

Arcadia has been overrun by a host of loosely associated vices: disloyalty, slander, sickness, property disputes, the introduction of cosmetics and fashionable clothing. Each of these vices is a departure from customary Arcadian honesty, chastity, and simplicity. The two elders decide to ferret out the causes of the decline by hiding themselves and spying on the interactions of the other shepherds and shepherdesses. They soon discover a small contingent of malefactors: Colax, a depraved foreign courtier; Techne, a foreign courtesan based on Guarini's Corsica; Alcon, a corrupt doctor nursing Arcadians to ill-health; Lincus, a lawyer trying to drum up business by encouraging ill-will and litigiousness. Colax in particular has destroyed a number of otherwise happy pastoral couples by slandering each to the other in order to work his own seductive wiles. The story centers predictably on the tribulations of the unhappy lovers, and on a plot laid by Colax and Techne to seduce the chaste paragon of Arcadia, Cloris.

It is impossible not to read the play's concern with lost Arcadian modesty as Elizabethan nostalgia. Indeed, Cloris – at once the most beautiful, chaste, and intelligent of the Arcadians – is reminiscent of numerous Elizabethan heroines, and was probably created with the type in mind. According to Techne

> sh'is as coy
> And hath as shrewd a spirit, as quicke conceipt,
> As any wench I brok'd in all my life.
>
> (1,271–73)

In an Elizabethan play, this combination of shrewdness, beauty, and virtue might enable Cloris herself to effect a solution to the Arcadian problems, much the way Rosalind in *As You Like It* (1600) is able to finagle a happy ending and solve that play's far-ranging problems. In Daniel's play, however, Cloris's virtue is literally incidental to the resolution of Arcadia's ills. The attempted seduction of the Elizabethan heroine provides what dramatic tension the play has, but her resistance has nothing to do with the play's solution. Cloris is in effect a dramatic red herring, a trace of an Elizabethan plot trajectory not finally followed.[59]

Instead, the play finds its solution when Ergastus and Melibaeus, observing the interactions and transactions of the community from their hiding-place, discover and subsequently denounce the decadent interlopers responsible for the innovations. Daniel's play, in other words, finds its solution in the opening up of the private to official scrutiny. In doing so, *The Queenes Arcadia* in effect reproduces a recurring Jacobean pastoral fantasy: the private is made public, exposed by the panoptic power of government. Thus, despite his common-law utopianism and Elizabethan nostalgia, Daniel's play participates in the Jacobean redefinition of pastoral. Moreover, Daniel's revisionary move – the private opened to public scrutiny – occurs everywhere in early

Jacobean pastoral. Think, for example, of the Satyr's observation of the faeries in Jonson's *Althorpe Entertainment*, or of Polixenes's discovery of the pastoral world in *The Winter's Tale*.[60]

The public exposure of the malefactors in the penultimate scene of Daniel's play is accompanied by a bizarre lapse into allegory. In addition to Alcon, Lincus, Colax, and Techne, the two Arcadian elders produce a fifth agent of corruption, Pistophoenax. The new character appears at first to be a foreign priest introducing religious dispute to Arcadia, but Ergastus suspects him of wearing a mask, has it pulled off, and reveals an allegorically rendered monster:

> a most deformèd ougly face,
> Wherewith if openly he should appeare,
> He would deterre all men from comming neere.
> And therefore hath that cunning wretch put on
> This pleasing visor of apparency,
> T'intice and to delude the world withall.
>
> (2,293–98)

The fact that Pistophoenax does not appear in the published play's list of characters suggests that he remained an afterthought, not felt to be integral to the story. At any rate, the abrupt introduction of an explicitly allegorical figure is a sharp departure from the representational decorum of the rest of the play.

With the sudden insertion of Pistophoenax, the conventional use of individual experience is abandoned altogether: the unexpected presence of an allegorical cipher announces that all the other malefactors are also to be taken as representative types. Rather than a story about the experiences of various characters, the play is revealed at the end to be a quasi-allegorical anatomization of social ills. Furthermore, the shift toward allegory occurs at precisely the moment in the play when private plots are publicly exposed by the two elders. In other words, the change in representational mode answers the development of the plot: the publicization of private machinations, coupled with a thoroughgoing erasure of private characterological space, signals the obsolescence of the representational decorum of pastoral drama itself. In effect, this too reproduces a fantasy of the Jacobean pastoral vision: the panoptic power of the government results in a dramatic redefinition of its subjects.

In the play's final speech, Melibaeus looks forward to the peace Arcadia is to enjoy once the five sources of corruption are removed:

let us recollect our selves
Dispers'd into these strange confusèd ills,
And be again *Arcadians*, as we were;
And so solemnize this our happy day
Of restauration, with other feasts of joy.
(2577–81)

Characteristically, social health is figured as re-collection of individuals into a national identity solidified by public sport.

A sharp contrast needs to be drawn here between the festive ending in Daniel's play and the conclusion of an Elizabethan pastoral drama such as *As You Like It*. Roughly speaking, *As You Like It* follows the tripartite structure of disintegration, education, and reintegration, which Walter Davis has suggested as the paradigmatic trajectory of pastoral romance.[61] The festivities with which the play ends celebrate and ratify a social reintegration made possible by a retreat into the love plot in Arden. By contrast, the festival promised at the end of Daniel's play is the result, not of passing through the private, but of erasing it altogether. Rather than celebrating a newly achieved harmony between individual and society, Daniel's festival is a model for a society in which the individual is fully collected into the public order.

There is something oxymoronic about the concluding vision of Daniel's play. On the one hand, it reproduces with surprising thoroughness the Jacobean pastoral line. On the other hand, the community restored is represented in nostalgic terms which are more readily assimilated to Elizabethanism than to the new king's self-presentation. The text's form seems Jacobean while its politics seem Elizabethan. This internal contradiction, it should be evident, parallels the tensions reproduced in Drayton's eclogue revisions.

As in Drayton's 1606 eclogues, the anatomization of social woes in *The Queenes Arcadia* brings with it a strain of explicit social satire which in the context of the play's mildly oppositional politics and Elizabethan nostalgia might be taken as criticism of the new court. Daniel – who had been called before the Privy Council for his play *Philotas* in early 1605 – probably did not want this play to be particularly controversial, but the very plainness of the allegory arising out of the erasure of the private increases the play's subversive potential: there can be no question but that Arcadia is beset by social ills demanding a governmental solution. Both Drayton and Daniel retain a characteristic Elizabethan *use* for pastoral, namely, "to insinuate and glaunce at greater matters" of the state, but their elision of Elizabethan inwardness brings with it a tendency towards dangerously pointed social anatomy. We might say, then, that in this case the indirect influence of the king's style contributed to the articulation of newly explicit criticism directed partly at his own government.

In Macherey's analysis, the kind of formal peculiarities manifested in Drayton's eclogues and Daniel's play always tells an otherwise silent ideological story:

it is not a question of introducing a historical explanation which is stuck on to the work from the outside. On the contrary, we must show a sort of splitting within the work: this division is its unconscious, in so far as it possesses one – the unconscious which is history, the play of history beyond its edges, encroaching on those edges.[62]

The "splitting" within these early Jacobean pastorals should remind us that when James ascended to the English throne he inherited a well-developed discursive system involved in complicated ways with the functioning of Elizabethan politics. Since Jacobean style conflicts with entrenched Elizabethan norms, there is a built-in interference between the social model James tries to install and the representational conventions inherited by his new subjects.

The fragmentations within these pastoral texts (though they are not always unconscious) are symptomatic of an interference between residual and emergent styles which may have proven costly in ways that James could never have been expected to know. We are accustomed to recognizing ways in which Elizabethan discursive conventions functioned strategically in the maintenance of her power and popularity. It is less clear how, or indeed if, discursive conventions which seem preeminently Jacobean could operate with an equivalent strategic force. In fact, with the exception of Goldberg, emphasis is generally placed on the political weakness of James's public style, either because he seems too blustery or because of his failure to establish a national cult like the so-called cult of Elizabeth.[63] These texts, I think, dramatize one way in which James's "success" as a ruler is mediated by a complex of interconnecting discursive practices: the Jacobean pastoral line – with its emphasis on communal clockwork and its impulse towards the flattening out of characterological depth – contributes to the articulation of satire and social anatomy because it collides with an Elizabethan sense of the political functioning of pastoral. In this case, the failure of the Jacobean pastoral line to function strategically can only be understood diachronically, in relation to inherited Elizabethan assumptions about the function and form of pastoral literature.

The process of generic renegotiation demonstrated by Jonson and Fletcher is carried out in Drayton's eclogue revisions and Daniel's *Queenes Arcadia* in a way that anticipates the more oppositional pastoral produced later by the group Joan Grundy has called the "Spenserian Poets."[64] These poets – Drayton, Wither, Browne, and the Fletchers – are largely satirical and Mantuanesque, and contribute to the development in England of a sense of nationalism divorced from the monarch's mythology.[65] Significantly, the extra-monarchic nationalism developed by this group can be seen as an extension of the movement towards social anatomy already present in the early texts we have looked at.

To a considerable degree, the social and generic polarization, of which later, more oppositional pastoral is evidence, is the result of the failure of Jacobean absolutist discourse to accommodate inherited Elizabethan representational strategies and assumptions – a failure that is captured in material form in early Jacobean pastoral production itself.[66] This in turn both confirms and extends Claudio Guillén's observation that while genre systems "will tend, generally speaking, to absorb change and assimilate innovation," this "assimilation becomes a small step in a larger process of change."[67] The same might be said of the larger systems of interaction between literature and society, for the process of generic renegotiation can itself be seen as part of a larger process of change which is at once literary and ideological.

PART TWO

Staging Jacobean kingcraft

Theatre of counsel: royal
vulnerability and early Jacobean political drama

> Of what use is a king, unless he has sound counsel? And of
> what use is counsel, unless the king trusts it?
>
> John Gower, *Vox Clamantis*[1]

The reciprocity of Gower's formulation nicely captures the importance
ascribed to counsel in early English expositions of state: it has been
remarked that "a great part of the constitutional history of England in
the medieval period might be said ... to be a commentary ... upon
the simple fact of the king's crying need for counsel and ever
more counsel."[2] The central importance of counsel was if anything
enhanced as Florentine republican humanism was adapted to a Tudor
courtly environment.[3] In F. J. Levy's words "it had always been a lord's
duty to give counsel to his king. Now, added to that, was the strong
conviction that it was a citizen's duty to serve his common weal."[4] The
author of *The Cabinet-Council*, a treatise falsely attributed to Ralegh by
its publisher and written by a mysterious "T. B." in the 1590s, describes
counsel as an indispensable part of government: "Without Counsel, no
kingdom, no state, no private house can stand; for experience hath
proved that commonweals have prospered so long as good counsel did
govern."[5] In effect, these expositions treated counsel as a cure-all,
necessary to compensate for the range of possible infirmities in the
monarch himself.

Within months of the accession of James I in England, observers
commented on a breakdown in his relationship to his counsellors, a
breakdown which seemed especially dangerous given the significance
traditionally ascribed to good counsel. In a report from the end of
July, 1603, Giovanni Carlo Scaramelli – the Venetian Secretary in
England – describes King James's domination at the hands of his
counsellors:

It is impossible to deny that these English statesmen have, so to speak, bewitched [*incantato*] the King; he is lost in bliss and so entirely in their hands that, whereas the late Queen knew them and put up with them as a necessity but always kept her eye on their actions, the new King, on the contrary, seems to have almost forgotten that he is a King … and leaves them with such absolute authority [*assoluto dominio*] that beyond a doubt they are far more powerful than ever they were before.[6]

Scaramelli's description suggests, in fact, that James's advisors had effectively usurped the "absolute authority" vested in the person of the king; the metaphorical association here between this usurpation and sorcery ("bewitched") is an index to the transgressive potential of this failure of counsel.

Scaramelli's perception – that James was entirely in the hands of his counsellors – was shared by English observers as well. In particular, I will argue that concern about a Jacobean crisis of counsel is rehearsed in a number of the political plays of the early Jacobean period. To get at the topical impact of this perceived crisis, I take as my subject the recurrence – in these early Jacobean plays – of what Robert Ornstein has called "unholy alliances between autocratic vanity and sycophantic opportunism."[7]

This alliance has a long dramatic history in which, generally speaking, sycophantic royal favorites are treated as symptoms of a king's flawed nature. Thus, for example, the character Felice in John Marston's *Antonio and Mellida* (1599) suggests that "limber sycophants" are caused by tyrannous kings, rather than vice versa: "No sooner mischief's born in regenty / But flattery christens it with policy."[8] The portrayal of the relationship between tyrant and flatterer in these early Jacobean plays reverses this equation, emphasizing in particular the powerlessness and isolation of the vain autocrat unable to see beyond the reflection of himself offered by the "glass-fac'd flatterer."[9]

Portrayed in this way, the "unholy alliance" provided a formula with which writers responded to and commented on a crisis of counsel which was in turn the result both of James's self-styling and of the makeup of his court. The reasons for these plays' emphasis on the echoic relationship between king and flatterer have to do both with the residual dissatisfactions of the late Elizabethan court and with James's governmental style. Each of these dramas is concerned with the ways that flatterers are able to "bewitch" the king, capitalizing on royal blindness to lead him towards tyrannic autocracy.

By emphasizing the powerlessness of kings, these plays destabilize the traditional distinction between the tyrant and the legitimate monarch. Insofar as the rhetoric surrounding the legitimate monarch constituted itself against the figure of the tyrant, this destabilization implies a critique of the conventional rhetoric of royalty. We can say, then, that even though these plays frequently voice deeply conservative political positions, their cumulative contribution to the rhetoric of kingship is decidedly radical. As a group, the dramatizations of counsel in early Jacobean England arise out of a specifically topical concern with James's new court, but wind up articulating positions which challenge basic assumptions about the majesty of the king.

PHILOTAS AND THE JACOBEAN CRISIS OF COUNSEL

The pressures of courtly performance often interfered in practice with ideals of conciliar duty. Hythlodaeus's apology in More's *Utopia* is perhaps the essential proof text on this point. As the ratio between office-seekers and available positions became increasingly disproportionate, the pressures of courtliness could only increase. By the last two decades of Elizabeth's reign the conflict between these pressures and established conciliar ideals contributed to what Levy has called a "general crisis of English political Humanism."[10] The dissatisfaction which polarized in the 1590s around the Earl of Essex is one specially acute instance of this late-Elizabethan social dissonance: the ongoing war with Spain – with its implications for the world religious climate – together with the uncertain and impending English succession made good counsel seem more important than ever even as Essex and his followers were being squeezed out of the decision-making processes by the Cecils and their faction.

When James VI of Scotland became James I of England, he also became the object of hopes and frustrations which had previously been attached to Essex.[11] Included in this inherited sentiment was widespread dissatisfaction with Cecil's domination of the machinery of government. Cecil, however, had worked to secure James's peaceful succession, and became the most influential of the new king's guides to the political terrain of the realm. If anything, Cecil's power increased during the earliest years of James's reign, and the anxiety and frustration of those opposed to him increased accordingly. Concern with the mechanisms of counsel, forged around the Essex crisis, could only be sharpened by Cecil's ongoing dominance.

The Essex affair has been proposed as the impetus behind a number of politically charged early Jacobean tragedies, especially those of Daniel, Greville, Jonson, and Chapman, and it is important to recognize how deeply the ongoing political reverberations of the rise and fall of Essex did influence early perceptions of James's court. Daniel's *Tragedy of Philotas* is a good place to look for this influence, since the relationship between the story of Essex and early Jacobean unrest is concretized in Daniel's play.

Philotas was acted by the Children of the Queen's Revels – the troupe for which Daniel himself served as licenser – in January of 1605. Shortly thereafter Daniel himself was called before the Privy Council, presumably to account for his play's handling of the Essex affair.[12] In response to the controversy, Daniel penned an Apology in which he claimed that he had written the first three acts of the extant text "neere halfe a yeere before the late Tragedy of ours [Essex's rebellion], (whereunto this is now most ignorantly resembled) unfortunately fell out heere in *England*" ("Apology," p. 156).

There does in fact seem to be a notable change of emphasis in the final two acts of *Philotas*. The first three acts share the dramatic interests of the so-called Wilton group, a late-Elizabethan collection of poets, including Greville and Daniel, who were responsive to the Countess of Pembroke's interest in the French Senecan accomplishments of Robert Garnier and others.[13] Accordingly, the play begins as a study in ambition. In fact, the Philotas of the first acts is the embodiment of what Gordon Braden has called the "Senecan self": he is above all autarchic, and the play promises to explore the necessary problematics of the relationship between such a character and the state.[14] This Philotas is capable of sincerely noble utterances – "I cannot plaster and disguise m'affaires / In other colours then my heart doth lay" (65–66) – and his quasi-treasonous pride springs from the same passionate martial spirit that makes him admirable by the play's standards.

This pride makes Philotas chafe under Alexander's absolutism ("thus must we fight, toyle, win, / To make that yong-man proud" [309–10]), and though Daniel does not endorse Philotas's treasonous impulses, he recognizes that both nobility and potentially anarchic pride stem from the soldier's declared need to "sayle by the Compasse of my minde" (169). At the same time, if Alexander's fear of his subject's greatness is not wholly justified, it is at least presented as understandable. In fact, to the chorus at the end of Act 1, Alexander's mistrust is partly Philotas's fault: "We see Philotas acts his goodnesse ill, / And makes his

passions to report of him / Worse than he is" (423–25). This paradox is
the philosophical core of the play's first three acts.

Beginning with the chorus at the end of Act 3, Daniel seems to be
less interested in the perils of ambition and more interested in ways
that "great men cloath their private hate / In those faire colours of the
publike good" (1,110–11). From this point onward, our sympathies are
more squarely with Philotas.[15] Moreover the last two acts, presumably
written in 1604, are more deeply critical of Alexander than the first
three. The chorus that begins Act 5, for instance, takes the form of a
dialogue between "Graecians" and Persians in which the latter point
out that "Those whom you call your Kings, are but the same / As are
our Sovereigne tyrants of the East" (1,771–72).

The change in emphasis is also the point at which Craterus –
Alexander's chief advisor – takes center-stage. Though Craterus and
Ephestion are depicted as flatterers in Act 2, suspicion of Philotas
stems from Alexander himself. Thus it is Alexander who introduces the
topic of Philotas's dangerous greatness at the beginning of the second
act (433ff), and when Dymnus's treasonous plot is revealed it is
Alexander who first assumes that Philotas must be its leader (823–25).
After Act 3, Craterus – instead of Alexander – is depicted as the prime
mover of the state's aggression. Thus, we learn in the play's fourth act
that Craterus, in order to overturn Alexander's impulsive clemency
towards Philotas,

> Falles downe before the King, intreates, implores,
> Conjures his Grace, as ever he would looke
> To save his person and the State from spoile,
> Now to prevent *Philotas* practises,
> Whom they had plainly found to be the man
> Had plotted the destruction of them all.
>   The King would faine have put them off to time
> And farther day, till better proofes were knowne:
> Which they perceiving, prest him still the more.
>
> (1,168–76)

Similarly, the Nuncius in Act 5 tells how

> The Councell being dismiss'd from hence, and gone,
> Still Craterus plies the King, still in his eare,
> Still whispering to him privately alone,
> Urging (it seem'd) a quicke dispatch of feare:
> For they who speake but privatly to Kings,
> Do seldome speake the best and fittest things.
>
> (1,964–69)

Alexander, in short, is led to act by Craterus's importunity. Philotas himself reads the situation properly when he exclaims,

> O *Alexander*! Now I see my foes
> Have got above thy goodnesse, and prevail'd
> Against my innocencie, and thy word.
> (1,218–20)

Alexander is also significantly absent during the bulk of Philotas's trial in Act 4, Scene 2, leaving its administration up to Craterus and Ephestion.

Laurence Michel has shown that Daniel used court records of Essex's trial in his own account of Philotas's.[16] Given this, it seems safe to say, with Albert Tricomi, that in the last two acts of *Philotas* Daniel uses the Essex material in order to "impersonate the liberty-destroying machinations of Cecil in the figure of . . . Craterus."[17] We know, at any rate, that Daniel felt the need in 1605 to write an apologetic letter to Cecil urging that "no misapplying wronge my innocent writing."[18] The "Argument" accompanying the printed text describes the actions of Craterus and his colleague Ephestion in a much more positive light than the play itself: Philotas's ambition, we are told

being by *Ephestion* and *Craterus*, two the most especiall Councellers of *Alexander*, gravely and providently discerned, was prosecuted in that manner as became their neereness and deerenesse with their Lord and Master, and fitting to the safety of the State, in the case of so great an Aspirer. ("Argument," lines 31–35)

It seems likely that fear of reprisals led Daniel to mobilize more flattering interpretations in hopes of deflecting Cecil's concerns.[19]

There is no reason to assume, however, that Daniel's interest in the events surrounding the Earl of Essex's revolt precludes an equally intense interest in early Jacobean politics. The trial of Sir Walter Ralegh in 1603, for example, may have underscored the lessons of Essex's trial and provided more recent Jacobean evidence of the frailty of all whom Cecil opposed. There are a number of similarities between Ralegh's trial and that of Philotas, particularly the lack of sufficient evidence, the defendant's ironic questioning of procedure, the use of accusatory invective, and the noble performance of the accused.[20]

The virtually all-powerful Craterus of the last acts of *Philotas* is in some ways an especially appropriate representation of early Jacobean Cecil who in 1606 was described by the Spanish ambassador to James's court as an "awesome person, the one who manages everything here, without whom no one plays a role."[21] Furthermore, while *Philotas* is in large part an attack on Cecil, it also voices more general complaints about the direction of the early Jacobean state. When the "Graecian" chorus points out that "where Kings are so like gods, there subjects are not men" and the Persians answer "Your king begins this course, and what will you be then" (1,815–56), for example, the play echoes the sort of parliamentarian response to Jacobean absolutism already codified by the Commons in *The Form of Apology and Satisfaction* (1604).

What *Philotas* shows us, then, is two-fold. First, it shows how the powerful questions evoked by the rise and fall of Essex led into and provided the impetus for a questioning of specifically Jacobean governmental practice. Cecil's continued domination of the bureaucratic machinery of early Jacobean England was felt by some as part of an ongoing crisis because of lessons learned in the earlier, Elizabethan débâcle. Second, it gives us some insight into contemporary criticism of Jacobean absolutism, since the criticism of Alexander becomes scathing at precisely the point in the play when he is first dominated by his counsellors. Daniel's condemnation of Alexander's absolutism takes on a distinctly Jacobean flavor in the last two acts of *Philotas*, while at the same time the dangers of that absolutism are revealed to be structurally related to Alexander's domination by corrupt, self-serving counsel. This, in turn, suggests that the perception that James was "bewitched" by his counsellors contributed to the development of anti-absolutist feeling in early Jacobean England.

The last acts of *Philotas* pinpoint the blame for Alexander's tyranny on Craterus, an attribution which has been taken to reflect Daniel's opposition to Cecil's domination of government. It is, however, important to remember that the ongoing influence of Cecil is only one facet of the Jacobean crisis of counsel, which means that it is possible to locate the topical meaning of Daniel's play within more inclusive contexts as well. Cecil, of course, was not the only statesman whose access to the king caused anxiety in the Jacobean court. In particular it was widely felt, and not without reason, that James's imported Scottish entourage insulated him from his new subjects by dominating service positions in the king's newly formed Bedchamber. With the exception of Sir Philip Herbert (made Earl of Montgomery in 1605), who was sworn a Groom of the Bedchamber in July of 1603, the Grooms and Gentlemen of the Bedchamber were all Scottish until after the emergence of George Villiers in 1615. There were English Pages of the Bedchamber, but their duties were menial, their prestige was limited, and they generally were unable to parlay their positions into any further advantage.[22] This Scottish domination was significant in that the Gentlemen, Grooms, and Pages of the Bedchamber were the only courtiers whose access to the king in his private capacity was guaranteed. Even Cecil, by 1608, had his access generally restricted to formal audiences, and from an earlier date he seems to have recognized the need to cultivate members of the Bedchamber like Herbert, Sir James Hay, and Sir Roger Aston.[23]

The structure and function of James's Bedchamber was dramatically unlike that of Elizabeth's Privy Chamber. Because the queen's chamber was staffed by women, who could not hold important bureaucratic positions, there was a unique separation between the right to access and formal office. To Privy Counsellors and other important Elizabethan courtiers, access was granted and restricted on an *ad hoc* basis dependent entirely on the will of the queen. As a result, no faction could ever count on monopolizing access to the private monarch; one imagines that this arrangement contributed significantly to Elizabeth's success in managing her court and balancing factions.[24]

Compared to the Elizabethan arrangement, James's Bedchamber was both novel and potentially insulating. With the Tudor Privy Chamber relegated to a largely ceremonial position within the court, the Bedchamber, established in 1603, became the new locus for the king's private life. Needless to say, the virtual Scottish monopoly of access within this new arrangement contributed mightily to anti-Scots feeling in the English court. The Scots seemed to be ruining the court, draining English finances, and insulating the king just when he had most need for good counsel. Once again, Scaramelli reports that

no Englishman, be his rank what it may, can enter the Presence Chamber without being summoned, whereas the Scottish Lords have free entree of the privy chamber, and more especially at the toilette, at which time they discuss those proposals which, after dinner are submitted to the council, in so high and mighty a fashion that no one has the courage to raise opposition.[25]

Something of the public response to this arrangement is conveyed in Chapman, Marston, and Jonson's *Eastward Ho* (1605), in an exchange between Sindefy and Quicksilver. Sindefy argues that the court is more uncertain than the sea, since it requires careful flattery of the Lord, to which Quicksilver responds, "Tush hee's no Journey-man in his craft, that cannot doe that."[26] Sindefy's response seems to be directed at the Scottish domination of the politics of access:

But hee's worse than a Prentise that does it, not onely humouring the Lorde, but every Trencher-bearer, every Groome that by indulgence and intelligence crept into his favour, and by Pandarisme into his Chamber; He rules the roste: And when my honourable Lorde sayes it shall bee thus, my worshipfull Rascall (the Groome of his close stoole) sayes it shall not be thus, claps the doore after him, and who dares enter? (2.2.80–87)

The Groom of the Stool was in fact one of the Henrician offices revived in James's newly formed Bedchamber. Despite what Neil Cuddy coyly calls its "eponymous lavatorial tasks," the Groomship was a prestigious position under James: the Groom slept at the foot of the royal bed, dressed the king in his undershirt, had the right to attend him wherever he went, and generally enjoyed a unique official intimacy with the Body Natural. James's Groom of the Stool was the Scottish Sir Thomas Erskine.[27] As Sindefy's declaration suggests, there was some fear that the Scots were using the intimacy of Erskine and others to dominate the king and "rule the roste" in England. Between Cecil's ongoing domination of the bureaucratic agencies of state and the new Scottish monopoly of the king's private ear, there was ample reason for Englishmen to suspect a generalized failure of counsel.

In fact, in its most general formulation, the Jacobean crisis of counsel has to do not only with the politics of access, but also with James's own public style. Elizabeth had used the rhetoric of advice and counsel much as she used most conventional symbolic systems: she assumed a variety of contradictory, strategic stances in order to deploy and protect her own authority.[28] James's style – as in so many areas – differed sharply from Elizabeth's and exacerbated the emergent crisis of counsel in a number of ways. His attention to and confidence in the science of kingcraft, together with his insistence that subjects can never fathom the drifts of kings, tended to de-emphasize the importance of counsel. In his *Basilikon Doron*, accordingly, James provides the following recipe for Solomonic judgment of advice-givers:

principally, excercise trew Wisedome; in discerning wisely betwixt trew and false reports: First, considering the nature of the person reporter; Next, what entresse he can have in the weale or evill of him, of whom hee maketh the report; Thirdly, the likely-hood of the purpose it selfe; And, last, the nature and by-past life of the dilated person.[29]

In the traditional formula, counsel was necessary to compensate for the inevitable flaws of the monarch; here, the "trew Wisedome" of the monarch is needed to correct the inevitable flaws of counsel! There is perhaps something of this Jacobean style in Shakespeare's Leontes, who also chooses to trust his own "wisedome" over the counsel of his lords:

> Our prerogative
> Calls not your counsels, but our natural goodness
> Imparts this; which if you – or stupefied
> Or seeming so in skill – cannot, or will not,
> Relish a truth like us, inform yourselves
> We need no more of your advice.[30]
>
> (2.1.199–204)

Small wonder, given this governmental tenor, that "there is ... a shift of emphasis, perceptible and important in the Jacobean mind, away from counsel and toward statecraft."[31]

At the same time, the wide circulation and putative stability of James's own published opinions made him especially vulnerable to flatterers, since in them he codified his own stances and positions. Once codified, these royal cues were available to anybody, which made James an easy mark for the "cunning flatterer" as described by Bacon in his essay "Of Praise":

Some praises proceed merely of flattery; and if he be an ordinary flatterer, he will have certain common attributes, which may serve every man; if he be a cunning flatterer, he will follow the arch-flatterer, which is a man's self; and wherein a man thinketh best of himself, therein the flatterer will uphold him most.[32]

In fact, James's self-styling encourages in his subjects a reiteratory aesthetic which tends in and of itself to verge on cunning flattery: on the one hand, if the king's declarations are true and plain the subject has access to truth by repeating them; on the other, since subjects cannot fully understand the ways of kings, they are encouraged to limit themselves to the plain truths disclosed to them. Jonathan Goldberg describes James's implied plain-style decorum this way: "the poet bound to represent his 'subject' exactly is thereby subjected to a law of decorous representation and to the reproduction of the structure of society."[33]

One problem with this reiterative aesthetic is that courtly modes of panegyric, which traditionally encouraged the monarch to live up to the terms of his praise, were less likely to stray from the king's own opinions and declarations. We have seen something of this in poems directed to James discussed in chapter 1. Consequently, the value of encomium as an indirect source of counsel was significantly diminished in the Jacobean court.[34] A second problem is that it is hard in practice to distinguish between reproduction and appropriation. Once the king's truths have been codified and circulated, they become a set of tools: writers learn to address the king using his own positions to make theirs seem more appealing. By seeming to reflect his stable truths back to him, these modes of address threaten to undermine the referential priority of James's "wisedome." The resultant royal blind-ness may be benign when the cunning flattery takes the form of a masque, pageant, or panegyric; when the flatterer is the king's immediate counsel, however, this mirror-relationship becomes more problematic.

It is just this potential that Bacon warns of, in his essay "Of Counsel," when he writes

councellors should not be too speculative into their sovereign's person. The true composition of a counsellor is rather to be skilful in their master's business, than in his nature; for then he is like to advise him, and not feed his humour.[35]

James's counsellors seemed too skillful in their master's nature, and this is partly because his humors were made so readily legible. Perhaps, then, the relationship between Alexander and Craterus in Daniel's *Philotas* – rather than being a criticism of Cecil or of Jacobean states-men generally – stands in for the complex of events and perceptions which made James seem specially vulnerable to such cunning flatterers.

RULING AND DISSIMULATION IN *THE FAWNE*

This description of James may come as a surprise to anyone who has come across either Arthur Wilson's claim that contemporaries paral-leled James "to *Tiberius* for dissimulation" or Anthony Weldon's attri-bution of the commonplace "*qui nescit dissimulare, nescit regnare*" to James as a familiar motto.[36] Thanks to these writers, an image of James as a master of subterfuge has persisted. More recently, Goldberg has made use of this version of the king to describe an obscurantist strain in James's rhetoric. Thus, for Goldberg, James's plain-style claims are balanced by a persistent discursive inscrutability needed in order to mystify and maintain absolutist power.[37] The Jacobean rhetoric of Tacitean *arcana imperii* is seen as a sort of built-in discursive dissimulation.[38]

While it is undoubtedly true that the inscrutability of state secrets is an important element of James's absolutist rhetoric, a few caveats are in order. First, there is a difference between claiming inscrutability and actually being inscrutable. There is a paradoxical quality to James's own discourse on the subject: it clarifies and describes its own supposed opacity. While James's rhetoric of kingship makes claims about royal inscrutability, these claims in themselves act as readily legible, stable cues. In fact, as Goldberg's analysis amply documents, James's obscurantist claims are themselves appropriated and used in reiterative formulae of address to and discussion of the king. Elizabeth's more performative and less declamatory style, while it lays less claim to secrecy, is effectively more opaque.

Second, Weldon's account of King James is a hatchet-job. Jenny Wormald has shown not only that Weldon's memoir of James's court was motivated by personal animosity, but also what a legacy of mis-understanding his piece has generated.[39] The Latin tag with which Weldon vilifies James was a proverb widely used, in late Elizabethan and early Jacobean England, to satirize court life. Thus, in Ulpian Fulwell's collection of satirical dialogues *Ars Adulandi, or the Art of Flattery* (1576), the first principle of the most liberal science of flattery is *"qui nescit simulare, nescit vivere."*[40] The fact that Weldon's phrase is a common-place of court intrigue detracts from its credibility as a comment on James's actual behavior. Wilson's corroborating comment is hearsay, and might well describe exactly the sort of ill-formed dissatisfaction expressed in Weldon's piece. Godfrey Goodman's memoir of James's reign describes the king quite differently: "all men do know he had an open heart, and did make little use of any kingcraft."[41]

Third, Leah Marcus has usefully pointed out that James's retreat into inscrutability increased dramatically in the middle and later years of his reign: "In defensive reaction to the repeated failure of his strategy of 'plainnesse,' he increasingly withdrew from that vulnerable open-ness and veiled himself in ideas about the impenetrability of the royal arcana."[42] Thus, she argues, the well-known passage on "plainnesse" from James's first speech to parliament in 1604 is to be taken at face value as one of his early ideals of kingship:

it becommeth a King, in my opinion, to use no other Eloquence then plain-nesse and sinceritie. By plainnesse I meane, that his Speeches should be so cleare and voyd of all ambiguitie, that they may not be throwne, nor rent asunder in contrary sences like the old Oracles of the Pagan gods. And by sinceritie, I understand that uprightnsse and honestie which ought to be in a Kings whole Speeches and actions: That as farre as a King is in Honour erected above any of his Subjects, so farre should he strive in sinceritie to be above them all, and that his tongue sould be ever the trew Messenger of his heart: and this sort of Eloquence may you ever assuredly looke for at my hands.[43]

Despite his invocations of the concept of *arcana imperii*, James's failure to dissemble effectively encouraged his subjects to use his own terms in their direct addresses to him.

The issue of effective royal dissimulation is treated explicitly in the so-called "disguised duke" plays produced during the first three years of James's reign: a list of them would include Marston's *Malcontent* (1604) and *The Fawne* (1604–06), Middleton's *The Phoenix* (1604), Sharpham's *The Fleer* (1606), and Shakespeare's *Measure for Measure* (1603–04). Though these plays vary in their treatment of topical material, their brief vogue represents a dramatic response to James's declarative public style and attendant problems of counsel.[44] Royal dissimulation – concretized in these plays as literal disguise – is explored as a strategic solution to the problem of the "cunning flatterer." Of these plays, Marston's *The Fawne* is most explicit in its satire of the vulnerability of James's style of self-presentation. In particular, it poses its disguised duke against a singularly ineffective ruler whose declarative plain-style is drawn broadly as a parody of James's.

Hercules, Marston's Duke of Ferrara, is an example of a ruler who knows how to dissemble effectively. He disguises himself as the courtier Faunus in order to visit the court of Duke Gonzago in Urbin, where he positions himself to manipulate his son Tiberio, who has in turn been sent into Urbin with instructions to negotiate a marriage between Hercules himself and Gonzago's daughter Dulcimel. Hercules, in fact, wants to marry Tiberio to Dulcimel: his own marriage proposal is merely a ruse to get the two royal offspring together. The complicated love-story of Tiberio and Dulcimel provides Marston with an occasion for a detailed satire of royal vanity and courtly sycophancy, for juxtaposed against Hercules's performative wiles are the declamatory, vain performances of Gonzago.

Gonzago's first speech betrays his vanity. Accompanied by Granuffo, a lord who never speaks and therefore seems always to concur, the Duke instructs his daughter to resist Tiberio's suit. His speech is punctuated by parenthetical comments about his own eloquence and intelligence which are addressed to the always-agreeable Granuffo: "is't not well thought, my lord"; "I think we yet can speak, we ha' been eloquent"; "My Lord Granuffo, pray ye note my phrase."[45] The style of Gonzago's self-pleasing eloquence is classical, and he constantly makes display of his own learning. Thus, when Tiberio begins to confer *sotto voce* with Dulcimel, Gonzago finds it inappropriate because, as he tells the omnipresent Granuffo, such discourse belongs only to "Men of discerning wit / That have read Pliny" (1.2.151–52). This rhetorical vanity is compounded, over the course of the play, by Gonzago's vain confidence in his own perceptions. Thus, Gonzago brags that he can read Tiberio's mind: "I read his eyes, as I can read any eye / Tho' it speak in darkest characters, I can" (2.1.498–99).

Gonzago's vanity, as we might expect, makes him uniquely vulnerable. Hercules – in his disguise as the flattering Fawn – rises virtually at once to prominence in Gonzago's court. As the personification of Bacon's cunning flatterer, the Fawn immediately seems to Gonzago to be "a rare understander of men" (3.1.296–97). An exchange between the two will give a taste of the play's satire. Gonzago enters with the Fawn and Granuffo after denouncing Tiberio for courting his daughter:

> [GONZAGO]: What, did he think to walk invisibly before our eyes?
> And he had Gyges' ring I would find him.
> [HERCULES]: 'Fore Jove, you rated him with emphasis.
> [GONZAGO]: Did we not shake the Prince with energy?
> [HERCULES]: With Ciceronian elocution?
> [GONZAGO]: And most pathetic, piercing oratory?
> [HERCULES]: If he have any wit in him, he will make sweet use of it.
>
> (3.1.277–84)

Here Hercules's rhetorical questions blend indistinguishably with Gonzago's, as if to suggest that the flatterer has insinuated himself into the royal "we." Here and elsewhere, Gonzago's vanity and predictability make it easy for Hercules to effect his own agenda.

Dulcimel is also able to rely on the blindness caused by her father's vanity and on the stable predictability of his responses. In fact, once she has fallen in love with Tiberio, she is able to use her father's predictable bluster as a means of communicating her desires: she tells Gonzago that Tiberio is wooing her, because she knows that the Duke will repeat her accusations to the young prince. This, as Dulcimel herself had planned, puts the idea into Tiberio's head. Later, after the prince has been made to love by Dulcimel's stratagem, Gonzago is used to set up an assignation: Dulcimel accuses Tiberio of suggesting a meeting at a specific time and place, Gonzago in turn accuses the prince, and Tiberio understands that the accusation is in reality Dulcimel's invitation. He meets Dulcimel at the time and place suggested and the two are wed. Sure that her father's vanity will make him relish the opportunity to discover a plot, and confident that his response to it will be plain and stable, Dulcimel is able to ventriloquize Gonzago and negotiate her own marriage. Gonzago's vanity leads him unwittingly to pander for his own daughter; given the family politics of the period, there could be no more decisive exposé than this.

The play's final act consists largely of a masque of Cupid, performed before Gonzago, which Hercules uses to expose the Duke of Urbin and his corrupt courtiers. In it, Cupid complains that love is being abused and has Hercules read his ancient statutes and administer his justice. One by one Hercules denounces the stock courtiers who populate Gonzago's court until finally he reads an act against "privy conspiracies" and "ambitions wisdom" aimed at Gonzago himself (5.1.395–96). Gonzago heartily concurs with the statute, declaring that "Of all the creatures breathing, I do hate those things that struggle to seem wise, and yet are indeed very fools" (5.1.403–05), and adds

I smile to think I must confess, with some glory to mine own wisdom, to think how I found out, and crossed, and curb'd, and jerk'd, and firk'd, and in the end made desperate Tiberio's hope. (5.1.416–19)

Gonzago's comeuppance follows hard upon this display of royal vanity, as Hercules "arrests" the boastful Duke by this very statute, and shortly thereafter reveals his real identity and the marriage of the two children. The play ends happily, with a reconciliation between Hercules in "his own shape" and the chastened Gonzago.

If *The Fawne* shows how Gonzago's vanity and stability make him vulnerable, the play also suggests that judicious dissimulation is necessary for effective government. Hercules, depicted as a clever schemer, discovers while disguised that he too has been vulnerable to flattery in his realm of Ferrara:

> I never knew till now how old I was.
> By Him by whom we are, I think a prince,
> Whose tender sufferance never felt a gust
> Of bolder breathings, but still lived gently fann'd
> With the soft gales of his own flatterers' lips,
> Shall never know his own complexion.
> Dear sleep and lust, I thank you; but for you,
> Mortal till now I scarce had known myself.
> Thou grateful poison, sleek mischief, flattery,
> Thou dreamful slumber (that doth fall on kings
> As soft and soon as their first holy oil),
> Be thou for ever damn'd; I now repent
> Severe indictions to some sharp styles;
> Freeness, so't grow not to licentiousness,
> Is grateful to just states.
>
> (1.2.325–39)

In addition to being an implicit justification of Marston's own sharp style, this speech pin-points what I have called royal blindness. Kings are structurally vulnerable to the lying mirror of flattery, Marston's play suggests; dissimulation and the encouragement of "freeness" are the only antidotes.

Marston's play was performed at Blackfriars by the Children of the Queen's Revels, probably in 1605. The venue is suggestive, since the queen's troupe staged a series of notoriously topical satires of James and his court during its short tenure. In a patent of February, 1604 James authorized the erstwhile Chapel Children to perform in Blackfriars under the patronage of the queen. The same patent gave Samuel Daniel the right to act as licenser to the troupe, an unprece- dented alienation of the authority of the Master of the Revels. Under Daniel's inattentive supervision, and perhaps encouraged by Queen Anne who, it has been suggested, enjoyed the satiric barbs directed at her husband, the Children of the Queen's Revels produced a number of daring topical satires before finally being deprived of the queen's patronage following the production of John Day's *Isle of Gulls* in 1606.[46] That the company was allowed to continue for as long as it did bespeaks unusual royal indulgence, and supports Janet Clare's sugges- tion that "the protection of the sovereign's mystique ceased to be one of the censor's priorities" under the new king.[47]

Despite the fact that *The Fawne*'s love plot softens Marston's satire, the play makes sense within this short-lived dramatic milieu: because of his classicism, his pompous rhetorical style, and his vain confidence in his own statecraft, Gonzago has been described as a satirical por- trait of James himself.[48] This may be an overstatement, but it seems to me at any rate that the figure of Gonzago emblematizes concerns about James's vulnerability to cunning flattery.[49] Learning and theoret- ical kingcraft notwithstanding, Gonzago, like James, has a style which admits of no disguise; like James, he makes himself unusually vulnera- ble to fawning manipulation. In other words, Marston's play validates the Latin motto *qui nescit dissimulare, nescit regnare*, but subtly suggests that James himself was unable to dissimulate.

THE CRISIS AND JONSON'S COUNSEL: *SEJANUS*

The early performance history of Jonson's *Sejanus* is vexed and uncer- tain. The title-page of *Sejanus* in Jonson's 1616 folio asserts that the play was performed by the King's Men in 1603. Since the public theatres were closed from the time of Elizabeth's death until early 1604, it has often been assumed that the play was performed in court before James himself in the fall or winter of 1603. We know, too, that Jonson was called before the Privy Council in 1605 to account for the play, a summons which is often supposed to have stemmed from the court performance.[50] Alternatively, the inquiry may have followed the publication of the play in 1605 – a simpler explanation, and one that requires less speculation.[51]

According to Jonson, *Sejanus* was substantially revised for publication, which means that we have no solid idea of what the play looked like when it was first performed.[52] But even discounting the suggestion that *Sejanus* was performed before James, the involvement of the Privy Council suggests that the play was seen as politically charged. And the politics of the play would presumably have become more, not less, topically Jacobean during the course of the revisions made in 1604–05. Consequently, I am not convinced by those who describe the play as it has come to us as a late-Elizabethan meditation on the Essex crisis.[53] Rather, it seems to me that the edition of *Sejanus* that we have at our disposal is part of the specifically Jacobean anxiety over the relation between monarch and advisor, though it may, like the finished text of *Philotas*, have had its seed in late Elizabethan political configurations.[54]

Jonson's play opens with a prolonged exchange between Sabinus and Silius, two of the few remaining virtuous Romans, the sort who are "rarely met in court" (1.2). They spot two of "SEJANUS clients" (1.23), which gives them occasion to describe the devious courtly skills necessary to flourish under Tiberius. Prominent among these courtly skills is flattery, and we soon learn that Sejanus's two clients are able to

> Laugh, when their patron laughes; sweat, when he sweates;
> Be hot, and cold with him; change every moode,
> Habit, and garbe, as often as he varies;
> Observe him, as his watch observes his clocke;
> And true, as turkise in the deare lords ring,
> Looke well, or ill with him: ready to praise
> His lordship, if he spit, or but pisse faire,
> Have an indifferent stoole, or breake winde well.
>
> (1.33–40)

The emphasis on the bedchamber functions of these flatterers is suggestive – there is perhaps a shred of anti-Scottish feeling behind it. More importantly, this passage acts within the play as an important introduction to the milieu of Tiberius's court in general. Sejanus, as we shall see, uses the same brand of reiterative flattery on Tiberius throughout the play.

Jonson's representation of the relationship between tyrant and flatterer makes it quite difficult to figure out which caused the other. It is Silius, once again, who first encapsulates the problematics of the relationship in the play's first act:

> he [Tiberius] permits himselfe
> Be carried like a pitcher, by the eares,
> To every act of vice: this is a case
> Deserves our feare, and doth presage the nigh,
> And close approach of bloud and tyranny.
> "Flattery is midwife unto princes rage:
> "And nothing sooner, doth helpe foorth a tyranne.
>
> (1.416–22)

Not only does flattery carry the emperor to tyranny, it also obviates the normal procedures by which a citizen might respond to such a threat. Arruntius's noble response to Silius's description – he impulsively suggests the sort of plain-spoken counsel that should reach a monarch's ears: "He should be told this" (1.425) – is quickly dismissed by Silius as impractical.

Implicit in Silius's metaphoric description of Tiberius and his flatterers is the suggestion that Tiberius has allowed himself to be controlled (carried away) by his own flatterers. Later, we see Sejanus bid explicitly to control the emperor by encouraging and subsequently directing Tiberius's suspicious nature. Sejanus himself summarizes his plot succinctly in a dark soliloquy towards the end of the play's second act:

> Work then, my art, on CAESAR's feares, ...
> ... till all my letts be clear'd:
> And he in ruines of his house, and hate
> Of all his subjects, bury his owne state:
> When, with my peace, and safty, I will rise,
> By making him the publike sacrifice.
>
> (2.399–404)

The exemplar of Bacon's cunning flatterer, Sejanus is an expert in the emperor's humors and plans to feed them in the service of his own agenda.

The sheer detail with which Jonson depicts counsel allows us to talk quite precisely about the role of the advisor in the political crisis of the play's milieu. The crucial scene in this regard – our first and closest glimpse into the actual scene of counsel – is the long private consultation held between the two in the play's second act (163–330). Fearful of Agrippina and the two offspring of Germanicus, the emperor inaugurates the counsel session with what is in effect a rhetorical question: "When the master-prince / Of all the world, SEJANUS, saith, he feares; / Is it not fatall" (2.165–67)? Sejanus, of course, cannot agree that the emperor is doomed. Instead, he responds as Tiberius expects him to: "Yes, to those are fear'd" (167). As the exchange develops it becomes clear that Tiberius is using Sejanus as a Machiavellian sounding-board against which to try platitudes of good government. Thus, Tiberius asks the rather abstract question "Are rites / Of faith, love, piety, to be trod downe? / Forgotten? and made vaine?" (175–77) To which Sejanus gives an equally abstract answer:

> All for a crowne.
> The prince, who shames a tyrannes name to beare,
> Shall never dare doe any thing, but feare;
> All the command of scepters quite doth perish
> If it beginne religious thoughts to cherish.
>
> (177–81)

After this exchange, Tiberius reveals just how closely he expects Sejanus to be following his intentions: "Knowes yet, SEJANUS, whom we point at" (188)? Sejanus, of course, admits that he does, and then launches into a long diatribe against the pridefulness of Agrippina and the Germanici, a diatribe which is intended to feed the emperor's fear and which has its desired effect. Finally, after Sejanus has over-ruled all of Tiberius's objections and advised him to kill off the potentially threatening family of Germanicus, Tiberius admits that he has been testing Sejanus all along:

> We can no longer
> Keepe on our masque to thee, our deare SEJANUS;
> Thy thoughts are ours, in all, and we but proov'd
> Their voice, in our designes, which by assenting
> Hath more confirm'd us, then if heartning JOVE
> Had, from his hundred statues, bid us strike.
>
> (278–83)

The formal question-and-answer structure of this scene has a ritual quality to it: it is clear on the one hand that there is no intellectual exploration involved in the exchange, while on the other hand it seems that both emperor and counsellor get what they want out of it.

As the ritualized quality of the exchange suggests, Tiberius's "masque" of goodness has been transparent all along to Sejanus. Moreover, since

Sejanus's advice has been cued all along to the expectations of Tiberius, the actual counsel is revealed to have been rather echoic than productive. There is a troubling irony, then, in the phrase "thy thoughts are ours, in all": Sejanus's professed thoughts in this scene of counsel are literally taken from the pattern of Tiberius's expectations, which means that Tiberius is operating under a sort of self-imposed solipsism. Rather than putting thoughts to the test, Tiberius's counsel with Sejanus subjects them to an empty ritual of confirmation; Sejanus, mirroring back Tiberius's expectations, is the perfect "glass-fac'd flatterer."

Sejanus's motives in Jonson's play are selfish. By echoing Tiberius he is able to direct and control the emperor. This is a second irony implicit in Tiberius's phrase "thy thoughts are ours, in all": despite the grasping possessiveness of the emperor's construction, the duplication of his thoughts makes possible the alienation of his authority. Having the emperor's thoughts means being able to make him have yours. This in turn means that the putatively hierarchical relationship between king and counsel is vulnerable to reversal. Sejanus's actions literalize this implicit irony, as he takes advantage of his familiarity with the emperor's opinions, hopes, and fears and, acting as the emperor's agent, begins to replace him.

This is most evident later in the play when Sejanus convinces Tiberius to retire from the city, leaving the government in his hands, but Sejanus's appropriation of Tiberius's role is already manifest in the exchange we have been looking at. Thus, after Sejanus promises to act on Tiberius's murderous wishes, Tiberius answers "But how? let us consult" (321). The counsellor then refuses to consult his ruler:

> Wee shall mispend
> The time of action. Counsels are unfit
> In businesse, where all rest is more pernicious
> Then rashnesse can be.
>
> (321–24)

Needless to say, this is a troubling moment: only the king's thoughts and intentions are supposed to remain unknown. In claiming the royal right to inscrutability – against the emperor himself! – Sejanus activates the dangerous potential of Tiberius's duplicated "thoughts."

In the end, Sejanus goes too far. When he asks Tiberius for the hand of Livia, it awakens the emperor's dormant suspicions. Tiberius has just enough kingcraft left in him to know that the royal blood is to be protected, and he hastily instructs Macro to keep an eye on Sejanus's machinations. At the end of the play, when Tiberius and Macro have negotiated Sejanus's fall from grace and power, Macro himself oversees the gruesome public executions of Sejanus's family, and takes his place as the absent Tiberius's agent in Rome. The exchange does the Roman citizens little good, for though Macro lacks Sejanus's improvisational virtuosity he is still the brutal agent of a brutal tyrant. In fact, the play is all the more pessimistic for the suggestion that one flatterer will inevitably be replaced by another.

To English readers, accustomed to reading Tacitus with the notion of *similitudo temporum* in mind, Jonson's play must have had some topical urgency.[55] We know that at least one contemporary saw the similarities between Tiberius's time and his own so clearly that he used passages from *Sejanus* freely in a topical satire of Jacobean court corruption.[56] And Philip Ayres has shown that Jonson's play alters Roman political history in order to make it cognate with contemporary monarchic theory. In particular, Ayres points out that while in Tacitus's *Annals* Arruntius is one of Augustus's potential successors (1.13), Jonson has the same character uphold the legitimacy of Tiberius's claim to the throne by reason of descent (1.244–46).[57] For Ayres, the moral core of *Sejanus* is Sabinus's speech against revolution in Act 4:

> No ill should force the subject undertake
> Against the soveraigne, more then hell should make
> The gods doe wrong. A good man should, and must
> Sit rather downe with losse, then rise unjust.
>
> (163–66)

This speech – like Arruntius's endorsement of Tiberius's lineal claim – expresses an important orthodoxy of English monarchic theory. Jonson, Ayres argues, changed the political history of Tacitus's *Annals* in order to underline these English orthodoxies for didactic purposes.

Ayres's reading of the topical thrust of *Sejanus*, it seems to me, overstates the affective power of Sabinus's orthodoxy. Since Tiberius's legitimacy is cause for alarm, not celebration, the function of Sabinus's call to quietism has to be more complex. In fact, I think it could be argued that by bringing its noble characters to the point where they have to even consider regicide, the play subjects its political orthodoxies to a dangerous degree of stress. The instability of the play's political moral is suggested most concretely by the critical debate it has engendered. Thus, Tricomi describes a didactic purpose diametrically opposed to the one Ayres responds to: "For Jonson's contemporaries with eyes to see and ears to hear, *The Tragedy of Sejanus* warned its readers to beware the possibility of a similar suffocation in England."[58] This critical disagreement over the play's politics is indicative of real ambiguity.

I would like to suggest that *Sejanus* was intended, in part, as a piece of self-advertisement, and that the rhetorical demands of Jonson's self-positioning help to explain the ambiguities of his peculiar tragedy. Since the play was revised and published during the years when Jonson was most eager to catch the eye of the court, it makes sense to imagine that the published quarto of 1605 conceives of James not only as part of its topical sub-text, but even perhaps of its audience, in the widest sense of that word. With this in mind, *Sejanus* must be taken as, among other things, an attempt on Jonson's part to establish himself as a frank, classically trained, and astute observer of the exigencies of politics and political discourse. *Sejanus*, accordingly, is Ayres's celebration of the legitimacy of blood because it imagined James and his court as its audience; it is also Tricomi's sagacious political admonition insofar as it tries to demonstrate its author's grasp of political complexities and *arcana imperii*. The text's scholarly, sometimes off-putting style can be seen as part of Jonson's attempt to establish his credentials as a writer with a scholar's grasp of political theory, for the text that has come down to us goes out of its way to demonstrate its author's understanding of the practical complexities of political discourse.

First, the play features a prominent incident in which the topical application of a scholarly text is debated, and its author punished. The historian Cremutius Cordus is accused by Sejanus of writing history as covert commentary on the present. Cordus denies the charges, but his books are burned. As Patterson has demonstrated, Jonson's treatment of the "hermeneutics of censorship" in Tiberius's Rome serves both to focus attention on the dangerous polyvalence of historical writing and to complicate Jonson's own claim to historical neutrality: the presence of the Cordus incident within Jonson's play effectively acknowledges the potential topicality of his own Roman history.[59] Rather than emphasizing either the justice of Cordus's Livian history or its political naiveté, Jonson's thematization of censorship focuses on the vulnerability of historical writing to interpretive appropriation and, consequently, on the uselessness of suppression.

Second, Jonson's play complicates its moral position by undercutting Arruntius's authority. During the play's long, stagey senate session in Act 3 (1–470), Arruntius's voice continually punctuates the action, commenting on the hypocrisy of the performance of state before him.

His criticism seems authoritative, and one takes him to be "the voice and exponent of the irrepressible critic and censor in Jonson himself."[60] Nevertheless, shortly after the senatorial theatrics, when Tiberius suggests that Arruntius might be worth killing, Sejanus responds

> By any meanes, preserve him. His franke tongue
> Being lent the reines, will take away all thought
> Of malice, in your course against the rest.
>
> (3.498–500)

Rather than being subversive in practice, Arruntius's performance is revealed to have been appropriated for the tyrant's purposes by Sejanus's trick of state. Even as we find Arruntius admirable, we are reminded of the complex malleability of discourse in a real political context.

Third, *Sejanus* ends with a gesture of closure which is manifestly inappropriate to the play. Concluding speeches by Arruntius and Terentius provide hackneyed morals which are far from satisfying in light of the play's political analysis. Arruntius warns against political hubris, drawing on the threadbare topos of fickle fortune: "Forbeare, you things, / That stand upon the pinnacles of state, / To boast your slippery height" (5.893–95); Terentius responds "Let this example moove th'<e> insolent man, / Not to grow proud, and carelesse of the gods" (898–99). These sentiments are imported from the *speculum principis* tradition and hardly seem appropriate at the end of a play which has been described as a fully material history so detailed that it leaves nothing to be explained by providentialism.[61] The effect of these inappropriate morals, it seems to me, is to call attention precisely to the play's lack of closure. In the words of Robert Ornstein, "the play is neither a tragedy of civic decadence nor one of insatiable ambition. We are not allowed to pity and we are not moved to fear."[62] Instead, we are reminded that closure is not always possible in complex material history.

So even as the analysis of the problematics of echoic advice in *Sejanus* warns of a potential crisis of counsel for James, the play demonstrates Jonson's own value in relation to precisely such a crisis. By positioning himself as a plain-spoken, knowledgeable, neo-stoic advisor, Jonson tacitly proposes himself as a solution to a crisis of counsel to which – he hints – James himself is vulnerable. Hence the admonitory tone of *Sejanus*: rather than saying "James is Tiberius," the play says "James is vulnerable to an analogous crisis; hiring me would help to avoid it." In effect, Jonson offers to James the services that

Seneca performed for Nero in Tacitus's *Annals*: plain advice and literary spokesmanship. As a gesture, this self-advertisement allows Jonson to be both celebratory and admonitory: the more audacious the play seems, the more plain-spoken and potentially useful its author promises to be.

Jonson's addresses to patrons tend in general to be subtly equivocal. Katharine Eisaman Maus, for example, argues that Jonson managed to deal with his own competitiveness by "making gestures that covertly challenge the powerful, even while they gratify them."[63] By the same token, Jonson's gestures of self-advertisement tend to play on the vulnerabilities of their recipients even as they ask for patronage. *Sejanus* does this: it uses the perceived Jacobean crisis of counsel in order to demarcate a need for Jonson's own brand of literary advice. Some years later, in his *Discoveries*, Jonson formulated the reciprocal relationship between king and counsel as one of mutual need:

> Learning needs rest: Soveraignty gives it.
> Soveraignty needs counsell: Learning affords it.
> There is such a Consociation of offices, betweene the
> Prince, and whom his favour breeds, that they may
> helpe to sustaine his power, as hee their knowledge.[64]

As we have seen, James's claim to "trew wisedome" made him unlikely to acknowledge his need for Learning's counsel. *Sejanus* in effect challenges James's self-sufficiency: it simultaneously highlights the king's need for good counsel and advertises its author as the perfect man for the job.

"KINGS ARE NOT SAFE WHOM ANY UNDERSTAND": *MUSTAPHA*'S WELL-MEANING TYRANT

The closest thing we have to an explicitly topical treatment of the Jacobean crisis of counsel is Greville's revised version of *Mustapha*. Like Daniel's *Philotas*, Greville's closet drama began as part of the Wilton group's experimentation.[65] Then the play underwent heavy revisions in manuscript – its Jacobean incarnation was completed between 1607 and 1610 – which changed it from a meditation on individual moral choice and the problem of succession into a treatment of political immorality and the dangers of counsel.[66]

There are purely biographical reasons for this play's explicit treatment of urgent political matters. Greville revised *Mustapha* during his forced retirement from court. Having earned the mistrust of Cecil for supporting Essex, Greville was effectively squeezed out of Cecil's Jacobean administration. In 1604 he was forced to resign his position as Treasurer of the Navy, and he did not hold an administrative position again until after Cecil's death.[67] In 1606 Greville's father died, leaving him his patrimonial lands. These rents, together with rents on his own lands and the income from fee-paying offices, gave Greville, in 1607, twice as much income as he enjoyed during his most lucrative year under Elizabeth.[68] Given Greville's real cause for discontent with James's administration, his increasing financial independence, and the fact that *Mustapha* was not written to be performed or published, one would expect the text to be more than usually frank.

As Ronald Rebholz has suggested, "most of Greville's revisions of Soliman's character pointedly stress qualities of James."[69] Among these are Solyman's vanity about his understanding of the "art of Monarchie," his propensity for plain-style declarations concerning this art, and his heavy reliance on absolutist dogma like "*Man comprehends a man, but not a King.*"[70] If the portrayal of Solyman is intended to be topical, so is Greville's representation of political crisis. The story upon which Greville's drama is based was widely known and frequently reported as an example of eastern despotic tyranny, but Greville works this material, in his second version of it, into a sustained treatment of the Jacobean vulnerability to insulating counsel.[71] Thus, in the second version Rossa becomes "less a figure in a moral *exemplum* and more a type of the ambitious courtier who, like Cecil or the Howards, attempts to dominate the monarch."[72]

The play opens with a conversation between Rossa and Solyman: the latter has begun to doubt the loyalty of his eldest son Mustapha, while the former schemes to put her own son, Zanger, on the throne in Mustapha's place. Rossa urges her husband to take action against Mustapha, but she presents her arguments in a manner that flatters Solyman's vanity, inviting him to use his royal insight to "looke into" Mustapha "by his outward wayes" (1.1.33). Rossa then presses her own agenda upon Solyman as if it was the fruit of his own privileged insight. The king's insecurity and vanity do their part as Rossa's advice begins to take hold. In effect, Rossa here acts on the principle later expounded by her son-in-law Rosten: "Sonnes love with selfe-love must be overthrowne" (3.1.55).

It is easy for Rossa to play on the king's "selfe-love." Solyman tends to state his opinions in plain speeches, laden with aphorisms, and the ease with which the king can be read makes it easier for his more dissembling interlocutors to control him. Achmat, Solyman's one faithful advisor and the play's moral authority, says as much in his long soliloquy at the beginning of Act 2:

> Princes humors are not like the *Glasse*,
> Which in it shewes what shapes without remaine,
> And with the body goe, and come again:
> But like the *Waxe*, which first beares but his owne,
> Till it the seale in easy mould receive,
> And by th' impression onely then is knowne.
> In this soft weaknesse *Rossa* prints her art,
> And seekes to tosse the Crowne from hand to hand;
> *Kings are not safe whom any understand.*
>
> (2.1.33–41)

Understanding a king makes it possible to use his vanity, his humors, and his assumptions against him. The result is that the king's "seale" – putatively the official expression of his will – is controlled by another. Rather than wielding the seal, the king, once understood, is wax to be imprinted by the will of another. Achmat suggests that Solyman's plain style deprives him in effect of his political agency. The image, here, explains nicely why "Kings are not safe whom any understand": understanding a king makes it possible to use his vanity, his humors, and his assumptions against him. Later in the play Rosten unknowingly confirms Achmat's description of Rossa's cunning flattery when he tells her to make Solyman "take impressions" from her "both of hope, and feare" (3.1.59). Similarly, the treacherous Beglerbie reiterates Achmat's perception that kings who are understood are consequently controlled:

> Ah humorous Kings? how are you tossed, like waves,
> With breaths, that from the earth beneath you move;
> Observed, and betray'd; knowne and undone.
>
> (4.4.1–3)

Mustapha is unusually explicit about both the conditions under which advisors can seize control and the potential consequences. First, given the commonplace analogy between king and father – an analogy which is brought up several times during the course of the play – the murder of a loyal son and heir is among the most terrible crimes a king can commit. Second, the wide-ranging results of Solyman's weakness are represented within the play by the choruses which "function not only as commentators but as institutional participants in the tragedy."[73]

The chorus of Bashas (advisors), in particular, depicts the compromised nature of councilors and courtiers under tyranny.

As in Jonson's *Sejanus*, the specter of revolution and revolt is raised only to be decisively rejected. Mustapha is executed – declaring as he goes that a king's will must not be resisted – Zanger commits suicide and an angry mob rises against Rosten, the new heir by default. The latter flees to Achmat, asking him to quell the mob, which provides Achmat with an opportunity to choose between the justice of the people's rage and the danger of anarchy. Here Achmat hesitates, as if to make clear that the decision is a real one. His first inclination is to urge the mob on:

> shall I helpe to stay the Peoples rage
> From this Estate, thus ruined with Age?
> No, People, No. Question these Thrones of Tyrants;
> Revive your old equalities of Nature.
>
> (5.3.90–93)

Finally, however, he decides that the mob is more dangerous than the crown: "No. *Achmat*! Rather, with thy hazard, strive / To save this high rais'd *Soveraignitie*" (5.3.112–13). Interestingly, the play is never clear about how, or indeed if, Achmat will be able to quell the mob. Apparently the scene of decision was enough for Greville's purposes. The play's final rejection of revolution is less ambivalent than the equivalent passages in the earlier version of the text. It can nevertheless be argued that in this play – as in Jonson's – the raising of the question is itself evidence of dissent. *Mustapha* ends in obedience because, in Tricomi's words, "as a seventeenth-century Calvinist who saw in the present age an irreversible pattern of corruption, Greville had no conception of effective political protest; it offended his metaphysics."[74]

The most remarkable thing about *Mustapha* – and in some ways the most radical thing as well – is the play's depiction of Solyman. Not only is he portrayed as a well-intentioned king who wants to rule for the betterment of his people, he is shown to be cognizant of the principles of statecraft, which should protect him from being "knowne and undone." He says, for example,

> A King ought therefore to suspect
> Feares, fearfull counsells which incline to blood,
> Wherein, but truths, no Influence is good.
> Else will inferior practise ever cast
> Such glassy shaddowes upon all our errors,
> As he that sees not ruine, shall see terrors.

> Power therefore should affect the Peoples stampe,
> "Whose good, or ill thoughts, ever prove to Kings,
> "Like aire, which either health, or sicknesse brings.
>   (1.2.27–35)

Solyman knows in theory that kings are prone to undue suspiciousness that must be checked. In fact, these precepts – Solyman calls them "straight lines" (1.2.36) – even lead him to perceive, however briefly, that his son is innocent:

> by these straight lines, if we sound
> The hollow depths of *Rostens* mysterie;
> He will the canker of this State be found.
> Long hath he wav'd betwixt my sonne, and me.
>   (1.2.36–39)

Even at the eleventh hour, just before he orders Mustapha to be executed, Solyman remembers the precept by which he should rule: "*Kings thoughts to Jealousie are over-tender*" (4.3.14).

Not only does Solyman understand the maxims of good kingcraft, he is shown to have access to good advice from two sources: his daughter Camena and Achmat. The former reminds Solyman of the importance of his blood relationship to Mustapha, and tells the king that his suspicions are the "mists of Greatnesse" (2.3.121). The latter decides, in a long soliloquy, that he must offer plain-spoken advice despite the peril that keeps the other Bashas silent. Solyman listens to both Camena and Achmat, promising to weigh their opinions but insisting (with King James) that "*Kings hearts must judge what Subjects hearts have wrought*" (2.2.159). Instead, Rossa and her faction effectively silence Solyman's two honest advisors. Camena is killed, and Solyman's carefully cultivated state of mind makes Achmat's advice ineffectual. The good Basha appears on stage with Solyman in Act 4, Scene 1, but he listens to the king's anguished raving without ever uttering a word. In that scene, Solyman forestalls Achmat's advice by declaring "God only is above me, and consulted" (4.1.2), and Beglerbie interrupts the Basha's audience.

Greville's play represents the strongest possible statement about the destructive effects of dominating counsel. Solyman is a fairly sympathetic character: he has the best interests of the state firmly in mind, and he has access to wise advice.[75] What is remarkable about *Mustapha* is that even in these circumstances the king can be made into the worst of tyrants by his advisors if he allows himself to be "understood."

The problems arising from this portrait of a failed king are manifested within the Bashas' formulation of the break-down of the system of counsel at the end of Act I:

> Bondage, and ruine, only wrought by those,
> That Kings with servile Flattery inclose,
> Hatching, in double heates of Power, and Will,
> *Thunder*, and *Lightning*, to amaze, and kill.
> Thus Tyrants deale with Peoples liberty;
> The nether Region cannot long live free.
> Thus Tyrants deale with us of higher place,
> As drawne up onely to disperse disgrace.
> (Chorus Primus, 23–30)

Those like Rossa who "Kings with servile Flattery inclose" are credited with having control over Solyman's malicious actions, while the king is himself held responsible for the social ills in general. This amounts to a puzzling anatomy of tyranny: Solyman is judged to be a tyrant even as he is seen to have little control over his own actions.

TYRANTS AND KINGS

The anatomy of the well-meaning tyrant in *Mustapha* literalizes what has been a troubling potential in many of the plays we have looked at. In Daniel's *Philotas*, for example, Alexander allows evil to be done in his name despite his better judgment. Craterus and Ephestion effectively make the putatively enlightened Greek king into the moral equivalent of a Persian despot. Jonson's Tiberius is, of course, less sympathetic to begin with, but it is not clear how much agency the play gives him. The contrast between Jonson's play and the other contemporary dramatic treatment of the story of Sejanus is instructive. The title character of the anonymous *Tragedie of Claudius Tiberius Nero* (1607) is a strong-willed tyrant from the start of his reign; the treatment of the Tacitean story depicts the relationship between Sejanus and Tiberius as a battle of depraved politicians. In this clumsy, anonymous version of the story, Tiberius's tyrannical nature creates an atmosphere in which Sejanus flourishes. In Jonson's, by contrast, Sejanus's mirror-like ministrations effectively control Tiberius.

What emerges in these plays is a less ethical and more structural analysis of the nature of the tyrannic king: bad kings are made, not born. This analysis of the vulnerabilities of even a well-meaning king has a special topical bite to it because of the perceived crisis of counsel under James. The immediate topical implication – generally only implicit in these plays – is that James's putative clarity and structural insulation might make him tyrannic despite the good intentions expressed in his published documents. Perhaps more importantly, this new structural analysis of tyranny suggests that the real distinction between kings and tyrants is situational and practical, rather than moral.

Traditional theoretical distinctions between king and tyrant were somewhat muddled in practice. In Tudor absolutist discourse, a tyrant was alternatively a usurper or a bad king. While the former might be (indeed, must be) lawfully overthrown, the latter had to be tolerated insofar as he ruled by God's decree. This last piece of absolutist orthodoxy, though widely associated with James, was given national currency as early as 1570 by the "Homily against Disobedience and Wilful Rebellion" which was delivered in churches across the land by royal command. According to this line of reasoning, moral character has nothing to do with legitimacy.[76]

More often than not, however, the relationship between tyrants and legitimate kings in Tudor drama shows signs of simplification, as moral criteria bleed into the question of legitimacy: in plays drawing from the *speculum principis* tradition, for example, usurpers are corrupt and dangerous as if by definition.[77] By the same token, as Rebecca Bushnell has argued, early Tudor drama also begins to emphasize the specifically moral basis of kingship, without fully exploring the potentially troubling figure of the evil and legitimate king. This emphasis continues – challenged perhaps by plays like Marlowe's *Edward II* and Shakespeare's *Richard II* – through the Elizabethan period.[78] There is a practical tendency, in other words, to reduce the theoretical complexity of the relationship between a king and a tyrant to a simple binary structure: good legitimate kings on the one hand, and amoral usurping tyrants on the other.

This binarism survives in James's writing. For while his *Trew Law of Free Monarchies* articulates the absolutist line and defends the legitimacy of even a bad king, we find in *Basilikon Doron* the following passage:

For the part of making, and executing of Lawes, consider first the trew difference betwixt a lawfull good King, and an usurping Tyran ... The one acknowledgeth himselfe ordained for his people, having received from God a burthen of government, whereof he must be countable: the other thinketh his people ordeined for him, a prey to his passions and inordinate appetites, as the fruites of his magnanimity.[79]

The slippage between "lawfull" and "good" is the mark of conceptual simplification within the discourse of the time. In other words, James's analysis of the distinction between king and "Tyran" relies on moral terms even as it explains putatively legal categories. Consequently, in the rhetoric of this passage, kings are good and usurpers are tyrants. Despite James's defense of absolute right, moral character is constructed as a subtly legitimizing or delegitimizing force. James's absolutist rhetoric, then, is somewhat selective: it is tempered in practice by traditional constructions of the morality of legitimacy. This is not surprising, for while absolutist theory claims unconditional legitimacy for the king, the conventionalized link between legitimacy and goodness makes its claims more palatable in practice.

Cumulatively, these early Jacobean dramatic explorations of the problematics of counsel constitute a powerful attack on the morality of legitimacy. The figure of the well-meaning, legitimate king made into an unbearable tyrant by counsel pressures the inevitability of the association between legitimacy and morality. More importantly, it calls into question the political relevance of morality itself. If a good man with the best of intentions can be made into a tyrant so bad that justifiable regicide is conceivable, then morality loses whatever legitimizing force it might have had. In fact since, in Bacon's analysis, all kings are subject by virtue of their position to "many representations of perils and shadows, which makes their minds the less clear," all kings should be vulnerable in theory to the sort of cunning flatterer capable of exerting this dangerous control.[80]

This line of analysis disallows whatever softening of absolutist claims is implicit in the conventional morality of legitimacy. Furthermore, it seems to me that the sort of structural or situational analysis of kingship and tyranny implicit in these plays would tend to encourage a more strictly consequentialist attitude towards the crown. Redefining the distinction between the good king and the bad king in terms of material relationships and structures demystifies the moral person of the king, privileging good or bad results over moral timbre as a criterion of judgment. Thus, rather than see the state of the realm as the passive reflection of the quality of the king, this new line of analysis would tend to reverse the equation, seeing an orderly realm as the only measure of the king's quality. By the same token, this consequential criterion would tend to authorize the subject's judgments about the performance of the king. Not only does this contradict Jacobean orthodoxy, one can see how the further development of this materialist, consequentialist perspective might contribute to the consolidation of oppositional politics under James and, later, under Charles.[81]

For these reasons, I see these plays as part of what Franco Moretti has called drama's "deconsecration of sovereignty": its ongoing role in the dissolution of old political orthodoxies and in the creation of a public capable of imagining regicide.[82] By now it should be clear, however, that these plays participate in larger historical paradigms only by means of their engagement with specific, topical concerns. Thus, in addition to serious-minded criticism of James's government (like *Philotas* or *Mustapha*), it is important to remember that the plays contributing to this deconsecrating Jacobean anatomy of kingship and counsel include both courtly self-advertisement (*Sejanus*), and entertaining topical satire (*The Fawne*). If these plays do respond to the Jacobean crisis of counsel in a way that is easy to assimilate to broad historiographical formulae like Moretti's, it should remind us that such overviews, though useful and even accurate in their own way, necessarily mislead by obscuring the sheer variety of contingencies involved in the micropolitics of authorial decision.

CHAPTER FOUR

Nourish-fathers and pelican daughters
Kingship, gender, and bounty in King Lear and Macbeth

BOUNTY, PLENTY, AND THE MATERNALITY OF KINGSHIP

Royal profligacy has long been a trope of Jacobean historiography, a central index to James's supposed foolishness, effeminacy, and weak will. Thus: "Choosing his favorites for no other merit but their charm as companions, he was too fond to deny them anything"; "He had a Scottish weakness for liking to please people."[1] Recent historical scholarship has been kinder, recognizing that James needed to be generous in order to secure loyalty in his new realm, and that generosity as such was seen as an important virtue in a monarch, an index to his majesty.[2] Contemporaries remarked on James's generosity with cash and titles, and resented the king's gifts to his Scottish entourage, but there is reason to believe that his initial generosity may have been seen as necessary and laudable, rather than as the harbinger of dangerous profligacy.[3] At any rate, it is clear that James's openhandedness, coming as it did on the heels of Elizabeth's stinginess, was seen as an important element of the new king's style of governing.[4]

Given the novelty and the scale of James's giving, it is not surprising to find issues of royal generosity treated in politically minded literary texts. Coppélia Kahn, for instance, has sketched a connection between the apparent recklessness of King James's gift-giving and the obsessive prodigality of Shakespeare's Timon.[5] In particular, Kahn calls attention to the maternal imagery which pervades the play's depiction of Timon's bounty in order to read *Timon of Athens* as "a doubly topical play, linked both to the economic world and the fantasy world of the Jacobean court," since "the extreme dependency created by patronage, in which advancement or obscurity, prosperity or ruin, hung on the granting of a suit, could have reawakened anxieties stemming from infantile dependency on the mother who, it seems to the child, can give or take away all."[6]

Thus, in Kahn's reading of the fable with which the Poet and the Painter describe Timon's ascent of Fortune's "high and pleasant hill"

(1.1.63), Timon is first figured as a baby at its mother's breast ("Bowing his head against the steepy mount / To climb his happiness" [1.1.75–76]), and then as a quasi-maternal source of bounty himself: ("his fellows ... through him / Drink the free air" [1.1.78–83]). In a related argument, C. L. Barber also called attention to the maternality of bounty in *Timon*, arguing that Timon's wealth is "likened, by a half-submerged image, to an inexhaustible breast" when the Poet describes "his large fortune / Upon his good and gracious nature hanging" (1.1.55–56).[7] Barber's unhistoricized findings might easily be assimilated to Kahn's more topical approach.

Instead of treating the maternality of bounty in *Timon* as an exclusively Shakespearean response to the psychic pressures of the patronage system, however, it is possible to locate Shakespeare's maternal imagery within broader pictorial and discursive contexts. Virtues such as generosity and charity, as well as benefits associated with them such as bounty or plenty, are commonly represented as maternal in contemporary iconographic and emblematic traditions. Cesare Ripa's influential *Iconologia*, for example, represents "Benignita" ("goodness," "generosity," "altruism" – the earliest English translation renders it as "Bounty") as "A noble Lady cloth'd in sky-colour's Apparel, with Stars of Gold: she presses her Duggs with both Hands, from which flows abundance of Milk, which several Animals drink up" (fig. 1).[8] Ripa's book was widely used in England, not only by emblem artists but also by poets and playwrights involved in a variety of kinds of production.[9] Though I am not proposing Ripa in particular as a source for Shakespeare's *Timon*, the *Iconologia* represents the kind of text that would appropriately surface as common ground during a dialogue between a Poet and a Painter: emblem books and mythographies were crucial not only as resources for visual artists but also as visual guides for poets.[10]

Ripa treats this maternal "Benignita" as an explicitly royal virtue, describing it specifically as a quality to be exercised towards subjects ("essercita verso i Sudditi"). Similarly, Kahn points out that James himself assimilates maternal functions to patriarchal kingship when, for example, he writes that a king should be "a loving nourish-father to the Church" or lists "nourishing" prominently among the paternal duties of a king towards his subjects.[11] More generally, maternal abundance and generosity were associated with peace and plenty – touchstones for early Stuart court panegyrists. The continuing association of these paired articles of Stuart propaganda with maternal bounty is

Figure 1. "Benignita" from Cesare Ripa, *Iconologia* (Rome, 1603).

suggested by a painting presented by Rubens to Charles I in 1630 entitled *Peace and War* (fig. 2). In the background, Minerva holds Mars at bay, while in the foreground women and children frolic with a civil satyr and a tamed tiger. In the center of the painting a naked woman squeezes her breast, producing a stream of milk (reminiscent of Ripa's "Benignita") which feeds a child perched at her side. In Rubens's canvas, the maintenance of Stuart peace is iconographically linked with images of plenty and generosity rendered as maternal.[12] The rhetoric of Stuart propaganda uses the iconographic richness of maternality in order to allegorize the success of monarchy.

Bounty, by analogy with the divine gift of grace, also participated in the structure of parallels between God and king which constituted

Figure 2. Peter Paul Rubens, *Peace and War*. The National Gallery, London.

absolutist rhetoric of divine right. Consequently, the rhetoric of royal
generosity tends to blur the distinction between fiscal and spiritualized
benefits.[13] Richard Knolles's 1606 translation of Jean Bodin's *The Six
Bookes of a Commonweale* makes the analogy, with its blurring of categories, explicit: "A good prince should imitat God, advancing the
poore and vertuous to honours and riches."[14] And, as Caroline Walker
Bynum has shown, the spiritual nurturance provided by Christ, like
the fiscal generosity of the king, was frequently associated with maternality at least through the sixteenth century. Bynum demonstrates a
persistent association between Christ's blood and Mary's maternal
breast.[15]

In England, the association between fiscal generosity, grace, maternal nourishment, and the blood of Christ lurks behind the depiction of
"Bountie" in *The Mirrour of Majestie* (1618), an emblem book thought to
have been compiled by Henry Godyere. Godyere (or H. G.) represents
"Bountie" as a female figure holding a wreath and a palm, with blood
flowing from her heart into the mouth of a kneeling supplicant (fig. 3).[16]
The iconography is unmistakably religious; by representing bounty as
blood flowing from a woman's side, the emblem conflates Christlike
generosity with maternal or feminine nurturance. The poem that
accompanies the engraving, however, describes what might well be
monetary dispersal:

> See *Bountie* seated in her best of pride,
> Whose fountaines never ebbe, ever full tide
> At every change: see, from her streaming heart,
> How rivulets of *Comfort* doe impart
> To *Worth* dryde up by *Want*.
>
> (1–5)

Godyere dedicates this emblem to "Lord Haye" – the same Sir James
Hay whose notoriously lavish expenditures have come to seem
emblematic of Jacobean wastefulness.[17] As one of the king's Scottish
favorites, Hay's profligacy was to a considerable degree bankrolled by
gifts and offices bestowed upon him by James. To Godyere, who may
have received some of his patronage, Hay was a conduit for royal
bounty. Godyere's description of bounty as an ever-flowing fountain of
God-like munificence is in keeping with contemporary conceptions of
royal bounty, associating the endless coffers of his patron with the
blood of a figure who shares attributes of both Christ and mother.[18]

Within this system of iconographic associations, the ideal king
should incorporate the maternal. The most vividly literal European

SEe *Bountie* seated in her best of pride,
Whose fountaines never ebbe, ever full tide
At every change : see, from her streaming heart,
How rivulets of *Comfort* doe impart
To *worth* dryde vp by *want*; and to assuage
The drought of *Vertue* in her pilgrimage.
Looke, how her wide-stretcht, fruit-befurnisht hand
Vnlockt to true *Desert*, do's open stand :
But if she should not be *Deserts* regarder,
Yet is it, in it selfe, its owne rewarder.
This *Emblem's* not presented (Noble Sir)
Your bounteous nature to awake, or stir :
For you are *Bounties Almner*, and do's know,
How to refraine, destribute, or bestow.

Figure 3. "Embleme 31" from H. G., *The Mirrour of Majestie* (1618).

depiction of this is the sixteenth-century wood-panel painting which depicts the French King Francis I as a combination of Minerva, Mars, Perseus, Diana, Amour, and Mercury.[19] Francis's bearded head, wearing a large plumed helmet, is perched atop a female body with a visibly rounded stomach.[20] One arm holds a sword aloft; the other cradles a caduceus and holds an unstrung bow. On his back, Francis wears a quiver of arrows, his sandals have wings, and over his robes he wears a breastplate emblazoned with the head of Medusa. A printed text accompanies the image, describing Francis as a great king who surpasses nature ("ton grand Roy qui surpasse Nature"). According to one recent commentator, Francis's hermaphrodite body represents the variety of ideal, gendered attributes he incorporates within his person: "wisdom, eloquence, generosity, personal integrity, fortitude, justice, love, caring."[21]

Jonathan Goldberg has argued that this ideology was typically Jacobean, describing it as follows: "As father and mother, the king is *sui generis*, self-contained as a hermaphrodite, an ideal form."[22] A useful Jacobean example, which also suggests a connection between male fertility and a larger principle of royal generosity, is provided by Henry Godyere's emblematic depiction of "Great Brytaines Monarchie" as a lion seated atop three mountains (which represent the three united kingdoms), carrying a sword and scale in one hand and a cornucopia in the other, and touched from above by a caduceus extended from the hand of God (fig. 4).[23] The cornucopia, extending from the lion's groin, is conspicuously phallic, so that the emblem pictorially appropriates natural plenty and fertility to patriarchal potency. The king's potency becomes a principle of natural generosity which in turn takes the place of mother earth. The "nourish-father" is part of an ideological construct which includes gift-giving but also resonates with a larger, resolutely patriarchal conception of nature as both cornucopian and safely masculine.

This system of iconographic associations undergirds the maternality of bounty in *Timon of Athens*. In order to represent Timon's gift-giving, Shakespeare draws on a conventional representation of bounty which also associates fiscal and spiritual generosity with the "inexhaustible breast." Contextualizing Shakespeare's imagery in this way does not contradict psychoanalytic readings of *Timon of Athens* based on the maternality of bounty, but it should shift the ground upon which they are argued: locating these images within a historically specific vocabulary of images should remind us that even Shakespeare's deep intuitions are

S Eated on this *three-headed Mountaine high*,
Which reprefents *Great Brytaines Monarchie,*
Thus ftand I furnifht t'entertaine the noife:
Of thronging clamours, with an equall poyfe:
And thus addreft to giue a conftant weight
To formall fhewes, of *Vertue*, or *Deceit* :
Thus arm'd with *Pow'r* to punnifh or protect,
When I haue weigh'd each fcruple and defect :
Thus *plentifully* rich in parts and place
To giue *Aboundance*, or a poore difgrace:
But, how to make thefe in iuft circl°moue,
Heav'n crownes my head with *wifedome* from aboue.
Thus Merit on each part, to whom 'tis due,
With God-like power difburfed is by you.
B 2

Figure 4. "Embleme 2" from H. G., *The Mirrour of Majestie* (1618).

neither autonomous nor timeless, and that psychoanalytical readings often need to be historicized in unexpected ways.[24] It also complicates the topical meaning of the "magic of bounty" in Shakespeare's play, for it becomes necessary to place Shakespeare's treatment of maternalized generosity within and against a series of idealizations of monarchic virtues. In particular, once it is recognized that generosity and bounty are conventionally depicted as maternal, it becomes possible to describe the assimilation of maternality to monarchy as already implicit in patriarchal royalism as such: good kings must be nourish-fathers. This in turn makes it possible to read the association between mother's milk and male bounty in *Timon of Athens* as Shakespeare's exploitation of a gender ambiguity already implicit within conventional ideals of kingship.

This thumbnail rereading of *Timon*'s generosity also adumbrates an important representational strategy of Shakespeare's two most powerful Jacobean explorations of kingship, *King Lear* and *Macbeth*. In what follows, I will argue that each of these plays sketches a fantasy of patriarchal kingship as quasi-maternal: Lear and Duncan are both introduced as bountiful, as representatives of a principle of cornucopian plenty, and as self-replicating fathers. Each play, moreover, takes advantage of the doubling of gender implicit in this idealizing rhetoric of kingship, treating the nourish-father as at once an ideal and symptomatically unstable. The failure of each monarch results in the eruption into the body politic of a different kind of maternality, one broadly associated with cultural hysteria surrounding female agency and appetite.[25] Since the maternal is represented as either assimilated to or beyond the control of patriarchy, the maternality of kingship is itself treated as either ideal or disastrous: both plays represent a terrifying maternality as being necessarily part of the body politic, and in each case its eruption is given as symptomatic of the failure of the king to be both father and mother.

This investigation of the gendered rhetoric of generosity is motivated not only by James's prodigality, but also by the simple fact that he was every inch a king: a man on the throne after five decades of female rule. For because of its analogy with grace, its association with cornucopian plenty, and its appropriation of the maternal to the king, the ideal of bounty lay at the center of a network of specifically patriarchal ideologies. Moreover, gender and generosity come to be intertwined, since the representation of royal bounty as maternal is itself part of a larger patriarchal fantasy of male autonomy, of appropriating maternal powers for the king. Shakespeare's tragedies of kingship capitalize on this overdetermined set of connections, retheorizing royal power in response to the accession of a new king.

To be sure, it was occasionally useful for Elizabeth to represent herself as bountifully nurturant: an example is Nicholas Hilliard's portrait in oils of Elizabeth with a medallion of a pelican, a bird traditionally associated with generosity because it was thought to feed its young with its own blood.[26] But bounty was never a central part of the cult of Elizabeth. Often, in fact, Elizabeth's panegyrists were able to take advantage of the queen's gender in order to represent her as maternal, and thus to finesse her real fiscal meanness. By depicting Elizabeth as a nurturant, chaste mother to her people, it was possible to use the sentimental associations of maternality to surround the queen with images associated with bounty while never insisting specifically on her material generosity.[27] Elizabeth's *de facto* association with the iconography of bounty gave her the aura of royal nurturance without forcing her to make a public display of her generosity. With the accession of James this iconographic resource was no longer available; conspicuous gift-giving and the rhetoric of material plenty came to play a more centrally explicit role in the crown's self-presentation.

KING LEAR AND THE FAILURE OF BOUNTY

There is by now a familiar litany of topical elements in *King Lear*, elements around which the play's historicist critics organize their readings; a brief résumé of these topoi will remind us how complicated *King Lear*'s engagement with issues of Jacobean kingship is. In 1603, Prince Henry was created Duke of Cornwall and Prince Charles became the Duke of Albany. Since these two Dukes are the suitors of Regan and Goneril respectively, and since Lear promises to give his kingdom to "Our son of Cornwall, / And ... our no less loving son of Albany" (1.1.41–42) before we learn that he even has daughters, we are in effect invited to see Lear as an analogue for James before we are invited to consider the differences between the two figures.[28]

Lear's desire to trade the cares of state for the joy of hunting has been seen as a reference to James's documented preference for hunting expeditions over business, while Lear's indulgent treatment of his Fool has been linked to James's own licensed royal fool, Archie Armstrong. Similarly, Lear's ultimately foolish autocratic rigidity has been described as a possible gibe at James's own declaratory absolutism.[29]

Kent's description of Oswald as a "beggarly, three-suited, hundred-pound, filthy worsted-stocking knave" (2.2.16–17) seems aimed in part at James's selling of titles, and at his retinue of putatively shabby Scottish followers, while the Fool's satirical descant on crown finances and monopolies (1.4.134–65) – heavily edited in the Folio – seems more broadly critical of courtly greed.[30]

Finally, and most importantly, Lear's division of the kingdom, as many critics have pointed out, both inverts and resonates with King James's projected reunification of Britain.[31] Issues of production and textual transmission further complicate matters of topicality: we know that some version of *Lear* was played before the king on St. Stephen's Day (December 26) 1606, but we do not know how or to what degree the crown's interests shaped the various texts of the play that have survived. In particular, questions remain not only about the function of the play within various performative milieux but also about the degree of censorship and self-censorship traceable in the differences (especially the omission of the Fool's remarks about monopolies in 1.4) between the Quarto and Folio texts.[32]

Generally speaking, the relevance of *King Lear* to the Jacobean state is both underscored within the play and given as an interpretive problem. If Lear seems the inversion of James at one moment, he seems quite like him at another; if the rowdiness of Lear's cohorts seems reminiscent of Jacobean diminishment of courtly decorum, Oswald – Lear's enemy – also reminds us of the rag-tag reputation of James's followers.

Topical meanings in *King Lear* are characteristically distilled, packed together, layered. This is central to my argument, for I begin with the observation, made in passing by Richard Halpern, that Lear's fatal abdication refers both to British legend and to contemporary fiscal concerns:

If in one sense Lear is James's opposite, sundering Britain as James sought to unite it, there is another sense in which the two are alike, for James's profligacy was widely regarded as a foolish waste of national and royal resources. Lear carves up his patrimony in one bold if misguided stroke, whereas James fritters his away through conspicuous consumption and the inflation of honors. But James's is a "division of the kingdom" nonetheless, which contrasts ironically with his attempts to forge a unified nation.[33]

Halpern's remarks sketch a reading made plausible in the play by the fact that Lear himself treats the division of the kingdom not entirely as abdication and division – he retains "the name, and all th'addition to a king" (1.1.136) – but as a dramatic performance of royal generosity:

> Tell me, my daughters
> (Since now we will divest us both of rule,
> Interest of territory, cares of state),
> Which of you shall we say doth love us most,
> That we our largest bounty may extend
> Where nature doth with merit challenge?
> (1.1.48–53)

Although we know from the start that Lear has already made an equal division of his kingdom ("curiosity in neither [of the Dukes] can make choice of either's moi'ty" [1.1.6–7]) the fiction of Lear's abdication ceremony is that the king's generous bounty can enlarge one third without diminishing another. It is possible, then, to read in the language of Lear's abdication a kind of *reductio ad absurdum* of the normative ideal of royal bounty as free-flowing and limitless: once the kingdom itself is given away it becomes evident that royal magnificence is not finally as abundant as grace.

The play's continuing interest in the principle of royal generosity is revealed later, when Lear discovers how the poor actually live, and criticizes himself for his failure to dispense largess widely enough:

> Poor naked wretches, wheresoe'er you are,
> That bide the pelting of this pitiless storm,
> How shall your houseless heads and unfed sides,
> Your loop'd and window'd raggedness, defend you
> From seasons such as these? O, I have ta'en
> Too little care of this! Take physic, pomp,
> Expose thyself to feel what wretches feel,
> That thou mayst shake the superflux to them,
> And show the heavens more just.
> (3.4.28–36)

One implication of this hard-won observation is that the king's bounty has been too limited. Read in conjunction with the play's first scene – and with Gloucester's call to let "distribution ... undo excess" (4.1.70) – Lear's imperative amounts to a massive demystification of the social idealism implicit in the principle of royal bounty itself.[34] The king's self-aggrandizing generosity is revealed to have been incapable of meeting the real needs of the subjects under his care.

The problem of royal bounty remains as one of the play's crucial unsolved questions, not only because the "young / Shall never see so much" (5.3.326–27) as Lear has, but also because the play's interest in financial generosity is thoroughly intertwined with an equally pressing interest in psychic, familial generosity. From the first scene on, the two kinds of generosity run parallel to each other, stand in for one another, and complicate each other. Peter Erickson's reading of Lear's call for social reparation is instructive here, for instead of responding as I do to the moral authority of Lear's material analysis, he sees the speech as a father's insufficient response to an essentially psychic crisis: "Patriarchal liberality that redistributes the superflux is not the appropriate 'physic' for Lear's central problem; this fantasy of reparation by a reformed male authority cannot serve as a substitute for the absence of maternal generosity."[35]

Erickson's argument underscores the degree to which politics and fantasy problematize each other in *King Lear*; much as I find his dismissal of the play's material politics unsatisfying, it is clear that any attempt to discuss royal bounty in the play must take into account the familial narrative within which Lear's kingship is cast. To do so, I will argue that *Lear*'s exploration of the ideal of royal bounty is in a revisionary dialogue with related but more conventional treatments of similar questions in *The True Chronicle Historie of King Leir* (1605).[36] In both plays, the investigation of royal generosity is undertaken in explicitly gendered, familial terms, but Shakespeare's revision exploits potential discrepancies in his source material between the familial and the political in order to raise questions about the ideal of the bountiful king.

In *The True Chronicle Historie*, the king's distribution of his lands is given more pragmatic justification than in Shakespeare's play, and the stubborn anger he directs at Cordella is based in part on her unwillingness to marry the suitor of his choice. Nevertheless, Leir – like Lear – understands Cordella's reticence as a monstrous ingratitude perpetrated in the face of his royal generosity:

> I am as kind as is the Pellican,
> That kils it selfe, to save her young ones lives:
> And yet as jelous as the princely Eagle,
> That kils her young ones, if they do but dazell
> Upon the radiant splendor of the Sunne.[37]

Leir's misapprehension of his daughter's character reverberates through the play, as his treatment at the hands of his other daughters is represented as a just re-enactment of his own unkindness. When Gonorill abridges Leir's allowance of men and money, she does so on the advice of a maxim which could be used to gloss Leir's own understanding of Cordella's ingratitude: "abundance maketh us forget / The fountaynes whence the benefits do spring" (803–04). Gonorill is a "viperous woman" (811), but Leir's tribulations are given as a kind of poetic justice all the same.

Leir and his faithful servant Perillus are forced to cast themselves upon the mercy of Cordella and her husband, but Leir despairs of help:

> I have throwne Wormwood on the sugred youth,
> And like to Henbane poysoned the Fount,
> Whence flowed the Methridate of a childs goodwill:
> I, like an envious thorne, have prickt the heart,
> And turnd sweet Grapes, to sowre unrelisht Sloes:
> The causeless ire of my respectlesse brest,
> Hath sowrd the sweet milk of dame Natures paps:
> My bitter words have gauld her hony thoughts,
> And weeds of rancour chokt the flower of grace.
> (2,054–62)

This speech, with all its scriptural allusion, transforms Cordella into a Christ-like figure of universal bounty. At the same time, it makes use of the maternal register of fecundity and generosity. In fact, Cordella in this speech loses her specificity, becoming an emblem for nurturant generosity as such: it is not entirely clear, for example, whose "hony thoughts" are "gauld," Cordella's or Nature's. Leir imagines that he has, in rejecting Cordella, destroyed the principle of natural generosity itself. Cordella's resulting generosity, when she feeds her tired father, is also given as an act of Christ-like benevolence: "Here father, sit and eat, here, sit & drink" (2,178).[38]

The True Chronicle Historie, like other non-Shakespearean treatments of the Lear story, ends happily: the old king is reconciled with his good daughter, and restored to the throne. There is every indication that Cordella's generosity results in the resuscitation of kingship as a benign institution within the play, for if Cordella – a woman – personifies a cluster of associated ideals of generosity, they are still the ideal attributes of the play's patriarchy. Cordella's exemplary husband, for instance, tells her the following:

> I am the stock, and thou the lovely branch:
> And from my root continuall sap shall flow,
> To make thee flourish with perpetuall spring.
> (1,245–47)

Leir's final gesture is one of thanks and promised royal generosity: "thou (*Perillus*) partner once in woe, / Thee to requite, the best I can, Ile doe" (2,653–54). The king's generous recognition of the worth of his loyal followers is an index to his new graciousness, to his fitness to be king once again. In effect, Leir's reconciliation with Cordella symbolizes the renewal of the principle of royal bounty; or, to put it another way, it symbolizes the reinstitution of that principle within the body politic. The "sweet milk of dame Natures paps" will flow henceforward from the no longer "respectlesse brest" of the king.

From the start of Shakespeare's play, Lear makes use of the rhetoric of bounty found in *The True Chronicle Historie*, embellishing his abdication ceremony with the language of dame Nature's milky generosity. Thus, as Halpern observes, "Lear gives speeches that metaphorically equate the natural fecundity of the land itself with his own royal magnificence."[39] To Goneril, Lear offers "plenteous rivers, and wide-skirted meads" (1.1.65); to Cordelia he promises "a third more opulent than your sisters'" (1.1.86). His description of Cordelia's two suitors is itself cast in terms redolent with associations of royal generosity, as if to suggest that he is giving her his bounty in marrying her off. Lear addresses Cordelia as

> our joy
> Although our last and least, to whose young love
> The vines of France and milk of Burgundy
> Strive to be interess'd.
>
> (1.1.82–85)

Milk and wine are both common symbols of royal and divine benignity. One of the arches in the pageant celebrating James's London entry, for example, was adorned with a fountain which, at the arrival of the king, flowed "through severall pipes, with milke, wine, and balme."[40] Similarly, compare the prophetic language of divine bounty from Isaiah: "every one that thirsteth, come ye to the waters, and he that hath no money; come ye, buy, and eat; yea, come, buy wine and milk without money and without price" (55:1). The allusiveness of Lear's language – its frequent use of conventional rhetoric of plenty and bounty – contributes to the sheer staginess of the event, revealing the degree to which his abdication is scripted to be a ceremony of regal generosity.[41]

Goneril and Regan reply to Lear in language entirely appropriate to his staged demonstration of bounteous abundance. Goneril's answer, for example, is structured by the same notion of superabundance that informs Lear's own performance: "I love you more than words can wield the matter ... Dearer than eyesight ... Beyond what can be valued ... Beyond all manner of so much" (1.1.55–61). Father and daughters participate in a shared ceremonial script, treating the division of the kingdom as an exchange of bounty for love within an economy of pre-venient superfluity. Moreover, as *The True Chronicle Historie* suggests, the ceremonial brief shared by Lear and his two daughters is not uncon-ventional. This means that what is troubling in the first scene of *King Lear* is not only the promised separation of "the name, and all th'addi-tions" of kingship from its material appurtenances, but also the fact that Lear's self-abnegating royal largess is itself kingly.[42]

In *The Trew Law of Free Monarchies*, James writes "By the Law of Nature the King becomes a naturall Father to all his Lieges at his Coronation: And as the Father of his fatherly duty is bound to care for the nourishing, education, and vertuous government of his children."[43] One can detect a slippage here between paternal and maternal func-tions – between "government," and "nourishment" – that is itself a commonplace of the rhetoric and iconography of early modern king-ship in general and of early Stuart kingship in particular. By insisting on the association between his own magnificent generosity and natural fecundity, Lear's "cornucopian rhetoric" of bounty casts itself in the same quasi-maternal register.[44]

Not only is Lear the quasi-maternal "nourish-father," he is first pre-sented as if he were the sole progenitor of his children as well: Shakespeare's reworking of the story conspicuously elides the figure of his wife. By way of comparison, Leir's decision to abdicate is catalyzed by the death of his wife, the "deceast and dearest Queen" (2). Shakespeare's alteration has generally been taken to be a strategic one. Kahn, for example, argues that the omission of Lear's wife allows the play to articulate "a patriarchal conception of the family in which children owe their existence to their fathers alone; the mother's role in procreation is eclipsed by the father's, which is used to affirm male pre-rogative and male power."[45] The excision of the maternal is sympto-matic of a patriarchal fantasy of perfect self-replication: if fathers are the sole creators of their offspring then legitimacy is assured. Within *Lear*'s first scene, then, nurturant maternal functions are appropriated by the king even as the potentially dangerous influence of the mother in procreation seems, fantastically, to be missing.

Together, Lear's cornucopian rhetoric and the unexplained absence of his wife constitute an ideal of autonomous patriarchal rule: one that flows independently with spring's "continuall sap," one that might be represented pictorially by Henry Godyere's emblem of phallic royal plenty. We can see from the start that this vision of kingship is flawed.

First, the fact that Lear has only daughters reminds us of the failure of male self-replication.[46] Second, Lear's angry response to Cordelia's unexpected reticence – "nothing will come of nothing" (1.1.90) – ironically exposes the hollowness of a ceremony whose purpose has been to demonstrate the king's divine and maternal ability to generate surplus.

Third, Lear's posture of autonomous milkiness is itself undercut by his expressed regret after disinheriting Cordelia: "I lov'd her most, and thought to set my rest / On her kind nursery" (1.1.123–24). This admission reverses the direction of Lear's bounty, suggesting that he himself desired to be its final recipient. As part of its parodic restaging of royal appropriation of the maternal, the first scene of *King Lear* exposes not only the hollowness of royal language of fecundity, but also the self-interest implicit in royal bounty regardless of its rhetorical construction.

In *The True Chronicle Historie*, the failure of bounty is represented as the departure of a particular king from the ideals of royal generosity. That play's kingly ideal, associated with the benignity of Christ and the fecundity of "dame Natures paps," is not itself criticized. By associating this kind of cornucopian rhetoric with the fantasy of patriarchal self-replication, Shakespeare's play insists that the language of bounty is itself part of a patriarchal ideology. In other words, where *The True Chronicle Historie* gives us the "continuall sap" of royal generosity as an ideal to be lived up to, *King Lear* gives it to us as part of a fantasy of royal autonomy, a fantasy which is revealed to be in crisis from the first scene, and which is subject to a thorough debunking shortly thereafter.

As *Lear*'s psychoanalytic critics have pointed out, the maternality that is simultaneously excluded from and appropriated by the body politic in the fantasy of the play's first scene returns with a vengeance as an anxiety about maternality which colors the whole play and provokes its powerful misogyny.[47] This angry uncertainty finds expression not only in the specially virulent misogyny of Lear's tirades ("to the girdle do the gods inherit, / Beneath is all the fiends" [4.6.126–27]), but also in the representation of the illegitimate Edmund as only his mother's son (1.1.11–12), and more subtly in the language with which characters generally discuss disguise and dissembling. Goneril, after instructing Oswald to neglect Lear's demands for service, declares, "I would breed from hence occasions" (1.3.24); Lear, during the mock trial scene, calls for an anatomy of Regan, to see "what breeds about her heart" (3.6.76–77); Goneril hints to Edmund that she wants him for a husband and adds "Conceive, and fare thee well" (4.2.24). In *King Lear*'s misogynistic scheme, maternal generation becomes associated

with everything that transgresses the opening scene's fantasy of patriarchal autonomy: illegitimacy, disguise, treason, betrayal, lust, the
uncontrollable force of nature.

Most terribly of all, Lear's recognition of his daughters' betrayal
provokes in him a madness which is itself called "mother":

> O how this mother swells up toward my heart!
> *Hysterica passio*, down, thou climbing sorrow,
> Thy element's below.
>
> (2.3.55–57)

As Janet Adelman points out, "'mother' is a technical term for the
uterus; 'Hysterica passio' . . . is the disease caused by its wandering."[48]
The failure of Lear's appropriation of the maternal is treated symbolically as the re-eruption of the all-too-maternal within the physical
body of the king himself. There is an analogous recognition one scene
later, when Lear acknowledges that Goneril, the play's exemplar of
dangerous female duplicity, is a part of him:

> thou art my flesh, my blood, my daughter –
> Or rather a disease that's in my flesh,
> Which I must needs call mine.
>
> (2.4.221–23)

One way to read this admission – responding more to the political
than to the psychological meaning – is to see in it the suggestion that
the dangerous, transgressive potential associated with the maternal
and crystallized in Goneril is of necessity always already present in the
patriarchal state.

Like the "disease" called Goneril or the wandering womb, the
failure of generosity is revealed to be a crisis internal to the normal
performance of kingship. In *The True Chronicle Historie*, Gonorill's treatment of Leir is given as an appropriate punishment for his failings, and
King Lear preserves that reversal. Begging for his daughters' generosity
could be seen as an apt comeuppance in the wake of Lear's own self-
serving bounty – the more so because it ironically anticipates his later
concern: "O, reason not the need! our basest beggars / Are in the
poorest thing superfluous" (2.4.264–65). In Shakespeare's play, however, Lear's punishment follows not from his departure from kingliness
but from his kingliness itself. Or, rather, the failure of the principle of
bounty is given, along with the play's abiding anxiety over female
generation, as a symptom of the failure of patriarchy's ideological
fantasies.

While it is Leir's sin that he is not in practice "as kind as is the Pellican," Lear describes his deprivations as the just reward for being precisely that: "Judicious punishment! 'twas this flesh begot / Those pelican daughters" (3.4.74–75). Lear in effect inverts the conventional iconography of the pelican, emphasizing not the kindness of the mother, but the destructive appetite of her children. This inversion foregrounds an implication ignored when Leir (or Queen Elizabeth) uses the pelican as a symbol of royal generosity, an implication with a strong topical basis in early Jacobean England: royal generosity depletes the king, possibly fatally. Moreover, by calling Regan and Goneril "pelican daughters," Lear suggests that in some sense to be a pelican (a generous monarch) is automatically to unleash the destructive, transgressive feminine potential that the bad daughters seem to represent: to be a pelican is to have pelican daughters. In his lucid hysteria, Lear suggests that he is undergoing "judicious punishment" for trying to embody a conventional patriarchal ideal.

Lear's invective against his pelican daughters expresses, in a remarkably condensed form, the perception that the cornucopian rhetoric of the play's first scene was misleading. The same recognition is taken to an extreme in his description of unaccommodated man as one that "ow'st the worm no silk, the beast no hide, the sheep no wool, the cat no perfume" (3.4.104–05). Whatever one has is taken from elsewhere: as blood from the pelican, so hide from the beast. Lear discovers that his is a world of scarcity, a world in which bounty cannot be bottomless, and in which resources must be husbanded with care. His belated sympathy for his country's "Poor naked wretches" is also based on this perception, as is his call to "shake the superflux" down to them.

There is an internal logic to the play's juxtaposition of Lear's hysterical misogyny with his lucid, moving concern for the impoverished. Both dramatize his response to the failure of the first scene's patriarchal fantasy of autonomous male generativity. The two are fused even more closely, for example, in Lear's angry denunciation of fecundity as such: "crack nature's moulds, all germains spill at once / That makes ingrateful man!" (3.2.8–9). This cry expresses not only misogynistic rage, but also a rejection of the cornucopian rhetoric of kingship. The ferocity of the storm (itself "the sign of the female place of origin" in Adelman's reading) sweeps away the opening scene's stately, generous nature, rich with wine and milk and plenteous streams.[49]

Implicit in the cornucopian rhetoric of bounty, in other words, is a version of nature which has little to do with the uncontrollable, hungry nature that Lear experiences. In fact, it is often suggested that Lear's apprehension of nature develops during the storm, as he relinquishes his pretense of command ("Blow, winds" [3.2.1]) and comes to recognize himself as nature's subject (that he is not "ague-proof" [4.6.105]).[50] Finally, the mad Lear who emerges after the storm appears dressed like some parodic emblem of the failure of royal bounty's "perpetuall spring." Cordelia describes his dress as follows:

> he was met even now
> As mad as the vex'd sea, singing aloud,
> Crown'd with rank femiter and furrow-weeds,
> With hardocks, hemlock, nettles, cuckoo-flow'rs,
> Darnel, and all the idle weeds that grow
> In our sustaining corn.
>
> (4.4.1–6)

When he appears on stage again, Lear symptomatically associates a king's "coining" (4.6.83) of money with uncontrollable adulterous generation:[51]

> The wren goes to't, and the small gilded fly
> Does lecher in my sight.
> Let copulation thrive.
>
> (4.6.112–14)

"Coining" expresses in concrete terms the fantasy of royal generativity, of the king's ability to generate value, but in Lear's stream-of-consciousness it is now associated (note that the fly is "gilded") with the play's pervasive, transgressive maternality. Where the rhetoric of patriarchal benignity still exists in the play, it is used by Goneril to insult Albany: "our mild husband" (4.2.1) she calls him, or "Milk-liver'd man" (4.2.50), and she refers to "the cowish terror of his spirit" (4.2.12). To be milky and mild, she suggests, is to be unfit to rule. We may have to agree with her: after the disasters of the play it is difficult to imagine what fitness to rule would consist of.

In *The True Chronicle Historie* Cordella's Christ-like intervention restores Leir both to his kingdom and to his kingliness. *King Lear*, of course, also surrounds Cordelia with a halo of scriptural allusion, describing her tears as "holy water from her heavenly eyes" (4.3.30), and naming her the

> one daughter
> Who redeems nature from the general curse
> Which twain have brought her to.
>
> (4.6.205–07)

Cordelia's ministrations to her aged father are also expressive of fertility, maternal generosity, and care:

> All blest secrets,
> All you unpublish'd virtues of the earth,
> Spring with my tears.
>
> (4.4.15–17)

But though Cordelia's ministrations are reminiscent of Cordella's in *The True Chronicle Historie*, they are not allowed to effect a happy solution to Lear's crisis. This is not only because we get, in Cordelia's benignity, "a full expression of Christian love without the Christian supernatural," but also because Lear's crisis has been revealed as a vulnerability within patriarchy itself.[52] Consequently, the play cannot offer a satisfactory political solution by restoring the patriarchy to its former stability. In fact, Lear's briefly sustained fantasy of a possible happy ending is a vision precisely of escape from the political:

> So we'll live,
> And pray, and sing, and tell old tales, and laugh
> At gilded butterflies, and hear poor rogues
> Talk of court news; and we'll talk with them too –
> Who loses and who wins; who's in, who's out –
> And take upon's the mystery of things
> As if we were God's spies.
>
> (5.3.11–17)

I find myself agreeing, here, with Jonathan Dollimore's criticism of "essentialist humanist" readings of *King Lear* which find something salvational in the emotionalism of the play's finale.[53] Whatever the pull of the reconciliation scene, it marks a political tragedy: a failure to imagine a political solution.

King Lear ends uncertainly, leaving the future of the state very much in doubt. It is not even clear who will succeed Lear. To be sure, Albany offers the crown to Kent and Edgar, but Kent turns it down and the texts of the play disagree about Edgar's response. In the Folio, Edgar seems to accept Albany's offer; he never acknowledges it explicitly, but his final speech is at least kingly in that it sums up the play's actions for everyone else: "we that are young / Shall never see so much, nor live so long" (5.3.326–27). In the Quarto, however, the final lines are given to Albany, and Edgar never responds to the proffered crown.

Albany – Lear's eldest surviving son-in-law, and king already over half the realm – presumably has the best claim, but neither he nor Edgar seems likely to heal the "gor'd state" (5.3.321). In fact, the final exchange underscores the continuing instability of the state by eerily recapitulating Lear's division of the kingdom. Albany's offer threatens to divide the kingdom yet again: "you twain / Rule in this realm" (5.3.320–21).[54] Marvin Rosenberg reports on one production of Lear which ends "with ominous sounds of storm gathering again."[55]

The play's bleak finale, of course, constitutes a major revision of the Lear story. In other versions, Lear is restored to the throne and succeeded by what Holinshed calls "the gunarchie of queene Cordeilla."[56] One of the striking things about this revision is that Shakespeare's version of Cordelia is, if anything, more fit to rule than most of her earlier incarnations. Not only is she made to represent a lost ideal of spiritual and natural bounty, but she also takes an unusually active role in the play's military campaign. In both Monmouth's version and *The True Chronicle Historie*, Cordella is always accompanied by her husband, who controls the military. In Holinshed's version, Cordeilla merely accompanies an army that her husband has gathered, going along only to take possession of the land after it is conquered.[57] In *Lear*, although the king of France leaves a Marshal to command his army, Cordelia is actively engaged in its deployment. Before the battle, for instance, a messenger reports to her about troop movement, and her response is businesslike (4.4.22–23); the decision to invade seems to have been hers, insofar as we learn of it in her letter to Kent (2.2.166–70).[58]

It is one of *Lear*'s ironies that the play's ideals of male kingship are most fully embodied in a woman who is never available to rule. However, since the fantasy of patriarchal autonomy with which the play began entailed the appropriation of maternal functions to the masculine ruler, it is an appropriate irony indeed. In *The True Chronicle Historie*, as I have argued, Cordella represents a principle of fecund benignity which comes once again to inform Leir's reign. In Shakespeare's revisionary treatment of this material, Cordelia's generosity is not given the chance to inform the government of the state, since the governmental failure of these ideals has been the point all along.

This, in turn, suggests that *King Lear* is primarily interested in exploring the governmental failure of royal benignity, not in trying to imagine its possible successes. If in many ways Cordelia represents the play's ideal ruler, her death is an indication that Shakespeare's play is not, finally, interested in "gunarchie": in the first years of James's reign, after a lifetime of Elizabeth's government, Shakespeare wanted to interrogate the rhetoric of male rulership. It is worth noting as well that this constitutes a response to Bradley's famous objection to the randomness of Cordelia's death.[59] By investing Cordelia with the ideals of kingship, making her an essentially ineffectual character, and dispensing with her almost casually, the play suggests that the ideals – benignity, Christlike generosity, maternal nurturance – of male kingship are themselves politically insufficient.

MACBETH'S SWELLING ACT

If anything, the topical meaning of *Macbeth* is even more difficult to unravel than that of *King Lear*. On the one hand, with its Scottish setting, its witches, and its explicit flattery of James as a representative of Banquo's line, *Macbeth* seems to go out of its way to entangle itself with the king's concerns. Since it seems likely that it was performed at court, it has always been tempting to see the play as having been tailored to James's interests and tastes.[60] On the other hand, *Macbeth*'s handling of the institution of kingship – like *Lear*'s – seems radical and pessimistic. Recent critics have tended to reject the notion that *Macbeth* was written to please James, and have pointed out a number of ways that it can be taken instead to be expressive of anti-Jacobean attitudes.[61]

In one of the more suggestive recent topical approaches to *Macbeth*, Leah Marcus has read Lady Macbeth as "a revivified scapegoat figure who gathers up once more the residual power of the image of Elizabeth." By demonizing the dominant woman, the argument goes, "*Macbeth* would celebrate the Jacobean succession and blacken the barren female authority associated with the previous monarch."[62] Instead, I want to argue that though *Macbeth* is shot through with the threat of feminine power, it imagines that threat as inevitably part of the patriarchal state. My reading of *Macbeth* reverses Marcus's, arguing that the play's depiction of threatening feminized agency arises only in tandem with its analysis of male kingship: instead of demonizing Elizabeth, the play dramatizes a side of patriarchy never fully explored in Shakespeare's Elizabethan plays.

Macbeth takes up the same material explored in *King Lear*, but with important differences. First, *Macbeth*'s treatment of gender and generosity is more abstract: driven by the witches, it contains nothing as rawly material as Lear's apprehension of poverty. Generosity, plenty, fertility, barrenness – all terms with material meanings in *Lear* – are more sheerly symbolic here. Second, *Macbeth* is more relentlessly pessimistic. It begins in a storm. The uncontrollable forces which Lear ultimately discovers are part of *Macbeth*'s world from the outset.

Moreover, where Lear's downfall is caused by a mistake, albeit a kingly one, Duncan's is not. The inscrutability of cause makes the crisis within Duncan's reign seem even more inevitable than that of Lear's.

To be sure, *Macbeth* welcomes misogynistic interpretation: the play seems, on the face of it, to blame the witches and Lady Macbeth not only for the corruption of Macbeth but also for the break-down of a putatively harmonious, patriarchal social order. From the bleeding Sergeant's description of Fortune as "a rebel's whore" (1.2.15) to Lady Macbeth's notorious and terrifying description of infanticide (1.7.54–59), *Macbeth* continually constructs the female, and especially the maternal, as uncontrollable and transgressive. At the same time, as recent critics have been concerned to show, the play expresses a fantasy of heroic male autonomy quite unlike the dream of patriarchal benignity expressed in *King Lear*.[63] Thus, for example, Macbeth's initial heroism in the war with Macdonwald – we learn that he "carv'd out his passage" (1.2.19) through the ranks of the enemy – adumbrates a vision of male autonomy by means of Caesarean birth which is made literal later in the play in the person of Macduff.[64] The witches' prophecy – "none of woman born / Shall harm Macbeth" (4.1.80–81) – in effect makes the exclusion of women into a pre-condition for the play's conclusion.

A reading of the play responsive to the text's misogyny might blame the demonized man-women for the tragic action and also find in the play's final configuration the restoration of a stable, autonomously masculine world. Reinforcing this fantasy of male autonomy is the fact that the witches' vision of Banquo's progeny seems to promise a male line of kings stretched "to th' crack of doom" (4.1.117), or at least to King James and his offspring. The first of these future kings is "like the spirit of Banquo," the second is "like the first," and so on (4.1.112–15); the vision, in other words, is one of endless paternal replication. Son mirrors father, without the dangers of maternal intervention. Indeed if, as has often been speculated, this vision of Stuart replication was constructed to please James himself, it would have had the advantage of effectively hiding the potentially embarrassing figure of James's own mother, Mary, Queen of Scots.

The fact that both Macduff's triumph and Banquo's succession are predicted by and contained within the witches' prophecy, however, destabilizes the play's promise of restored masculine autonomy.[65] Since the play neither explains nor removes them, the witches escape the play's gestures of closure. Whatever they are, we can assume that the

Weird (or, alternatively, "Weyard" or "Weyward") Sisters will continue to haunt Malcolm's Scotland. In Goldberg's phrase, "what escapes control is figured in the witches": they are ciphers who, as if by definition, evade not only the literal control of *Macbeth*'s other characters but also whatever interpretive control we bring with us to the text.[66] Category deconstruction ("Fair is foul, and foul is fair" [1.1.11]) is their defining characteristic; they continually transgress the play's conceptual boundaries.

As the embodiment of patriarchal social order, Duncan ought to counterbalance the witches, to be their antithesis. This would make sense not only in terms of the play's system of oppositions, but also in terms of King James's thinking, since the antithesis between the king (God's deputy) and the witch (Satan's) was part of the reason for his interest in witchcraft.[67] However, as Goldberg has pointed out, Duncan is given language derived from Holinshed's witches on at least one occasion, which suggests that the transgressiveness they embody is already part of whatever paternal social order the play can imagine.[68] This, in its most general formulation, is the disturbing message which *Macbeth* encodes.

This account of the witches also challenges the simple misogynistic reading which the text seems to call for, since the sheer transgressiveness of the Weird Sisters in fact destabilizes the gender categories upon which such a reading would rest: despite her call to "unsex me here" (1.5.41), we know that Lady Macbeth is a woman; a definitive judgment concerning the witches' gender, however, is problematic not only because they are supernatural (i.e. because they may transcend natural gender categories), but also because their gender is given to us as an interpretive puzzle from the beginning. Banquo, when he sees the witches, exclaims

> You should be women
> And yet your beards forbid me to interpret
> That you are so.
>
> (1.3.45–47)

Banquo's response is symptomatic rather than judgmental. What we get, instead of a satisfyingly clear account of the witches' gender, is a depiction of Banquo's inability to apprehend the witches within received gender categories.[69] The effect of this is not only to emphasize and specify the transgressive quality of the witches, but also to direct our attention to the constructions of gender within the natural (as opposed to supernatural) world of the play. We are invited to pay special heed to the ways in which the normative, political world of the play deploys gender, and to keep in mind as well that there is a perspective from which those deployments will always seem insufficient.

Within the "natural" world of the play, gender is also ambiguous, as if in weak reflection of the "supernatural." Lady Macbeth is one manifestation of this principle of gender ambiguity; Duncan himself is another. In fact, the two figures, oddly enough, can be seen as inversely related to one another within the play: if Lady Macbeth is a mother ("I have given suck" [1.7.54], she says) with a man's "undaunted mettle" (1.7.73), Duncan is a king who stands for generosity and fecundity, enfolding these gendered, maternal attributes within his royal self-sufficiency. Both characters are unsexed, and although Lady Macbeth is far more terrifying, Duncan's doubleness is arguably more destructive. Similarly, if Lady Macbeth is a barren mother (to whom has she "given suck"?), Duncan – like Lear – seems to be an independently fertile father (where is the mother of his children?). These lacunae indicate the degree to which maternality and the agency of generation are problematic in *Macbeth*.

Duncan's appropriation of maternal functions is also reflected in his kingcraft. Having heard of their martial exploits, Duncan finally meets Macbeth and Banquo in front of the royal palace in Act 1, Scene 4. He is understandably grateful, and in a highly ceremonial exchange he promises to reward and nourish his two captains:

> [DUNCAN:] I have begun to plant thee [Macbeth], and
>   will labor,
>   To make thee full of growing. Noble Banquo,
>   That hast no less deserv'd, nor must be known
>   No less to have done so, let me infold thee
>   And hold thee to my heart.
> [BANQUO:] There if I grow,
>   The harvest is your own.
> [DUNCAN:] My plenteous joys,
>   Wanton in fullness, seek to hide themselves
>   In drops of sorrow.
>
>   (1.4.28–35)

Duncan takes upon himself the role of "nourish-father," and although his metaphoric register pointedly ignores the role of the mother in childbirth, his language appropriates the maternal nevertheless. Thus, giving birth to the new Macbeth is described as undergoing "labor," while Banquo is imagined enfolded in a quasi-maternal embrace: he is enveloped like a child, held to the kingly bosom. Even the king's tears of joy are described as being "wanton in fullness," as if they sprung from an eroticized maternal fecundity. Duncan, too, is full of "th' milk of human kindness" (1.5.17).

In Holinshed, Duncan's gentleness is treated as a failing, since it makes him unable to rule the warlike Scots:

Duncane was so soft and gentle of nature, that the people wished the inclinations and maners of these two cousins [Macbeth and Duncan] to have beene so tempered and enterchangeablie bestowed betwixt them, that where the one had too much of clemencie, and the other of crueltie, the meane vertue betwixt these two extremities might have reigned by indifferent partition in them both, so should Duncane have proved a woorthie king, and Makbeth an excellent capteine.[70]

Holinshed's Macdonwald, recognizing that the milk of human kindness in Duncan makes him vulnerable to attack, dismisses him as "a faint-hearted milkesop."[71] In *Macbeth*, by contrast, there is little in the way of overt criticism of Duncan's quasi-maternal benignity. Instead, it is treated as appropriate to the ceremonial decorums of kingship, a virtue. The exchange between Duncan as "nourish-father" and his captains, for example, is represented as a ceremony of state in which both monarch and subject have a part: Banquo's response – "There if I grow, / The harvest is your own" – makes use of the same register as Duncan's promise in a way that suggests that the language of the scene is familiar and shared.

As we might expect, Duncan's maternal generosity is associated with a cornucopian vision of nature. Banquo, speaking with the king upon their first appearance at Macbeth's castle, praises it as a site of teeming plenty:

> This guest of summer,
> The temple-haunting marlet, does approve,
> By his lov'd mansionry, that the heaven's breath
> Smells wooingly here; no jutty, frieze,
> Buttress, nor coign of vantage, but this bird
> Hath made his pendant bed and procreant cradle.
> Where they most breed and haunt, I have observ'd
> The air is delicate.
>
> (1.6.3–10)

Duncan, in his royal capacity, is surrounded by the rhetoric of plenty. It is worth noting, however, that breeding and haunting – redolent of plenty in the context of this passage – can also be associated with the demonized maternal agency of Lady Macbeth or the witches. Duncan's cornucopian rhetoric even now contains its own inversion.

After Duncan's body is discovered, Macbeth's public exclamation makes the death out to be the loss of a principle of bountiful gentleness in the world: "The wine of life is drawn, and the mere lees / Is left this vault to brag of" (2.3.95–96). Moreover, shortly after Duncan's assassination, Rosse describes regicidal ambition as in itself the violation of a principle of plenty, apostrophizing it as "Thriftless ambition, that will ravin up / Thine own live's means" (2.4.28–29). Here ambition is seen as a parodic, self-consuming version of maternal nurturance, ravening up its own sustaining milk – a grotesque inversion of the maternalized principle of generosity assimilated to Duncan's fecund, "milky gentleness."[72]

Macbeth's career is also given to us in terms of incorporated maternality, but where Duncan's appropriation of the maternal is seen as normative, Macbeth's is given as grotesque. The first indication of Macbeth's parodic maternality coincides with the first stirring of Macbeth's ambition:

> Two truths are told,
> As happy prologues to the swelling act
> Of the imperial theme.
>
> (1.3.127–29)

"Swelling act" taps into a conventional language of tyranny and ambitious desire as male tumescence and / or pregnancy.[73] Thus, for example, in the induction to John Marston's *Antonio and Mellida* (1599), the actor about to play the role of the tyrant is advised to "Grow big in thought / As swoll'n with glory of successful arms."[74] Similarly, in a sermon preached before James in Whitehall and published in 1604, Richard Eedes describes treason as a kind of monstrous pregnancy:

no treason shall be conceived and hatched in the heart, as it were in the wombe of discontentment, or so cunningly contrived and carried in vowed silence, as it were in the safe conduct of an hidden conspiracie, but *the birds of the aire shall reveale it, & that which hath wings bring it to light, Eccles.* 10:20.[75]

In *Macbeth*, "swelling act" names a process of self-creation, characterizing the change of Macbeth as a grotesque male pregnancy in which ambition gives birth to its own tyrannous image. Macbeth's self-division – his loss of the "single state of man" (1.3.140) – is represented as a parodic version of maternal creativity. Later, when he learns that Macduff has escaped to England, Macbeth reveals the result of his "swelling act," describing his murderous impulses as offspring:

"The very firstlings of my heart shall be / The firstlings of my hand" (4.1.147–48).

The association of Macbeth's kingship with grotesque maternality is strengthened by the troubling figure of Lady Macbeth, to whom Macbeth himself seems to cede autonomous creative power:

> Bring forth men-children only!
> For thy undaunted mettle should compose
> Nothing but males.
>
> (1.7.71–73)

Macbeth's admiring exclamation raises the question, again, of Lady Macbeth's absent children, and the pun on mettle and male praises her as a virago. More troubling, it seems to me, is Macbeth's suggestion that his wife's nature will predominate in her offspring. In what Thomas Laqueur has called the "one-sex / one-flesh model" of sexual difference (prevalent, in his account, to the end of the seventeenth century), men and women are versions of the same physiological blueprint, differing by degrees of potency and completion.[76] These differences are seen as sharply hierarchical, a fact crucial to the understanding of generation: "the female always provides the material, the male that which fashions it."[77] Like Banquo's all-male line (mirror images of their respective fathers) male offspring should duplicate their male fashioners. Within this model of generation, the possibility of a woman's seed having the generative potency of a male is seen as a "manifest absurdity," since that woman would then be able to get herself pregnant.[78] Macbeth's tribute to his wife labels her as just such an absurdity, for if her "mettle" is to be replicated by "male children" then it follows that her (male) seed will have fashioned them. Lady Macbeth is given here as figure of monstrous parthenogenesis, as the inversion of Duncan's autonomous paternalism. Note also that Lady Macbeth is in this regard the inverse of Lear, who brought forth female children only.

Kahn's reading of this same passage associates the generative power of Lady Macbeth with her ability to shape her husband: "He speaks of her as though she were a sole godlike procreator, man and woman both. And she does have the terrible power to make him her kind of bloody man."[79] In this reading, Lady Macbeth is the primary agent behind Macbeth's tyrannous desire. The play, of course, makes the question of Macbeth's agency a notoriously murky one. Responsibility seems to be shared by the witches, Lady Macbeth, and Macbeth himself. If the play at moments does give Macbeth to us as Lady Macbeth's creation, it also, as we have seen, gives him to us as self-creating. This latter possibility makes him very much his wife's equivalent: both are figures of monstrous, barren parthenogenesis, both invert the ideal of paternal fruitfulness. Consequently, though the agency involved in the play's tragic action remains unclear, it is possible to say that Macbeth and Lady Macbeth are inextricably representative of a clear anxiety about patriarchy and generation.

Macbeth's kingship, of course, is anything but fecund. As Kahn puts it, "his character and his career pivot on the crucial distinction made in the witches' prophecies between being a king and being a father."[80] Macbeth himself comes to recognize the force of this distinction, and to understand that he and Banquo are consequently opposites:

> prophet-like,
> They [the witches] hail'd him father to a line of
> kings.
> Upon my head they plac'd a fruitless crown,
> And put a barren sceptre in my gripe,
> Thence to be wrench'd with an unlineal hand,
> No son of mine succeeding.
>
> (3.1.58–63)

This perception spurs a fear of Banquo – "under him / My Genius is rebuk'd" (3.1.54–55), says Macbeth – which seems hysterical: as far as we know, Macbeth has no son, so there is no reason for him to resent any particular successor. The suddenness and irrationality of Macbeth's fear (he has heard the witches prophecy long before he begins resenting it) suggest that he perceives a cleavage between kingship and fatherhood, a cleavage whose significance to him dwarfs that of specific political machinations. Banquo's paternal fruitfulness – or, paternal fruitfulness as such – indicates to Macbeth the limitations of his own "swelling act." Mother to himself, Macbeth cannot father: the "continuall sap" of patriarchy is dried up.

The problematics of gender and generation implicit in Macbeth's "swelling act" locate him within a longstanding, overdetermined association between the appetitive ambition of the tyrant and effeminacy which has been traced by Rebecca Bushnell.[81] Among the constitutive elements of that association are, for example, the domination of Tiberius and Claudius by mothers and mistresses in Tacitus' widely read *Annals of Imperial Rome*.[82] The representation of Macbeth's tyrannous appetite as maternal, the argument might run, puts a new spin on an old theme, as does the association between Macbeth's maternality and the domineering figure of Lady Macbeth.

Bushnell's own reading of *Macbeth* focuses in fact on the relationship between Macbeth and Lady Macbeth, seeing their relationship as Shakespeare's rewriting of the tyrant's traditional domination by women. Instead of being uxorious or luxurious – which in Bushnell's account would be the norm – Macbeth is gradually distanced from the effeminacy of desire over the course of the play: he is "most 'manly' – and most depleted – in his full tyranny."[83] As I read the play, however, the grim scarcity of Macbeth's Scotland is a symptom of the inversion of Duncan's milky benignity. Macbeth's self-consuming kingship inaugurates a scarcity which depletes everyone: "Naught's had, all's spent" (3.2.4), as Lady Macbeth puts it. Thus, I do not think the play represents depletion – to use Bushnell's term again – as manliness *per se*, but rather as a kind of failed manliness, the sign of a crisis in patriarchy's appropriation of feminized functions. Lady Macbeth, too, is representative of that crisis, and she too represents an unnatural interruption of maternal bounty: "take my milk for gall" (1.5.48).

Each could be described as a symptom of the failure of Duncan's paternalism to satisfactorily incorporate maternal functions. If *Macbeth* opens in a Scotland that is ruled by a fruitful "nourish-father," it is also vulnerable to the disorderliness represented alternatively by the witches and by civil strife. From a certain perspective, Duncan's orderly patriarchal appropriation of maternality is doomed to failure from the outset, and its failure is made manifest by the eruption into the political milieu of grotesque, parthenogenic maternality. The play, in other words, seizes on a doubleness within the conventional rhetoric of benignant monarchy, showing first the king's maternality, then characterizing the impulse behind his murder as its parodic inversion. Swelling regicide and barren tyranny are the signs of the failure of Duncan's kingship.

This is also implicit in Macbeth's lurid description of Murder moving towards the king "With Tarquin's ravishing strides" (2.1.55). Macbeth's unexpected figure of speech – a striking literalization of Duncan's gender ambiguity – aligns Duncan's trusting weakness with the feminized powerlessness of Lucrece.[84] Murderous usurpation is figured as the rape of the feminized royal body. Macbeth's image here provides an anamorphic new perspective on the idealized figure of the royal "nourish-father," for it is a shocking variation on Duncan's feminized language of nurturance earlier in the play: the maternality of the bountiful king brings with it the feminized vulnerability of the "milkesop." Moreover, since Shakespeare's Duncan is ostensibly a good king, this internal gender division – and the crisis to which it seems to give rise – can be seen as part of the play's generalizable conception of kingship itself.

What happens when Macduff kills Macbeth? When Macbeth compares the murder of Duncan to the rape of Lucrece, he unwittingly establishes a set of equivalences which might color our apprehension of the end of the "swelling act." For just as the expulsion of the usurping Tarquin is simultaneously the starting-point for a new Roman republic, might not the overthrow of the usurping Macbeth simultaneously signal the start of a new Scotland, one in which Banquo's offspring will someday rule, culminating gloriously in the reign of James VI? If so, one would argue that the elimination of the maternal – the defeat of Macbeth by Macduff, who is "not of woman born" – provides the solution to the crisis that dominates the play's tragic action.

There are, however, a number of reasons to be less than satisfied with the play's final excision of the maternal. First, the same Macduff whose Caesarean birth allows him to wield putatively autonomous masculine power is anamorphically revealed to be a failure as a father: in the same scene in which his family is murdered, Macduff's wife complains that her husband "wants the natural touch" (4.2.9) and calls her son "fatherless" (4.2.26).[85] Martial and generative power, the power of Macbeth and that of Banquo, remain irreconcilable as Macduff takes on Macbeth's military prowess.

One might say that where *Lear* expresses one failed fantasy of male autonomy, *Macbeth* expresses two: the quasi-maternal patriarchal autonomy of Duncan (and possibly Banquo), and the military autonomy of Macbeth and Macduff. The rule of each fails, and each failure is given as the inability to keep the frighteningly transgressive version of the maternal in check. The former brings with it the spiritualized generosity, paternal fertility, and principle of plenty so important to the justifying rhetoric of kingship, but it also brings with it a feminized weakness, a symptomatic vulnerability. The latter seems to reject the female altogether, but it is associated with tyranny and revealed to be in fact a grotesque inversion of maternality that is barren and depleted. It is surely troubling, given these two possibilities, that the basic relationship between legitimate king and martial captain with which the play began is reinstated at the end: if, at the beginning of the play, Duncan relies on the figuratively Caesarean Macbeth, at the end of it Malcolm relies on the literally Caesarean Macduff.[86]

The play ends with Malcolm's promise of bounty and love:

> We shall not spend a large expense of time
> Before we reckon with your several loves,
> And make us even with you.
>
> (5.9.26–28)

Since Duncan's maternal bounty was both ideally gracious and also a sign of his feminized weakness, Malcolm's imminent generosity should raise as many questions as it settles about the peacefulness of his reign. If anything, *Macbeth* should have taught us that

> The king-becoming graces,
> As justice, verity, temp'rance, stableness,
> Bounty, perseverance, mercy, lowliness,
> Devotion, patience, courage, fortitude,
>
> (4.3.91–94)

are no guarantee against the worst kinds of political débâcle. In fact, *Macbeth* may have taught us that they lead to disaster: having these graces threatens to make Malcolm as much a "Milkesop" as his gracious father.

Alternatively, it is possible to see Malcolm as a new kind of king, one whose largess is predicated on a more careful reckoning of his subject's "several loves." Instead of making a display of his conspicuous, over-abundant generosity, Malcolm's more modest promise is simply to repay loyalty: to "make us even." If so, he may represent a shift to a new, more careful and pragmatic style of government, one predicated on the careful husbanding of resources and on the perception that the crown's wealth is limited. This, too, would represent a loss within the world of the play, for it would signal the final replacement of a grand if insufficient ideal of royal responsibility with a more bureaucratic sense of the office. Read as signs of a new style of monarchy, Malcolm's inaugural acts promise to accept and adapt to a world of scarcity rather than to reinstate the cornucopian abundance which Duncan stood for. If the ideals of kingship which Duncan stood for are revealed to be inevitably insufficient, the alternative is also a diminishment. And though the ideal of the nourish-father is shown to be unsustainable, we see that its passing is to be mourned as well.

"MARK, KING OF SCOTLAND, MARK": SPECULATIONS ON TOPICAL MEANING

Although I am proposing that these plays respond to topically specific

developments – the accession of a generous king after a stingy queen –
I am not suggesting, finally, that they be taken as commentary on
James's performance. I do not think that they are particularly
interested in criticizing or in praising James in particular, though it is
possible to detect elements of each in both plays.[87] For one thing, I am
not convinced that the ambiguities of application characteristic of the
topical references in these plays can be explained away as evasive
maneuvers prompted by the institution of censorship.[88] James's censors
were relatively lax, and many contemporary plays staged much more
explicitly applicable material without significant repercussions.[89]

For another thing, though affairs of state provided ideas for dramatists and generated interest in their audiences, the closeness of the connection between the theatre and the court is often overstated. Leeds
Barroll has recently destabilized the familiar assumptions used to
buttress many treatments of Shakespeare's topical meanings, namely
"that King James was a lover of plays and a royal sponsor of artistic
activities, and that Shakespeare's genius was recognized by his aristocratic patrons in much the same way we recognize it today."[90] Arguing
against these two givens, Barroll suggests that even court performances of
Shakespeare's plays were of little import to James himself, and that
readers of Shakespeare's plays have overestimated the influence of the
Jacobean court upon them. Loosening the connection between Shakespeare and King James, Barroll directs our attention toward different
audiences, different financial exigencies, and different political concerns.
With this in mind, we can see that though *Lear* and *Macbeth* are clearly
interested in James and in the institution of kingship, they do not necessarily contain a consistent, recoverable line of commentary on James
himself.

Instead, it seems to me that both plays take up the newly topical
rhetoric of royal bounty, using its richly vulnerable deployment of
gendered language in order to subject patriarchal kingship to a kind of
symbolic deconstruction. These plays use concepts and rhetoric made
topical by James's accession in order to make political points about
kingship as such. The pointed but conflicting references to James and
his courtiers, in addition to merely being the material at hand, serve
two purposes: as risqué in-jokes, they give each play a kind of
scandalous excitement; as intentionally cryptic topical references they
add urgency, reminding audiences of the materiality of political concepts even as they thwart rigorous topical application.

This is not the same as arguing that Shakespeare is "not of an age, but for all time." I am not arguing that these plays strive to be apolitical, or that they contain no political intent. I am suggesting that spurred by James's gender as well as his generosity, Shakespeare uses the ambiguous, overdetermined affect surrounding maternality – expressive of a complex of patriarchal ideals and, at the same time, a sign of the limits of patriarchal control – in order to represent both a sustaining ideology of kingship and its inevitable fictionality.

Linda Levy Peck's *Court Patronage and Corruption in Early Stuart England*, to which I have already referred, discusses the breakdown of the patronage system and the emergence in England of modern notions of governmental corruption. Changes in the political landscape of England – increased centralization, for example, and new marketplace conditions – meant that the patron / client relationship became less effective as a principle of government. Attempts to respond to governmental crises with *ad hoc* adjustments in the patron / client structure were doomed to failure, and yet given the customary centrality of this relationship in the government of England, Peck argues, it was not easy to see beyond them to any alternative governmental structure. Accordingly, the emergence of a modern notion of corruption is a symptom of the failure of an older notion of government based on patronage and its interrelated ideals of generosity and loyalty.

Though Shakespeare's investigation of royal generosity anticipates the full crisis of the patronage system by decades, *King Lear* and *Macbeth* can be seen as part of the larger cultural process whose political skeleton Peck anatomizes. If the handling of the ideal of bounty in these plays seems proleptic, it may be because the rhetoric of gendered generosity which accompanied James's accession catalyzed a fresh interrogation of long-standing patriarchal ideals. By treating bounty as part of a necessarily insufficient, sustaining fiction of patriarchy, *King Lear* and *Macbeth* provide what in Marxist terminology might be called a critique: they demystify the ideology of patriarchal generosity, making it newly legible as an ideological construct.

PART THREE

Structures of feeling

The politics of nostalgia
Queen Elizabeth in early Jacobean England

for the Queen, she was ever hard of access, and grew to be very covetous in her old days: so that whatsoever she undertook, she did it to the halves only, to save charge; that suits were very hardly gotten, and in effect more spent in expectation and attendance than the suit could any way countervail; that the court was very much neglected, and in effect the people were very generally weary of an old woman's government ... But after a few years, when we had experience of the Scottish government, then in disparagement of the Scots, and in hate and detestation of them, the Queen did seem to revive; then was her memory much magnified – such ringing of bells, such public joy and sermons in commemoration of her, the picture of her tomb painted in many churches, and in effect more solemnity and joy in memory of her coronation than was for the coming in of King James.

Bishop Godfrey Goodman[1]

The Jacobean magnification of Elizabeth's memory – which Godfrey Goodman was here describing from the perspective of a moderate Anglican in the 1650s – is by now a familiar phenomenon.[2] Recent accounts of this nostalgia have for the most part joined Goodman in accepting it as a natural response to Jacobean failures of government. The shared assumption is that justifiable dissatisfaction with the new king forced Englishmen to retroactively re-evaluate their departed queen, seeing her in a more positive light by contrast with her successor.

This account of the late queen's famous memory needs to be revised in a number of ways. For one thing, far from being universally critical of James, depictions of Elizabeth produced during the first decade of his reign in England stand in a variety of relationships to Jacobean orthodoxies. There is a considerable body of early Jacobean literature, for example, which emphasizes precisely the continuity between the queen and her successor. And even those early Jacobean texts which reproduce versions of Elizabethan glory incompatible with James's policies and style are not always motivated by dissatisfaction with the current king.

For another, any account of the uses of Elizabeth in Jacobean England must recognize that they vary according to the milieux in and for which they are produced. Bishop Goodman's account of the rise of Elizabethan nostalgia in Jacobean England makes reference to the interests both of the neglected Elizabethan courtiers and of "the people," but he elides whatever differences there may have been between the two, describing the emergence of Jacobean dissatisfaction as a collectively shared experience: "after a few years, when *we* had experience of the Scottish government ..." Nevertheless, there is a curious rift in Goodman's account, in which dissatisfactions of Elizabethan courtiers are replaced by a public nostalgia expressed in bell-ringing, sermons, and other displays of a much wider public's "joy." If nothing else, Goodman's juxtaposition of courtly and public sentiment, awkwardly linked under the rubric of the collective pronoun, should focus our attention on the need for a more differentiated analysis of the various interests involved in this emergent nostalgia.

Jacobean deployments of the late queen's famous memory tended to cluster into three distinct groups. First, many writers including James himself attempted to emphasize those elements of the Elizabethan cult which could be transferred effectively to the new king.[3] Second, the relative autonomy of Queen Anne and Prince Henry, each with a separate court, created new sources of patronage and protection on the margins of James's court; the versions of Elizabeth shaped under Anne and Henry differ markedly from those of the Jacobean orthodoxy. Third, the citizen classes of London must be considered as a separate contributor to Elizabethan nostalgia: the plays, pamphlets, and published sermons produced by and for this public include a version of Elizabeth with its own distinct emphases.

Borrowing Raymond William's vocabulary, we can describe the presence of the late queen's cult in Jacobean culture as a "residual" element. And in Williams's influential model, the selective deployment and suppression of such residual material is an essential part of the process by which the dominant culture reproduces itself.[4] That is to say, the relationship between perceptions of James and memories of Elizabeth must be seen as twofold: while dissatisfaction with James no doubt contributed to the production of nostalgia for Elizabeth, idealized images of the late queen also helped to shape England's apprehension of James.

Accordingly, the contest over the legacy of Elizabeth was an important one, and as Goodman's account suggests, the satisfactory incorporation of residual Elizabethanism was never fully accomplished by James and the writers who shaped his public image. In order to understand the production and ideological functions of these competing nostalgic images of Elizabeth in early Jacobean England, it is necessary to see how the queen's memory came to be represented in each of the three groups I have alluded to. Furthermore, in order to assess the varied influence of these nostalgic images on perceptions of James, it will be necessary as well to trace the ways that they circulated, and to examine the kinds of cultural negotiation that occur whenever these different images of Elizabeth contradict or reinforce each other.

THE KING JAMES VERSION OF QUEEN ELIZABETH

Upon his accession to the English throne, King James gave orders that Elizabeth's funeral should take place in his absence. As the Venetian secretary Giovanni Carlo Scaramelli reported, the decision was seen as a sign of the new king's lingering resentment of his predecessor:

they say he wishes to see her neither alive nor dead, for he can never expel from his memory the fact that his mother was put to death at the hands of the public executioner ... Elizabeth's portrait is being hidden everywhere, and Mary Stuart's shown instead.[5]

Private emotion notwithstanding, the memory of the late queen could not be so easily hidden. As James realized, the new government had to construct for itself a popular image that would take into account inherited Elizabethan expectations about the role of the English monarchy. On the one hand, comparisons between the old queen and the new king were inevitable; on the other, Elizabeth's glorious memory was a mine of discursive resources for the glorification of the English throne, and (by extension) of its new occupant.

In his first speech to parliament in 1604, James was careful to describe the advantages of his accession in terms of familiar elements of the Tudor myth:

the second great blessing that GOD hath with my Person sent unto you, is Peace within, and that in a double forme. First, by my descent lineally out of the loynes of Henry the seventh, is reunited and confirmed in mee the Union of the two Princely Roses of the two Houses of LANCASTER and YORKE, whereof that King of happy memorie was the first Uniter, as he was also the first ground-layer of the other Peace. The lamentable and miserable events by the Civill and bloody dissention betwixt these two Houses was so great and so late, as it need not be renewed unto your memories: which, as it was first setled and united in him, so is it now reunited and confirmed in me, being justly and lineally descended, not onely of that happie conjunction, but of both the Branches thereof many times before. But the Union of these two princely Houses, is nothing comparable to the Union of two ancient and famous Kingdomes, which is the other inward Peace annexed to my Person.[6]

Here James goes to some trouble to adapt his own claims to the Elizabethan legacy, pointing out not only that he is literally descended from Henry VII, but also that the union of England and Scotland effected by his accession is analogous to the union York and Lancaster brought about by his Tudor ancestor.[7] The continuity suggested in James's speech between the Tudor peace and the Jacobean union is one of the commonplaces of early Jacobean panegyric. Samuel Daniel encapsulates the gesture nicely in his "Panegyric Congratulatory": "Our former blessed union hath begot / A greater union that is more intire."[8]

The emphasis on continuity is strategic, intended to co-opt and capitalize on the popularity of Elizabeth. And several early Jacobean panegyrists responded to the crown's need for representations of royal continuity, perhaps none more explicitly than Alexander Craig, an expatriated Scotsman whose *Poeticall Essayes* (1604) consist mostly of verse congratulations for the new royal family. In a poem entitled "Elizabeth, Late Queene of England, Her Ghost," Craig puts words into the mouth of the late queen, making her praise James and urge her subjects to be loyal to him: "All you my subjects deire, do homage dew to him, / And that shal make my blessed ghost in boundles joyes to swim."[9] The volume in which this poem appeared earned Craig a pension from the king.[10] Michael Drayton's failure to mention Elizabeth in his panegyric "To The Majestie Of King James" is thought to have hurt the poet's chances with courtly patrons and the king himself.[11]

In a sermon preached before the king at Whitehall in 1604, Henry Hooke goes out of his way to describe James's accession as providential, since God

did in the change of state so order all things, as that it might seeme no change at all. For when the rare Phoenix of the world, the queene of birds, which had for many yeeres gathered together, and safely covered Jerusalems children under her wings, was now through age to be turned into dust and ashes, though she appeared unto men to die, yet she died not, but was revived in one of her owne bloud; her age renewed in his younger yeeres; her aged infirmities repaired in the perfection of his strength; her vertues of Christianitie and princely qualitie rested on him, who stood up a man as it were out of the ashes of a woman, retaining in his life the memorie of her never-dying honour, expressing in his government the patterne of her clemencie and justice, preserving to his glorie, and his peoples comfort, the state of the kingdome, as he found it.[12]

In order to capitalize fully on the propagandistic value of asserting continuity between Elizabeth and James, sharp distinctions between the two rulers had to be finessed. For to ignore them often meant praising James in ways that were awkward or tactless. The pageantry written by Thomas Dekker to celebrate James's entry into London in 1604, for example, has been described as "a form of initiation rite introducing the new King to the roles created for Queen Elizabeth and left vacant by her."[13] For these pageants bestowed upon James many of the motifs of Elizabethan imperialist mythology, and so can be seen as an attempt to assert continuity between the two reigns in much the same manner as Hooke or James himself.

But there is reason to believe that James or some associate of his was dissatisfied with Dekker's pageant. Dekker's epistle to the reader of *The Magnificent Entertainment Given to King James* complains that "a regard being had that his Majestie should not be wearied with teadious Speeches, a great part of those which are in this booke set downe were left unspoken."[14] Jonson was belatedly commissioned to contribute to the pageant, and his additions make no allusion to Elizabeth. It seems that Dekker's pageantry failed to please the king because, unlike Jonson's, it relied on an Elizabethan notion of how a king should behave in public: where Elizabeth thrived on public performance, James found the prolongation of the pageant "teadious."[15] So though Dekker's attempt to invest James with the trappings of the Elizabethan mythos is in keeping with the crown's attempts to establish continuity, his composition failed to accommodate James's very un-Elizabethan approach to public performance.

In other cases, James's recycled Elizabethan motifs were subjected to radical change in order to align them with the policies and style of the new government. If under Elizabeth the Trojan origins of Britain were generally used to associate the Tudor dynasty with its Arthurian heritage, with chivalry, and with military prowess, the Jacobean use of the material had to be renegotiated to fit the policies of *Rex Pacificus*.[16] The mythic history of Britain as New Troy contained in Monmouth's chronicles continued to be invoked in celebrations of James, but with a new emphasis on union and internal peace. Similarly, in James's court, King Arthur was more likely to be used as a symbol of national unity than as an exemplar of Britain's chivalric might.[17]

One important component of the multi-faceted cult of Elizabeth saw her as the representative of Protestant England's special relation to God. Popularized by John Foxe's *Actes and Monuments*, this conception of the English crown had a lot to offer James, since it emphasized the close relationship between royal and divine authority. The influence of this image of the queen has been described by William Haller, who notes that "by the time James came to the throne the Book of Martyrs and the stream of annals, chronologies and histories in similar vein had gone far to establish in the public mind . . . a quite definite conception of the part rulers might be expected to play henceforth."[18] But the unequivocal damnation of Catholicism and justification of militant Protestantism implied by the Foxean tradition were not easily squared with James's Spanish peace, nor with his policy of religious moderation.

In 1610, Foxe's *Actes and Monuments* was reprinted for the sixth time, with a comparatively brief epistle by Edward Bulkeley appended in order to bring the book up to date. Bulkeley's addendum is interesting because it reflects what is essentially a Jacobean change in emphasis. For Bulkeley retains Foxe's interest in the true church, while de-emphasizing the centrality of England's role as its defender. In fact, the appendix begins with a history of the St. Bartholomew's Day massacre, continues with a list of other French atrocities, and finally comments on "the murthering of Henry the third, and Henry the fourth, late French kings, by papists."[19] Since Bulkeley's epistle shifts the focus away from Foxe's English nationalism, it would tend to weaken the association between the needs of the true church and English military destiny. Consequently, it would tend to make the book as a whole more compatible with James's policies and with his public image.

Bulkeley also adds the experiences of James himself to Foxe's catalogue:

the barbarous and monstrous powder plot shall follow; whereby it was intended and purposed, to have blowen up the Parliament house; when our gracious king James, prince Henry, all the nobility, bishops, knights and burgesses should be assembled therein. To the effecting of which divellish device, about thirtie foure barrels of gunpowder were laid under the said Parliament house, and there found. This bloodie conspiracie was practiced by precise papists; whose consciences would not permitte them to come to our churches; but did easily suffer and allow them to attempt this savage and horrible practice ... This bloodie device should have beene executed the fifth of November, 1605. but was by Gods great mercie discovered and defeated, to the just destruction of those detestable traitors, who fell into the pit that they digged for others, and to the eternal shame and confusion of that bloodie Babylon of Rome, and her favourers and followers. (1952a–b)

The attempt on James's life makes him a victim of Catholic persecution, and the prevention of the plot shows that God in His mercy protects His agent on earth. Seen in this way, the Gunpowder Plot becomes analogous to the persecution suffered by Elizabeth during the reign of Queen Mary in Foxe's history. Bulkeley's appendix ratifies James's divine right by casting his escape in the mold of Elizabeth's exemplary experiences.

Of course Bulkeley's continuation is dwarfed by the reprinted *Actes and Monuments* itself, and so we should not imagine that the tone of the book as a whole is significantly transformed. The 1610 edition of Foxe's volume preserves plenty that is incompatible with Bulkeley's revisionary appendix: like James's entry into London – written by multiple authors, fragmented, unable fully to reconcile Elizabethan nostalgia and Jacobean kingship – the reprint of Foxe makes manifest crucial vulnerabilities inherent in the translation of Elizabethan royal motifs onto James. Each of these productions reveals at the level of form incompatibilities between James's rule and Eliza's legacy.

In order to celebrate James as the perpetuator of Elizabethan glory without stumbling on the sharp differences between the two monarchs, writers associated with James's court had to recast Elizabeth's memory. Instead of trying to bring James in line with Elizabethan practices, these writers created a version of Elizabeth strikingly similar to James's image of himself. One of the more elegant examples of this reconstruction is Francis Bacon's "In Felicem Memoriam Elizabethae," composed and circulated in manuscript in 1608.[20]

Bacon's memoir is unabashedly celebratory from the start: "ELIZABETH both in her nature and her fortune was a wonderful person among women, a memorable person among princes" (305). At the same time, Bacon makes it clear that he understands the politics of nostalgia and intends to serve the king:

Her death was followed by two posthumous felicities, more lofty and august perhaps than those which attended her in life; her successor, and her memory. For successor she has got one who, though in respect of masculine virtue and of issue and of fresh accession of empire he overtop and overshadow her, nevertheless both shows a tender respect for her name and honour, and bestows upon her acts a kind of perpetuity; having made no change of any consequence either in choice of persons or order of proceedings; insomuch that seldom has a son succeeded to a father with such silence and so little change and perturbation. And as for her memory, it is so strong and fresh both in the mouths and minds of men that, now death has extinguished envy and lighted up fame, the felicity of her memory contends in a manner with the felicity of her life. (311)

As this passage suggests, Bacon reinvokes the queen's glorious legacy in part to make James its rightful heir. But in order to make his claim convincing, Bacon must construct a version of the Elizabethan legacy compatible with Jacobean policies.

Elizabeth is praised in Bacon's memoir for resisting widespread public desire for war, and for presiding over a prolonged peace:

Observe too that this same humour of her people, ever eager for war and impatient of peace, did not prevent her from cultivating and maintaining peace during the whole time of her reign. And this her desire of peace, together with the success of it, I count among her greatest praises; as a thing happy for her times, becoming to her sex, and salutary for her conscience. Some little disturbance there was in the northern counties about the tenth year of her reign, but it was immediately quieted and extinguished. The rest of her years flourished in internal peace, secure and profound. (308)

This may be surprising to a reader more accustomed to seeing Elizabeth praised as the scourge of the Armada, or to those who remember Elizabeth's policy in Ireland. Bacon glosses over these aspects of Elizabeth's reign, insisting that these skirmishes merely "had the effect of keeping both the warlike virtues of our nation in full vigour and its fame and honour in full lustre" (308). After down-playing the militarism of Elizabeth's reign, Bacon returns to his emphasis on her cultivation of peace, reiterating his earlier assertion: "upon another account also this peace so cultivated and maintained by Elizabeth is matter of admiration; namely, that it proceeded not from any inclination of the times to peace, but from her own prudence and good management" (309).

It is true that Elizabeth – especially towards the end of her reign – tempered the gung-ho militarism of Essex and others. Finances tied her hands in this regard, though, and she was never fully opposed to foreign intervention. In Simon Adams's words, "the frequently bitter disputes over foreign policy in the Elizabethan Privy Council remained

... debates over means rather than ends."[21] In fact, Bacon's praise for Elizabeth applies more closely to King James's policy than to the late queen's. Unlike Elizabeth, James made peace an important part of his public self-styling despite the popular anti-Spanish sentiment which constituted the "inclination of the times." As Sir Henry Neville put it in a letter of 1606, "the Kingdom generally wishes this peace broken, but *Jacobus Pacificus* I believe will scarce incline to that side."[22]

Bacon's account of Elizabeth's good fortune "in escaping the treacherous attempts of conspirators" (309) also shows subtle signs of having been tailored to fit James's own rhetoric, when it emphasizes the detection, as well as the providential defeat, of treachery: "not a few conspiracies aimed at her life were in the happiest manner both detected and defeated" (309). The tradition upon which Bacon's narrative draws here is that of Foxe's chronicle, which details the dangers faced by Elizabeth under Mary, and which helped shape perceptions of later conspirators like William Parry. However, in Foxe's representation of Elizabeth's providential escapes, emphasis is placed on her almost naive innocence in the face of peril. James and his mouthpieces, by contrast, made the detection of the Gunpowder Plot into evidence not only of providence, but of the king's special agency in its operations: the statute of 1606 that made the anniversary of the discovery a holiday states that all would have been lost "had not it pleased Almighty God, by inspiring the king's most excellent majesty with a divine spirit, to interpret some dark phrases of a letter shewed his majesty."[23] Bacon's emphasis on the detection of conspiracies, as well as on their defeat, subtly recasts the Elizabethan legacy in the mold of Jacobean propaganda.

Bacon praises the king for respecting the memory of Elizabeth while simultaneously reconstructing that memory to fit James. The neat circularity of the move underscores the cagy purposefulness of Bacon's memoir, a piece of writing which meets the needs of Jacobean propaganda by transforming the Elizabethan legacy into an authorizing precedent for Jacobean claims and policies, erasing differences between the two reigns which might seem to reflect badly on James's, and at the same time managing to appear politically disinterested. Written at a time when his own political ambitions were only partly fulfilled, it seems possible that Bacon's piece was meant precisely to demonstrate its author's mastery of the politics of nostalgia, and to underscore his usefulness to government.[24]

That Bacon wrote his "In Felicem Memoriam" in order to bolster his credit with the crown is corroborated by the fact that he sent a copy to Sir George Carew, ambassador to France, asking him to show it to the French historian Jacques-Auguste de Thou.[25] The ongoing production of de Thou's *Historiae Sui Temporis* was a collaborative project of international scope, and a matter of some interest to James, who took an interest in the work upon the appearance of his first volume in 1603, and tried to influence its accounts of recent Scottish and English history for a decade thereafter.[26] By sending his memoir to de Thou, Bacon aligns himself with James's interest, and signals his willingness to apply his rhetorical talents to the king's own international public relations project.

Another participant in James's ongoing attempt to influence de Thou was William Camden, whose *Annales Rerum Anglicarum et Hibernicarum Regnante Elizabetha* was originally intended to be a contribution to the French historian's massive project. James's eagerness to provide de Thou with an accurate Scottish history and a sympathetic account of Mary Stuart provided the original impetus for Camden's project in 1608. In 1611 a portion of Camden's history, edited for the crown by Robert Cotton, was sent in manuscript to de Thou. The French historian refused to revise his Scottish material, so James apparently ordered Camden to publish the first part of his alternative account (through 1588) in 1615.[27] Although the degree to which royal intervention influenced its writing will continue to be debated, it seems clear that Mary Stuart is treated with great care in Camden's history, and the figure of Elizabeth that emerges has more in common with Bacon's depiction of her than with Foxe's.

Though Camden's history does on occasion celebrate Elizabethan military achievements, its cumulative picture of Elizabeth has more in common with James's image of himself than has generally been recognized.[28] First, Camden goes out of his way to praise James wherever occasion arises, as for example his description of James's birth: "In June following was the Queene of Scots, to the perpetuall felicity of *Britaine*, happily brought to bed of her sonne *James*, who lately was Monarch of *Britaine*."[29] Second, Camden sometimes emphasizes ways in which the new king's policy is an improvement.[30] Third, negotiated peace is repeatedly the aim of Camden's Elizabeth, especially in the section (up to 1572) which was sent to de Thou. In 1559, "a peace was proclaimed over all *England* betwixt the Queene of *England*, the King of *France*, the Dolphin, and the Queene of Scots; which was ill taken by the people ... " (25). This treaty is broken, in Camden's history, because of intrigues between France, Spain, and Scotland; later, peace with Scotland is re-established (42), but Spain refuses it (44–45). The Elizabethan foreign policy reported by Camden matches the objectives of early Jacobean foreign policy. Indeed, in the case of Scotland, the mere presence of James solves a persistent problem: Camden describes Elizabeth's attempts to establish "a mutuall amity betwixt the two Kingdomes" (35) and notes that James's union ensures the amity for which Elizabeth had to go to war (32–37).

It is important to remember that James saw himself as a moderate *politique*, exercising craft to negotiate a balanced response to international and internal problems. The portrait of Elizabeth that emerges from Camden's account – and about this there is something like critical consensus – has precisely those virtues that James attributed to himself. Camden's Elizabeth upheld the *via media* in religion, maintained the balance of power in Europe, avoided war unless absolutely necessary, and ruled by insight and what James might have called "kingcraft." In the words of D. R. Woolf, "it was this image of Elizabeth which appealed to James I as much as Camden's portrait of Mary Stuart, because most of what he praised in Elizabeth was still Jacobean practice, at least as far as the king was concerned."[31]

Neither Bacon's "In Felicem Memoriam" nor Camden's *Annales* would have had a wide English reading public, the more so since both texts were written in Latin and only Camden's was published. Given James's concern elsewhere to capitalize on the popularity of Elizabeth and the skill with which these two texts recast Elizabeth in accordance with Jacobean practices, this seems an important oversight. Indeed, the practical failure of these texts as propaganda is illustrated by the fact that when a translated version of the first section of Camden's *Annales* was finally published in 1625, it was adorned with graphic and poetic depictions of the military triumphs of the lost Elizabethan golden age. No longer even recognizable as an expression of Jacobean orthodoxy, Camden's text was repackaged and made to oppose it in response to the proposed match between Prince Charles and the Infanta of Spain.[32]

Adherence to James's personal interest in de Thou's history directed the efforts of Bacon and Camden towards a project whose influence on English popular opinion was negligible. This is a striking example of an important difference between Elizabethan and Jacobean court literature. One reason for the development of the so-called cult of

Elizabeth was, paradoxically, the queen's unwillingness to finance artists. In lieu of royal patronage, what we think of as Elizabethan court culture was financed by a variety of courtly patrons, each vying for limited royal favor. This competition encouraged increasingly ingenious propaganda, and also widened the circle involved in its production and dissemination.[33] By contrast, James's open-handed bounty seems to have contributed to the insularity of Jacobean court production. Direct royal bounty meant that writers were more concerned with echoing the king's own opinions and tastes than with independent elaborations of his greatness. And as the king became the source of bounty, he also became the most important audience for works of propaganda, which tended to limit their circulation and social effectiveness. Had James not been so directly the audience for the kind of work done by Bacon and Camden, their version of Elizabeth might have reached a wider English audience, been elaborated in a broader range of texts, and ultimately been more influential.

But despite the limited circulation of its major embellishments, the King James version of Elizabeth did find public expression, and not only in the early panegyrics which welcomed James to England by stressing the continuity between the old queen and her successor. Cranmer's prophesy in the final scene of Shakespeare and Fletcher's *Henry VIII* (1613), for example, promises that in Elizabeth's day every man shall "sing / The merry songs of peace to all his neighbors" (5.4.34–35). After promising this peace in the reign of the future queen, Shakespeare's Cranmer makes it clear that the Elizabethan peace is to be seen as continuous with the policy of *Jacobus Pacificus*:

> Nor shall this peace sleep with her; but as when
> The bird of wonder dies, the maiden phoenix,
> Her ashes new create another heir
> As great in admiration as herself,
> So shall she leave her blessedness to one
> (When heaven shall call her from this cloud of darkness)
> Who from the sacred ashes of her honor
> Shall star-like rise as great in fame as she was,
> And so stand fix'd. Peace, plenty, love, truth, terror,
> That were the servants to this chosen infant,
> Shall then be his, and like a vine grow to him.
>
> (5.4.39–49)

Though its function within the play as a whole remains problematic, the vision expressed here of continuous peace beginning under

Elizabeth and upheld by the policies of James was a recognizable – if never fully naturalized – early Jacobean encomiastic gesture.[34]

OLD ELIZABETH AND THE NEW ROYAL FAMILY

Early Jacobean panegyrists also welcomed the new royal family, applying conventional tropes of the Elizabethan cult to both Queen Anne and Prince Henry as well as to James himself. Anne in particular was the recipient of much of the gendered encomiastic language formalized under Elizabeth.[35] Thus, Daniel's *Vision of the Twelve Goddesses* (1604) – the first masque performed before the new court – presents the queen and her ladies as a procession of goddesses personifying an Elizabethan array of virtues:

As unto *Juno* the Goddesse of Empire and *regnorum praesedi*, they attributed that blessing of power. To *Pallas*, Wisedome and Defence: to *Venus*, Love and Amity: to *Vesta*, Religion: to *Diana*, the gift of chastity: to *Proserpina*, riches: to *Macaria*, felicity: to *Concordia*, the union of hearts: *Astraea*, Justice: *Flora*, the beauties of the earth: *Ceres*, plenty: to *Thetis* power by Sea.[36]

Not only are a number of these figures standard Elizabethan fare in themselves, but the grouping depends on a sense of the congruence of female and imperial virtues, which is also distinctly Elizabethan. Daniel's pageant is a celebration of naval power, military defence, and empire on the one hand, and chastity, loveliness, and religious purity on the other. The Elizabethan logic according to which these virtues are linked illustrates both Daniel's own nostalgic politics and the early Jacobean tendency to celebrate the new queen in terms of the old.[37]

The association of imperial power and female virtue – reminiscent of the rhetoric of the elect nation, and of the Protestant militarism associated with the late queen – relies on a version of the Elizabethan legacy almost incompatible with James's pacific, diplomatic style.[38] However, in the conceit of Daniel's masque, Anne and her ladies represent gifts and blessings bestowed upon James by the various goddesses. This frames the potentially subversive system of associations lavished upon the goddesses themselves, locating them in the service of James, whose reign is here figured as a Temple of Peace. Since the goddesses hearken back to a version of Elizabethan glory which includes militarism, their service to the Temple of Peace creates some rhetorical dissonance in the text.[39]

This raises familiar questions about subversion and containment. It is easy to see Anne's Elizabethanism here as a challenge to James's authority, and to argue that its staging of popular militaristic affect carries an oppositional charge. But by making Anne carry a powerful and dangerous nostalgic image of Elizabeth, while at the same time dramatizing her obedience, it was possible to invoke the affective memory of Elizabeth in such a way as to disarm potentially threatening comparisons between her reign and that of James. In this latter argument, Anne becomes a safety-valve for what is already a dangerous structure of feeling, which in turn depressurizes whatever subversive potential Elizabeth's memory might have carried.

Recent scholarship has corrected shop-worn notions of Anne as flighty, and has shown that Anne and the important members of her court actively cultivated political and artistic influence. The queen resisted James's royal authority on more than one occasion, and it has been argued that she used her patronage of the court masque in order to express her resistance to, or at least independence from, James.[40] At the same time, the writers employed for the masques could hardly ignore the major ceremonial brief of such an occasion, which was to celebrate James and his court. This means that by virtue of their fundamental patronage situation, Anne's masques are self-divided at the level of conception and production. That subversive Elizabethan affect can coexist, in a text like Daniel's, with powerful gestures of containment is evidence of this internal division: the text's deployment of Elizabeth's memory is available for both radicalizing and conservative readings.

The role played by Prince Henry in the politics of nostalgia is similarly ambiguous, though the stakes were somewhat higher.[41] For the prince's court was the site of an ambitious Elizabethan revival which fostered support for a number of positions opposed to James's policies. Most centrally, from the time of James's accession Henry was projected as the heir to England's military glory.

It quickly became conventional to celebrate Prince Henry as "The *Index*, *Abstract*, or *Compendium* of the very greatest Princes whatsoever," a mode of celebration which aligned the Tudor myth with the chivalric glory of Henry V.[42] As the culmination of this ancient tradition of British imperial power, Henry inherits the mantle specifically of Elizabethan Protestant imperialism. In Daniel's *Tethys' Festival*, written "to solemnize the creation of the high and mighty Prince Henry, Prince of Wales" in 1610, the transfer of Elizabethan military glory is made explicit.[43] A messenger from Tethys gives to the prince the

sword of Astraea, together with what amounts to an imperialist
mandate:

> there will be within the large extent
> Of these my waves, and watry Government
> More treasure, and more certaine riches got
> That all the Indies to Iberus brought.[44]
>
> (172–75)

Henry encouraged this Elizabethan inheritance, allowing himself to be
represented as a throwback to an Elizabethan brand of chivalry.[45] In
1608, for instance, Queen Elizabeth's old champion at tilt, Sir Henry
Lee, presented Henry with a valuable suit of armor and, symbolically,
with the ceremonial mantle of Elizabethan knighthood.[46] As part of his
imperial self-presentation, Henry took an active interest in England's
naval power and in the ongoing process of colonization. Sir John
Holles described the prince's involvement in the glorious projects of
"Queen Elizabeth, whose memory and government this worthy prince
ever much reverenced" in an elegiac letter written shortly after
Henry's death: "all actions profitable or honourable for the kingdom
were fomented by him, witness the North West passage, Virginia,
Guiana, The Newfoundland, etc., to all which he gave his money as
well as his good word."[47]

Henry cultivated the support of James's naval administrators, pro-
tecting master shipwright Phineas Pett and others from investigation
on charges of graft; in 1610 Pett unveiled a magnificently ornate new
ship, called the "Prince Royall" in Henry's honor. Though the ship
proved ultimately to be unseaworthy, its construction underscores
the prince's close relationship with the navy.[48] Henry also took an
interest in the case of Sir Walter Ralegh, a representative of the past
generation's imperial ambition languishing in prison under James.
Though it is not clear that the two ever met, Henry sought Ralegh's
advice, publicly praised him, and attempted to intercede with James
when the Ralegh estate was about to be given to Robert Carr in
1609.[49]

The prince also surrounded himself with an aggressively Protestant
and culturally cosmopolitan circle in his court at St. James's. It is in
this context that Roy Strong describes Henry as the heir to a tradition
of militant Protestantism and culturally innovative internationalism
handed down from Leicester to Sidney to Essex, and lost upon Henry's
death.[50] Arthur Gorges's elegy for Prince Henry, "The Olympian
Catastrophe," makes this lineage concrete, recycling some of the lines

that he had previously used in his elegy for Sidney.[51] Given that so many of the elements of Elizabethan imperial glory were taken up in the young prince's self-fashioning, Strong describes it as "inevitable" that his court became "the focal point of the hopes of the old Elizabethan war party."[52]

It was inevitable as well that the prince's bellicosity should not only focus but also generate dissatisfaction with the Jacobean Peace. When, in his "Ballad of Agincourt" (1606), Drayton concludes his résumé of Henry V's heroism by pointedly asking

> O, when shall *English* Men
> With such Acts fill a Pen,
> Or *England* breed againe,
>   Such a King HARRY?[53]

it becomes clear that the poet is using the martial promise of the prince to criticize the pacifism of the king. And Henry rewarded Drayton with an annual stipend of £10.[54]

Drayton's increasingly oppositional politics include their own version of Elizabeth's legacy. The first part of Drayton's *Poly-Olbion* (1612), which was written under the prince's protection and subsequently dedicated to him, couples explicit criticism of James with a rousing celebration of Elizabethan military glory. In the seventeenth song of Drayton's chorographical epic, the river "Tames" catalogues the glories of the English kings through Elizabeth:

> *Elizabeth*, the next, this falling Scepter hent;
> Digressing from her Sex, with Man-like government
> This Iland kept in awe, and did her power extend
> Afflicted *France* to ayde, her owne as to defend;
> Against th' *Iberian* rule, the *Flemmings* sure defence:
> Rude *Ireland's* deadly scourge; who sent her Navies hence
> Unto the either *Inde*, and to that shore so greene,
> *Virginia* which we call, of her a Virgin Queen:
> In *Portugall* gainst *Spaine*, her English ensignes spread;
> Took *Cales*, when from her ayde the brav'd *Iberia* fled.
> Most flourishing in State: that, all our Kings among,
> Scarse any rul'd so well: but two, that raign'd so long.
> Here suddainly he staid . . . [55]

Not only does Drayton exclude James from his catalogue, he calls attention to the gesture by insisting that Tames's list end "suddainly." It should be clear how far removed Drayton's version of the late queen's famous memory is from the crown's. As things turned out, of course,

Henry's death cheated the poet out of royal support, but it remains suggestive that Drayton generated this distinctly oppositional version of Elizabethan nostalgia under the *aegis* of the prince's patronage.

Henry encouraged a structure of feeling that tended to chafe under Jacobean pacifism. But, since most writers tended in practice to have conflicted loyalties and goals, Henry's nostalgic self-projections were often forced into uneasy reconciliation with Jacobean orthodoxy. The most explicit example here is the masque-like *Speeches at Prince Henry's Barriers* constructed by Inigo Jones and Ben Jonson and performed on Twelfth Night, 1610. Though its occasion is self-evidently chivalric – the show itself is merely the culmination of twelve nights of role-playing begun with a ceremonial challenge issued to the knights of the realm by the Arthurian figure Meliadus – Jonson's text goes out of its way to de-emphasize military glory.[56] Our first indication of Jonson's unusual use of his Arthurian characters comes early, when Arthur ("translated to a star"[57]) instructs the Lady of the Lake to bestow a shield upon Meliadus in order "To arm his maiden valor, and to show / Defensive arms th'offensive should forego" (98–99). Further following Arthur's instructions, the Lady of the Lake frees Merlin's spirit and calls forth Meliadus and his attendants. This sets the stage for Merlin's protracted reading of the proffered shield, an oration which traces ideal monarchic virtues and which, uninterrupted, makes up only slightly less than half of the whole text.

As virtually all of the masque's critics have noted, Merlin's speech begins by explicitly turning away from the implicit values of Arthurian legend:

> No giants, dwarfs or monsters here, but men.
> His arts must be to govern and give laws
> To peace no less than arms.
>
> (166–68)

What follows is a long, peculiar catalogue praising those British monarchs whose reigns saw civic advances: "th'increase / Of trades and tillage" (179–80), for example, or the development of "The trade of clothing" (186). The benefits bestowed upon the nation by these kings and queens are polemically mundane: they act to deflate the aura established by Jonson's battery of Arthurian characters.[58] Finally, Merlin's list culminates with a version of "great Eliza" that the king might have approved of – she is praised for building a "wall of shipping" (200–01) – before an eminently Jacobean conclusion:

> These, worthiest prince, are set you near to read,
> That civil arts the martial must precede,
> That laws and trade bring honors in and gain,
> And arms defensive a safe peace maintain.
>
> (203–06)

Having said all of this, Merlin proceeds with a second catalogue – this time in order to show how a king should behave if battle is unavoidable. This list looks more familiarly chivalric: "Richard, surnaméd with the lion's heart" (213), the "Black Prince Edward" (248), "Harry the fifth" (278), and Elizabeth. Reading from the shield, Merlin describes the military heroism of Eliza:

> I could report more actions yet of weight
> Out of this orb, as here of eighty-eight
> Against the proud Armada, styled by Spain
> The Invincible, that covered all the main,
> As if whole islands had broke loose and swam,
> Or half of Norway with her fir-trees came
> To join the continents, it was so great;
> Yet by the auspice of Eliza beat,
> That dear-beloved of heaven, whom to preserve
> The winds were called to fight and storms to serve
>
> (291–300)

This second, more protracted, description of Eliza's glory draws on the patriotic sentiments of the myth of the elect nation. Needless to say, it would have been more closely cognate with the feelings of Prince Henry's circle than was Merlin's original catalogue of bureaucratic managers.

The final forty lines of Merlin's speech praise "Royal and mighty James" (345), describing at length his mastery of the civil arts. To Strong, these lines register as hopelessly flat after the celebration of Elizabeth's naval conquest. He writes: "The speech had somehow to reach its apogee in James I, but not even Jonson could be faithful to such a brief, except by floundering into a hymn of praise."[59] But it is important to recognize that this discontinuity is intended strategically. Instead of trying to crescendo after the praise of Elizabeth, Merlin's speech aims at containment. Jonson in effect isolates his catalogue of warriors, surrounding it by praise of civil rulers on one side and of James as a civil ruler on the other.

When the Lady of the Lake finally speaks, she reinforces the Jacobean reading of Merlin's speech, enjoining Meliadus to obey the king and to learn from his kingcraft:

Aye, this is he, Meliadus, whom you
Must only serve and give yourself unto,
And by your diligent practice to obey
So wise a master, learn the art of sway.
(359–62)

This done, Chivalry awakens, the House of Chivalry flies open, and the actual barriers begin. Jonson strenuously sets limits around the Elizabethan chivalric virtue of the prince. By subjugating martial prowess to civic art, and by insisting on the total obedience due to James by the young Meliadus, Jonson is able simultaneously to invoke and contain the affective power of Elizabethan elect nation patriotism. The strategy is analogous to Daniel's treatment of Anne in *The Vision of Twelve Goddesses*.

The printed text of Jonson's script for the *Barriers* is only a small part of the ceremonial event: the barriers themselves lasted through the night and would in all probability have dwarfed Jonson's speeches.[60] Though the text may give us the impression that the chivalric appeal has effectively been blunted, the actual event was probably a good deal more stirring to Henry and like-minded courtiers. There is some evidence, moreover, that neither of Jonson's two patrons was entirely satisfied. It has been suggested that Daniel got the commission for *Tethys' Festival* because the prince wanted to find a writer less loyal to Jacobean orthodoxy than Jonson, while James in turn refused to allow the same kind of staged barriers to be produced the following year.[61]

Instead of a sequel, the following year Jonson and Inigo Jones collaborated on *Oberon* (1611). Like *Prince Henry's Barriers*, *Oberon* displays the prince in nostalgic, Elizabethan terms: Silenus refers to Oberon as "the fairy prince" (39), for example, while in both *The Faerie Queene* itself and in Dekker's *The Whore of Babylon* (1607) the name Oberon is given to King Henry VIII. Either way, Henry is located within the framework of the Elizabethan Tudor myth. In *Oberon*, however, the containment of volatile material is more complete: the trappings of Elizabethan chivalric figures remain, but the potentially oppositional value system that goes with them has been gutted. Indeed, as the "foremost sylvan" (236) explains it, the prince's total obedience to the throne constitutes the fictional occasion of the masque. The celebration is to be

A night of homage to the British court,
And ceremony due to Arthur's chair,
From our bright master, Oberon the fair;

> Who with these knights, attendants, here preserved
> In fairyland, for good they have deserved
> Of yond' high throne, are come of right to pay
> Their annual vows.
>
> (240–46)

Jonson includes knights, fairies, and even Arthurian material, but his text is finally a celebration not of arms but of James's ability to rule by "the sweetness of his sway, / And not by force" (263–64).[62]

Henry's Elizabethan revival had a split impact on the politics of nostalgia. His court at St. James's provided a more or less containable site for dangerously oppositional passions, as overlapping loyalties, deferral, and the fact that no heir wants to encourage disobedience in his future subjects kept the oppositional energy surrounding the prince in check. James's willingness to countenance his son's rising popularity despite its oppositional tenor may have been the result of wise kingcraft rather than of impotence.[63] The prince's sudden death unleashed this nostalgic energy, with the result that a more coherent oppositional voice emerged, but this unforeseeable turn of events does not reflect any failure in the state's strategic containment of the prince's court.[64]

That said, the prince's vivid persona undoubtedly gave purpose to a brand of nostalgic military patriotism antithetical to the policies of James's government. Moreover, if the King James version of Elizabeth failed to take on the ring of truth, the Chivalric Nationalism fostered by Henry inevitably contributed to its failure: during his lifetime, the prince's self-fashioning added to the cacophony of voices making up the legacy of Elizabethan glory, and consequently interfered with the transmission of the royalist line.

THE CITIZENS AND THEIR QUEEN

A description of Queen Elizabeth's coronation entry of 1559, entitled *The Royall Passage of Her Majesty From the Tower to White-hall*, was reprinted in 1604. One imagines that its publication was sparked by popular enthusiasm both for the pageantry celebrating James, and for the late queen's memory. Apparently the two were not seen as contradictory: the appetite of London book-buyers for Elizabethan nostalgia remained strong (during the first decade of James's reign and beyond) despite fluctuations in popular attitudes towards the crown. Thus, among the many religious pamphlets directed at the London citizen audience were texts like William Leigh's *Queene Elizabeth, Paraleld in her Princely Vertues, with David, Joshua and Hezekia* (1612), a collection of sermons preached during Elizabeth's reign, or Thomas Sorocold's *Supplications of Saints. A Booke of Prayers: Divided into Three Parts. Wherein are Three Most Excellent Prayers Made by Queene Elizabeth* (1612, entered 1608).[65] Looking elsewhere, we find texts like Christopher Lever's *Queen Elizabeth's Tears* (1607), and plays like Thomas Dekker's *The Whore of Babylon* (1607) or Thomas Heywood's popular two-part drama *If You Know Not Me, You Know Nobody* (1605–6).[66]

Heywood's plays in particular are indicative of the popularity of Elizabethan material. It is generally accepted that the two plays were originally composed not as a unit but as a treatment of Elizabeth's trials under Queen Mary in the one, and a depiction of the life of the merchant Thomas Gresham in the other. The two texts, it is speculated, were then scrambled and amalgamated by their printer Nathanael Butter, with the result that an account of the naval victory of 1588 is improbably appended to the life of Gresham with only the most tenuous of connections.[67] Both plays sold extremely well, and it seems at least possible that the always opportunistic Butter altered his texts in order to capitalize on the popularity of Elizabethan material. By adding the Armada to the life of Gresham, Butter would have been able to use the appeal of Elizabethan nostalgia to sell both books. At any rate, Butter does seem to have seen commercial potential in Elizabethan nostalgia: in addition to Heywood's plays he also printed Dekker's *The Whore of Babylon*.

Elizabeth's memory retained its popular appeal among the various strata of London citizenry in large part because Elizabeth herself was remembered as the special friend of her non-noble subjects. The queen's public performances played a considerable role in the making of this image. Thus, her coronation entry in January 1559 served as a defining moment in her cultural memory, especially since the account of that entry was so frequently republished. Having received an English Bible presented by the figure of Truth, Elizabeth kissed it, held it up, hugged it to her breast, and offered her thanks to the city. The vividness of the scene, and its importance to the citizen audience, is attested to by the fact that it is staged both at the end of the first part of Heywood's *If You Know Not Me* and in the dumb show that precedes the first act of Dekker's *The Whore of Babylon*.[68] The former in particular stresses the special relationship established between the queen and the city. In Heywood's play the Lord Mayor

presents Elizabeth with a Bible on behalf of the City of London, and
the queen replies:

> We thanke you all: but first this booke I kisse,
> Thou art the way to honor; thou to blisse.
> An English Bible, Thankes, my good Lord Maior,
> You of our bodie and our soule have care,
> This is the Jewell that we still love best.
>
> (1,578–82)

Elizabeth continued to dramatize her gracious love for her subjects
throughout her reign. In November 1601, forced by widespread dissatisfaction to redress grievances in the system of monopoly patents,
the queen conceded to parliamentary demands in what has come to be
called the "Golden Speech." Using this political crisis as an opportunity to publicize her concern for the welfare of her subjects,
Elizabeth's speech declares that "there is no prince that loves his subjects better, or whose love can countervail our love":

There will never Queen sit in my seat with more zeal to my country, care for
my subjects, and that will sooner with willingness venture her life for your
good and safety, than myself. For it is my desire to live nor reign no longer
than my life and reign shall be for your good. And though you have had and
may have many princes more mighty and wise sitting in this seat, yet you
never had nor shall have any that will be more careful and loving.[69]

Published accounts of this virtuoso performance bolstered the patriotism of the London reading public, reinforcing the notion that
Elizabeth was their special protector. After the queen's death the
speech was continually reprinted, and remembered as an exemplary
expression of her idealized graciousness.[70]

If the second part of Heywood's *If you Know Not Me* is any indication,
Elizabeth was remembered fondly for her close relationship with
wealthy London merchants and guildsmen. In Heywood's play, the
queen sends a messenger to Hobson – a wealthy haberdasher and one
of the play's two citizen-heroes – asking for the loan of £100. Hobson's
effusive answer makes his patriotic royalism quite clear:

> How, bones a mee, *Queene* know *Hobson*, *Queene* know *Hobson*?
> And send but for one hundred pound? Friend come in;
> Come in friend, shall have two, *Queene* shall have two:
> If *Queene* know *Hobson*, once her *Hobsons* purse,
> Must be free for her she is Englands Nurse.
>
> (1,115–19)

Later, Hobson and the queen meet in Gresham's newly built exchange building, and reiterate the terms of their economic relationship:

> [HOBSON:] by this hand Queene *Besse*, I am olde *Hobson*
> A Haberdasher, and dwelling by the Stockes:
> When thou seest money with thy Grace is scant,
> For twice five hundred pound thou shalt not want.
> [QUEEN:] Upon my bond.
> [HOBSON:] No, no my Soveraigne,
> Ile take thine owne word without skrip or scrowle.
> [QUEEN:] Thankes honest *Hobson*, as I am true mayde,
> Ile see my selfe the money backe repayd:
> Thou without grudging lendest, thy Purse is free,
> Honest as plaine.
>
> (2,086-96)

In this same scene, the queen demonstrates her further care by naming Gresham's bourse the Royal Exchange and knighting Gresham himself. The naming of the exchange was the cause of considerable civic pride, as is indicated by its inclusion in Stow's *Survey of London*.[71]

The queen did cultivate her wealthy merchants. She had to. Once the English crown ceased to rely on the international money market, the London Corporation and the powerful trading companies of the city gradually became almost exclusive sources for royal loans. Thus Elizabeth gave the Merchant Adventurers a virtual monopoly on the export to Europe of white-cloth in 1564 in large part because she needed the financial services that this powerful group was then able to advance.[72] This same predicament also contributed to the queen's policy of relying on the statesmanship of such able administrators as Gresham and William Cecil from the ranks of the new rich: relations with the City Corporation and with the merchant companies were an important aspect of the management of crown finances.[73]

The advantages accrued to the average citizen as a result of the policies implemented by these merchants and statesmen were probably negligible. J. H. Hexter acknowledges that "an undeniably close relationship was maintained between the government of Elizabeth and a small inner coterie of Tudor merchant-bankers," but adds that the policy sponsored by this coterie "was clearly and immediately to the disadvantage of almost every member of the middle class except themselves."[74] Nevertheless, civic pride taken in the prominence of some London citizens, coupled with patriotic pride in London's contributions to the bankrolling of Elizabethan military exploits, contributed to the nostalgic memory of Queen Elizabeth's special bond with her London citizens. Heywood's play, with its concurrent celebration of Gresham and of the freely given loan, capitalizes on this nostalgic pride. I would argue, in fact, that civic pride relating to London's contributions to Elizabeth's war chests provides the thematic link between the story of Gresham and Hobson and the hastily appended description of the defeat of the Armada.

A third source for London's memory of Elizabeth as the champion of her citizens is Foxe's widely read account of the future queen's treatment under Mary. Though published early in Elizabeth's reign, it remained a staple of Elizabethan culture and was, as we have seen, reissued in 1610. Foxe's narrative continually emphasizes both the queen's common touch and the immediate, unanimous sympathy between her and her common subjects. Thus, when Elizabeth is taken to the Tower, Foxe shows us not only the queen's exemplary behavior, but also her effect on the poorer members of the Tower's staff: "the poor men kneeled downe, and with one voice desired GOD to preserve her grace" (1,896b). Similarly, transportation of Elizabeth from one prison to the next provides occasion, in Foxe's account, for impromptu displays of public affection, despite the fact that her keeper Sir Henry Bedingfield prohibits such celebration and indeed puts one group of bell-ringers into the stocks (1,898a–b). These anecdotes and others are used by Foxe to establish a contrast between Elizabeth, who in her access to simple truth enjoys a bond of sympathy with the people at large, and Mary, under whose tyrannical rule both Elizabeth and her future subjects suffer.

The first part of Heywood's *If You Know Not Me* relies heavily on Foxe's narrative, and intensifies Foxe's emphasis on Elizabeth's bond of sympathy with her common subjects.[75] In Heywood's play, Elizabeth's household servants continue to attend to her after her household has been broken up and dissolved, following her to prison. Even the soldiers transporting the queen agree that her punishment is wrong. Since they are afraid to state such opinions, they express themselves in veiled language: "Masse I say this: That the Lady *Elizabeth* is both a lady, / and *Elizabeth*, and if I should say she were a vertuous Princesse, / Were there any harme in that" (478–80)? Finally, Heywood stages the tribute paid to Elizabeth by three "poor men" and other assorted townsmen during her transportation. This scene is drawn from Foxe, but in Heywood's account we see not only the exemplary love evoked among the commoners by Elizabeth but also her sympathetic reactions to them. Upon first hearing the clamor, Elizabeth tells her servant to thank them and give them gold; then, when Beningfeild [*sic*] tells his soldiers to stop the celebrants, Elizabeth asks him to be kind to them ("the poore are loving, but the rich despise, / And though you curbe their tongue, spare them their eyes" [856–57]). When Beningfeild hears bells and sets out after the ringers, Elizabeth utters an exclamation of pity: "Alas poore men, helpe them thou God above, / Thus men are forst to suffer for my love" (874–75). It is worth noting how unlike the Jacobean style this populism might have seemed: as the Venetian Ambassador Nicolo Molin reported, the new king refused to "caress the people nor make them that good cheer the late Queen did."[76]

Associated with London's memory of Elizabeth's populism was an equally prevalent nostalgic construction of her authority: time and again in these texts we see that Elizabeth's power is associated with her access to simple, honest truth in the form of naive political morality and pure scriptural godliness. Thus, Heywood's Elizabeth reduces complex issues of political finance to the most basic and accessible sort of morality when she promises to repay Hobson's loan: "as I am true mayde, / Ile see my selfe the money backe repayd." Not only does Heywood here associate fiscal responsibility with truth and chastity, but he underscores Elizabeth's willingness to deal plainly and directly with the Haberdasher by attending to his money herself. By the same token, Christopher Lever's versification of material from Foxe, *Queene Elizabeth's Teares*, depicts the queen's uncomplicated religious truth triumphing over the "Machevillian" political intrigue of Steven Gardiner.[77] She says, for example,

> I am not cunning for to make dispute;
> I thanke yourselfe, but not your sophistrie,
> In my religion I am resolute;
> Yet here is one your learning can confute;
> (And then she points whereas her Bible lay)
> Here's one (she saith) will teach me what to say.
> (719)

Needless to say, the naive purity attributed to the queen in this nostalgic reconstruction has little to do with the cagy, *Politique* Elizabeth of Camden's *Annales* or with the Elizabeth who we now tend to see as a cipher at the center of a "whole field of cultural meanings personified in her."[78]

James, by contrast, prided himself precisely on being "cunning for to make dispute," as is evidenced among other things by his sponsorship of the Hampton Court Conference. Indeed, a sharp distinction can be drawn between the accessible plainstyle of London's Elizabeth and the more authoritative style of James: while London's nostalgic version of the queen draws authority from her perfect embodiment of self-evident moral truths, James himself assumes the authority to dictate truths to his subjects. Emblematic of this stance is James's youthful dedication of his "Schort Treatise" on the rules of Scottish poetry to "the docile bairnes of knawledge."[79] The word docile meant "teachable" in early modern English and, as D. J. Gordon and others have shown, James's claim to pedagogic authority continued to influence the literature produced by his court. In Gordon's account, a text like Ben Jonson's *Hymenaei* encodes precisely this Jacobean model of pedagogic king and "docile" subject:

> knowledge of truth, which is knowledge of the intelligible world and the eternal Unity, cannot be reached by the discourse of reason unless reason be aided by divine inspiration: only sapience or wisdom brings knowledge of truth. Such wisdom King James has – James who is the British Solomon. Such wisdom, and such knowledge are his to impart to his adoring subjects.[80]

The version of Elizabeth popular among early Jacobean London's citizen classes, by contrast, need not demand docility since she herself operates according to universally apprehended standards of morality and truth.

Despite the clarity of the contrast between London's Elizabeth and the public image of the new king, there is no clear evidence that the figure of Elizabeth is used in these London texts to comment on James. The texts that constitute this civic version of the late queen's legacy not only dwell on her populism, fiscal responsibility, and naive simplicity – emphases which are potentially dangerous to James – they also tend to endorse Elizabethan military imperialism and anti-Spanish sentiment without being openly critical of the policies of the new *Rex Pacificus*.[81] In general, they tend to praise James in his terms while enthusiastically reiterating the glories of Eliza in hers. Of course, one would not expect these texts to criticize James openly, and it remains possible that criticism of James in these London texts remains veiled in order to circumvent the attentions of the censor. My own impression of these texts, however, is that they contain none of the tell-tale signs of oblique political commentary described by Annabel Patterson: elaborate disclaimers, carefully crafted ambiguity of application, delicate positioning *vis-à-vis* patrons, and so on.[82] There is little here to direct a reader's attention toward topical application of the Elizabethan material.

Among the many texts which contribute to the production of London's memory of Elizabeth, Thomas Dekker's *The Whore of Babylon* stands out as the most unstinting celebration of Elizabethan Protestant imperialism produced during the first decade of James's reign. Dekker's allegorical celebration of Elizabethan glory is also unusually thorough in its thematization of an idealized version of the Elizabethan legacy incompatible with Jacobean orthodoxy. If there is an early Jacobean text in which London's memory of Elizabeth is used to critique James's performance it is *The Whore of Babylon*.

Dekker makes his polemical stance clear from the outset:

The Generall scope of this Drammaticall Poem, is to set forth (in Tropicall and shadowed collours) the Greatnes, Magnanimity, Constancy, Clemency, and other the incomparable Heroical vertues of our late Queene. And (on the contrary part) the inveterate malice, Treasons, Machinations, Underminings, and continual blody stratagems, of that Purple whore of *Roome*.[83]

In order to set forth these matters, Dekker presents Elizabeth as Titania, the Fairy Queen, and pits her against the Whore of Babylon who represents an international popish empire. The allegory is simple: Titania poses a threat to the global domination of the Whore, and the latter makes four failed attempts to disrupt her. First the Whore sends three kings to woo Titania; second, she employs agents to encourage drunkenness and dissatisfaction within Faery Land; third, she sends Doctor Paridel (i.e., Parry) to assassinate Titania; finally, she sends the Spanish Armada. In its use of Eliza as an allegorical representative of elect nation status, *The Whore of Babylon* fits squarely into the Foxean tradition. And the association of Elizabethan military imperialism with elect nation Protestant eschatology in Dekker's play runs directly counter to the Jacobean policies of negotiated peace and religious moderation.

The moral and aesthetic assumptions around which Dekker's play is organized also reflect the potentially oppositional nature of London's version of the late queen. In the play's prologue, for example, Dekker writes,

         wee present
Matter above the vulgar Argument:
Yet drawne so lively, that the weakest eye,
(Through those thin vailes we hang betweene your sight,
and this our peice) may reach the mistery:
What in it is most grave, will most delight.

                     (3–8)

Dekker's desire to expose the mysteries of state to the "weakest eye" contradicts the published opinion of James himself, who once wrote and continued to believe that such mysteries were "to grave materis for a Poet to mell [meddle] in."[84] Instead, Dekker's aesthetic of disclosure resonates with London's image of the late queen's authority in which, as we have seen, her power stems from the embodiment of universally obvious moral truths. Dekker's project is appropriate only because Elizabeth, in London's memory of her, operates according to principles that always remain available to the "weakest eye." An organizing premise of Dekker's aesthetic brief is the assumption that Elizabethan government did not rely on *arcana imperii.*[85]

Dekker's aesthetic of clarity gathers moral significance within the play's allegory. Titania faces the Whore's threats with precisely the sort of simple purity and Protestant faith dramatized in Lever's *Queene Elizabeth's Teares* and in the Foxean tradition. Her response to the gathered Armada, for example, is powerful in its simplicity: "Let it come on: our Generall leades above them" (5.2.9). The allegorical personifications of both "Plain-dealing" and "Truth" are among Titania's sworn subjects. Even Titania's physical person adumbrates this moralized aesthetic of transparency: her faithful councillor Fideli refers to her eyes as "christal / Faire, double-leaved doores" (1.2.172–73).

Rather than by *arcana imperii*, Titania governs by adhering to basic moral codes. Her plain, personal chastity stands in for the impenetrability of Faery Land as a whole:

> Her kingdome weares a girdle wrought of waves,
> Set thicke with pretious stones, that are so charm'd,
> No rockes are of more force: her Fairies hearts,
> Lie in inchanted towers (impregnable)
> No engine scales them.
>
>   (1.1.97–101)

In order to break the charmed borders of Titania's kingdom, the Whore sends her three European kings to woo Titania "like lovers" (1.1.104): breaching the body of the queen means breaching the boundaries of her realm.[86]

At the same time, the Whore and her compatriots are consistently associated with disguise, courtly arts, stratagems, and arcane learning. The three kings sent by the Whore to Faery Land present a "maske" to Titania, and when they discover themselves Titania exclaims, "Your painted cheeks beeing off, your owne discovers, / You are no Faeries" (1.2.82–83). The masquers' painted cheeks adumbrate their dissembling moral character. Later the Whore recruits Campeius, a poor scholar, because she knows that "none sooner rent / A Church in two, then Schollers discontent" (2.2.49–50). Since Titania's religious and moral truths are simple and clear, the role of the scholar is to create confusion where none need be. Dekker's play distinguishes between Truth and "that common harlot, / That baseborne trueth, that lives in *Babylon*" (3.3.11–12). Plain-dealing asks Truth "how shall I know, thou art the right truth?" Truth answers, "Because I am not painted" (3.3.1–2). The play, in other words, establishes a binary opposition between two associative clusters. Popish stratagems are associated with courtly arts, painted faces, unnecessary and contentious learning, and sexual promiscuity; English patriotism with clarity, simplicity, chastity, and pure Protestant faith.

What seems to me most striking about *The Whore of Babylon* is that, if pushed, the assumptions and values upon which his binary system is built would condemn James's style and align it with that of the Catholic Whore. For in addition to his assertion that affairs of state must remain hidden from the weakest eyes, the king took pride in his own arcane learning and admired learning for its own sake in others. The aesthetic of James's court tended to favor scholarly arcana, not the least of which were those mysteries expressed for the benefit of the learned in the masques of Ben Jonson and Inigo Jones.[87] As Roy Strong and Stephen Orgel describe it, the means of the court masque "was spectacle, its end was wonder, and the whole was an expression of the glory of princes."[88] In Dekker's play, however, it is the Whore of Babylon who relies on spectacle and wonder in order to rule, as she puts it, "in pompe, in peace, in god-like splendor, / With adoration of all dazeled eies" (1.1.1–2). Within the moral landscape of the play, this is yet another sign of the Whore's corruption since, by contrast, Titania's transparently moral government need never dazzle even the weakest eyes. The moral and aesthetic assumptions around which Dekker's play is constructed are part of the structure of Elizabethan nostalgia in London: to apply them to James's court would be to denounce it.

But even allowing for the features I have just described, any critique of James that we might intuit is balanced by gestures that point in the opposite direction. The only time James is alluded to in *The Whore of Babylon* he is given high praise. One of the Whore's Cardinals argues that the death of Elizabeth will bring no comfort to their empire, since her successor would be just as mighty:

Say that *Titania* were now drawing short breath,
(As that's the Cone and Button that together
Claspes all our hopes) out of her ashes may
A second Phoenix rise, of larger wing,
Of stronger talent, of more dreadfull beake,
Who swooping through the ayre, may with his beating
So well commaund the winds, that all those trees
Where sit birds of our hatching (now fled thither)
Will tremble, and (through feare strucke dead) to earth,
Throw those that sit and sing there, or in flockes
Drive them from thence, yea and perhaps his talent
May be so bonie and so large of gripe,
That it may shake all *Babilon.*

(3.1.232–44)

Lest anybody miss the point of this speech, a marginal note identifies its subject as James. On the strength of this panegyric, it has even been suggested that we read *The Whore of Babylon* as a pro-Jacobean play written in the spirit of patriotic nationalism occasioned by James's triumphant evasion of the popish Gunpowder Plot in 1605. In this account Elizabeth's defeat of the Armada is seen, plausibly enough, as analogous to James's defeat of Guy Fawkes.[89] In other words, Dekker's play is certainly available for an anti-court reading, but it is also available for a royalist, Jacobean reading. There is no way to be certain either that oppositional meanings were intentionally encoded in the text by Dekker or that they would have necessarily been recognized by the play's early Jacobean audience.

Other London pieces strike me as being demonstrably naive rather than subtly indeterminate in their juxtapositions of Elizabethan recall and Jacobean panegyric. Perhaps the perfect example is Thomas Heywood's baggy verse chronicle, *Troia Britanica: or, Great Britaines Troy* (1609), a text that doggedly praises both Elizabeth and James in obviously contradictory terms. The bulk of Heywood's folio is a versification of Caxton's fifteenth-century *Recuyell of the Histories of Troye*, a text which had itself been reprinted as recently as 1607.[90] But Heywood, trying to capitalize on contemporary interest both in Britain's Trojan origins and in chronicle history, interjects dedicatory invocations and illustrative examples from recent English history, and appends a chronicle of Great Britain's kings and queens that culminates in Elizabeth and James. Elizabeth and James both figure prominently throughout Heywood's chronicle, which often praises the one for war and the other for peace without favoring either, or betraying any sign of rhetorical discomfort.

Heywood's celebrations of the king are dispersed throughout his long poem. In canto 1, he addresses the king as a Protestant devotional poet might address God: "Oh, may these Artlesse numbers in your eares, / (Renowmed JAMES) seeme Musically strung."[91] He echoes the king's absolutist dogma in canto 2: "*Princes* are earthly Gods and placst on high, / Where every common man may freely gaze" (2.49.1–2). At the start of canto 3, Heywood praises the king's peace at length (stanzas 1–3), and in the middle of the fourth, he compares Jove making peace with Troy to James making peace with Spain (stanzas 48–49). Wherever possible, Heywood includes Scottish legend in his text in order to demonstrate that he considers England and Scotland to be united, and in a long catalogue of treason (canto 15) he includes the Gunpowder Plot (stanzas 5–7). The final canto of Heywood's poem mentions both the battle of Lepanto – the subject of James's best-known poem – and the Gowrie conspiracy, but pointedly ignores both the fate of the Queen of Scots and the Essex conspiracy, each of which would tend to highlight potential friction between James and his predecessor.

But Heywood celebrates the military glories of Elizabeth as frequently as he praises the pacific policies of James. In canto 7, for example, he compares the conquests of Drake and Essex to those of Hercules (stanza 87), while in canto 11 he demonstrates the imperial superiority of England by comparing its heroes favorably to those of Greece, Troy, and Rome. These invocations begin with Arthur, but go on to include surprisingly recent Elizabethan figures:

> And those whose Woorths these late times have displaid
> *Howard, Grey, Norris, Sidney, Essex, Veare*:
> These, had they liv'd in aged Priams dayes,
> Had dim'd the Greekes, and matcht the Trojans prayse.
> (11.8.5–8)

The opening of canto 2 juxtaposes an encomium on the Jacobean peace with a rousing celebration of the explicitly chivalric glory of the defeat of the Armada (stanzas 6–7). If Heywood himself noticed the contradictions built into his encomiastic scheme, he certainly did not let on.

The naive association of nostalgic Elizabethan patriotism and Jacobean panegyric in Heywood's chronicle suggests that it was at least possible for Londoners during the first decade of James's reign to support the crown while cherishing a memory of Elizabeth replete with oppositional potential. It is for this reason that I am reluctant to see Dekker's more programmatic play as oppositional in any concrete, putatively intentional fashion. Instead, it seems likely to me that while early Jacobean London promulgated a version of the late queen whose implicit values were in conflict with Jacobean orthodoxies, the oppositional energy this version carried remained largely dormant during the first decade of James's reign. If the generation of frankly oppositional feeling lagged behind the production of possibly oppositional affective structures, there are undoubtedly good reasons for the delay. Among them, we might name the habitual royalism of London's citizens, and a spectacular economic boom keyed by peacetime mercantile expansion between 1604 and 1614.[92]

It has been argued that James completed the break between the monarchy and the citizen classes of London.[93] The ideological conflict concretized in these memorial texts suggests that this may be so: the fact that the discrepancies between the popular memory of Elizabeth and Jacobean practice go unacknowledged suggests that the Jacobean line was not effectively disseminated among London's populace. By the same token, these texts suggest that whatever tangible effects this break may have had were slow in coming.

MAKING OPPOSITION

The early years of James's reign saw a great deal of nostalgic energy invested in the figure of Queen Elizabeth. There is no evidence to suggest that the majority of this memorial literature was conceived of as oppositional, or that it was used explicitly to compare Jacobean failure to Elizabethan success. This is the case even with those texts not produced within or for James's court. As we have seen, oppositional potential in texts produced for Queen Anne or Prince Henry tends to be dampened by the obedience owed to the king by the patron, or by connections with the king's court on the part of the client. Alternatively, those texts produced in and for the city often contained material for damning comparisons between James and his predecessor, but those comparisons themselves are never pushed.

Instead, the political consequences of the nostalgic voices outside of James's court were twofold. First, as I have suggested, they interfered with the dissemination of the King James version of the late queen, drowning it out as it were. Insofar as that version was intended to transfer Elizabeth's popularity to James and to ratify Jacobean policies, this interference contributed to the failure to establish and naturalize an emotionally effective cult of monarchy in Jacobean England.

Second, these alternative versions of the late queen promoted ideal standards of royal behavior and policy by which James in the long run was judged, and judged wanting, by his subjects. The texts may not have been constructed in order to compare Elizabeth and James but they inevitably contributed negatively to the way James and his court were seen.

Take, for example, the account of Elizabeth's honest fiscal dealings with Hobson in *If You Know Not Me* part two. There is no reason to believe that the London citizen would have seen this as a negative commentary on James's policy in 1606. In fact, there is considerable evidence to the contrary: as Robert Ashton points out, James inherited a debt of £60,000 from a loan raised for Elizabeth by the Corporation of London; the same body raised two further loans – one interest-free – before the original debt was fully repaid in 1608.[94] After 1610, however, James's inability to repay loans manifested itself in the deterioration of the crown's credit with the Corporation.[95] During this process, the idealized picture of royal financial responsibility shaped in earlier Elizabethan nostalgia would have contributed to the perception that the crown's fiscal difficulties were an indictment of James himself. In other words, James's failure to live up to standards of royal behavior popularized in earlier nostalgic texts may have contributed to the erosion of James's credit, in more than one sense of that word.

Alternatively, even if the various versions of Elizabethan military and chivalric glory promulgated in London and around Prince Henry were not always intended to be critical of James's policy of peace, they prolonged the affective lure of military glory and contributed to an overall climate of opinion in which Jacobean relations with Spain were likely to provoke discontent. In either case – and similar arguments could be made about other facets of Elizabeth's cultural legacy – the point is that rather than arising in response to James's failures, these idealized memories of the queen's actions and policies in fact contributed to the formation of public perceptions of the new king and his government.

In time, and thanks in part to the cultural work done by the texts with which we have been concerned here, Jacobean praise for Elizabethan glory became more programmatically oppositional. The best known proof-text here is Fulke Greville's *A Dedication to Sir Philip Sidney* (written between 1610 and 1612, published in 1652). In that piece, Greville follows up his romanticized account of the life and death of Sidney with an account of the virtues of Elizabeth and her government that insistently underscores parallel shortcomings in her successor. Thus, if James made peace with the popish Spaniard and increased the crown's fiscal difficulties, Greville's Elizabeth not only vowed to repair the "ruins of our Saviour's militant church," but managed to do so in such a way that "her wars maintained her wealth, and that wealth supplied her war."[96] In a thinly veiled reference to James's ongoing struggle with the House of Commons, Greville writes

neither did she, by any curious search after evidence to enlarge her prerogatives royal, teach her subjects in Parliament, by the like self-affections, to make as curious inquisition among their records to colour any incroaching upon the sacred circles of monarchy. (103)

Similarly, in an obvious reference to James's habit of vesting his authority in favorites like Carr, Greville writes, "in the latitudes which some modern princes allow to their favourites, as ... middle walls between power and the people's envy; it seems this queen reservedly kept entrenched within her native strengths and scepter" (105). Together with the equally nostalgic account of Sidney, the text is constructed in order to hold up the "large complexions of those active times" as an example for James's "effeminate age" (7). Greville wrote his *Dedication* during his years of exile from James's court and, as Ronald Rebholz argues, its paired accounts of lost exemplarity constitute "a claim by Greville that, given an opportunity to serve the new age with strengths developed in the old, he might help save Jacobean England from its imminent death."[97]

Greville's *Dedication* circulated only in manuscript form during his lifetime. Thus, despite its subsequent fame, it must be remembered that it can have played only a marginal role in the ongoing cultural negotiations surrounding the figure of the late queen which we have been concerned to trace. That said, it is worth noting that the *Dedication* is a concrete manifestation of the ultimate failure of the Jacobean court to effectively control residual Elizabethan material. To return to the terminology of Raymond Williams with which we began, it is the job of the dominant culture to alter and incorporate the active residual elements of culture "by reinterpretation, dilution, projection, discriminating inclusion and exclusion."[98] We have seen that the use of these strategies by James and his court was in effect drowned out by alternative reinterpretations: the variety of interfering voices is an expression of the variety within even mainstream Jacobean culture. In Greville's text we see the result beginning to take shape.

A Dedication to Sir Philip Sidney is a relatively early example of a critical strain of Elizabethan nostalgia which not only lasted in England for generations but also, according to some, had serious political repercussions. H. R. Trevor-Roper, for example, has argued that Oliver Cromwell's concept of parliamentary freedom was based on an inaccurate, idealized notion of Elizabeth's governmental practice, while C. V. Wedgwood has suggested that nostalgia for Elizabeth was "an element in the climate of opinion which made a Civil War possible."[99]

In other words, if nostalgia for the late queen in early Jacobean England did little more than contribute to systems of values which impeded the king's propaganda, the same nostalgia came also to be a means of expressing emergent dissatisfaction with James. Thus, after helping to create negative perceptions of James, the late queen's famous memory eventually became their vehicle. This change has made it tempting retroactively to read opposition into early Jacobean productions of Elizabethan nostalgia. The nostalgic texts produced in early Jacobean London, however, suggest that this oppositional tenor, which in the long run they themselves helped to shape, may not yet have been fully available to either their producers or their primary audiences.

CHAPTER SIX

Royal style and the civic elite in early Jacobean London

LONDON'S ELITE AND CIVIC PRIDE

It is difficult to generalize about a city as large as Jacobean London. The economic interests and governmental structure of the old city within the wall were not the same as those of the parishes to the west; both of these areas were unlike the northern, eastern, and southern extramural parishes on the edge of the old city where manufacturing interests came to predominate.[1] Moreover, it has been argued that the loyalties of the majority of London's inhabitants were involved and invested more heavily in institutions at the level of ward or parish than in the city itself, so civic attitudes probably varied considerably by locality even within one of these larger civic groupings.[2] The increasing number of visitors to London each year compound the difficulty. Insofar as this transient population was an important market for London's public entertainments it is notoriously difficult to extrapolate anything like a stable civic ideology from the printed matter of the period.[3]

One can, however, speak of a loosely homogeneous civic elite, an elite distinguished from the mass of London's inhabitants on the one hand, and from courtiers and courtly entrepreneurs on the other. Consisting of liveried members of the twelve major companies of London, this group directed the city's major economic institutions, possessed London's greatest fortunes, and dominated the influential positions in London's civic government.[4] The business interests of this group brought them into contact with courtiers and other dealers in royal concessions and patents, but members of this civic elite made their homes in the center of the old city even as London's resident gentry and nobility moved to the West End and beyond. As a result, there was an increasing segregation of the courtly class from the mercantile class in seventeenth-century London.[5] In the words of R. G. Lang, members of the civic elite were bound together "by their apprenticeships ... by their marriages to the daughters and sisters of citizens, by their business affairs, by civic office, by their circles of city friends, and most of all by the respect, prestige, and honour that attended success in the city."[6] Their loyalties were engaged by the city, for which they served as sheriffs, aldermen, common councilmen, Lord Mayors, and in a variety of other influential positions.[7]

In addition to their considerable economic and political importance, these men were the symbolic representatives of a brand of civic pride which engaged the imaginations of a much larger and less homogeneous class of citizens.[8] Valerie Pearl has argued that the unusually high ratio of officials (generally on the level of ward or parish) to household heads in seventeenth-century London contributed to a communality of spirit among the city's enfranchised citizens in spite of hierarchical differences.[9] Moreover, since the city's wealthy were seen as an open elite by the rest of the populace, they were regarded as examples of attainable civic glory and were the focus of popular ambition rather than of popular resentment.[10]

The city's pride in its elite is manifested in a variety of texts produced for various London consumers throughout the late Elizabethan and early Stuart periods. John Stow's *Survey of London* – first published in 1598 and subsequently republished and enlarged – celebrates the historical magnificence of London's elite for a reading public presumably somewhat larger than that elite itself. Alternatively, representatives of this group are the subjects of a number of folksy fictional accounts produced during the 1590s and thereafter.[11] Expressions of London's pride in her elite continued unabated under James as, for example, the portrayal of Sir Thomas Gresham's comportment and gentlemanly disregard for wealth in the second part of Thomas Heywood's *If You Know Not Me, You Know Nobody* (1606) and the popularity of the Dick Whittington legend around this time suggest.[12]

This strain of specifically civic pride coexisted in late Elizabethan London with patriotic royalism, but traces remain of the potential for conflict between the two. Stow remembers that

an Alderman of London reasonably (as me thought) affirmed, that although London received great nourishment by the residence of the Prince, the repaire of the Parliament, and Courtes of Justice, yet it stoode principally by the advantage of the scituation upon the River: for whenas on a time it was told him by a Courtier, that Queene *Mary*, in her displeasure against London, had appointed to remove with the Parliament and Terme to Oxford, this playne man demaunded, whether she meant also to divert the River of Thames from London, or no? and when the Gentleman had answered no, then, quoth the Alderman, by Gods grace wee shall do well enough at London, whatsoever become of the Tearme and Parliament.[13]

The alderman's pride in London's self-sufficiency is supported by Stow's tacit juxtaposition of the reasonableness of the "playne man" and the self-important arrogance of the queen and her courtier. Though the anecdote is blunted by the fact that the alderman stood up to the detested Mary, his arguments apply equally well under Elizabeth. Moreover, in distinguishing between honest, civic comportment and courtly self-importance, the passage adumbrates an anti-courtly strain in civic pride which is more overt elsewhere.

The strident tone of this one passage is balanced in Stow's *Survey* by anecdotes which specifically draw on royalist patriotism to glorify the city and its governors. The pride of Elizabethan London coexisted with national pride despite potential tension between the two. This coexistence was in large part related to the queen's active cultivation of a gracious and loving public persona in her capital, for this persona engaged the civic elite in a structure of mutual obligations with the crown.[14] It is the argument of this chapter that King James's departures from Elizabeth's civic persona released London from the affective bond of these mutual obligations and consequently contributed to alterations in the civic self-fashioning of the first decade of his reign in England. In particular, I will argue that in response to Jacobean style civic pride found modes of expression – in the annual Lord Mayor's pageant and elsewhere – which, if not strictly oppositional, were increasingly incompatible with the city's traditional patriotic royalism.[15] Civic pride becomes more autonomous as the city's special relationship with the crown ceases to play a central role in it; the distinction between the citizen (Stow's "playne man") and the gentleman becomes blurred.

Providing impetus for this revisionary process were a number of localized conflicts between the civic elite and the crown. A few of them deserve special mention here. Recurring conflicts between James and the city over royal charters given to groups of manufacturers trying to break away from established companies underscored the limits of London's self-government.[16] In 1606 the merchant John Bates provoked a legal test of the king's right to set impositions by refusing to allow customs officers access to a cargo of imported currants. The royal prerogative was upheld in the Court of Exchequer, but the incident – together with the subsequent setting of new impositions in 1608 – publicly set royal and civic economic interests at odds.[17] In 1609, the construction by Cecil of a new Exchange on the Strand, named "Britain's Bourse" by James, was seen as a courtly challenge to the symbolic heart of London's trade. A letter from the Lord Mayor to

Cecil expressed the fear that the access of the new Bourse to the privileged denizens of the West End and Westminster would make the older Royal Exchange obsolete: "It will have such advantages of our Exchange as will make it of noe use for salesmen at all."[18] In fact, Cecil's Bourse was never the threat it promised to be, but by establishing an alternate Exchange Cecil called attention to the divide between the court and the city. By pitting the interests of London's mercantile elite against those of the crown and court, these incidents put a strain on the cooperation between the two groups. More importantly, they publicized the discrepancies between royal and civic interest and consequently contributed to the increasing autonomy of civic pride.

ROYAL PERFORMANCE AND CITIZEN STYLE

It is common, in Renaissance bourgeois fiction, for the hero to feast the monarch. The narrative purpose of these banquets, in such texts as Thomas Deloney's *Jack of Newbury* (1597) and Thomas Dekker's *The Shoemakers' Holiday* (1599), is generally to demonstrate that the non-noble hero is wealthy, willing to spend, and "as useful to the commonwealth as the aristocracy and the gentry."[19] Yet even as these tales articulate a brand of bourgeois pride, they nevertheless rely on and reinscribe orthodox social hierarchies. Part of the virtue of a Jack of Newbury or a Simon Eyre consists of knowing his proper sphere and staying in it. Like Stow's alderman, these heroes are "playne": they are generally depicted as boisterous, mirthful, and free from gentility's pretensions. Deloney's Jack jests boldly with King Henry VIII, feasts him, and finally refuses to be knighted, saying "I beseech your Grace let mee live a poore Clothier among my people, in whose maintenance I take more felicity, than in all the vaine titles of Gentility."[20] By the same token, Dekker's Simon Eyre becomes Lord Mayor of London, feasts the king, but manages to retain his folksy touch: he invites London's apprentices to his royal banquet, and personally entertains the king with a distinctly low-brow brand of humor. In these bourgeois fictions merchants and manufacturers may be as essential to the state as aristocrats, but the two classes are generally represented as being irreducibly distinct.

The monarchs in these tales also participate in the patriotic, essentially royalist, traditions of popular literature. Tales of kings disguising themselves and mingling with commoners were plentiful among English ballads and jestbooks, and the monarch's willingness to not only forgive but also appreciate indecorous behavior in these stories is always an index of his or her graciousness.[21] The kings and queens in these bourgeois fictions demonstrate grace by appreciating and joining in with the rowdy good fellowship of Simon Eyre and his ilk. Gracious condescension on the part of the monarch and plain virtue on the part of the citizen are both part of the popular structure of feeling represented in these texts: they are interrelated as part of the same sentimental structure of reciprocal obligations.

This structure of feeling was not an exclusively Elizabethan phenomenon; its elements were popular before the queen's accession and remained in circulation after her death. Nevertheless, the queen's virtuoso displays of gratitude and condescension in London were both made to exploit it and bound to contribute to its affective power. While queen and citizen shared this contract of sentiment, the queen's public expressions of grateful love held an essentially loyalist version of bourgeois pride in place. That the queen played her role in the city so well, one imagines, is part of the reason for her ability to maintain the balance between mercantile and aristocratic interests which Paul Siegel has called "the Elizabethan compromise."[22]

King James did not participate in this drama of kingship. Instead, his popular reputation in London was shaped by his strongly worded absolutist publications, and by public performances like his ceremonial entry into London, which displayed a more distant style of majesty. The difference in performance between Elizabeth's coronation procession and James's entry was noted by contemporary observers such as Arthur Wilson, and has become a touchstone for subsequent comparisons of Elizabethan and Jacobean style.[23] The essence of the comparison is put most succinctly by Jonathan Goldberg, who writes that while "Elizabeth played at being part of the pageants, James played at being apart."[24]

James's absolutist style emphasized hierarchical distinctions, calling for obedience rather than welcoming reciprocity. This Jacobean conception of the relationship between king and citizen is epitomized in a remarkable anecdote from Gilbert Dugdale's *Time Triumphant* (1604), which describes an impromptu visit to the Royal Exchange by the king and queen. As Dugdale tells it, the royal visit occasioned a mob scene, as subjects expressed their love "with such unreverent rashnes, as the people of the Exchange were glad to shut the staire dores to keepe them out." Once inside the building, the king observed the merchants from a window as they conducted business below. The merchants, in turn, were so smitten by the unexpected presence of the king that, "like so many pictures civilly seeming all care," they stood at attention. In Dugdale's account, this pleased James no end:

[this] sight so delighted the King, that he greatly commended them, saying, he was never more delighted then seeing so many of divers and sundry Nations so well ordred and so civill one with the other, but with all discommended the rudeness of the multitude, who, regardles of time, place, or person, will be so troublesome.[25]

Here the royal visit becomes an allegorical tableau: the king looks on from above and civic enterprise is conducted in a well-ordered manner under his royal eye. The scene is transformed into an emblem of the king's supervisory authority. But where Elizabeth's enactment of her role in the culturally plotted drama of reciprocity had provided a means of expression for growing civic pride by channelling it into a structure of loyalty and mutual obligation, James's style left no room for satisfactory expression from below. Instead, as Dugdale's anecdote suggests, James's supervisory stance imagines subjects as mere "pictures" of orderly efficiency, and demands from them a loyalty consisting of passive subjection.

James paid for his departure from Elizabeth's public persona with losses in popularity. Nicolo Molin, the Venetian ambassador, suggested as much in an often-quoted report dispatched in 1607. The king, Molin reports,

does not caress the people nor make them that good cheer the late Queen did, whereby she won their loves; for the English adore their Sovereigns, and if the King passed through the same street a hundred times a day the people would still run to see him; they like their King to show pleasure at their devotion, as the late Queen knew well how to do; but this King manifests no taste for them but rather contempt and dislike. The result is he is despised and almost hated.[26]

James's more autocratic public style threatened to dismantle the sentimental royalism built up within the reciprocal structure of Elizabethan royal performance.

Molin describes the erosion of the monarch's mass appeal, but the king's departure from the Elizabethan style of self-dramatization also affected his relations with more select civic elites. To illustrate this development, we can juxtapose the banquets offered by Jack of Newbury and Simon Eyre with an actual feast held for King James at the Merchant Taylors' hall in the summer of 1607. On June 27 of that year, the Merchant Taylors' court learned that "the King's most excellent Maj^tie. with our gracious Queene and the noble Prince and diverse Honble. Lordes and others determyne to dyne at our Hall."^27 The logistics involved in preparing for the king's visit were staggering, and arrangements had to be made with breakneck speed: extra furniture, silver, and plate had to be hired; enormous quantities of food had to be procured and prepared; music and other entertainment had to be arranged; architectural changes had to be made in the hall itself; substantial cash gifts had to be provided.

James dined at the Merchant Taylors' hall on July 16, which means that preparations were completed in just twenty days. The cost and effort involved bespeaks the magnitude of the event. For the king, the visit was an opportunity to demonstrate concern for and fellowship with the business classes of London. As such, the banquet was apparently part of a concerted effort to improve relations with London's elite: earlier that summer James had dined with the Lord Mayor, Sir John Watts, and agreed to be made free of the Clothworkers, Watts's Company.^28 For the Merchant Taylors, the royal visit provided a unique opportunity to enhance their company's status by demonstrating and laying claim to a specially privileged relationship with royalty and nobility. In keeping with this objective, a vellum roll containing the names of nobles and royalty made honorary members of the company since the reign of Edward III was given, along with gold, both to James and to Prince Henry.

The Merchant Taylors' preparations reveal throughout the special decorum with which the king had to be handled: a window was cut into the wall of a separate chamber in which the king was to eat, so that he would be able to look in upon the feast in the main hall if he so desired; in order that patrons of an adjacent tavern with roof-top seating not see the king, an existing brick wall was hastily enlarged; the king's own cooks were brought in to prepare a separate meal for James (including an impressive array of imported fruits for the king's own table, intended, no doubt, to underscore the benefits of international trade); Ben Jonson was consulted, and hired to orchestrate an entertainment suitable to the king's taste, since – in the words of the company court record – "the Company doubt that their Schoolmaster and Schollers be not aquainted with such kinde of Entertainments."^29 Hidden from prying eyes, fed special food, and welcomed by an entertainment fashioned to his taste by a familiar court poet, James is elevated, set apart, and put in a supervisory position over the rest of the banqueters.

Such treatment dramatizes James's absolute power by distinguishing him from the rest of the group. Consequently, the sheer stateliness of the king's treatment emphasizes precisely the status distinctions which the royal banquets in bourgeois fiction are made to overcome. Rather than dramatizing James's willingness to participate in a civic function, the event displays the ability of the Company to comply with courtly decorum. Of course, the comparison should not be carried too far: the protocol involved in James's banquet at the Merchant Taylors' hall is not unusually elaborate for an important state dinner, and Elizabeth herself seems often to have dined in a private chamber adjacent to the hall occupied by palace guests.[30] The point here is not that James's treatment at the Merchant Taylors' hall is necessarily unusual, but rather that such a feast was poorly chosen as an occasion for public performance. For in the place of Elizabeth's dramatized common touch, James's entertainment in the city concretizes the distinction and elevation of his exalted majesty.

The Merchant Taylors clearly saw the king's visit as an opportunity to increase the Company's prestige. However, since James's autocratic style made the normative Elizabethan structure of such a visit obsolete, the Company was unsure of how to stage the meeting between crown and Company. In particular, there seems to have been a considerable debate in the Merchant Taylors' court as to whether the Lord Mayor and aldermen should be invited. On the one hand, it was suggested that "to see soe many sitt togeather in their Scarlet Robes" could only enhance the honor generated for the company by the occasion.[31] On the other hand, it was objected that the presence of the city dignitaries would "much derogate from the private Companie ... and soe make it seeme as an entertainment done at the charge of the whole Cytty." Moreover, it was pointed out, inviting the civic government would lead inevitably to problems of protocol:

Some houlding opynion that if wee preferred my Lord Maior and Alderman to a principal Table it woulde offend the nobles and honorable gentlemen who would reckon my Lord Maior in the presence of the King, to be but an ordinary Knight *Quia in praesentia Majoris cessat potestas minoris*: others houlding it the duty of us citizens to have a very special care to give satisfaction and preferr the Governours of the Cytty.

Neither the mayor nor the aldermen were invited. The feast went forward without them, despite the intervention of the Recorder of London who "did use many perswasive speeches" in his attempt to soften the Company's resolve.[32]

At stake in the Company's debate is not only the relative status of city and court elites (as manifest in the question of protocol), but also the source and style of the Company's self-proclaimed dignity. For some members of the Merchant Taylors' court, the banquet was to be a sign of the mutual respect shared by London and the crown. Inviting an array of civic dignitaries would tend to emphasize this meaning. And James, who saw his visit as an opportunity to demonstrate the union of the king and his court with the city as represented by one wealthy Company, presumably shared this conception of the event. This ceremonial brief, however, relies on the assumption that the city is unified, univocal, and distinct from the court. Blurring the distinction between the city and the court, or undermining the Merchant Taylors' representativeness, diminishes the ceremonial meaning of the king's visit.

Other members of the Merchant Taylors' court apparently saw the feast itself as an opportunity to blur the distinction between court and city by appropriating courtly dignity for the Company and its wealthy membership. For them, the banquet represented not the cooperation of crown and city, but rather a chance to increase the gentility of the Company. It was this group who carried the day: by hiring court artists, excluding the mayor and Aldermen, and making an ostentatious demonstration of the Company's noble and royal members, the Merchant Taylors presented themselves as courtly rather than civic.

The Merchant Taylors' banquet is emblematic of the changing relationship between city and crown during the early years of James's reign: it demonstrates both James's propensity to "play at being apart," and also the resulting development of subtle status conflicts among the city elite and between city and court. The two phenomena are related, for by refusing to play his part in the mutually obligating Elizabethan exchange between king and commoner, the king releases civic pride from its structured relationship with royal condescension without providing any alternative, state-sanctioned means for its expression. There is, then, an irony implicit in James's appearance at the Merchant Taylors' hall: the king's own conception of the ceremony relies on the stable social hierarchies which Elizabethan public style helped to hold in place. James's performance, in other words, contributed to the breakup of the very social distinctions upon which it relied.

A striking postscript to James's banquet is provided by Anthony Munday's dedicatory epistle to the Merchant Taylors in his wonderfully titled *A Briefe Chronicle, of the Successe of Times, from the Creation of the World, to this Instant* (1611). In it, Munday rehearses the Company's royal membership without mention of James or Prince Henry. The omission reinforces the notion that James's style diminished whatever public relations benefits he might have accrued from the banquet of 1607:

> Seaven Kings have borne Bretherens name of that Society, (viz:) *Edward* the third; *Richard* the second; *Henrie* the fourth; and *Henrie* the seaventh, and (as is credibly affirmed) wearing the Liveryhood on their shoulders, they have gone on the election day, from the Hall, to the Pallace of Saint *Johns*, in Saint *Johns* Streete, there to heare divine service, and graciously permitted the Maister to goe on the upper-hand, such (in those times) was the milde nature of Princes, shewing (by their owne example) how Magistrates, and other their meaner Ministers, ought to be held in honor and respect.[33]

Given the fact that James and Henry had dined so triumphantly at the hall within recent memory, and the fact that the latter had been made free of the Company, the failure of the epistle to mention the event can hardly be an oversight. Instead, the omission is tantamount to a criticism of James, one seconded by the nostalgic memory of better, less rigidly autocratic rulers. Not only does this formulation concretely invoke the loyalty generated by "graciously" condescending monarchs, it implicitly criticizes the less gracious style of the current king. The suggestion, then, is that James's failure to dramatize his "milde nature" cost him his place in the Company's loyalties.

James's visit to Sir John Watts in 1607 seems to have had a similarly ambiguous effect on his image in London. In Thomas Dekker's *The Dead Tearme* (1608), London (personified as a "provident Mistris over so many families," and as the *"Mother* of the twelve *Companies"*[34]) complains that Westminster has stolen her lover the king, and reminisces about past royal visits:

> A Cittizen of mine (to his immortal memory) dyd in one day, feast at his Table *Foure Kings* ... and now of late (imitating that example) did another of my *Praetors* feast (tho not foure kinges) one equall in power, in Majesty, and in Dominion, to all these 4. (even the Heyre and present *Inheritor* of 4. mighty Empires, our soveraign Lord & maist. *James* the 6.) To looke but back upon which happy daies (because I have séene but few of them) makes my hart beate against my ribbes for joy. (62)

A marginal note indicates that Dekker refers to James's entertainment at the hands of Watts, but the implication of London's complaint (especially of the aside: "I have seene but few of them") is that the king's efforts at public relations in the summer of 1607 failed to remedy the perception that even London's business elite had seen but little of him. Combined with Munday's dedication, Dekker's pamphlet suggests that James's efforts actually exacerbated London's feelings of betrayal.

Munday's *Brief Chronicle* is aimed at an audience of liverymen and civic rulers, a group with whom Munday had been, and would continue to be, involved as overseer for several Lord Mayor's pageants. In addition to the dedication to the Merchant Taylors, the book is dedicated to the Goldsmiths and to "THE RIGHT HONORABLE, SIR WILLIAM CRAVON, Knight, *Lord Maior of the Cittie of London; Sir* HENRIE MONTAGUE, Serjant at Law to his Majestie, *and Recorder of London: And to all the Knights, Aldermen, and Worshipfull Bretheren, the carefull Fathers and Governours of this Honourable Estate*" (sig. A2). These dedications resulted in small cash gifts to Munday from each of the Companies.[35] Finally, brief dedications to specific London officials are strewn throughout the text. Aimed at and rewarded by the financial and governmental elites of London, Munday's book is also an example of the growing autonomy and boastfulness of early Jacobean civic self-fashioning; even where civic texts are not critical of James or his programs, they often make manifest the breakdown of sentimental reciprocity between city and king both by ignoring him and by generating transgressive formulations of civic status.

The historiography of Munday's *Brief Chronicle* is notable both for its lack of interest in the deeds of kings and for its ennobling memorials of London's governors. Though the book runs through a quick survey of the kings of England, it never lingers over any particular monarchic hero. More remarkably, though the book mentions James during its survey, it displays neither more nor less interest in him than in his predecessors (sig. MM4–4^v). Neither oppositional nor laudatory, the treatment of James in Munday's history is simply disinterested. Similarly, a quick survey of the Princes of Wales mentions Henry only in passing, and fails to mention his membership in the Company of Merchant Taylors (sig. MM5).

Instead of lavishing attention on royalty, the book takes pains to account for the parentage of each Lord Mayor of London since 1483, explaining that "many have often desired, to know the country and parentage of our *Lord Maiors of London*, in regard that divers worthy houses have descended of them" (sig. QQ8). By going to such lengths to record the genealogy of the many Lord Mayors – by assuming that their blood matters – Munday treats them as an alternative sort of nobility. Similarly, in his dedication to the Lord Mayor and aldermen, Munday derives aldermanic dignity from explicitly royal stock:

the name of Alderman declareth both verie Reverend Originall, and great Antiquitie; I find recorded, that in the time of King *Eadgar*, one *Ailwin*, a man of the bloud Royall, and, for the speciall great authority and favour hee had with the King (being Sir-named *Healf-Koning*, that is, *Half-king*) was Alderman of all England.[36] (sig. A3)

Like Munday's ennobling attention to the office of the Lord Mayor, this derivation implies a re-evaluation of the status of London's aldermen which would, if pressed, transgress or at least challenge orthodox social hierarchies. However benign the assertions of civic dignity are in the context of Munday's text, they are typical of the civic literature of the period: the city's pride is expressed in increasingly autonomous and thus potentially transgressive terms in the early years of James's reign. As Munday's *Brief Chronicle* suggests, this development is related to a comparative lack of involvement in the iconography of state which is, in turn, partly the result of James's style. In particular, it is the result of James's failure to enact any drama of mutuality with his citizens, and consequently of his failure to channel civic pride into a contained relationship with the crown and court.

THE LORD MAYOR'S PAGEANT AND THE STYLES OF CIVIC PRIDE

We can get at least a skeletal sense of this emergent civic autonomy by looking at the development of the annual Lord Mayor's pageant.[37] Though gaps in the historical record make generalization unreliable, the early Jacobean Lord Mayor's shows for which texts survive become more elaborate even as the versions of civic pride they stage become less bound up in the tropes of royalist panegyric. As M. C. Bradbrook puts it, "it is as if the disappearance of the Elizabethan legend ... released for London a new sense of her own identity."[38] James Knowles's more recent study of civic ritual also describes an "explosion in civic ceremony after 1603."[39]

The annual Lord Mayor's pageant celebrated the installation of each new Lord Mayor on October 29. The return by barge of the new mayor from his swearing-in at Westminster was the occasion for pageantry on the water, and his subsequent procession first to the Guildhall for a feast and subsequently back to St. Paul's provided the occasion for a show of pageant devices. Theodore Leinwand has described these pageants as "the quintessential instance of self-presentation on the part of those men who ruled and enlivened the City."[40] But small gifts were often thrown to the crowd from pageant floats, and we know that the poets who were hired to produce and oversee the pageants were expected as part of their responsibility to publish pamphlets describing each show. So we can safely assume that the pageant was supposed to legitimate the civic elite in the eyes of a wider viewing and reading public.

The latest extant Elizabethan Lord Mayor's pageant is George Peele's *Descensus Astraeae* (1591).[41] As its name suggests, the pageant was immersed in Elizabethan state iconography, and concerned primarily with reaffirming the city's loyalty to the queen. It embodies perfectly the Elizabethan mutuality of civic pride and royal glory, for the city is celebrated in terms of its special relationship with England's Astraea.[42] Celebration of royal inhabitants was in turn understood to be a conventional trope of the praise of cities, prominently featured, for instance, in Giovanni Botero's internationally read *Treatise Concerning The Causes of the Magnificency and Greatness of Cities* (as the 1606 translation by Robert Peterson calls it). Understood as part of the formal brief of the Lord Mayor's show, the celebration of the city as *camera regis* is not surprisingly prominent in Anthony Munday's *Triumphes of Re-United Brytannia* (1605), the first show performed after James's accession.

The text of Munday's pageant begins with an account of the legend of Brute's conquest of Britain and of the realm's subsequent division; and as in so many examples of Jacobean propaganda, Munday uses the story to set up praise of the Jacobean union and endorse the Jacobean peace:

> And what fierce war by no meanes could effect,
> To re-unite those sundred lands in one,
> The hand of heaven did peacefully elect
> By mildest grace, to seat on Britaines throne
> This second Brute, then whom there else was none.[43]

The text of the pageant goes on to celebrate and enumerate the continuing relationship between English royalty and the Merchant Taylors, the Company to which the new Lord Mayor, Sir Leonard Holliday, belonged.

Here the message of the pageant is reminiscent of the meaning conveyed by the vellum roll presented to James and Henry at the Merchant Taylors' banquet two years earlier. In each case, the Company stresses its close alliance with royalty. But in the context of Munday's pageant the emphasis is placed more on the graciousness of royal condescension than on the elevated status of the Merchant Taylors: "Princes loose no part of dignity, / In beeing affable, it addes to Majesty" (386–87). Munday's pageant closely follows the inherited formula for such an event: it celebrates the city in terms of its relations with the crown, and it emphasizes the reciprocal nature of royal affability and civic pride.

Company records allow us glimpses of the next few pageants, usually by reporting payments for dramatic properties, but the next pageant for which anything like a full text exists is Munday's *Camp-bell, or The Ironmongers Faire Feild*, written for the installation of Sir Thomas Campbell in 1609. The text that does exist for this pageant is apparently fragmentary, but what we have of it displays a suggestive ambivalence about the relative authority of the Lord Mayor and the king. At stake, in the pageant's allegorical apparatus, is the nature of majesty itself: "In a goodly Island styled *Insula Beata*, or the land of Happynes, we suppose that true *Majesty* holdeth her government ... There, in a golden Feild or Garden ... do we erect *Majesties* watch Tower" (1–8); Majesty, as well as her six attendants (Religion, Nobility, Policy, Vigilance, Memory, and Tranquility) are seated on this tower. One recognizes in this the beginning of a fairly conventional allegorical rendering of England as the land of happiness and seat of true majesty, and so when Munday brings forward Saint George and Saint Andrew – patrons of England and Scotland respectively – one expects to find that England's majesty resides in King James, and in the union between the two nations made possible by his accession. In fact, Dekker had planned to use the same two patron saints to welcome King James to London on the occasion of the royal entry in 1604, and Dekker's published account is almost certainly Munday's source here.[44]

Munday uses the two saints as presenters, explaining the device to Campbell, but the first explanation takes the allegory in a peculiar direction:

Honourable Lord, this first devise, had it but a tongue whereby to expresse it selfe, would use this or the like language to you. It derives it [*sic*] owne best conceit from the borrowed Caracter of your name, *Faire Feild*, and your name being *Campbell*, dooth argue and expresse the very same. It is a Feild, wherein, besides the goodly Trees, Fruites, and faire Fountaine that gives it ornament, you may discerne a farre fayrer embellishment. Those seaven royall and unparalled Vertues, that are this lifes best glory, and the futures Crowne, do make it seeme a Feild of heavenly happines. (112–20)

Saint Andrew seems to be suggesting that majesty (and the majestic "Vertues") reside in the Fair Field, which is to say in Camp-bell.

Rather than attributing it to James, as the conjunction of the two
national patron saints seems to predict, Munday's Saint Andrew
locates "true majesty" in the Lord Mayor of London. Moreover, as
Andrew explains, the "seaven royall and unparalled Vertues" in the
Feild serve

> to foretell or prognosticate, seaven gladsome and fayre nourishing yeares of
> comfort, to extenuate or wipe out the remembrance of those seaven sad and
> disconsolate yeares passed. For in their heaven-borne natures, they declare a
> true sense and feeling, of those woes, wants, and calamities, which so long
> time hath lyen heavie upon this Cittie. (122–27)

Munday's meaning here is cryptic; he probably refers to intermittent
eruptions of plague in the seven-year period from 1603 to the end of
1609. Nevertheless, it is suggestive that the "seven sad and disconsolate
yeares" to which Saint Andrew refers coincide with the reign of King
James in England. Given both the apparent attribution of majesty to
the Lord Mayor and the complaint about unspecified problems during
the king's tenure, Andrew's gloss of the pageant device could be taken
as a boldly oppositional statement: London, tired of seven years of
"woes, wants, and calamities" under James's administration, exalts her
own Lord Mayor in the king's place in hopes that the former will be
able to redress grievances caused by royal oversight.

Saint George's speech, which immediately follows Saint Andrew's in
the text, presents a more conventional gloss of the pageant device: "the
tipe or figure of true born *Majestie*, is caractered in this glorious
Monument, presenting a fortunate and happy Island, where awfull
power commaundeth, true Religion with honourable Care and
Councell assisteth, and Loyalty in all Dutye obeyeth" (138–42). Here,
the allegory expresses patriotic royalism at its most orthodox and conventional. Though Saint George does not specifically allude to James –
a suggestive oversight when compared with extant predecessors – it is
clear enough that he is celebrating the English crown. This second
gloss provides a counterbalance to the radical potential of the first,
making *Camp-bell* as a whole an unusually disjointed celebration of
governmental power.

The radical implications of Saint Andrew's gloss may have more to
do with authorial clumsiness than with veiled political intention. We can
say with confidence only that the distribution of praise in Munday's
pageant marks a departure from earlier Lord Mayor's shows. The
specificity of praise given to Campbell and to the "truely Worshipfull
Company of Ironmongers" (152) in Munday's Show, juxtaposed with

the vague, generalized praise of the English crown, points toward an alteration in the formal encomiastic expectations of the event. Rather than celebrating London and the Lord Mayor in terms of their loyalty to the crown, the celebration of Campbell is oddly unrelated to the pageant's residual royalism. In fact, the two panegyrics are presented as alternative and potentially opposed glosses for the same device.

We know that our text of *Camp-bell* is truncated, and that the actual pageant failed to please the Ironmongers.[45] It would be unwise, consequently, to consider the pageant to be broadly indicative of the relationship between the London Corporation and the crown. But the equivocal nature of Munday's pageant is at least suggestive of conflicting generic demands: Munday seems to have felt the need to place the pageant's praise within a national, royalist context while responding simultaneously to a powerful sense of mayoral centrality. The disjunction between praise for Campbell and praise for the crown may reflect the breakdown of Elizabethan reciprocity.

Munday's pageant celebrating Sir William Craven's mayoralty in 1610 is lost, but his *Chruso-thriambos. The Triumphes of Golde*, written for the inauguration of Sir James Pemberton in 1611, survives.[46] In it, Munday consolidates some of the implications of his earlier pageant, while retreating from its more radical possibilities. The pageant is concerned with the authority of the Lord Mayor, and its relation to the authority of the king; the most orthodox statement of the relationship is presented by Time toward the end of the pamphlet:

> Consider likewise, *James* thy gracious King,
> Sets *James* (his subject) heere his Deputy.
> When Majeste doth meaner persons bring
> To represent himselfe in Soveraignty,
> Is't not an high and great authority?
>   Let it be said, for this high favour done:
>   King *James* hath found, a just *James Pemberton*.
>
> (436–42)

The implication here is that the power of the Lord Mayor derives from the "high favour done" by the king in deputizing him: a nod, perhaps, to the loyalty oath sworn by the mayor at his inauguration earlier in the day.[47]

This is hardly the version of mayoral power that the pageant emphasizes throughout, however. The day's first speech is delivered to the new mayor by "*Leofstane* a Gold-Smith, the first Provost that bare authoritie in London" (31–32). Leofstane conducts the mayor to a tomb, beside which is a chariot containing Richard the First and his brother and successor John. The two kings are included because they both contributed to the institution of the mayoralty:

Richard was the first that gave London the dignity of a Lord Maior, reducing it from the rule of Portgreves, Provosts, and Bayliffes, to that more high and honourable Title: yet with this restriction, that the election of the Maior consisted then in the King himselfe, as it did all King *Richards* life time, and so continued til the fifteenth yeare of King John, who then (most graciously) gave the Cittizens of London absolute power, to elect a Lord Mayor amongst themselves. (40–47)

Emphasis on the "absolute power" over the election of mayors given to the "Cittizens of London" by King John belies the formulation of deputized power with which the text describes the "high favour done" for James Pemberton by his royal namesake. In the one formulation, the mayor derives his power from the "absolute" customary right of the electorate, while in the other his power descends to him from above by favor of the absolute power of the king. The two formulations are not literally contradictory, but their emphases are clearly quite different. Though the pageant praises the cooperation of king and mayor, it also stresses the city's autonomous power within the partnership.

The aggressive claim-staking involved in the pageant's assertion of absolute customary right is accompanied by an unstinting celebration of the office of the mayor and of his company, which takes center-stage here for the first time. Indeed, the show rehearses Company history over and over again: in addition to Leofstane's appearance, the history of the mayoralty is traced in a speech by Time (172–227), who repeats the historical material with which the text begins and also names a few legendary Goldsmith mayors: the first Lord Mayor, Henry Fitz-Alwine, was a Goldsmith, as was Nicholas Faringdon, a four-times Lord Mayor whose accomplishments are memorialized in Munday's text; Time wakes Faringdon from his tomb to celebrate the inauguration of a new Goldsmith's mayoralty.

The absence here of the conventional praise of London as the *camera regia* is suggestive, for in those earlier pageants for which a text survives this conventional motif ensured that praise for the monarch framed the praise of the mayor. Instead, *Chruso-thriambos* is the first extant Jacobean Lord Mayor's pageant to do entirely without gestures towards monarchic, patriotic framing: it includes praise for King James only as an addendum whose message, as we have seen, is directly challenged by the bulk of the pageant's encomiastic thrust. It is also worth noting that Munday's praise for Richard and John reverses the Elizabethan panegyric hierarchy: rather than celebrating the mayor for his loyalty to the crown, this pageant celebrates past kings for their contributions to the power of the mayor's office.

The title-page of Munday's *Chruso-thriambos* makes it clear that the text will be an exercise in civic plain style: it is "Devised and written by A. M. Cittizen and Draper of London," "Imprinted by William Jaggard, Printer to the Honourable Citty of London," and sponsored by the "harty love" of the Goldsmiths.[48] The phrase "harty love," in particular, locates the text within a tradition of unpolished, bluff loyalty associated with the native virtue of Thomas Deloney's craftsmen and with the "playne" speech of Stow's Alderman. Moreover, by calling attention to the Goldsmiths' funding, listing only the author's initials, and describing him as a citizen and Company-man, the title-page of Munday's pamphlet reflects the perception that the Lord Mayor's pageant is a communal celebration of civic values.

By way of contrast, the title-page of Thomas Dekker's *Troia-Nova Triumphans*, written for the inauguration of Sir John Swinnerton into the office of Lord Mayor in the following year, describes itself as "The Solemne, Magnificent, and *Memorable Receiving of that worthy Gentleman*, Sir JOHN SWINERTON Knight, into the Citty of LONDON, after his Returne from *taking the Oath of Maioralty at Westminster*."[49] The style of this description is unmistakably more elevated than that of Munday's title-page, both in terms of the language used to describe the event, and of the language used to describe the incoming mayor. In fact, the title-page description echoes the title of Dekker's *Magnificent Entertainment* for the king (1604).

Unlike Munday's pageants, *Troia-Nova Triumphans* also comes equipped with a dedicatory epistle from the author. Dekker is newly concerned to establish the text as his own authorial property and to mark it as his personal gift to Swinnerton. Thus, if Munday's text presents itself as a communally produced expression of the "harty love" offered to a special member of the community, Dekker's is packaged as the gift of a client to a noble patron. This change in the author function represents another elevation in mayoral styling: Dekker's claim to his literary property responds to (and mirrors) the perception that Swinnerton is an individual dignitary rather than merely a representative of the community.

The pamphlet itself insists on the courtly magnificence of the pageant, but distinguishes between civic and courtly costliness:

Tryumphes, are the most choice and daintiest fruit that spring from *Peace* and *Abundance*; *Love* begets them; and *Much Cost* brings them forth ... They are now and then the *Rich* and *Glorious Fires* of *Bounty*, *State* and *Magnificence*, giving light and beauty to the *Courts* of *Kings*: And now and then, it is but a debt payd to *Time* and *Custome*: And out of that debt come *These*. *Ryot* having no hand in laying out the *Expences*, and yet no hand in plucking backe what is held decent to be bestowed: A *sumptuous Thriftinesse* in these *Civil Ceremonies* managing *All*. (1–13)

The paradoxical quality of "sumptuous thriftiness" captures nicely the delicate positioning of the city *vis-à-vis* the court evident through-out Dekker's pageant. On the one hand, Dekker is anxious to dis-tinguish between "Civil ceremonies" and those of the court. In fact, there is probably a surreptitious dig at the less-than-thrifty style of James's court entertainments here. On the other hand, Dekker is equally eager to demonstrate that the Lord Mayor's pageant is a magnificent display of conspicuous consumption in its own right. The emphasis on expenditure as an index of dignity is normally reserved for courtly performances, but Dekker wants to style the Lord Mayor's show in accordance with a courtly model of ceremonial magnificence. Dekker's desire to appropriate courtly style for the city while simul-taneously distinguishing civic style from courtliness gives his text an oxymoronic quality.

An analogous ambivalence characterizes the conception of the Lord Mayor implicit in Dekker's show. On the one hand, *Troia-Nova Triumphans* uses courtly models of royal panegyric to dignify the mayor. In a speech reminiscent of court masques, for example, the pageant's first "triumph" dramatizes the coercive power of the Lord Mayor's name ("*a strange* Spell" [128]) over the god Neptune.[50] Later, Justice advises Swinnerton that, like a king, he is set on stage before "*the quicke Eye / Of this prying world*" (553–54), and must keep his conscience clear. The global scrutiny to which the mayor is to be subjected suggests that his influence will be equally global. On the other hand, Dekker takes pains to insist that unlike a king the Lord Mayor is "*not like a* Pinnacle, *plac'd / Onely to stand aloft*" (242–43), and he introduces an admonitory tone to the proceedings which becomes part of the generic norm for subsequent pageants.[51] In other words, Dekker simultaneously styles the mayor according to courtly panegyric models and strives to distinguish between civic and regal magnificence.

Swinnerton was a Merchant Taylor, and Dekker's pageant makes use once more of the Company's well-worn list of noble and royal members. Fame invites the new mayor to look upon his own name inscribed in "Fames *Voluminous booke*" (365), and warns him not to do anything that might

> *dishonour the high* Merits
> *Of thy* Renown'd Society: Roiall Spirits
> *Of* Princes *holding it a grace to weare*
> That Crimson Badge, *which these about them beare,*
> *Yea, Kings themselves 'mongst you have* Fellowes *bene,*
> *Stil'd by the Name of a* Free-citizen.
>
> (370–75)

A long list follows, making it clear that royal and noble membership remains an important part of the Company's pride. In Dekker's account, however, the Company's relationship with its "Roiall Spirits" is recast: Munday's rehearsal of the same material in his *Triumphes of Re-United Britannia* expresses "what great grace each majesty, / Gave to the Merchant-Taylors Company" (344–45); here the Company's badge gives grace instead to princes. Instead of having renown bestowed upon it by its royal membership, the Company's merit now attracts princes and kings who consider it a "grace" to sport its badge. Royal membership is still a sign of the Company's quality, but the causal relationship between the two has been reversed. It is as if in Dekker's pageant, "Free-citizen" is a title of honor coveted by princes, with the crimson badge as its emblem. Of course, the recasting of the relationship between court and Company is consistent with Dekker's appropriation of courtly magnificence and style for his civic pageant. It attributes courtly merit to the city while carefully retaining the sense that the two are separate: "Free-citizen" becomes both a specifically civic style and a princely honorific.

Thomas Middleton's *The Triumphs of Truth*, written to celebrate the mayoralty of the poet's namesake Sir Thomas Middleton in 1613, resembles Dekker's pageant of a year earlier in its appropriation of courtly styles of grandeur. The title page to the published account of Middleton's pageant provides the most inflationary description of a pageant to date: the pageant is touted as "A Solemnity unparalleld for Cost, Art, and Magnificence."[52] By the same token, the pageant text itself begins with a ringing boast about the "unparalleld" stateliness of the mayor's show:

SEARCH all chronicles, histories, records, in what language or letter soever; let the inquisitive man waste the dear treasures of his time and eyesight, he shall conclude his life only in this certainty, that there is no subject upon earth received into the place of his government with the like state and magnificence as is the Lord Mayor of the city of London. (233)

The word "subject" excepts kings from comparison, but this subtle disclaimer is easy enough to lose amidst the rhetorical flourishes lavished upon the mayor. The pride in costly magnificence manifested here (and later in the same introduction, when Middleton attributes the pageant's magnificence to the "generous and noble freeness of cost and liberality" [233]) indicates that Middleton relies on the model of courtly spectacle first appropriated for the Jacobean Lord Mayor's show by Dekker a year earlier.[53] Middleton's boastfulness is justified: the £1,300 spent to produce the pageant makes it the most costly Lord Mayor's show of the English Renaissance.[54]

Another indication of the courtly style of Middleton's pageant is its repeated borrowing from royal entertainments: the dramatization of the five senses in Paul's Churchyard echoes a similar presentation within the arch at Soper Lane for the king's entry in 1604;[55] Time and Truth are paired in Middleton's pageant, as they were in Elizabeth's coronation pageant years earlier. Middleton imagines London as a city on a hill, screened by mists of Error which are dispelled by Truth at the arrival of the mayor: as Glynne Wickham has pointed out, this is adapted from Jonson's *Hymenaei* (1606).[56] In an apparent visual quotation from the *Masque of Blackness* and the *Masque of Beauty*, a ship containing the king and queen of the Moors sails towards the mayor bearing the legend "*Veritate gubernor*, – I am steered by Truth" (247). The mayor elect may not be able to "blanch an Ethiop," as the king does in the first of Jonson's masques, but it turns out that the missionary efforts of London merchants have converted the Moors with analogous results: "However darkness dwells upon my face, / Truth in my soul sets up the light of grace" (248).[57] As a ritual of legitimation, *The Triumphs of Truth* demonstrates a regal style of mayoral dignity that hardly resembles the humility and royalism of Munday's *Triumphs of Re-United Britannia.*

As the costliest pageant of its kind, Middleton's *The Triumphs of Truth* is hardly representative. Subsequent pageants are often considerably cheaper and less sophisticated in their conceits.[58] But however exceptional in the history of such shows, the equation of conspicuous expense with grandeur in Middleton's show points toward a courtly version of civic pride which would probably not have been thinkable a decade earlier. More broadly, given the gaps in the historical record, I think it best to see the developments suggested by these pageants not as points on a graph leading to increased opposition between the city and the court, but as successive reformulations of civic pride occasioned by James's withdrawal from the center of London's political consciousness.

Wickham has described the relationship between the Jacobean Lord Mayor's pageant and Jacobean court culture as one of rivalry and mounting tension, explaining that "in the underlying basis of flattery and inflated self-esteem, in the extravagance of the expenditure, and in the spectacular quality of both types of entertainment, there is a similarity so remarkable as to be more than coincidence."[59] Though responding to the same developments, I would argue that the self-importance manifested in these early Jacobean pageants is the result of a relationship between court and city more complicated than simple rivalry. For since London's wealthy elite were frequently dependent upon privileges and concessions bestowed by the crown, it would be extraordinary if Lord Mayors and their peers saw themselves as its enemies.

Rather than being symptomatic of a growing rivalry between the city and the court, the magnificence and autonomy celebrated in individual pageants reflects a necessary renegotiation of civic self-fashioning occasioned by the breakdown of affective reciprocity between subject and king. First, the growing autonomy of civic self-fashioning in these pageants is the result not only of James's failure to woo the city, but of his failure to make room for such civic pride within the conception of the state implied by his writings and actions. In contrast to the Elizabethan style, as we have seen, James's supervisory style defines loyalty as obedience to orthodoxy handed down from above. Consequently, self-glorification and loyalty are subtly at odds in that the one involves staking a claim and the other involves passive subjection. Since the Lord Mayor's show continued to be the quintessential expression of an aggressive strain of civic pride, it became necessary to diminish its traditional emphasis on London's loyalty, and to shift its focus gradually to London's own history without recourse to royalist framing.

Second, within the structure of Elizabethan performance, civic pride takes the form "I may not have gentlemanly pedigree or postures, but I am as loyal and as useful to the state as a gentleman nonetheless." The prideful citizen is defined in binary opposition to the gentleman, and his personal style, accordingly, is resolutely plain and anti-courtly. This conservative expression of citizen pride depends for ratification on the gracious condescension of the monarch, and James's dictatorial public style offered no such gesture. In sophisticated pageants like *Troia-Nova Triumphans* and *The Triumphs of Truth*, socially conservative civic plainness is replaced by a magnificence modelled on courtly entertainments. This shift in emphasis is made possible by James's departure from Elizabethan performance, for by interrupting the reciprocal relationship between royal condescension and plain-style civic virtue, James left civic pride without a stylistic mandate. In order to fill the void, the fashioners of the civic pageants are able to turn toward courtly styles, appropriating them because they are the privileged celebratory modes of the day. The similarity to which Wickham responds, in other words, is the result not necessarily of rivalry, but rather of the breakdown of the structure of reciprocity which in turn maintained the differences between courtly and civic styles.

CIVIC PRIDE AND SOCIAL TENSION

In 1937, L. C. Knights attempted to relate the drama of Jonson, Shakespeare, and their contemporaries to the economic tensions of early capitalism.[60] Knights's book has become a classic, and numerous scholars have followed his lead, finding in the early Jacobean efflorescence of satiric, urban comedy symptoms of the emergence of a new economic formation and foreshadowings of revolution.[61] In its ongoing elaboration, this materialist account has proved useful, but its Olympian perspective has generally led critics away from tracing more localized interactions between satiric comedy and its social surroundings. Critics concerned primarily with situating literary texts against this spacious backdrop of social change are unlikely to ask why a particular set of texts is produced at any more specific moment. Thus, although the plays generally regarded as "city comedies" were for the most part products of early Jacobean London, critics have had relatively little to say about their relation to or emergence out of this specific urban milieu.[62]

The early Jacobean renegotiation of civic pride with which we have been concerned provides an important context for the simultaneous popularity of the satiric comedy with which these critics are concerned. For these comedies cumulatively reflect, stage, transmute, parody, and reinforce the attitudes and discourses provoked by this process of renegotiation. More specifically, changes in the style of civic pride contributed to status tension in early Jacobean London, while early Jacobean popular forms betray an almost obsessive interest in staging and restaging such conflicts.

We have seen – specifically in the debate in the Merchant Taylors' court and more generally in the courtliness and autonomy of civic self-fashioning – the potential for status conflict between the London elite and the elite of blood in London's West End and towards Westminster. Ironically, even as it signalled a reallocation of status that pressured the distinction between merchant and gentleman, the elevation in civic style also seems to have been the cause of tensions between the Lord Mayor and aldermen on the one hand, and the mass of less dignified Londoners on the other. George Unwin has described the consolidation of power by London's government, adding that the power of the Lord Mayor's office in particular reached a peak during the reign of James I, "when the Lord Mayor put forward the claim that he was master of all the Companies."[63] This is an indication of the increasing dignity of the Lord Mayor, but it is also an indication of his appropriation of James's style, for it echoes the absolutist style of the king's own claims.

It is easy to see how the appropriation of this style might lead to conflicts between the high-ranking civic dignitaries and, for example, the less influential members of London Livery Companies. Richard Johnson's jestbook *The Pleasant Conceits of Old Hobson* (1607) concretizes this intra-urban conflict: recalling the sentiment once lavished on Stow's "playne" alderman, Johnson's book celebrates Hobson as a "homely plaine man" clad in "ancient fashion."[64] Hobson, however, pokes fun not at courtiers, but at the gentlemanly affectations of city dignitaries. In one anecdote, Hobson arrests a kinsman of the Lord Mayor for debt and then sneers at the verbosity of the mayor's officer who comes to relieve the prisoner: cutting him off, Hobson announces "what thou saydst in the beginning I doe not like of: and what was in the middle, I doe not well remember, and for thy conclusion, I understand it not" (sig. F1ᵛ). If Johnson's book is any indication, the increased dignity of the civic governors made them seem symbolic not of plain-spoken London virtue but rather of puffed-up courtly self-styling.

That such conflicts are dramatized in the period's satiric urban comedies hardly needs to be argued, especially in light of Leinwand's *The City Staged*, which argues specifically that urban comedies dealing with status rivalries between merchant-citizens and gentry flourished during the first decade of James's reign. It is important to remember, however, that while these plays take part in London's heightened concern with status-group rivalries, they cumulatively take a variety of representational approaches to tensions between the civic elite and other groups. For example, though class conflicts between wealthy London drapers and gentlemen are staged in Part One of *The Honest Whore* (1604), *Michaelmas Term* (1604–06), and *Greene's Tu Quoque* (1611), they are thematized quite differently in each case.

The sub-plot of Middleton and Dekker's *The Honest Whore* centers on Candido, a wealthy linen draper famed in his native Milan as "the mirror of patience."[65] Candido is a fine specimen of a citizen: he refuses to drink or cheat, he insists that the customer is always right – even when a young gallant asks for a pennyworth of lawn cut from the center of the cloth – and he is a member of an aldermanic court where

> grave men meet each cause to understand,
> Whose consciences are not cut out in brybes,
> To gull the poore mans right: but in even scales,
> Peize rich and poore, without corruptions veyles.
> (3.1.165–68)

Candido's patience is tested throughout the play, first by a trio of gallants who try for sport to enrage him, and then by his own wife, whose attempts to break his patience lead him into public ridicule, physical abuse, and finally get him committed to "Bethlem monastery."[66] By way of contrast, the play's nobles inhabit a world of stereotypical Italianate intrigue; the duke in particular is portrayed as an unscrupulous Machiavel. In the end, the duke is made to see the error of his ways, and the play cements its ethical conclusions by staging his exemplary exchange with the newly released Candido. First, Candido explains his position in a way that explicitly compares his plain virtue favorably to the duke's behavior, arguing that "stock of *Patience* then cannot be poore, / All it desires it has; what Monarch more" (5.2.495–96)? Then, recognizing the citizen's wisdom, the duke invites him to court: "Come therefore you shall teach our court to shine" (5.2.514). Thus, although the play pokes gentle fun at its bourgeois hero, the final implication is that the draper's honest, aldermanic virtue is in fact the mirror of true nobility. There is a kind of nostalgia in the celebration of plain civic virtue as an alternative to courtly corruption.

Middleton's *Michaelmas Term* also juxtaposes the wealthy draper Quomodo with traditional gentility, but in this play the citizen is villainous, a representative of a range of urban depredations. Covetous of the land owned by the nobility and gentry, Quomodo cozens the Essex landowner Easy. His motivation, throughout, is twofold. On the

one hand, he wants to gentrify himself, to be "divulg'd a landed man /
Throughout the livery."[67] On the other hand, he is driven by what is
portrayed as a Londoner's basic hatred of the gentry:

> There are means and ways enow to hook in gentry,
> Besides our deadly enmity, which thus stands,
> They're busy 'bout our wives, we 'bout their lands.
>   (1.1.110–12)

This enmity, in Quomodo's formulation, is fueled by economic rivalry
within the London marketplace, for within the representational logic
of city comedy both wives and lands are exchangeable commodities.[68]

Michaelmas Term ends conservatively, with the punishment of
Quomodo and the rest of the play's upwardly mobile citizens. In fact,
the legal examination of Quomodo in the play's final act reduces him
to an almost allegorical figure for urban corruption, a character
defined exclusively by his function as "cozener":

> JUDGE: Now, what are you?
> QUOMODO: I'm Quomodo, my lord . . .
> JUDGE: How are we sure you're he?
> QUOMODO: O, you cannot miss, my lord!
> JUDGE: I'll try you:
> Are you the man that liv'd the famous cozener?
> QUOMODO: O no, my lord!
> JUDGE: Did you deceive this gentleman of his right,
> And laid nets o'er his land?
> QUOMODO: Not I, my lord.
> JUDGE: Then you're not Quomodo, but a counterfeit. –
> Lay hands on him, and bear him to the whip.
> QUOMODO: Stay, stay a little,
> I pray. – Now I remember me, my lord,
> I cozen'd him indeed; 'tis wondrous true.
> JUDGE: Then I dare swear this is no counterfeit:
> Let all doubts cease; this man is Quomodo.
>   (5.3.16–32)

"Quomodo," of course, means "how," and here the Judge provides
him with a juridical identity in keeping with his name. Rather than a
character understood to possess internal motivations and desires, the
Judge defines him by his actions, describing him in effect as a cozening
machine. This depiction of the wealthy London businessman – as
deceitful by definition – subtends a vision of the city as a dangerous
place, a place in which the marketplace of cash, women, and land
threatens the matrix of social hierarchies, and a place populated by

grasping, greedy citizens. The conservative judgment that gives
Michaelmas Term its closure reverses the sentimental conclusion of *The
Honest Whore*, in which Candido's civic steadiness is seen as a cure for
courtly corruption.[69]

Joshua Cooke's *Greene's Tu Quoque* investigates the status of still
another upwardly mobile draper, Sir Lionel Rash. Rash has purchased
a knighthood, and seeks to leave his trade behind:

> the sword of Knighthood sticks stil upon my shoulders, and I feele the blow in
> my purse, it has cut two leather bagges asunder; but all's one, honour must be
> purchac'd: I will give over my Citty coate, and betake my selfe to the Court
> jacket.[70]

Sir Lionel gives his shop to his apprentice Spendall, declaring that he
will move to the Strand, and adding "To day Ile go dine with my Lord
Maior: to morrow with the Sherifes, and next day with the Aldermen.
I will spread the Ensigne of my knighthood over the face of the Citty"
(147–49). The draper's rash yearning for gentrification is gently
mocked later in the play when he insists that his two daughters marry
Bubble and Scattergood – a couple of broadly drawn new-money
buffoons with comically inappropriate affectations of gentility.

Spendall of course proves profligate, mixing a decidedly civic
ambition to "bee Lord Maior of London before I die, and have three
Pageants carried before me, besides a Shippe and an Unicorne"
(372–73) with the behavior of a young gallant. The slightly oxymoronic
quality of his character is emphasized when he engages in a duel with
Staines, a gentleman by birth who has lost his fortune. When Staines
expresses his desire to challenge Spendall provided he is a gentleman
the latter answers that he is "a Citizen" but nevertheless promises to
duel "as fairely / As the best Gentleman that weares a sword"
(1,136–68). The two fight to a standstill, which prompts Staines to
declare, "Thou art the highest spirited Cittizen, / That ever Guild-hall
tooke notice of" (1,347–48). Like Rash, Spendall is both civic and
courtly, and while Cooke's play uses Sir Lionel and Spendall to satirize
the gentrification of civic pride, it also clearly approves of Spendall's
ambitious spiritedness.

The figures of Rash and Spendall are set against a London in which
fortunes, and titular gentility, change hands routinely. At the start of
the play, Bubble is a wealthy gentleman and Staines – gentle of blood
but penniless – is forced to be his man-servant. The prehistory of this
arrangement is that though Bubble used to serve Staines, the latter lost

his fortune to Bubble's father (a usurer), who in turn left the stolen fortune to his son. By the end of the play, Staines dupes Bubble, regains his fortune, and hires his erstwhile master to be his man once again. Despite its central interest in the fluidity of wealth and rank ("honour must be purchac'd"), and its staging of characters who violate social categories, *Greene's Tu Quoque* is a sentimental comedy in which there are no real villains. Rash is neither a monster like Quomodo nor a paragon like Candido. Instead – as a knighted draper – Rash exemplifies a social turmoil which is reflected all around him, played for its comic potential, and gently satirized by the play.

Each of these plays uses a wealthy draper to caricature the liveried elite, and each pivots around the contested relationship between civic status and courtly status. It is easy enough, then, to see how all of these plays, despite the variety of their representations of civic ambition and pride, take part in and arise in response to the same process of social renegotiation. The spectrum of attitudes towards the problem of civic and courtly status represented by these plays, however, should make it clear that early Jacobean comedy – despite returning to the same stock characters, situations, and themes time and time again – represents a cacophony of responses to the redefinitions of status that we have been looking at.

Moreover, Middleton's *Michaelmas Term* is the only one of these plays generally described as a "city comedy"; since the plays evidently share similar thematic concerns, it is important to recognize that these different kinds of civic comedy are all part of early Jacobean London's working out of social conflicts. This, in turn, corroborates Douglas Bruster's contention that adherence to categories of subgenre within civic comedy has contributed to oversimplified notions of the relationship between the city and the theatre. Bruster's recommendation – that instead of "grouping plays together by surface forms" we look for deeper thematic concerns – is based on the observation that the sheer variety of kinds of early modern English drama arises in response to and within the polyvocality and fluidity of exchange characteristic of London itself.[71]

Due to the renegotiation of the relationship between the civic elite and the court, and to the changing relationship between this elite and its constituencies, London's social order during the formative years of Jacobean England was perceived to be unusually volatile. The self-fashioning of the civic elite is only one part of a larger, ongoing process of fashioning social relations, a process in which a wide range of civic dramas and printed material participated. It should be remembered too that James added to this volatility by creating an extraordinary number of new knights during the first two years of his reign. By diluting the pool of knights, and by strengthening the link between money and rank, this inflation of honors reinforced the stylistic gentrification of civic pride which we have seen.[72]

Still, relations between London's civic elite and the alternative centers of authority represented by the king, his Privy Council, and his court during this first decade were generally cordial. Robert Ashton has written, of the first decade of James's reign, "on the whole there is little to suggest that during these years the Elizabethan *mariage de convenance* between the government and metropolitan big business was very seriously threatened."[73] Generally speaking, the two groups needed each other. The crown relied on the financial resources of London's elite, while London's merchants in turn relied on privileges and concessions from the crown. The revisionary process to which I have alluded, then, cannot be considered oppositional. Instead, this process of revision prepared the way for more overt conflict later by eroding the traditional loyalty of London's citizens, increasing the polarization of crown and city interests, and developing the oppositional potential always implicit in London's pride.

If Jonson's *Christmas His Masque* is any indication, tensions between the crown and the city were in fact more overt by the end of 1616. By then, the king's endorsement of William Cockayne's ill-fated project to monopolize the dyeing and export of English cloths had put an end to the early Jacobean period of mercantile expansion, and the city had begun to balk at the king's demands for loans.[74] In *Christmas His Masque*, Jonson stages an entertainment brought before the king from "out o'the Citie" (H&S VII: 18) where, as Gregory Christmas its maker admits, "it was intended ... for Curryers Hall" (21). The actors reveal themselves to be both incompetent and mercenary; Cupid – who is said to represent the "Love o' the cittie" for her king – forgets his lines (193)![75]

That Jonson stages the silence of the "Love o' the cittie" before the king suggests that by 1616 the failure of the city's loyalty was recognized in court. As we have seen, however, the actual love for the king, as expressed in London's pageants, had fallen silent some years earlier. There is, in other words, a hiatus between the development of a more autonomous civic identity and the emergence of recognizable financial and political manifestations of the attitudes that go with it. During the early, prosperous years of James's reign, social relations were re-negotiated, and this renegotiation in turn helped to give shape to the gradual dissolution of monarchic authority during the early Stuart period. As always, it is by means of such historically localized appropriations, renegotiations, and exclusions that more global historical trends take place.

Warrant and obedience in Bartholomew Fair

In an essay that still ranks among the most insightful readings of *Bartholomew Fair* (1614), the critic Ray Heffner Jr. described the play's central theme as "the problem of what 'warrant' men have or pretend to have for their actions."[1] Though for Heffner this question is primarily an ethical and epistemological one, Jonson's play insists on the material and political implications of the question as well.[2] In fact, *Bartholomew Fair* takes as its central and recurring problem the relationship between a subject's actions and the structures of authority putatively governing them.

The first published edition of *Bartholomew Fair* (1631) suggests strongly that royal authority be considered part of the play's investigation of warrant. It includes the prologue and epilogue from the play's court performance, and the title page heralds "A COMEDIE, ACTED IN THE YEARE, 1614 ... And then dedicated to King JAMES, of *most Blessed Memorie*; By The Author, BENJAMIN JOHNSON."[3] One cannot be sure, on the basis of this, when Jonson dedicated the play to James, or even if the dedication was made after James's death in 1625. Nevertheless, that *Bartholomew Fair* is the only one of Jonson's stage plays to be so dedicated suggests that he considered the play to have a special relevance to the king. One imagines that this dedication was intended to reinforce the panegyric tone of the court performance. The dedication may also suggest that the play's satire of Puritan hypocrisy was prompted by royal request, since John Aubrey's sketch of Jonson notes that "King James made him write against the Puritans, who began to be troublesome in his time."[4]

Jonson's treatment of "warrant" and action, however, raises questions about the limits of authority and its imposition. And insofar as these apply to the king, the play must be seen as both flattering and admonitory to its royal dedicatee.[5] These questions have been at the core of the case-studies in this book: How does governmental authority interact with the individual agendas of subjects? What are its limits? What happens to authority when it enters circulation? What constitutes obedience? And since *Bartholomew Fair* caps for Jonson a decade of uniquely successful involvement with the articulations of Jacobean authority, it is worth ending the present study by attending to the way the play theorizes these important questions of state.

The immediate authority figure presiding over Jonson's fair is Justice Adam Overdo, a somewhat smug magistrate determined to spy out the fair's many abuses. Though the nature of the relationship has been the subject of some debate, Jonson's play repeatedly establishes parallels between the Justice and King James: Overdo's harangue against tobacco – which echoes James's own *Counterblaste to Tobacco* (1604) – his fondness for the proverbial wisdom of government, his overstated confidence in his own powers of judgment, and his propensity to make ostentatious display of his classical learning.[6] Furthermore, Overdo's final dinner invitation to the assembled fairgoers ("my intents are *Ad correctionem, non ad destructionem; Ad aedificandum, non ad diruendum*: so lead on"[7]) echoes a speech given by James to the assembled Houses of Parliament in March 1610: "[the head] may apply sharpe cures, or cut off corrupt members, let blood in what proportion it thinkes fit, and as the body may spare, but yet is all this power ordeined by God *Ad aedificationem, non ad destructionem*."[8] This parallel calls attention to a distinction between the humbled Overdo (who allows others to lead him), and the king (who insists on his own sharp power to lead), but the echo contributes nonetheless to the general impression given by the play that royal authority is somehow at stake in the failure of Overdo's supervision.

In addition to specific echoes of James's public voice, the prologue and epilogue added to the play for its court performance delicately emphasize parallels between Overdo and James. When he writes "Your Majesty is welcome to a Fayre" (Prologue, 1), Jonson casts James as an outside authority visiting the fair, which is of course Overdo's role within the frame of the play. More explicitly, the end of the play as it was performed at court juxtaposes Overdo's failure as a judge of the fair's enormities with an invitation to the king to judge the play: "*Your* Majesty *hath seene the* Play, *and you / can best allow it from your eare, and view*" (Epilogue, 1–2). This can be read as flattery ("James will succeed where Overdo fails"), but it can also be read as an admonition ("if James condemns my play, he is as bad as Overdo"). Either way, the association between the two figures is reinforced.

Leah Marcus, in an effort to distinguish between Overdo's errors and the judgment of James, has suggested that Overdo represents the authority of the law, and that the politics of the play hinge on conflicts between law and royal prerogative. According to this reading, the humbling of Overdo and the epilogue's invitation to James to judge the play add up to an endorsement of James's final authority over the law.[9] This interpretation, it seems to me, relies on an exaggerated account of the antagonism between the king and his judges, overemphasizing conflicts over prerogative and ignoring the king's broader alliance with the courts. For judges – who were after all the crown's employees – generally saw their function as an extension of royal authority, and tended in general to support royal interests.[10] Within the play, Adam Overdo describes his judicial authority as part of the larger project of royal government, swearing to act "in Justice name, and the Kings; and for the common-wealth" (2.1.1–2). His failures of judgment are manifested not in his opposition to royal authority, as Marcus's paradigm might imply, but rather in the vanity of his belief in his own royally sanctioned powers of judgment. Overdo's legal authority seems in fact to rely on James's absolutist style, and to present itself as an extension of the king's special powers of supervision.

To complicate matters, Overdo also aligns himself repeatedly with the authority of Sir Thomas Middleton, the man who became Lord Mayor of London in 1613.[11] Overdo is referring to Middleton, for example, when discussing the wisdom of disguise:

Never shall I enough commend a worthy worshipfull man, sometime a capitall member of this City, for his high wisdome, in this point, who would take you, now the habit of a Porter; now of a Carman; now of the Dog-killer ... and what would hee do in all these shapes? mary, goe you into every Alehouse, and down into every Celler; measure the length of puddings, take the gage of blacke pots, and cannes, I, and custards with a sticke ... Would all men in authority would follow this worthy president! For (alas) as we are publike persons, what doe we know? (2.1.12–28)

Middleton himself reported to the Lord Chamberlain, in a letter of July 8, 1614, that he had used disguises to detect the enormities perpetrated by brewers and bakers in London.[12]

Later, in a final surge of vanity, Overdo exclaims

looke upon mee, O *London*! and see mee, O *Smithfield*; The *example of Justice* and *Mirror of Magistrates*: the true top of formality, and scourge of enormity. (5.6.33–36)

This, as David McPherson has shown, alludes to Richard Johnson's pamphlet of 1613 entitled *Looke on me London: I am an Honest English-man*, *ripping up the Bowels of Mischiefe, lurking in thy Sub-urbs and Precincts*. As its name suggests, the pamphlet is a "small discovery of abuses" perpetrated in gambling houses and the like.[13] More to the point, the pamphlet is dedicated to Middleton, whom it praises as an exemplary reformer of civic abuses. McPherson also notes that a significant portion of *Looke on me London* is plagiarized from an older pamphlet, George Whetstone's *A Mirour for Magestrates of Cyties* (1584), and argues that Jonson was reminded of the older pamphlet by the newer. Consequently, Overdo's reference to the "Mirror of Magistrates" can be seen as an allusion to Whetstone rather than to the well-known collection of cautionary tales for rulers.[14]

Jonson himself seems to have anticipated this kind of argument. His induction for performance at the Hope theatre criticizes anyone offering "to affirme (on his owne *inspired ignorance*) what *Mirror of Magistrates* is meant by the *Justice*" (142–43). Indeed, it would be a diminution of the play's considerable richness to reduce Overdo to a mirror of any one kind of magistrate, for he is given to us as an amalgamation of judicial, royal, and mayoral models of authority. And this hotchpotch accurately reflects the multiplicity of authorities governing the actual Bartholomew Fair: the court of Pyepowders heard commercial disputes arising during the time of the Fair, the Corporation of London oversaw the government of the Fair and profited from its fees and tolls, and James (in a proclamation prompted by the outbreak of plague in 1603) declared the Bartholomew Fair and other fairs illegal "till they shall be licensed by Us."[15]

By associating judicial, mayoral, and royal modes of authority with Overdo, *Bartholomew Fair* points toward a shared Jacobean rhetoric of authority and supervision.[16] Overdo's vanity leads him to appropriate for himself the king's supposedly unique powers of insight and judgment, as if justice (and mayor[17]) necessarily took their cues from above. And the play is everywhere concerned to show that the appropriation by lesser authorities of the royal style of supervisory absolutism implies a challenge to it.[18]

This point is comically underscored, for instance, by the watchman Bristle, who offers an extraordinarily narrow definition of obedience as he patrols fairgrounds:

> TROUBLE-ALL. My Masters, I doe make no doubt, but you are officers.
> BRISTLE. What then, Sir?
> TROUBLE-ALL. And the Kings loving, and obedient subjects.

BRISTLE. Obedient, friend? take heede what you speake, I
advise you: *Oliver Bristle* advises you. His loving
subjects, we grant you: but not his obedient, at this
time, by your leave, wee know our selves, a little better
then so, wee are to command, S^r. and such as you are to
be obedient. Here's one of his obedient subjects, going
to the stocks, and wee'll make you such another, if you talke.
(4.1.1–10)

Though he and his fellow watchman Haggis profess themselves to be
loving subjects, Bristle says he is not obedient because he is not actively
being subjugated by royal commands. Instead they "are to command,"
as if the two were mutually exclusive. The joke here is that Bristle
imagines even his minute authority to be absolute: command is
imagined to be total, the antithesis of obedience.

Bristle's bristly response makes another important point about
authority in *Bartholomew Fair* as well: alienated authority is implicitly
disobedient to its source. This serves within the play as a commentary
on Overdo's vain authoritarianism, which leads him – as a representative of the king – to claim for himself the Solomonic powers of insight
and judgment which in theory should accompany only the king's
absolute power. Overdo's authority, in other words, is given as a kind
of alienated, and hence disobedient, absolute power.

As if to underscore the paradoxical nature of this authority,
Bartholomew Fair surrounds Overdo with a series of examples of the
material circulation of warrants, licenses, and patents, demonstrating
again and again that when governmental authority is alienated it is
vulnerable to a variety of abuses.[19] The marriage license stolen from
Wasp by Edgworth, for example, represents a legal authority at once
commodified and reified ("you must have a *Marke* for your thing here"
[1.4.22–23], says Wasp), and consequently both vendible and subject
to theft. After the license has been stolen, it proves easy to alter its
function: "I have a *License* and all, it is but razing out one name, and
putting in another" (5.2.82–83). Elsewhere in the play we see
Knockem's forged warrants, as well as the blank, signed warrant given
by Overdo to a man he thinks is Trouble-all but who is really Quarlous
in disguise.

The play's interest in such documents is part of its larger exploration
of functional authority, and the implication of all these anecdotes
within the play seems to be that alienated authority functions beyond
official control: it enters circulation, and consequently must be subject

to appropriations and contingencies beyond the reach of any authoritative intent. This is true in *Bartholomew Fair* of reified authority – warrants, licenses, and so on – and also of the delegated authority vested in Overdo and Bristle who cannot, strictly speaking, be both absolutist and obedient.

If Overdo represents a Jacobean style of supervision, his perfect foil is the madman Trouble-all. Trouble-all, we learn, was formerly an officer in the court of Pyepowder until being relieved of his duties by Justice Overdo. His madness is a response to Overdo's power:

hee will doe nothing, but by Justice *Overdoo's* warrant, he will not eate a crust, nor drinke a little, nor make him in his apparell, ready. His wife ... cannot get him make his water, or shift his shirt, without his warrant. (4.1.58–62)

For Heffner, Trouble-all's obsessive concern with authorization serves as a central thematic unifying device for the play, because it represents "the widespread and not unnatural human craving for clearly defined authority."[20] Recent interest in the representation of political authority has led critics to politicize and reverse Heffner's basic observation, seeing in Trouble-all's madness not a human need for authority but rather authority's fantasy of total obedience from its subjects. Thus, Marcus argues that Trouble-all "represents human nature as it would have to be in order for the justice's ideology to function as he wishes."[21] As Jonathan Goldberg's *James I and the Politics of Literature* makes abundantly clear, Trouble-all also represents the kind of obedient subject imagined in King James's absolutist rhetoric. In fact, Goldberg seems to describe some of James's actual subjects as Trouble-alls: Donne, for example, is described by Goldberg as being "named by another and given identity – and robbed of self-determination at once; this is like the condition Donne imagines for himself in the letters, totally submissive so that he may gain a place in the world."[22] But where for Goldberg this submissiveness describes a real response to James's discursive power, for Jonson it is rather a parody of the kind of impossibly docile subject posited by an absolutist rhetoric of supervision. Trouble-all is a walking reminder that such a subject would in fact be no more than a hollow shell of a man.

By staging Trouble-all's obsessive obedience as grotesque parody, *Bartholomew Fair* reminds us of the failure of authority to elicit total obedience from even loving subjects. Seeing a character who will not respond to bodily needs or selfish desires without warrant underscores precisely the degree to which needs and desires normally escape control. We should be reminded here also of Bristle who, by distinguishing so sharply between the fully obedient and the fully authoritative, suggests that even the performance of a delegated duty can be driven by selfishness: that this is the case with Bristle himself is suggested by his proud iteration of his own name ("I advise you; *Oliver Bristle* advises you"). If Trouble-all's total obedience is grotesque, the alternative is a kind of unavoidably disobedient self-interest.

Trouble-all's obedience is refigured towards the end of the play in a troupe of puppets under the direction of Lanthorn Leatherhead. Leatherhead describes these puppets as a "well govern'd" company (5.3.103), which is hardly surprising since, as he proudly puts it, "I am the mouth of 'hem all" (5.3.78–79). In the play's penultimate scene, one of the puppets engages in a debate with the self-congratulatory Puritan zealot Busy, who has attacked the puppets with stock arguments from the anti-theatrical tradition. Quarlous comments on the appropriateness of this pairing, noting that there is "no fitter match, then a *Puppet* to commit with an Hypocrite" (5.5.50–51).[23] Indeed, there is a certain symmetry to the pairing of puppet and hypocrite at the end of the play, since the figures represent the two kinds of obedience figured in *Bartholomew Fair*: the dehumanizing total obedience of a puppet (or a madman), and the selfishly motivated façade of adherence to authoritarian principles which characterizes Busy, Wasp, and Overdo.[24]

The play's interest in the alienation and circulation of authority implies as well an exploration of the limits of authoritative judgment. Throughout the play, Overdo considers himself authorized to see through subterfuge, but his overconfidence makes him instead uniquely vulnerable to it. Typically, Jonson uses the judgment of literature as a central figure for the difficulty of objective understanding, theorizing in the process literature's complex relationship to authority. The signal example of Overdo's blindness in the play, for example, casts him specifically as a misreader of the balladeer Nightingale's song warning about the danger of pickpockets. Overdo, taking the meaning of the poem at face value, remarks that the song "doth discover enormitie," and adds that he "ha' not lik'd a paltry piece of poetry, so well, a good while" (3.5.112–13). In fact, the song is performed only in order to draw a crowd in which Edgworth can steal Cokes's purse.

What Overdo cannot see is that the poem's use determines its meaning (rather than vice versa), and that as used by Nightingale it is itself a dangerous "enormity." His misreading is a kind of formalist fallacy, the belief that literary meaning can be detached from social context. To add injury to insult, the disguised Overdo is himself accused of the theft, and is put in the stocks for his troubles. This anecdote within the play aligns literature with the licenses and warrants circulating through the fair, since the functional variability of each is shown to escape any authoritative imposition of meaning from above.

Overdo's inability to interpret Nightingale's ballad is both a symptom and a symbol of his failure as a governor. Throughout the play, Overdo's blindness to the social functions of literature is always associated with his overblown belief in objective knowledge and absolute authority. We learn, for instance, that because Overdo cannot see any use for literary representation beyond idle escapism, he draws a sharp distinction between those fit for state service and those stricken with the disease of poetry:

> my *Project* is how to fetch off this proper young man, from his debaucht company: I have followed him all the *Fayre* over, and still I finde him with this songster: And I begin shrewdly to suspect their familiarity; and the young man of a terrible taint, *Poetry*! with which idle disease, if he be infected, there's no hope of him, in a state-course. *Actum est*, of him for a common-wealths-man: if hee goe to't in *Rime* once. (3.5.2–9)

This despite the fact that numerous Tudor and Stuart writers – Jonson prominent among them – used poetry as an avenue into a variety of careers at court! Since Overdo's idea of "a state-course" is predicated on his notions of objective and authoritative supervision, he imagines no government use for the rhetorically skilled.

The Epilogue to the play's court performance tacitly associates James with Overdo's arrogant blindness, praising him for his "power to judge" the play:

> Your Majesty hath seene the Play, and you
>   can best allow it from you eare, and view.
> You know the scope of Writers, and what store
>   of leave is given them, if they take not more,
> And turne it into licence: you can tell
>   if we have us'd that leave you gave us, well:
> Or whether wee to rage, or licence breake,
>   or be prophane, or make prophane men speake?
> This is your power to judge (great Sir) and not
>   the envy of a few. Which if wee have got,
> Wee value lesse what their dislike can bring,
>   if it so happy be, t' have pleas'd the King.

Though insisting on James's authority to judge in Overdo's place, the repeated insistence on "licence" is a troubling pun after a play in which a stolen and altered license has played a major role. As Richard Burt points out, the Epilogue refers to the fact that the play has already been licensed by the Revels Office ("that leave you gave us"), and implies consequently that for the king to condemn it now would be to contradict the crown's own delegated authority.[25] No wonder the poem seems so confident of the king's approbation. Moreover, the awkward phrase "if they take not more, / And turne it into licence" seems to allow the writer a good deal of agency beyond the power of the king to give "leave." Following this reading, one might argue that the Epilogue simultaneously affirms and questions the ability of the king to effectively oversee writers. The emphasis on the use to which royal license is put should remind us of Overdo's inability to recognize literature's variable uses. Perhaps, the Epilogue suggests, James is also unable to judge and control what writers are actually doing.

This hint – that James's relation to writers might be more complicated than that of authoritative judge to submissive subject – is seconded within the frame of the play by a curious incident in which we learn that the royal image also circulates within the fair itself. Thus, towards the end of the play, the puppeteer Lanthorn waxes elegiac about narrative subjects that have proven to be especially lucrative. Among them is the Gunpowder Plot, about which Lanthorn exclaims, "there was a get-penny! I have presented that to an eighteene, or twenty pence audience, nine times in an afternoone" (5.1.12–14). The discovery of the Powder Plot in 1605 occasioned a spate of royalist propaganda in which James himself was given credit for uncovering the treachery: in one tract, for example, the king is praised for his "fortunate judgment in clearing and solving of obscure riddles and doubtful mysteries."[26] This is a high point for Jacobean propaganda, allowing James to be credited with the kind of authoritative judgment and insight into enormities which Overdo also longs to demonstrate. Lanthorn's remark, however, registers the multiplicity of interests involved in the dissemination of the king's image, reducing James's glory to a "get-penny." Judging from his comically inept performance of the story of Hero and Leander, one imagines that Lanthorn's depiction of the Powder Plot might in fact have held the king up for ridicule. If Overdo's blindness to literature stems from a mistaken belief in the absolute objectivity of his authority, this anecdote reminds us that social authority is itself circulated as a series of representations. Jonson, of course, wants to insist on this point, since as a laureate writer he can serve the state by intervening in this process of circulation.[27]

More broadly, Jonson recognizes that literary representations – from Nightingale's ballads, to Lanthorn's puppet show, to Richard Johnson's pamphlet, to *Bartholomew Fair* itself – are constitutive of ideals, ideologies, and attitudes of the kind that shape behaviors and perceptions. This returns us to the most general politicized formulation of Heffner's description of the play's thematic core, namely "the problem of what 'warrant' men have or pretend to have for their actions." The kind of broad warrant for behavior supplied by a culture's fictions is impossible to control.[28] Overdo cannot recognize this, and so it is one of the central ironies of his character that he is himself so hackneyed, a disguised duke and a discoverer of abuses. His own actions are patently influenced – warranted – by notions of magisterial behavior circulated in the popular literature and drama which he himself would undoubtedly dismiss as idle.

The fair, of course, is an event bounded within a specific location and time. So how do its lessons about judgment and misrule apply to the world outside? This question is underscored by the hint at the end of the play that misrule will simply move to Overdo's banquet: Cokes says "bring the *Actors* along, wee'll ha' the rest o' the *Play* at home." Those critics who have seen the play through the lens of Bakhtin's notion of carnival have argued that the carnivalesque "moves out from the fair to enter and transform the space of official law and order."[29]

But the fair is itself remarkably inclusive, containing an unusually wide range of types and classes.[30] Jonson seems to go out of his way to include among the play's cast of characters a variety of regional figures, including the Irishman Whit, the Welsh Bristle, as well as "a Northren Clothier, and one *Puppy*, a Westerne man" (4.3.113–14). In fact, the fair's social and geographical heterogeneity – together with its heteroglossia – makes it a kind of microcosm for James's realm as a whole.[31] Rather than see the fair as a festive space which moves into and transforms a world of order, I like to see *Bartholomew Fair* this way, as a microcosm for a realm in which order and disorder, authority and disobedience, judgment and uncontrollable heteroglossia necessarily coincide. The play's lessons – about alienation and delegation, about obedience, and about authoritative judgment – apply more broadly than a narrow focus on festival misrule will allow.

Seen this way, *Bartholomew Fair* is a complex and measured response to the problematics of absolutist authority, its imposition, and its relation to literary representation. As such, we can take from it several important observations. First, the play encourages us to recall that the reproduction of the style of official authority need not demonstrate obedience. Appropriation of royal style, as Bristle demonstrates, can designate a kind of disobedience as well, a kind of discursive usurpation.[32] Second, the errors of Overdo coupled with the grotesque obedience of Trouble-all remind us never to believe that the rhetoric of absolutism accurately describes the relationship between magistrate and subject. This in turn means that to study the king's power of discursive imposition in the literature produced by subjects requires us to take into account the agencies of the various writers attempting to negotiate between personal desires and beliefs and the demands of various audiences and occasions. Third, in order to avoid Overdo's interpretive error, we are encouraged to ask not only what the text says, but what it was used to do.

Finally, the play reminds us that authority is necessarily imbricated within the discourse of the society it is supposed to supervise. Consequently, the king's actions and his reception by his subjects are both to some extent determined by ideals and expectations in wider circulation. This complicates our understanding of the negotiations that take place in literature, since it suggests that the interests and stances of all parties concerned are themselves made up of both the pragmatic and the formulaic. To be responsive to this as a critic means paying close attention not only to the uses of literature – as self-advertisement, as propaganda, as "get-penny," and so on – but also to the intersecting demands of genre, precedent, and decorum. These kinds of category determine the form and the forum in which literary negotiations between various interests take place.

These chapters have attempted to follow Jonson's critical program. That is to say, they have attempted to isolate different ways in which James's public image was circulated, to locate these within and against Elizabethan expectations, and to describe their various social effects. In doing so, they have depicted James as the purveyor of a style to be imitated, as an audience to be addressed, as a misunderstood victim of Elizabethan expectations, as a strategic rhetorician, as a body natural, as a locus of governmental power, as the subject of public relations campaigns, as the object of political satire, as a symbol of his realm, as a foreigner, as the central figure in court networks and factions, and as the public exponent of political dogma to be commented upon, criticized, and applauded. That all these often contradictory versions of James coexist is itself an index of the uncontrollable symbolic richness surrounding early modern monarchy, and should serve as a caution to those who would oversimplify the office's central position in the political imagination of Renaissance English culture.

Notes

INTRODUCTION

1. Positioning *vis-à-vis* predecessors is always an important public relations task. For a discussion of the ways that Mary Tudor and Elizabeth responded to the memory of their father, see Leah S. Marcus, "Erasing the Stigma of Daughterhood: Mary I, Elizabeth I, and Henry VIII," in *Daughters and Fathers*, Lynda E. Boose and Betty S. Flowers, eds. (Baltimore: The Johns Hopkins University Press, 1989), 400–17. See also Susan Frye's discussion of Mary Tudor as a "pre-text" for the gendered iconography of Elizabeth I's coronation entry: *Elizabeth I: The Competition for Representation* (New York: Oxford University Press, 1993), 26–30.

2. Pioneering studies here include Gary Schmidgal's *Shakespeare and the Courtly Aesthetic* (Berkeley: University of California Press, 1981), 101, and Leonard Tennenhouse's *Power on Display: The Politics of Shakespeare's Genres* (New York: Methuen, 1986).

3. B. E. Supple, *Commercial Crisis and Change 1600–1642; a Study in the Instability of a Mercantile Economy* (Cambridge: Cambridge University Press, 1959), 28–32.

4. Foucault, *The History of Sexuality, Volume 1: An Introduction*, Robert Hurley, trans. (New York: Random House, 1978), 93.

5. Weeks, "Foucault for Historians," *History Workshop* 14 (1982): 115.

6. Foucault, *The Order of Things: An Archaeology of the Human Sciences* (New York: Vintage Books, 1973), xx.

7. Foucault, *Power/Knowledge: Selected Interviews & Other Writings, 1972–1977*, Colin Gordon, ed., Colin Gordon, Leo Marshall, John Mepham, and Kate Soper, trans. (New York: Pantheon, 1980), 122. In *The History of Sexuality* Foucault writes, "by power, I do not mean…a group of institutions and mechanisms that ensure the subservience of the citizens of a given state" (92).

8. Foucault, *Discipline and Punish: The Birth of the Prison*, Alan Sheridan, trans. (New York: Vintage, 1979), 27.

9. Foucault, *History of Sexuality*, 94. Frank Lentricchia has described an analogous notion of power in new historicist criticism generally, and in Stephen Greenblatt's work in particular, in his *Ariel and the Police: Michel Foucault, William James, Wallace Stevens* (Madison: University of Wisconsin Press, 1988), 95.

10. Goldberg, *James I and the Politics of Literature: Jonson, Shakespeare, Donne, and Their Contemporaries* (Baltimore: The Johns Hopkins University Press, 1983), xi.

11. James Holstun, "Ranting at the New Historicism," *English Literary Renaissance* 19 (1989): 197.

12. Thompson, *The Poverty of Theory & Other Essays* (New York: Monthly Review Press, 1978), 153.

13. Ibid., 4–5.

14. White, "Foucault Decoded: Notes From Underground," in *Tropics of Discourse: Essays in Cultural Criticism* (Baltimore: The Johns Hopkins University Press, 1978), 230–60.

15. Montrose, "Professing the Renaissance: The Poetics and Politics of Culture," in *The New Historicism*, H. Aram Veeser, ed. (New York: Routledge, 1989), 17.

16. Leah Marcus's *Puzzling Shakespeare*, a book published by the University of California Press in Greenblatt's New Historicism series in 1988, makes explicit its call to return to old historical analytical tools like authorial intent (41–42).

17. See Holstun, "Ranting at the New Historicism," 197, and also David Norbrook's review article, "Absolute Revisionism," *English* 33 (1984): 251–63.

18. Foucault writes, "resistance is never in a position of exteriority in relation to power" (*History of Sexuality*, 95). Think here of Thompson's remarks about players being gamed.

19. Holstun, in "Ranting at the New Historicism," describes the subversion-containment model as used in a range of new historical studies, and uses the writings of the Ranters to point out the possibility of a truly radical "oppositional collective self-fashioning" (209). Kevin Sharpe and Peter Lake, in their introduction to *Culture and Politics in Early Stuart England* (Stanford: Stanford University Press, 1993), 5, note that both the "new historicism" in literary studies and the "revisionism" of historians tend to "present a severely constricted account of both the capacity and indeed the propensity of contemporaries successfully to challenge or subvert the structures of power with which they found themselves confronted."

20. R. C. Munden, "James I and 'the growth of mutual distrust': King, Commons, and Reform, 1603–1604" in *Faction and Parliament: Essays on Early Stuart History*, ed. Kevin Sharpe (Oxford: Clarendon Press, 1978), 43–72, and Maurice Lee Jr., *Great Britain's Solomon: James VI and I in His Three Kingdoms* (Urbana: University of Illinois Press, 1990), 102–04.

21. Munden, "James I and 'the growth of mutual distrust,'" 55.

22. J. P. Kenyon, ed. *The Stuart Constitution, 1603–1688: Documents and Commentary* (Cambridge: Cambridge University Press, 1966), 27.

23. Barroll, *Politics, Plague, and Shakespeare's Theater: The Stuart Years* (Ithaca: Cornell University Press, 1991).

24. See Theodore B. Leinwand's useful discussion of negotiation and subversion-containment models of culture in his "Negotiation and New Historicism," *PMLA* 105 (1990): 477–90.

25. Greenblatt, *Shakespearean Negotiations: The Circulation of Social Energy in Renaissance England* (Berkeley: University of California Press, 1988).

26. Jones, *The Currency of Eros: Women's Love Lyric in Europe, 1540–1620* (Bloomington: Indiana University Press, 1990), 201n.6. Jones describes a negotiated subject position as "one that accepts the dominant ideology encoded into a text but particularizes and transforms it in the service of a different group" (4). Leinwand makes similar suggestions in his "Negotiation and New Historicism," pointing out that Greenblatt's "notion of negotiating is a great deal more abstract than the more literal sense that I want to develop" (479).

27. Drayton, *Works*, 1: 488, 1.5.

28. Jonson, *Epigrammes*, no.43.1, in H&S VIII: 40.

29. Philip J. Finkelpearl, "The Role of the Court in the Development of Jacobean Drama," *Criticism* 24 (1982): 158. More generally, see J. Leeds Barroll's claim that the concerns of the crown and the interests of the theatre were quite separate, in *Politics, Plague, and Shakespeare's Theater*.

30. Bevington, *Tudor Drama and Politics: A Critical Approach to Topical Meaning* (Cambridge: Harvard University Press, 1968), 25.

31. Jacobean drama has seemed to many critics to put special pressure on a number of the age's political and social orthodoxies by staging them in ways that made it possible to see their limitations and failures. The most influential statement of this case is Jonathan Dollimore's *Radical Tragedy: Religion, Ideology and Power in the Drama of Shakespeare and His Contemporaries* (Chicago: University of Chicago Press, 1984).

32. Williams, *The Sociology of Culture* (New York: Schocken Books, 1982), 158. See also Franco Moretti, "'A Huge Eclipse': Tragic Form and the Deconsecration of Sovereignty," trans. D. A. Miller, in *The Power of Forms in the English Renaissance*, Stephen Greenblatt, ed. (Norman: University of Oklahoma Press, 1982), 7–40.

33. Williams adds: "the relations between these [structures] and formal or systematic beliefs are in practice variable (including historically variable), over a range from formal assent with private dissent to the more nuanced interaction between selected and interpreted beliefs and acted and justi-fied experiences" (*Marxism and Literature* [Oxford, Oxford University Press, 1977], 132).

34. By virtue of its attention to micro-historical change, this study can be seen as part of an ongoing revision of James's poor historical reputation. See the following: Marc L. Schwarz, "James I and the Historians: Towards a Reconsideration," *The Journal of British Studies* 13.2 (1974): 114–34; Kevin Sharpe, "Parliamentary History 1603–1629: In or out of Perspective," in *Faction and Parliament*, ed. Kevin Sharpe, 1–42; Jenny Wormold, "James VI and I: Two Kings or One?," *History* 68 (1983): 187–209. More recently, Maurice Lee Jr. has provided a sympathetic book-length study of James's life in *Great Britain's Solomon*. Traditionally, James has been lampooned as a pedant, criticized as a spendthrift, dismissed as weak-willed, and reviled

as decadent and effeminate. These shop-worn criticisms have been reinforced by James's place in the larger narrative of Whig history, which saw his failure as a landmark on the path leading to the Civil War and the rise of modern government. Macaulay, for example, wrote that "on the day of the accession of James the First England descended from the rank which she had hitherto held, and began to be regarded as a power hardly of the second order" (*The Complete Works of Lord Macaulay*, 12 vols. [1898; rpt. New York, AMS Press, 1980], 1: 72). This study rarely addresses James's skill as a politician directly, but its attention to the contingencies – of reception, of circulation – involved in the dissemination of his words and image in England should make it clear that the causes of his well-known public relations problems were necessarily more complicated than has sometimes been assumed.

1 PANEGYRIC AND THE POET-KING

1. G. P. V. Akrigg, *Jacobean Pageant; Or, The Court of King James I* (1962; rpt. New York: Athaneum, 1974), 29.
2. This common spatial metaphor – the king as the symbolic center – is theorized by Clifford Geertz in his essay "Centers, Kings, and Charisma: Reflections on the Symbolics of Power" in his *Local Knowledge* (New York: Basic Books, 1983), 121–46.
3. Goldberg, *James I and the Politics of Literature: Jonson, Shakespeare, Donne, and Their Contemporaries* (Baltimore: The Johns Hopkins University Press, 1983), xi.
4. Elizabeth wrote poems, but she neither published nor shared James's level of vanity about her productions. See Leicester Bradner, ed., *The Poems of Queen Elizabeth* (Providence: Brown University Press, 1964). See also Kevin Sharpe, "The King's Writ: Royal Authors and Royal Authority in Early Modern England," in *Culture and Politics in Early Stuart England*, Kevin Sharpe and Peter Lake, eds. (Stanford: Stanford University Press, 1993), 117–38.
5. George Puttenham, *The Arte of English Poesie*, Gladys Doidge Willcock and Alice Walker, eds. (Cambridge: Cambridge University Press, 1936), 4–5.
6. Daniel, *Works* II: 176, stanza 9.
7. Spenser, *Poetical Works*, J. C. Smith and E. de Selincourt, eds. (Oxford: Oxford University Press, 1912), 434.
8. Montrose, "The Elizabethan Subject and the Spenserian Text," in *Literary Theory/Renaissance Texts*, Patricia Parker and David Quint, eds. (Baltimore: The Johns Hopkins University Press, 1986), 320. See also Thomas H. Cain, *Praise in The Faerie Queene* (Lincoln: University of Nebraska Press, 1978), 14–24.
9. Chettle, *Englandes Mourning Garment* (London, 1603), sig. A4^{v}.
10. Roy Strong writes: "The strength of the Elizabethan image lay in its

capacity to be read and re-read many ways and never to present a single outright statement which left no room for manoeuvre" (*The Cult of Elizabeth: Elizabethan Portraiture and Pageantry* [Berkeley: University of California Press, 1977], 112).

11. I borrow the term "symbolic capital" from Pierre Bourdieu's *Outline of a Theory of Practice*, Richard Nice, trans. (Cambridge: Cambridge University Press, 1977), 171–97.

12. *Political Works*, 3. Goldberg's reading of this sonnet makes the point explicitly (*James I and the Politics of Literature*, 26–27).

13. *The Poems of James VI of Scotland*, 2 vols., James Craigie, ed. (Edinburgh: William Blackwood & Sons, 1955–8), 1: 9. Subsequent citations from James's poetry will be given parenthetically.

14. Goldberg, *James I and the Politics of Literature*, 20.

15. Craigie's edition (*Poems*) of James's poetry is equipped with a glossary. "Dytement" is there defined as "a literary composition." All subsequent definitions will be included in the text in brackets.

16. Helgerson, *Self-Crowned Laureates: Spenser, Jonson, Milton and the Literary System* (Berkeley: University of California Press, 1983), 25, 28.

17. Ibid., 30.

18. Goldberg, *James I and the Politics of Literature*, 20.

19. Unpublished during his lifetime, these poems were written between 1589 and 1595, and were grouped together (in a manuscript prepared considerably later) under the heading "amatoria."

20. For an account of James's literary education, and of the preponderance of French books in his Scottish library, see Craigie, *Poems*, 1: xi–xxv.

21. Craigie (ibid. 11: 208) indicates that the last four words of the title, which distance the production from the will of the king by attributing it to the queen's desire, were added late to the manuscript in Prince Charles's hand. The final sonnet is written on an inserted leaf in James's hand. It seems that the process of distancing the king from love conventions took place in several stages.

22. The king's authorial self-fashioning later manifested itself in his publication of selected political writings as "works" in 1616, and also in his sponsorship of the King James Bible. Kevin Sharpe has described James's sponsorship of the Bible as being "as much an act of power as of piety," since "an official translation proscribed the Geneva Bible and sought to define the parameters of hermeneutic freedom opened by the translation of the Scriptures" ("The King's Writ," 118–19).

23. John Bodenham, ed., *Bel-vedére, or the Garden of the Muses* (London, 1600), sig. A4ᵛ. *Bel-Vedére* consists of interwoven and often altered excerpts from a wide variety of sources. It is organized by subject, and lacks an author index, which means that a reader would be unlikely to know who the author of any particular snippet really was. Rather, *Bel-Vedére* simply makes use of the authorizing name of the poet-king in order to lend weight to what might otherwise be seen as a purely ephemeral production.

24. Stephen W. May, "Tudor Aristocrats and the Mythical 'Stigma of Print',"
    Renaissance Papers 1980, 16–17.
25. *Englands Parnassus* and *Bel-Vedére*. David McPherson's reconstruction of
    Ben Jonson's library reveals that Jonson had only nine original works of
    literature in English including James's *Poeticall Exercises* ("Ben Jonson's
    Library and Marginalia: An Annoted Catalogue," *Studies in Philology* 71.5
    [1974]: 55–56).
26. Franklin B. Williams, Jr., *Index of Dedications and Commendatory Verses in
    English Books Before 1691* (London: Bibliographical Society, 1962). After 1607
    the number of dedications to James drops somewhat, though it still
    surpasses average Elizabethan levels.
27. For a useful, if not comprehensive, bibliography of tracts on the accession
    and coronation of James I see Nichols, I: xxxvii–xli.
28. Daniel, *Works*, I: 146, stanza 10.
29. Barbara K. Lewalski, *Donne's Anniversaries and the Poetry of Praise: The
    Creation of A Symbolic Mode* (Princeton: Princeton University Press, 1973),
    18. See also O. B. Hardison Jr.'s *The Enduring Monument: A Study of the Idea
    of Praise in Renaissance Literary Theory and Practice* (Chapel Hill: University of
    North Carolina Press, 1962). On Daniel's poem see Joan Rees, *Samuel
    Daniel* (Liverpool: Liverpool University Press, 1964), 89–90.
30. For a more detailed analysis of James's relation to counsel, see chapter 3.
31. Greene, *A Poets Vision, and a Princes Glorie* (London: 1603). Similarly, Joseph
    Hall's *The King's Prophecie: or Weeping Joy* (London: 1603) calls James "The
    onely credit of *our* scorned skill" (stanza 52 – emphasis mine). For a discus-
    sion of James's influence on poetry in England that stresses the way the
    accession of the poet-king seemed to signal an elevation of poetry, see
    James Doelman, "The Accession of King James I and English Religious
    Poetry," *Studies in English Literature, 1500–1900* 34 (1994): 19–40.
32. Nichols, I: 52.
33. Drayton, *Works*, I: 488.
34. Fletcher's poem is included in the 1603 Cambridge anthology "Sorrowes
    Joy," which in turn is reprinted in Nichols, I: 1–24. These quotations
    appear on page 22.
35. I quote Harbert's *A Prophesie of Cadwallader, last king of the Britains* from the
    Miscellanies of the Fuller Worthies Library, 4 vols., Alexander B. Grosart, ed.
    (1871; rpt. New York: AMS Press, 1970), I: 249.
36. Curtius, *European Literature and the Latin Middle Ages*, Willard R. Trask,
    trans. (Princeton: Princeton University Press, 1953), 159–62.
37. Bacon, *Works*, III: 264.
38. "The Kinges Welcome" is reprinted in *The Poems of Sir John Davies*, Robert
    Kreuger, ed. (Oxford: Clarendon Press, 1975), 228–30.
39. Nichols, I: 82.
40. Goldberg, *James I and the Politics of Literature*, 230.
41. The "Panegyre" is reprinted in H&S, VII: 113–17. Subsequent citations
    will be given parenthetically by line.

42. See David M. Bergeron, *English Civic Pageantry 1558–1642* (Columbia: University of South Carolina Press, 1971), 65–87, and Graham Parry, *The Golden Age Restor'd: The Culture of the Stuart Court, 1603–42* (New York: St. Martins Press, 1981), 1–39.

43. In particular, Themis echoes James's formulation of the divine right of kings, and his notion that "Kings being publike persons, by reason of their office and authority, are as it were set...upon a publike stage ... where all the beholders eyes are attentively bent to looke and pry in the least circumstance of their secretest drifts" (*Political Works*, 5). Jonathan Goldberg makes interesting use out of what he sees as Jonson's tellingly partial renditions of James's positions (*James I and the Politics of Literature*, 120–22).

44. I quote Jonson's *Epigrammes* from H&S, VIII. "To King James" is no.4; subsequent citations will be given by number and line.

45. Jonathan Z. Kamholtz, "Ben Jonson's *Epigrammes* and Poetic Occasions," *Studies in English Literature, 1500–1900* 23 (1983): 77–94.

46. For a discussion of how the fifth and thirty-fifth of Jonson's *Epigrammes* engage specific cues from James's work see Jennifer Brady, "Jonson's 'To King James': Plain speaking in the *Epigrammes* and the Conversations," *Studies in Philology* 82 (1985): 380–99.

47. Helgerson, *Self-Crowned Laureates*, 101–84.

48. *The Letters and Epigrams of Sir John Harington Together with The Prayse of Private Life*, Norman Egbert McClure, ed. (Philadelphia: University of Pennsylvania Press, 1930), 321. This epigram was delivered to James along with other poems and a number of elegant and allegorical gifts; James is supposed to have liked Harington's gift: Nichols, I: 48–51.

49. On Jonson's strategy of reminding his subjects of their insecurities see Robert C. Evans, *Ben Jonson and the Poetics of Patronage* (Lewisburg: Bucknell University Press, 1989), 89–128. On Jonson's poems to Cecil see also Robert Wiltenburg, "'What need hast thou of me? or of my *Muse?*': Jonson and Cecil, Politician and Poet" in *'The Muses Common-Weal': Poetry and Politics in the Seventeenth Century*, Claude J. Summers and Ted-Larry Pebworth, eds. (Columbia: University of Missouri Press, 1988), 34–47.

50. Fish, "Authors–Readers: Jonson's Community of the Same" in *Representing the English Renaissance*, Stephen Greenblatt, ed. (Berkeley, University of California Press, 1988), 239.

51. Greene, "Ben Jonson and the Centered Self," in *The Vulnerable Text: Essays on Renaissance Literature* (New York: Columbia University Press, 1986), 194–217.

52. Kevin Sharpe (in *Sir Robert Cotton 1586–1631* [Oxford: Oxford University Press, 1979], 195–222) traces Cotton's circle by looking at: contemporaries at the Middle Temple and in college; kinship; patronage networks; coteries. The density and range of the interconnections described in this case-study suggest that fashions could be quickly disseminated throughout the court world with relative ease.

53. Whigham, *Ambition and Privilege: The Social Tropes of Elizabethan Courtesy Theory* (Berkeley: University of California Press, 1984), 32.

54. Michael McCanles's *Jonsonian Discriminations: The Humanist Poet and the Praise of True Nobility* (Toronto: University of Toronto Press, 1992) traces Jonson's epideictic stances through the entire corpus of his non-dramatic poetry. This study, focusing on continuities in Jonson's work, is a useful counterweight to my arguments here, which emphasize the determinate relationship between Jonson and his early Jacobean milieu.

55. Goldberg, *James I and the Politics of Literature*, 217.

56. See Annabel Patterson, "John Donne, Kingsman?" in *The Mental World of the Jacobean Court*, Linda Levy Peck, ed. (Cambridge: Cambridge University Press, 1991), 251–72, and David Norbrook, "The Monarchy of Wit and the Republic of Letters: Donne's Politics," in *Soliciting Interpretation: Literary Theory and Seventeenth-Century English Poetry*, Elizabeth D. Harvey and Katharine Eisaman Maus, eds. (Chicago: University of Chicago Press, 1990), 3–36. These essays argue against the notion that Donne was subsumed by absolutism, a notion promulgated most influentially by Goldberg and by John Carey's *John Donne: Life, Mind and Art* (New York: Oxford University Press, 1981).

57. Patterson, "John Donne, Kingsman?," 255.

58. Donne, *Pseudo-Martyr* (London, 1610), sig. A3–A3ᵛ.

59. Fish, "Masculine Persuasive Force: Donne and Verbal Power," in *Soliciting Interpretation*, Harvey and Maus, eds., 224.

60. Marotti, *John Donne, Coterie Poet* (Madison: University of Wisconsin Press, 1986), 207. For related arguments see: Carey, *John Donne: Life, Mind and Art*, 117–118; Meg Lota Brown, "'In that the world's contracted thus': Casuistical Politics in Donne's 'The Sunne Rising,'" in *'The Muses Common-Weal'*, Summers and Pebworth, eds., 23–33; Margaret Maurer, "The Real Presence of Lucy Russell, Countess of Bedford, and the Terms of Donne's 'Honour Is So Sublime Perfection,'" *ELH* 47 (1980): 212–14.

61. Lewalski, *Donne's Anniversaries and the Poetry of Praise*, 46.

62. See Margaret Maurer, "John Donne's Verse Letters," *Modern Language Quarterly* 37 (1976): 234–59, and Jay Arnold Levine, "The Status of the Verse Epistle Before Pope," *Studies in Philology* 59 (1962): 658–81.

63. W. Milgate, ed., *The Satires, Epigrams and Verse Letters* (Oxford: Clarendon Press, 1967), 91–94. These are the first two stanzas of this epistle. Subsequent citations will be given parenthetically by line number.

64. Aers and Kress, "'Darke Texts Need Notes': Versions of Self in Donne's Verse Epistles," in *Literature, Language and Society in England, 1580–1680*, David Aers, Bob Hodge, and Gunther Kress, eds. (Dublin: Gill and MacMillan, 1981), 23–48.

65. Ibid., 29.

66. Marotti, *John Donne, Coterie Poet*, 202. See also Maurer, "The Real Presence of Lucy Russell."

67. Marotti, *John Donne, Coterie Poet*, 207.

68. "The Sunne Rising" is generally accepted as an early Jacobean poem on the basis of strong circumstantial evidence: the line "Goe tell Court-huntsmen, that the King will ride" (7) seems to allude to James's taste for hunting; the poem has generally been taken to express the sentiments of a writer excluded from court; the rhetoric with which Donne establishes the royal centrality of the lovers has been compared to James's absolutist rhetoric. My text of the poem is from *The Poems of John Donne*, 2 vols., Herbert J. C. Grierson, ed. (Oxford: Clarendon Press, 1912), I: 11–12.

69. Carey, *John Donne: Life, Mind and Art*, 109. See also Goldberg, *James I and the Politics of Literature*, 107–12, and Marotti, *John Donne, Coterie Poet*, 156–57.

70. Norbrook, "The Monarchy of Wit and the Republic of Letters," 15.

71. *Satires, Epigrams and Verse Letters*, Milgate, ed., 107–10.

2 ARCADIA RE-FORMED: PASTORAL NEGOTIATIONS IN EARLY JACOBEAN ENGLAND

1. Macherey, *A Theory of Literary Production*, Geoffrey Wall, trans. (London: Routledge & Kegan Paul, 1978), 13.

2. Ibid., 41–42.

3. Ibid., 80.

4. Ibid., 92, 39.

5. Ibid., "Translator's Preface," ix.

6. A number of pastoral conventions have provided resources for the theorization of questions of tradition: elegiac longing for a golden age often doubles as a sense of literary belatedness, and the Virgilian pastoral debut provides an opportunity for the new poet to locate himself in relation to the tradition as both an innovator and a borrower. Thomas G. Rosenmeyer points out that the pastoral emphasis on tradition and imitation is itself borrowed by the modern world from Virgil (*The Green Cabinet: Theocritus and the European Pastoral Lyric* [Berkeley: University of California Press, 1969], 3–5). On the generic self-consciousness of Renaissance pastoral see Patrick Cullen, *Spenser, Marvell, and Renaissance Pastoral* (Cambridge: Harvard University Press, 1970), 1–26.

7. *The Poems of James VI of Scotland*, 2 vols., James Craigie, ed. (Edinburgh: William Blackwood & Sons, 1955–58), II: 193, lines 43–48.

8. H&S, VII: 121, line 21. Subsequent references to Jonson's entertainment will be given parenthetically by line number. For James's speech see *Political Works*, 272.

9. Nichols, I: 49.

10. Williams, *Marxism and Literature* (Oxford: Oxford University Press, 1977), 121–27. I refer to Goldberg's *James I and the Politics of Literature: Jonson, Shakespeare, Donne, and Their Contemporaries* (Baltimore: Johns Hopkins University Press, 1983).

11. Sukanta Chaudhuri, *Renaissance Pastoral and Its English Developments* (Oxford: Clarendon Press, 1989), 157. Chaudhuri's book, together with W. W.

Greg's *Pastoral Poetry and Pastoral Drama* (1906; rpt. New York: Russell & Russell, 1959), provides a useful bibliographical guide.

12. See Patterson, *Pastoral and Ideology: Virgil to Valéry* (Berkeley: University of California Press, 1987), and Montrose, "Of Gentlemen and Shepherds: The Politics of Elizabethan Pastoral Form," *ELH* 50 (1983): 415–59, and "The Elizabethan Subject and the Spenserian Text" in *Literary Theory/Renaissance Texts*, Patricia Parker and David Quint, eds. (Baltimore: The Johns Hopkins University Press, 1986), 303–40.

13. Anne Ferry, *The "Inward" Language: Sonnets of Wyatt, Sidney, Shakespeare, Donne* (Chicago: University of Chicago Press, 1983), 4. In *Inwardness and Theater in the English Renaissance* (Chicago: University of Chicago Press, 1995), Katharine Eisaman Maus discusses many different uses for the Renaissance language of inwardness.

14. Alpers, "Pastoral and the Domain of Lyric in Spenser's *Shepheardes Calender*," *Representations* 12 (Fall 1985): 83–100. For a discussion of the interplay between the private lyrics of Colin and the communality of verse, see Roland Greene's "*The Shepheardes Calender*, Dialogue, and Periphrasis," *Spenser Studies*, 8 (1990): 1–33.

15. Helgerson's study (*The Elizabethan Prodigals* [Berkeley: University of California Press, 1976]) of Elizabethan prodigality includes, but is not limited to, pastoral texts.

16. As Lisa Jardine has suggested (*Still Harping on Daughters: Women and Drama in the Age of Shakespeare* [Sussex: Harvester Press, 1983], 169–98), this characteristic pastoral representation of Elizabeth also helped to contain the threat of a powerful woman by associating her power with traditionally female virtues. Elizabeth's gender encouraged the formation of certain courtly conventions; James's contributed to the perception that Elizabethan conventions were no longer appropriate.

17. On the courtly strategies of Petrarchism, see for example Arthur F. Marotti, "'Love Is Not Love': Elizabethan Sonnet Sequences and the Social Order," *ELH* 49 (1982): 396–428. Marotti's reading of Fulke Greville's sonnet sequence *Caelica* describes a break between Greville's Elizabethan and Jacobean lyrics which reflects the kinds of discursive changes I am positing here: the Elizabethan section of *Caelica*, in Marotti's reading, is a self-contained amorous sequence, while the predominantly philosophical and religious poems written after the queen's death are "Jacobean lyrics in a different sociocultural idiom" (420).

18. Among these, as Louis Adrian Montrose has demonstrated in "Of Gentlemen and Shepherds," are questions about the assumed superiority of courtly nobles over the lower classes.

19. MacCaffrey, "Place and Patronage in Elizabethan Politics," in *Elizabethan Government and Society*, S. T. Bindoff, J. Hurstfield, and C. H. Williams eds. (London: Athlone Press, 1961), 108.

20. Puttenham, *The Arte of English Poesie*, Gladys Doidge Willcock and Alice Walker, eds. (Cambridge: Cambridge University Press, 1936), 38.

21. Compare David Riggs's claim that the *Althorpe Entertainment* "does little more than recapitulate the motifs that Jonson's Elizabethan predecessors had used on such occasions" (*Ben Jonson: A Life* [Cambridge: Harvard University Press, 1989], 98). Since the Elizabethan portion of the pastoral entertainment is directed toward Anne, we might say that this entertainment begins by transferring Elizabethan affect to the new queen – a common move discussed in chapter 5 below – and then gestures past her to the absent king.

22. Marcus, *The Politics of Mirth: Jonson, Herrick, Milton, Marvell, and the Defense of Old Holiday Pastimes* (Chicago: University of Chicago Press, 1986), 4–5.

23. *Political Works*, 27.

24. Marcus, *Politics of Mirth*, 8.

25. Ibid.

26. "Sorrowes Joy," is reprinted in Nichols, 1: 1–24. These lines appear on page 22.

27. Chettle, *Englandes Mourning Garment* (London, 1603), sig. 3; further references given in parentheses.

28. This Jacobean notion of active sport, with its attendant definition of the subject, does not describe how James's rural subjects saw themselves. See David Underdown, *Revel, Riot and Rebellion: Popular Politics and Culture in England 1603–1660* (Oxford: Oxford University Press, 1985), 44–105.

29. Also interesting in this regard is Sir George Buc's *Daphnis Polystephanos. An Eclog Treating of Crownes, and of Garlands, and To Whome Of Right They Appertaine* (1605), which brings a rigid social hierarchy to the pastoral realm. Its chief conceit is the explanation of something like pastoral sumptuary laws decreed by Apollo and interpreted by a wise old shepherd named Silenus. James, as Daphnis, is installed atop the structure and allowed to wear the appropriate garland. Where earlier pastoral praised Elizabeth in terms that served to mystify the structural reality of royal power ("Eliza" rules by virtue and beauty rather than by rank), Buc's eclogue emphasizes precisely the structural and hierarchical nature of James's divine right. Buc, who was among those knighted by James on the day before the coronation, was given a reversionary grant to the mastership of the revels in 1603. He presumably had a good sense of royal taste, and the eclogue is clearly tailored to it.

30. Florence Ada Kirk summarizes the evidence relating to the date and stage history of *The Faithful Shepherdess* in the introduction to her critical edition of the play (New York: Garland, 1980), vi–xx. I use this edition of the play and all subsequent citations will be given parenthetically by act, scene and line, or by page number when I refer to the play's apparatus.

31. James J. Yoch, "The Renaissance Dramatization of Temperance: The Italian Revival of Tragicomedy and *The Faithful Shepherdess*," in *Renaissance Tragicomedy: Explorations in Genre and Politics*, Nancy Klein Maguire, ed. (New York: AMS Press, 1987), 125.

32. Clorin's natural influence over the satyr is reminiscent of the natural

ability of Calepine and Serena to tame the savage man in book 6 of *The Faerie Queene*.

33. Leah Marcus describes the role-playing of Portia and Rosalind among others as re-enactments of Eliza's characteristic tactics in *Puzzling Shakespeare: Local Reading and Its Discontents* (Berkeley: University of California Press, 1988), 98–100.

34. Yoch, "The Renaissance Dramatization of Temperance," 125.

35. Perhaps Fletcher borrows this plot-twist from *The Faerie Queene*: the false Amoret is reminiscent of the false Una in book 1 and the false Florimel in book 3.

36. Yoch, "The Renaissance Dramatization of Temperance," 132. On the symbolic meanings of Pan in Jacobean pastoral see also Martin Butler, "Ben Jonson's *Pan's Anniversary* and the Politics of Early Stuart Pastoral," *English Literary Renaissance* 22 (1992): 371–78.

37. Philip Finkelpearl, *Court and Country Politics in the Plays of Beaumont and Fletcher* (Princeton: Princeton University Press, 1990), 104–10.

38. Leech, *The John Fletcher Plays* (Cambridge: Harvard University Press, 1962), 43–44.

39. Finkelpearl, *Court and Country Politics*, 110. This argument has been seconded more recently by Gordon McMullan in *The Politics of Unease In the Plays of John Fletcher* (Amherst: University of Massachusetts Press, 1994), 55–70.

40. Robert Ashton, ed., *James I by his Contemporaries* (London: Hutchinson & Co., 1969), 248.

41. Bliss, "Defending Fletcher's Shepherds," *Studies in English Literature, 1500–1900* 23 (1983): 307; Yoch, "The Renaissance Dramatization of Temperance," 132.

42. Bliss, "Defending Fletcher's Shepherds," 297–98.

43. For the text of Drayton's 1593 pastorals I use Drayton, *Works*. Since Hebel does not reproduce the 1606 version of Drayton's eclogues, citations from that text refer to the original London edition. Citations will be given parenthetically by line number.

44. For a discussion of Drayton's debt to Spenser in this book see Richard Hardin, *Michael Drayton and the Passing of Elizabethan England* (Lawrence: University of Kansas Press, 1973), 11–14. On the structural similarities of the two poems see Michael D. Bristol, "Structural Patterns in Two Elizabethan Pastorals," *Studies in English Literature, 1500–1900* 10 (1970): 33–48.

45. Chaudhuri points out that three of the new songs found in the 1606 version were included in *England's Helicon*, meaning that they were written by 1600 (*Renaissance Pastoral and Its English Developments*, 207). Most of the revisions, however, were undertaken as Drayton became dissatisfied with James's court.

46. For another early Jacobean example of didactic, plain style pastoral, see the three eclogues that survive of the twelve supposedly written by

Edward Fairfax, which are reproduced in *Godfrey of Bulloigne: A Critical Edition of Edward Fairfax's Translation of Tasso's Gerusalemme Liberata, Together with Fairfax's Original Poems*, Kathleen M. Lea and T. M. Gang, eds. (Oxford: Clarendon Press, 1981).

47. See Patterson, *Pastoral and Ideology*.

48. Part of the purpose for this beginning, I think, is Drayton's desire to begin where Spenser's *Shepheardes Calender* leaves off.

49. On Drayton's revision of the first eclogue see also Jane Tylus, "Jacobean Poetry and Lyric Disappointment" in *Soliciting Interpretation: Literary Theory and Seventeenth-Century English Poetry*, Elizabeth D. Harvey and Katharine Eisaman Maus, eds. (Chicago: University of Chicago Press, 1990), 183–85.

50. John Day's *Isle of Gulls* (1606) is cognate in some ways with Drayton's revisionary project here: it borrows its plot from Sidney's *Arcadia*, but transforms it into a satiric Jacobean comedy of comeuppance. By flattening out the personal space developed in Sidney's text, Day unleashes a different kind of satiric potential. In the place of Sidney's carefully modulated orchestration of private manias and disfiguring obsessions, Day's play focuses on the comic possibilities of the social structure as a whole. Gulling is the name of the game, and everybody gets into the act.

51. This seems to refer to Virgil's fifth eclogue, in which the lamented shepherd Daphnis is also imagined transformed into a "shepheardes starre."

52. Bernard H. Newdigate, *Michael Drayton and His Circle* (1941; rpt. Oxford: Basil Blackwell, 1961), 133.

53. For a more detailed discussion of Drayton, his patronage problems, and the satirical thrust of the 1606 eclogues see Jean R. Brink, *Michael Drayton Revisited* (Boston: Twayne, 1990), 75–80.

54. Godyere, *The Mirrour of Majestie* (London, 1618), 5. See also the invocation of Elizabethan pastoral settings and personae in the dedicatory poem to Anne in Aemilia Lanyer's volume *Salve Deus Rex Judeorum* (London, 1611).

55. My text is from Daniel, *Works*. All citations will be given parenthetically by line number. The speech against tobacco, spoken by a wicked doctor who is giving the weed out in order to undermine the health of the Arcadians, is lines 1,112–1,138.

56. Pocock, *The Ancient Constitution of the Feudal Law* (Cambridge: Cambridge University Press, 1957), 30–69.

57. Once his *Panegyrick Congratulatorie* failed to evoke royal favor, Daniel seems to have shifted his literary attentions to the Countess of Bedford and the queen with some success. See Joan Rees, *Samuel Daniel* (Liverpool: Liverpool University Press, 1964), 89–121.

58. Craigie, ed., *Poems*, 1: 79.

59. In addition to Elizabethan models, Daniel's play is the first sustained attempt to reproduce the pastoral drama of Tasso and Guarini in English. Daniel himself probably met Guarini in 1590–91 (Rees, *Samuel Daniel*, 8, 113; on Daniel's use of Italian models see Greg, *Pastoral Poetry and Pastoral*

Drama, 251–56). *Il Pastor Fido* makes use of the same strategic internalization of social problems that I have been concerned with in Elizabethan pastoral. In Guarini's play, Arcadia suffers under a curse imposed by the Goddess Diana to punish the faithlessness of one nymph, Lucrina. An Oracle names virtuous love shared by mortal children of the gods as the condition for the lifting of this curse, thereby making the comic ending of the love plot into the cure for a widespread social miasma. Had Daniel followed the lead of his Italian model his play would have been cognate with Elizabethan uses of the private.

60. Lewes Machin's ephemeral "eclogue of Menalcas and Daphnis" – published along with William Barksted's *Mirrha the Mother of Adonis* (London, 1607) – also imagines a private dialogue of love made public by a hidden observer: the eclogue centers on the voyeuristic experience of the speaker, who spies on the love-play of the couple – presumably Menalcas and Daphnis. Finally the pair retire to the woods, leaving the narrator thinking about the pair and "wishing for such a Nimph, I were a Swaine" (line 106). By interposing the narrator between the reader and the scene, Machin effectively strips his characters of private sentiment.

61. Walter Davis, *A Map of Arcadia: Sidney's Romance in Its Traditions* (New Haven: Yale University Press, 1965), 38–39.

62. Macherey, *A Theory of Literary Production*, 94.

63. For a discussion of this failure see R. Malcolm Smuts, *Court Culture and the Origins of a Royalist Tradition in Early Stuart England* (Philadelphia: University of Pennsylvania Press, 1987), 26–29.

64. Grundy, *The Spenserian Poets* (London: Edward Allen, 1969).

65. On the pastoral produced by the "Spenserian poets" see Grundy, ibid., 72–106; Chaudhuri, *Renaissance Pastoral and its English Developments*, 218–28; David Norbrook, *Poetry and Politics in the English Renaissance* (London: Routledge, 1984), 195–214. On the development of an extra-monarchic nationalism see Richard Helgerson, *Forms of Nationhood: The Elizabethan Writing of England* (Chicago: University of Chicago Press, 1992), 107–47.

66. Martin Butler's "*Pan's Anniversary* and the Politics of Early Jacobean Pastoral" describes a "hardening" of pastoral's wonted political flexibility in Jonson's masque, arguing that ambiguities implicit in the masque's pastoral traditions have been "overridden in the interests of affirming the transcendence of king and court" (394–95).

67. Guillén, *Literature As System: Essays Towards the Theory of Literary History* (Princeton: Princeton University Press, 1971), 385.

3 THEATRE OF COUNSEL: ROYAL VULNERABILITY AND EARLY
JACOBEAN POLITICAL DRAMA

1. *Vox Clamantis*, 6.7.31–32. Quoted from *The Major Latin Works of John Gower*, Eric W. Stockton, trans. and ed. (Seattle: University of Washington Press, 1962), 231.

2. S. B. Chrimes, *English Constitutional Ideas in the Fifteenth Century* (Cambridge: Cambridge University Press, 1936), 39.

3. J. G. A. Pocock, *The Machiavellian Moment: Florentine Political Thought and the Atlantic Republican Tradition* (Princeton: Princeton University Press, 1975), 334.

4. Levy, "Francis Bacon and the Style of Politics," *English Literary Renaissance* 16 (1986): 102. See also: Pocock, *Machiavellian Moment*, 333–60; G. K. Hunter, *John Lyly: The Humanist as Courtier* (Cambridge: Harvard University Press, 1962), 26–35; Arthur B. Ferguson, *The Articulate Citizen in the English Renaissance* (Durham: Duke University Press, 1965), 162–99.

5. *The Cabinet-Council: Containing the Chief Arts of Empire and Mysteries of State* is quoted here from *The Works of Sir Walter Ralegh, Kt.*, 8 vols. (Oxford: Oxford University Press, 1829), VIII: 55. On the authorship and dating of the *Cabinet-Council* see Ernest A. Strathman, "A Note On the Ralegh Canon," *The Times Literary Supplement* (April 13, 1956): 228.

6. *CSP Ven* x (1603–07), 70.

7. Ornstein, *The Moral Vision of Jacobean Tragedy* (Madison: University of Wisconsin Press, 1960), 30.

8. Marston, *Antonio and Mellida*, W. Reavley Gair, ed. (Manchester: Manchester University Press, 1991), 1.1.75–77.

9. A coinage of the Poet in Shakespeare's *Timon of Athens*: 1.1.59.

10. Levy, "Francis Bacon and the Style of Politics," 1–4.

11. Conrad Russell, *The Crisis of Parliaments: English History 1509–1660* (Oxford: Oxford University Press, 1971), 256.

12. Laurence Michel's edition of *The Tragedy of Philotas* (New Haven: Yale University Press, 1949, 36–66) contains a useful account of the play's relation to the Essex affair and of Daniel's resultant difficulties. For a more detailed analysis of what would have seemed seditious in the play see Richard Dutton, *Mastering the Revels: The Regulation and Censorship of English Renaissance Drama* (Iowa City: University of Iowa Press, 1991), 165–70. Citations from *Philotas* refer to Michel's edition and are given parenthetically by line number.

13. On the Wilton group in particular and French Senecan drama in England in general see the introductory essay on the Senecan tradition in *The Political Works of Sir William Alexander Earl of Stirling*, 2 vols., L. E. Kastner and H. B. Charlton eds. (Edinburgh: William Blackwood and Sons, 1921–9), I: clxxvi–cxc. See also Alexander M. Witherspoon, *The Influence of Robert Garnier on Elizabethan Drama* (New Haven: Yale University Press, 1924), 65–180.

14. Braden, *Renaissance Tragedy and the Senecan Tradition: Anger's Privilege* (New Haven: Yale University Press, 1985), 2–3.

15. Michel, *Philotas*, 62–63.

16. Ibid., 36–66.

17. Albert Tricomi, *Anticourt Drama in England, 1603–1642* (Charlottesville: University of Virginia Press, 1989), 64.

18. Michel, *Philotas*, 38.

19. Dutton (*Mastering the Revels*, 165–70) offers a detailed analysis of Daniel's involvement with the Privy Council, arguing that though the representation of Cecil was the immediate cause for official concern, Daniel's handling of the interrogation further inflamed things by stirring up sensitive memories of the Essex faction and thereby offending the Earl of Devonshire.

20. See the account of Ralegh's trial in *A Complete Collection of State Trials and Proceedings for High Treason and other Crimes and Misdemeanors from the Earliest Period to the Year 1783*, 21 vols. (London: 1816), II: 1–30. The staginess of Ralegh's performance is commented on by Dudley Carleton in a letter to John Chamberlain written on November 27, 1603: "Sir Walter Raleigh served for a whole act and played all the parts himself" (*Dudley Carleton to John Chamberlain, 1603–1624: Jacobean Letters*, Maurice Lee, Jr., ed. [New Brunswick NJ: Rutgers University Press, 1872], 38–39).

21. As translated and cited in Albert J. Loomie, "Sir Robert Cecil and the Spanish Embassy," *Bulletin of the Institute of Historical Research* 42 (1969): 34.

22. On the politics of access in James's court see Neil Cuddy's "The Revival of the Entourage: the Bedchamber of James I, 1603–1625" in David Starkey *et al.*, *The English Court: From the War of the Roses to the Civil War* (London: Longman, 1987), 173–225.

23. Ibid., 193, 197–98.

24. Pam Wright, "A Change in Direction: the Ramifications of a Female Household, 1558–1603" in Starkey *et al.*, *The English Court*, 147–72.

25. *CSP Ven* x (1603–07), 33. On the wide-ranging effects of English suspicion of James's Scottish imports see Jenny Wormald, "James VI and I: Two Kings or One?" *History* 68 (1983): 187–209. Wormald also points out that in Scotland James was known as a king unusually receptive to counsel. There, she argues, he settled problems face to face by debate and compromise and allowed his parliaments to speak freely to him. The formalities of English governmental bureaucracy made this type of direct solution impossible and forced James to adopt the declamatory style of kingcraft so familiar to us.

26. H&S, IV: 2.2.78. Subsequent references will be given parenthetically by act, scene, and line.

27. Cuddy, "The Revival of the Entourage," 185–86.

28. See Mary Thomas Crane, "'Video et Taceo': Elizabeth I and the Rhetoric of Counsel," *Studies in English Literature, 1500–1900* 28 (1988): 1–15.

29. *Political Works*, 42.

30. Stuart M. Kurland offers a substantially different account of the relationship between the Jacobean stage and the issue of counsel in "'We need no more of your advice': Political Realism in *The Winter's Tale*," *Studies in English Literature, 1500–1900* 31 (1991): 365–86.

31. Pocock, *The Machiavellian Moment*, 353.

32. Bacon, *Works*, VI: 502.

33. Goldberg, *James I and the Politics of Literature: Jonson, Shakespeare, Donne, and Their Contemporaries* (Baltimore: The Johns Hopkins University Press, 1983), 19.

34. On the use of panegyric for counsel, and on the difficulty of reconciling the need to flatter with the desire to advise, see Martin Butler, "Ben Jonson and the Limits of Courtly Panegyric," in *Culture and Politics In Early Stuart England*, Kevin Sharpe and Peter Lake, eds. (Stanford: Stanford University Press, 1993), 91–115.

35. Bacon, *Works*, vi: 426.

36. Wilson's observation on James can be found in Robert Ashton, *James I by his Contemporaries* (London: Hutchinson & Co., 1969), 18; I quote from Weldon's *The Court and Character of King James* as it appears in *The Secret History of the Court of James the First*, 2 vols. (Edinburgh, 1811), 1: 412.

37. Goldberg, *James I and the Politics of Literature*, 68–9.

38. Alan Bradford, in "Stuart Absolutism and the 'Utility' of Tacitus," *Huntington Library Quarterly* 46 (1983): 127–55, argues that far from being a careful student of Tacitean tactics, James actually supported the anti-Tacitean rhetoric of Edmund Bolton and others.

39. Wormald, "James VI and I: Two Kings or One?"

40. Fulwell, *Ars Adulandi, or the Art of Flattery*, Roberta Buchanan, ed. (Salzburg: Institut für Anglistik und Amerikanistik, Universität Salzburg, 1984), 33. For other Elizabethan uses of the motto see Morris Palmer Tilley, *A Dictionary of the Proverbs in England in the Sixteenth and Seventeenth Centuries* (Ann Arbor: University of Michigan Press, 1950), D386.

41. Goodman, *The Court of King James the First*, 2 vols., John S. Brewer, ed. (London, 1839), 1: 10. This is the first published edition of Goodman's memoir, which was written during the 1650s to counter the slanders of Weldon's piece.

42. Marcus, *Puzzling Shakespeare: Local Reading and its Discontents* (Berkeley: University of California Press, 1988), 116.

43. *Political Works*, 280.

44. There have been various attempts to explain the emergence of this distinct subgenre in terms of James's accession. The plays have been described alternatively as a reaffirmation of the natural supremacy of kings (see Leonard Tennenhouse, "Representing Power: *Measure for Measure* in its Time" in *The Power of Forms in the English Renaissance*, Stephen Greenblatt, ed. [Norman: Pilgrim Books, 1982], 139–56), and as an admonitory call for royal attention to national grievances (see Tricomi, *Anticourt Drama*, 13–24). I do not think that the political comment behind these plays can be so easily generalized. Indeed, the distance separating these two approaches suggests as much.

45. I use the text from *The Works of John Marston*, 3 vols., A. H. Bullen, ed. (Boston, 1887). *The Fawne* appears in the second volume, and the speech in which these remarks appear is 1.2.83–99. Subsequent citations will be given parenthetically.

46. Tricomi, *Anticourt Drama*, 10–12 and 42–50. See also Dutton, *Mastering the Revels*, 165–81.

47. Janet Clare, *'Art made tongue-tied by authority': Elizabethan and Jacobean Dramatic Censorship* (Manchester: Manchester University Press, 1990), 99. On the surprising leniency of Jacobean censorship, and on the wide range of variables determining the effectiveness in practice of censorship, see also Philip J. Finkelpearl, "'The Comedians' Liberty:' Censorship of the Jacobean Stage Reconsidered," *English Literary Renaissance* 16 (1986): 123–38.

48. See Philip Finkelpearl, *John Marston of the Middle Temple: An Elizabethan Dramatist in His Social Setting* (Cambridge: Harvard University Press, 1969), 223–27.

49. Linda Levy Peck has recently described the play as "a deliberately multivalent reading of the Jacobean court rather than a realistic portrait of King James." See her "John Marston's *The Fawn*: Ambivalence and Jacobean Courts" in *The Theatrical City: Culture, Theater and Politics in London, 1576–1649*, David L. Smith, Richard Strier, and David Bevington, eds. (Cambridge: Cambridge University Press, 1995), 118.

50. The suggestion originates in E. K. Chambers, *The Elizabethan Stage*, 4 vols. (Oxford: Clarendon Press, 1922), III: 367. David Riggs treats this performance and the resulting summons as fact in his *Ben Jonson: A Life* (Cambridge: Harvard University Press, 1989), 105–06.

51. Dutton (*Mastering the Revels*, 11–12) sees both as unlikely and offers a useful résumé of alternative solutions.

52. Jonson mentions revisions in his dedicatory epistle to the edition of 1605. I will quote *Sejanus* from H&S, vol. IV. Citations will be given parenthetically by act and line. On our ignorance of the original, see Annabel Patterson, *Censorship and Interpretation: The Conditions of Writing and Reading in Early Modern England* (Madison: University of Wisconsin Press, 1984), 49–58.

53. See, for example, Jonas Barish's introduction to his edition of *Sejanus* (New Haven: Yale University Press, 1965), 16. Annabel Patterson points out that since Jonson had depicted Essex sympathetically in *Cynthia's Revels* it would be peculiar if he saw Essex as Sejanus only a few years later (*Censorship and Interpretation*, 55–56).

54. Dutton (*Mastering the Revels*, 10–12) argues that the involvement of Earl of Northampton in the disturbance over *Sejanus* ties the play instead to the more recent débâcles of Ralegh and Cobham, with which Northampton was involved.

55. On the habit of reading Tacitus with contemporary situations in mind see J. H. M. Salmon, "Seneca and Tacitus in Jacobean England," *Journal of the History of Ideas* 50 (1989): 199–225.

56. Alan T. Bradford, "Nathaneal Richards, Jacobean Playgoer," *John Donne Journal* 2.2 (1983): 63–78. Richards copied down passages from *Sejanus* into his commonplace book and used them to flesh out his topical satire "The Vicious Courtier."

57. Ayres, "The Nature of Jonson's Roman History," *English Literary Renaissance* 16 (1986): 166–81.
58. Tricomi, *Anticourt Drama*, 79.
59. Patterson, *Censorship and Interpretation*, 60–61.
60. H&S, II: 13.
61. J. W. Lever, *The Tragedy of State: A Study of Jacobean Drama* (London: Methuen, 1971), 59–69.
62. Ornstein, *Moral Vision*, 97.
63. Maus, *Ben Jonson and the Roman Frame of Mind* (Princeton: Princeton University Press, 1984), 9. On Jonson's penchant for reminding the subjects of his epigrams of their own insecurities while praising them, see Robert C. Evans, *Ben Jonson and the Poetics of Patronage* (Lewisburg: Bucknell University Press, 1989), 89–128.
64. H&S, VIII: 565.
65. Like *Philotas*, the original version of *Mustapha* had a great deal to do with the crisis surrounding the Earl of Essex and the succession problem. Greville's revisions, like Daniel's, flesh out the concerns of the late Elizabethan crisis where applicable, making his new play deeply invested in its Jacobean context.
66. For the dating of Greville's versions of *Mustapha* see Ronald A. Rebholz, *The Life of Fulke Greville First Lord Brooke* (Oxford: Clarendon Press, 1971), 325–40.
67. Ibid., 155–99.
68. Ibid., 188–89.
69. Ibid., 201.
70. I use the text of *Mustapha* from *The Poems and Dramas of Fulke Greville First Lord Brooke*, 2 vols., Geoffrey Bullough, ed. (New York: Oxford University Press, 1945), vol. II. These quotations are from 1.2.233 and 1.2.262 respectively. Subsequent citations will be given parenthetically.
71. See the discussion of the many possible source-texts for Greville's play in the introduction to Bullough's edition, II: 8–25.
72. Rebholz, *Life*, 203.
73. Tricomi, *Anticourt Drama*, 68.
74. Ibid., 70. See also Jonathan Dollimore, *Radical Tragedy: Religion, Ideology and Power in the Drama of Shakespeare and his Contemporaries* (Chicago: University of Chicago Press, 1984), 133.
75. On the ways that Greville's Solyman is "self-divided rather than evil" see Tricomi, *Anticourt Drama*, 70.
76. For an interesting study of Elizabethan dramatic explorations of this doctrine of obedience, see David Bevington, *Tudor Drama and Politics: A Critical Approach to Topical Reading* (Cambridge: Harvard University Press, 1968), 156–67.
77. W. A. Armstrong has given an account of the normative conception of tyranny in two closely related pieces: "The Elizabethan Conception of the Tyrant," *Review of English Studies* os 22 (1946): 161–81; "The Influence of

Seneca and Machiavelli in the Elizabethan Tyrant," *Review of English Studies* os 24 (1948): 19–35.

78. Bushnell, *Tragedies of Tyrants: Political Thought and Theater in the English Renaissance* (Ithaca: Cornell University Press, 1990), 37–79.

79. *Political Works*, 18.

80. From "Of Empire": Bacon, *Works*, 6: 419.

81. This reading of this set of plays corroborates Rebecca Bushnell's contention that Jacobean drama tends to "address the complex relationship between the prince's moral behavior and his legitimacy" in a newly direct way (*Tragedies of Tyrants*, 158).

82. Moretti, "'A Huge Eclipse': Tragic Form and the Deconsecration of Sovereignty," trans. D. A. Miller, in *The Power of Forms in the English Renaissance*, Stephen Greenblatt, ed. (Norman: University of Oklahoma Press, 1982), 7–40.

4   NOURISH-FATHERS AND PELICAN DAUGHTERS: KINGSHIP, GENDER, AND BOUNTY IN *KING LEAR* AND *MACBETH*

1. G. M. Trevelyan, *England Under the Stuarts* (1904; rpt., London: Methuen, 1965), 71, and David Harris Willson, *King James VI & I* (1956; rpt., New York: Oxford University Press, 1967), 195.

2. On the former see Conrad Russell, *The Crisis of Parliaments: English History, 1509–1660* (Oxford: Oxford University Press, 1971), 259; on the latter see Linda Levy Peck, *Court Patronage and Corruption in Early Stuart England* (Boston: Unwin Hyman, 1990), 1–46.

3. Derek Hirst suggested to me that royal profligacy became an urgent complaint after 1606, when James was granted a special subsidy by parliament to help meet the growing royal debt and celebrated by giving £44,000 to three of his Scottish favorites (see Hirst's *Authority and Conflict: England, 1603–1658* [Cambridge: Harvard University Press, 1986], 109). Though there was resentment about James's gifts to his Scots before 1606, his open-handedness with the extra income provided by this subsidy defined and clarified the problem for concerned subjects. Cash gifts were not the only troublesome form of royal largess. Cecil's "Book of Bounty," drafted in 1608 and printed in 1610, was designed to curb the king's generosity with monopoly grants.

4. Peck, *Court Patronage and Corruption*, 4.

5. Kahn, "'Magic of Bounty': *Timon of Athens*, Jacobean Patronage, and Maternal Power," *Shakespeare Quarterly* 38 (1987): 34–57.

6. Kahn, "'Magic of Bounty'," 57.

7. Barber and Richard Wheeler, *The Whole Journey: Shakespeare's Power of Development* (Berkeley: University of California Press, 1986), 305.

8. I quote from the first English translation of Ripa's *Iconologia* (London, 1709) as reprinted in facsimile under the direction of Stephen Orgel (New York: Garland, 1976), 10. Ripa's *Iconologia* was first published in Rome in

1593, first published with illustrations in Rome in 1603, and quickly went through many international editions.

9. Rosemary Freeman discusses Ripa's influence on Henry Peacham's emblem book *Minerva Britanna* (1613), and also on masques by Jonson and Carew in *English Emblem Books* (London: Chatto & Windus, 1970), 79–81, 95–96. D. J. Gordon discusses the use of Ripa by Jonson and others in many of the essays collected in *The Renaissance Imagination*, Stephen Orgel, ed. (Berkeley: University of California Press, 1975).

10. The title page of the first edition of *Iconologia* (Rome, 1593) describes it as a work designed for poets, painters, and sculptors. Subsequent editions expand this advertisement to include an even wider range of crafts.

11. Kahn, "'Magic of Bounty,'" 43–44. The quotations from James are from *Basilikon Doron* and *The Trew Law of Free Monarchies* respectively and are quoted from *Political Works*, 24, 55. James's argument that kings should be "nourish-fathers" to the church is a conventional one, and has its roots in Isaiah 49: 23 ("kings shall be thy nursing fathers"). Debora Shuger describes the idealized image of generous paternal authority in *Habits of Thought in the English Renaissance: Religion, Politics, and the Dominant Culture* (Berkeley: University of California Press, 1990), 218–49.

12. In the early seventeenth century, art collecting was an international endeavor shared by many leading statesmen. It became common to utilize art-world networks for minor diplomatic projects and as sources of information about international affairs. Rubens's painting celebrates a peace between England and Spain that he himself helped to negotiate. See C. V. Wedgwood, *The Political Career of Peter Paul Rubens* (London: Thames and Hudson, 1975), 7, 45–49.

13. The ideological importance of royal generosity makes sense in the context of larger ideals of circulation and plenty. As Patricia Fumerton has argued (*Cultural Aesthetics: Renaissance Literature and the Practice of Social Ornament* [Chicago: University of Chicago Press, 1991], 29–66), gift-exchange contributed to the ideological fantasy of an aristocratic community unified by shared interest and communal plenty. Fumerton's analysis draws heavily on anthropological studies of gift-giving which emphasize the way that the circulation of gifts creates bonds of reciprocal indebtedness. Royal bounty is of course a special case here. While a king was understood to participate in a reciprocal relationship with his subjects, and thus finally to profit by his own gift-giving, the image of the king as the creator of wealth is a staple image in the rhetoric of kingship. The emphasis placed upon this image of royal generosity by James is of a piece with his implicit claim to be the origin of symbolic capital, as discussed in chapter 1.

14. I quote from Kenneth Douglas McRae's facsimile edition of Knolles's translation (Cambridge: Harvard University Press, 1962), 595.

15. See Bynum, *Fragmentation and Redemption: Essays on Gender and the Human Body in Medieval Religion* (New York: Zone Books, 1992), 93–108, 157–65,

205–22. See also her *Jesus as Mother: Studies in the Spirituality of the High Middle Ages* (Berkeley: University of California Press, 1982), 110–69.

16. Godyere, *The Mirrour of Majestie: or, The Badges of Honour Conceitedly Emblazoned* (London, 1618), no. 31, p. 61.

17. For example, Lawrence Stone's classic treatment of conspicuous expenditure (*The Crisis of the Aristocracy, 1558–1641* [Oxford: Clarendon Press, 1965], 561) uses details from one of Hay's banquets as its centerpiece.

18. Peck (*Court Patronage and Corruption*, 1) argues that the image of the king as an inexhaustible fountain recurs in this period, an emblem of monarchy as "a never-ending source of reward, the earthly embodiment of god, who was the original spring or wellhead."

19. For a detailed and contextualized description of the painting see Barbara Hochstetler Meyer, "Marguerite de Navarre and the Androgynous Portrait of François Ier," *Renaissance Quarterley* 48 (1995): 287–325.

20. Though there is no reason to assert, with Robert Kimbrough (*Shakespeare and the Art of Humankindness: the Essay Toward Androgyny* [Atlantic Highlands: Humanities Press International, 1990], appendix III), that the figure is pregnant, it remains possible that the look of fertility – broadly construed – is part of the cluster of associated attributes lavished on Francis here. See also Raymond B. Waddington, "The Bisexual Portrait of Francis I: Fontainebleau, Castiglione, and the Tone of Courtly Mythology" in *Playing With Gender: A Renaissance Pursuit*, Jean R. Brink, Maryanne C. Horowitz, and Allison P. Coudert, eds. (Urbana: University of Illinois Press, 1991), 99–132.

21. Kimbrough, *Shakespeare and the Art of Humankindness*, 186.

22. Goldberg, *James I and the Politics of Literature: Jonson, Shakespeare, Donne, and their Contemporaries* (Baltimore: The Johns Hopkins University Press, 1983), 142.

23. Godyere, *The Mirrour of Majestie*, no. 2, p. 3.

24. Historical changes in family structure underscore the need to historicize psychoanalytic readings of Renaissance texts. If most wealthy noblewomen had wet-nurses, for example, then for this group the bond between mother and child would have different bases and valences than the relationship described by Freud.

25. For one account of the cultural anxiety surrounding the figure of the mother, see Phyllis Mack, *Visionary Women: Ecstatic Prophesy in Seventeenth-Century England* (Berkeley: University of California Press, 1992), 34–44. Maternality – as associated with the uncertainty of paternity, the uncontrollable in generation, and female appetite – comes to represent what Natalie Zemon Davis has called the "disorderliness" of the female sex: see her *Society and Culture in Early Modern France* (Stanford: Stanford University Press, 1965), 124–51.

26. Roy Strong, *Gloriana: The Portraits of Elizabeth I* (London: Thames and Hudson, 1987), 80. On the iconography of the pelican see Victor E. Graham, "The Pelican as Image and Symbol," *Revue de Littérature Comparée* 36 (1962): 235–43.

27. Elkin Calhoun Wilson, *England's Eliza* (Cambridge: Harvard University Press, 1939), 217–20. Louis Adrian Montrose has located Elizabeth's maternality within a matrix of gendered representations, noting how her association with the virginal, the erotic, and the maternal contributed to the queen's compelling power in the imaginations of her subjects ("'Shaping Fantasies': Figurations of Gender and Power in Elizabethan Culture," *Representations* 2 [1983]: 61–94).

28. On the names of the princes, see Glynne Wickham, "From Tragedy to Tragi-Comedy: 'King Lear' as Prologue," *Shakespeare Survey* 26 (1973): 36. On the "carefully induced surprise at the sudden substitution of daughters" for sons in this scene see Janet Adelman, *Suffocating Mothers: Fantasies of Maternal Origin in Shakespeare's Plays, Hamlet to the Tempest* (New York: Routledge, 1992), 107–08. Commenting in her *Shakespeare and the Popular Voice* (Oxford: Basil Blackwell, 1989), on the substitution of daughters for these sons, Annabel Patterson writes "at the very least, this ruse would have encouraged a flexible hermeneutics, a wary approach to the play's exceptionally complex representational structure" (107).

29. Patterson summarizes these associations in her account of the "striking number of characteristics" shared by Lear and James in her *Shakespeare and the Popular Voice*, 106–07. On Archie Armstrong, see also Theodore B. Leinwand, "Conservative Fools in James's court and Shakespeare's Plays," *Shakespeare Studies* 19 (1987): 219–37.

30. On both points, see the notes in Kenneth Muir's Arden edition of the play (1952; London: Methuen, 1972). On the latter, see also Gary Taylor, "Monopolies, Show Trials, Disaster, and Invasion: *King Lear* and Censorship" in *The Division of the Kingdoms: Shakespeare's Two Versions of King Lear*, Gary Taylor and Michael Warren, eds. (Oxford: Clarendon Press, 1983), 101–09, and Richard Halpern, *The Poetics of Primitive Accumulation: English Renaissance Culture and the Genealogy of Capital* (Ithaca: Cornell University Press, 1991), 229–31.

31. John W. Draper's "The Occasion of *King Lear*" (*Studies in Philology* 34 [1937], 176–85) argues that the play compliments James by illustrating "the evils of disunion" (182). Draper's hypothesis – that the play is basically a compliment to the new king – is taken up by a number of subsequent critics including Glynne Wickham ("From Tragedy to Tragi-Comedy") and Richard Dutton in his *"King Lear, The Triumphs of Reunited Britannia, and 'The Matter of Britain'"* (*Literature and History* 12 [1986]: 139–51). Other critics have found the relationship between Lear's division and James's union to be more equivocal. Marie Axton (*The Queen's Two Bodies: Drama and the Elizabethan Succession* [London: Royal Historical Society, 1977], 131–47) sees *Lear* as a speculative investigation of issues of kingship brought to the surface by the discrepancy between propaganda for the Jacobean union and the ongoing political squabbles between king and Commons over the union itself. Other readings of *Lear* which emphasize equivocations in the topical meaning of the division of the kingdom include Leah

S. Marcus, *Puzzling Shakespeare: Local Reading and its Discontents* (Berkeley: University of California Press, 1988), 148–59, and Annabel Patterson, *Censorship and Interpretation: The Conditions of Writing and Reading in Early Modern England* (Madison: University of Wisconsin Press, 1984), 58–73.

32. On the former, see Marcus, *Puzzling Shakespeare*, 148–59. For differing arguments about censorship in the *Lear* texts see Gary Taylor, "Monopolies, Show Trials, Disaster, and Invasion," and Patterson, *Censorship and Interpretation*.

33. Halpern, *The Poetics of Primitive Accumulation*, 231.

34. Leah Marcus has suggested that the play's call to "shake the superflux" would have radically different meanings in different performative contexts. Performed at court on St. Stephen's Day, the emphasis on poverty would be explained and contained to a certain extent by liturgical emphases on charity and hospitality. Elsewhere, she argues, the same messages could be taken to be critical of parliament or of James: see *Puzzling Shakespeare*, 148–59. See also Patterson, *Shakespeare and the Popular Voice*, 106–16.

35. Erickson, *Patriarchal Structures in Shakespeare's Drama* (Berkeley: University of California Press, 1985), 112.

36. Claire McEachern's "Fathering Herself: A Source Study of Shakespeare's Feminism" (*Shakespeare Quarterly* 39 [1988]: 269–90), argues that *Lear* interrogates its source's more-or-less conventional handling of the analogy between father and king.

37. *Narrative and Dramatic Sources of Shakespeare*, 8 vols., Geoffrey Bullough, ed. (London: Routledge and Kegan Paul, 1957–75), VII: 349, lines 512–16. Subsequent citations from *Leir* will be given parenthetically by line number.

38. Compare Luke 12: 37: "Blessed are those servants, whom the lord when he cometh shall find watching: verily I say unto you that he shall gird himself, and make them sit down to meat, and will come forth and serve them."

39. Halpern, *The Poetics of Primitive Accumulation*, 252.

40. Nichols, I: 357.

41. If, as Patricia Fumerton has argued, in Elizabethan England "the language and spirit of generosity repeatedly surfaced in the giving of children" (*Cultural Aesthetics*, 41), then Lear's conflation of the distribution of bounty and the marriage of his daughters may have a basis in convention.

42. The former question – what is a king without his fiscal and political resources? – is addressed by both Richard Halpern's *The Poetics of Primitive Accumulation* and Leah Marcus's *Puzzling Shakespeare*.

43. *Political Works*, 55.

44. I borrow the term from Halpern, *The Poetics of Primitive Accumulation*, 252.

45. Coppélia Kahn, "The Absent Mother in *King Lear*," in *Rewriting the Renaissance: The Discourses of Sexual Difference in Early Modern Europe*, ed.,

Margaret W. Ferguson, Maureen Quilligan, and Nancy J. Vickers (Chicago: University of Chicago Press, 1986), 35–36. See also Adelman, *Suffocating Mothers*, 107–09.

46. Adelman, *Suffocating Mothers*, 108.

47. See ibid., and the following: Kahn, "The Absent Mother"; Erickson, *Patriarchal Structures*; Madelon Gohlke, "'I wooed thee with my sword': Shakespeare's Tragic Paradigms" in *Representing Shakespeare: New Psychoanalytic Essays*, Murray M. Schwartz and Coppélia Kahn, eds. (Baltimore: The Johns Hopkins University Press, 1980), 175–77; Gayle Whittier, "Cordelia as Prince: Gender and Language in *King Lear*," *Exemplaria* 1 (1989): 367–99.

48. Adelman, *Suffocating Mothers*, 114.

49. Ibid., 110.

50. See ibid., 110–12, and Marilyn French, *Shakespeare's Division of Experience* (New York: Summit Books, 1981), 221–22.

51. In the Folio text of *Lear*, "coining" is replaced by "crying," an alteration which Leah Marcus, in her *Puzzling Shakespeare*, describes as part of a motivated revision of the text: "an attribute associating King Lear specifically with King James I is neutralized into a trait Lear shares with all humanity" (150).

52. Barber and Wheeler, *The Whole Journey*, 293. Owing to the juxtaposition of scriptural allusion and materialism, the question of religious meaning in *Lear* has been a vexed one. The classic study, which first called the play's Christianity into question, is William Elton's *King Lear and the Gods* (San Marino: The Huntington Library, 1966). Useful subsequent treatments of scriptural meaning in the play include Rosalie Colie's sure-handed essay "The Energies of Endurance: Biblical Echo in *King Lear*" in *Some Facets of King Lear: Essays in Prismatic Criticism*, Rosalie Colie and F. T. Flahiff, eds. (London: Heinemann, 1974), 117–44, and Joseph Wittreich's "'Image of that horror': the Apocalypse in *King Lear*" in *The Apocalypse in English Renaissance Thought and Literature*, C. A. Patrides and Joseph Wittreich, eds. (Ithaca: Cornell University Press, 1984), 174–206.

53. Dollimore, *Radical Tragedy: Religion, Ideology and Power in the Drama of Shakespeare and his Contemporaries* (Chicago: University of Chicago Press, 1984), 189–203.

54. Marvin Rosenberg, *The Masks of King Lear* (Berkeley: University of California Press, 1972), 322.

55. Ibid., 323.

56. Bullough, *Narrative and Dramatic Sources*, 319.

57. The only exception here is Spenser's highly compressed version of the story in *The Faerie Queene* (Book 2, Canto 10), in which Cordelia herself levies an army. Spenser's departure probably has to do with Queen Elizabeth; Spenser also expands the duration of Cordelia's reign from five years to an undisclosed "long time" (32.4).

58. See Barbara C. Millard, "Virago with a Soft Voice: Cordelia's Tragic

Rebellion in *King Lear*," *Philological Quarterly* 68 (1989): 143–65. Gayle Whittier, in her "Cordelia as Prince," describes Cordelia as Lear's "phantom son," and notes that "she partakes of the best qualities of an heir" (387).

59. A. C. Bradley, *Shakespearean Tragedy* (1904; rpt. London: Macmillan, 1957), 206–07.

60. The classic study is Henry N. Paul's *The Royal Play of Macbeth: When, Why and How it was Written by Shakespeare* (New York: Macmillan, 1950). See also John W. Draper, "*Macbeth* as a Compliment to James I," *Englische Studien* 72 (1937–38): 207–20; George Walton Williams, "*Macbeth*: King James's Play," *South Atlantic Review* 47.2 (1982): 12–21; Garry Wills, *Witches and Jesuits: Shakespeare's Macbeth* (New York: Oxford University Press, 1995).

61. See the following: Michael Hawkins, "History, Politics, and *Macbeth*," in *Focus on Macbeth*, John Russell Brown, ed. (London: Routledge, 1982), 155–88; Alan Sinfield, "*Macbeth*: History, Ideology, and Intellectuals," *Critical Quarterly* 28.1–2 (1986): 63–77; David Norbrook "*Macbeth* and the Politics of Historiography," in *Politics of Discourse: Literature and History of Seventeenth-Century England*, Kevin Sharpe and Stephen N. Zwicker, eds. (Berkeley: University of California Press, 1987), 78–116; Jonathan Goldberg, "Speculations: *Macbeth* and Source," in *Shakespeare Reproduced: The Text in History & Ideology*, Jean E. Howard and Marion F. O'Connor, eds. (New York: Methuen, 1987), 242–64; Steven Mullaney, "Lying Like Truth: Riddle, Representation, and Treason" in his *The Place of the Stage: License, Play, and Power in Renaissance England* (Chicago: University of Chicago Press, 1988), 116–34.

62. Marcus, *Puzzling Shakespeare*, 105.

63. See Adelman, *Suffocating Mothers*, 130–47; Erickson, *Patriarchal Structures*, 116–22; Coppélia Kahn, *Man's Estate: Masculine Identity in Shakespeare* (Berkeley: University of California Press, 1981), 172–92; Leonard Tennenhouse, *Power on Display: The Politics of Shakespeare's Genres* (Methuen: New York, 1986), 127–32.

64. Adelman, *Suffocating Mothers*, 142–43.

65. Goldberg, "Speculations: *Macbeth* and Source."

66. Ibid., 260.

67. Stuart Clark, "King James's *Daemonologie*: Witchcraft and Kingship," in *The Damned Art: Essays in the Literature of Witchcraft*, Sydney Anglo, ed. (London: Routledge, 1977), 156–81.

68. Goldberg, "Speculations: *Macbeth* and Source," 248–49; Adelman also discusses Duncan's alliance with the witches, and points out that, like Macbeth's, Duncan's language unconsciously echoes that of the witches (*Suffocating Mothers*, 132).

69. Marjorie Garber describes "gender undecidability as such" (110) as the central source of both power and anxiety in *Macbeth* (*Shakespeare's Ghost Writers: Literature as Uncanny Causality* [New York: Methuen, 1987], 87–123).

70. Bullough, *Narrative and Dramatic Sources*, VII: 488.

71. Ibid., 489.
72. I borrow the phrase from Janet Adelman's *Suffocating Mothers*, 133.
73. Kenneth Muir's edition of *Macbeth* in the new Arden series (London: Methuen, 1951) glosses the phrase by citing lines 3–4 of the prologue to *Henry V*: "A Kingdom for a stage, princes to act, / And monarchs to behold the swelling scene" (p. 20). Given the prologue's description of the theatre as a "cockpit" (11) located "within the girdle of these walls" (19), it can be argued that "swelling" here is part of a systematic association between pregnancy and the acts of imaginative creation that take place in the theatre.
74. Marston, *Antonio and Mellida*, W. Reavely Gair, ed. (Manchester: Manchester University Press, 1991), "Induction," 11–12.
75. Eedes, *Six Learned and Godly Sermons* (London, 1604), sig. G1.
76. Laqueur, *Making Sex: Body and Gender from the Greeks to Freud* (Cambridge: Harvard University Press, 1990), 25–148. I quote here from page 25.
77. Aristotle's *Generation of Animals*, quoted from Laqueur, *Making Sex*, 30.
78. Laqueur, *Making Sex*, 58. See also Marie-Hélène Huet's book-length study of the relationship between maternality and monstrous progeny, *Monstrous Imagination* (Cambridge: Harvard University Press, 1993).
79. Kahn, *Man's Estate*, 173.
80. Ibid., 175.
81. Bushnell, *Tragedies of Tyrants: Political Thought and Theater in the English Renaissance* (Ithaca: Cornell University Press, 1990), 20–25, 34–36, 63–69.
82. Ibid., 34.
83. Ibid., 126–31. I quote here from page 130.
84. Adelman, *Suffocating Mothers*, 133.
85. Janet Adelman, ibid., describes Macduff's abandonment of his family as inexplicable and unforgivable and adds that the "unexplained abandonment severely qualifies Macduff's force as the play's central exemplar of a healthy manhood that can include the possibility of relationship to women" (144). I think Macduff's absence could be explained differently – as a tragic but comprehensible underestimation of Macbeth's tyranny – but agree that the basically unhealthy inverse relationship between martial power and nurturing fatherhood is maintained even in the case of the otherwise sympathetic Macduff.
86. On the similarities between the end of the play and its beginning see Sinfield, "*Macbeth*: History, Ideology, and Intellectuals."
87. It is important to remember also that *Lear* and *Macbeth* may have been written in 1605/6, in which case they would predate the heightened concern over James's profligacy which was catalyzed by gifts to Scottish favorites in 1606. We would not, then, expect any investigation of the ideology of bounty to be necessarily critical of James's behavior at this point.
88. Annabel Patterson's suggestion in *Censorship and Interpretation*.
89. For an account of the censorship exercised by the Revels office which

emphasizes its *ad hoc* quality see Richard Dutton's *Mastering the Revels: The Regulation and Censorship of English Renaissance Drama* (Iowa City: University of Iowa Press, 1991).

90. Barroll, *Politics, Plague, and Shakespeare's Theater: The Stuart Years* (Ithaca: Cornell University Press, 1991), 67.

5 THE POLITICS OF NOSTALGIA: QUEEN ELIZABETH IN
  EARLY JACOBEAN ENGLAND

1. Goodman, *The Court of King James the First*, 2 vols. (London, 1839), I: 96–98. This is the first published edition of Goodman's memoir, which was originally written in the 1650s in response to Anthony Weldon's *The Court and Character of King James* (London, 1650).
2. See J. E. Neale, "November 17" in his *Essays in Elizabethan History* (London: Jonathan Cape, 1958), 9–20; Judith Doolin Spikes, "The Jacobean History Play and the Myth of the Elect Nation," *Renaissance Drama* 8 (1977): 117–49; Frances Yates, *Majesty and Magic in Shakespeare's Last Plays* (Boulder: Shambhala, 1978), 17–37; Anne Barton, "Harking Back to Elizabeth: Ben Jonson and Caroline Nostalgia," *ELH* 48 (1981): 706–31; R. Malcolm Smuts, *Court Culture and the Origins of a Royalist Tradition in Early Stuart England* (Philadelphia: University of Pennsylvania Press, 1987), 22–42; John N. King, "Queen Elizabeth I: Representations of the Virgin Queen," *Renaissance Quarterly* 18 (1990): 30–74.
3. For a survey of such texts, see D. R. Woolf, "Two Elizabeths? James I and the Late Queen's Famous Memory," *Canadian Journal of History* 20 (1985): 167–91.
4. Williams, *Marxism and Literature* (Oxford: Oxford University Press, 1977), 121–27.
5. *CSP Ven*, x (1603–07), 9–10.
6. *Political Works*, 271.
7. The conceit by which Elizabeth is represented as the one rose uniting the warring houses of York and Lancaster is, as Frances Yates puts it, "an all-pervasive commonplace of Elizabethan symbolism" (*Astraea: The Imperial Theme in the Sixteenth Century* [London: Routledge, 1975] 50–51).
8. These lines, from the third stanza of Samuel Daniel's "Panegyric Congratulatory," can be found in Daniel, *Works*, I: 144. As discussed in chapter 1, Daniel's insistence on the continuity between the two rulers is both encomiastic and admonitory.
9. *The Poetical Works of Alexander Craig of Rose-Craig* (Glasgow, 1873), 24, lines 37–38.
10. J. W. Saunders, *A Biographical Dictionary of Renaissance Poets and Dramatists, 1520–1650* (Sussex: The Harvester Press, 1983), *sub nomine*.
11. Bernard H. Newdigate, *Michael Drayton and His Circle* (1941; rpt. Oxford: Basil Blackwell, 1961), 124–35.
12. Hooke, *A Sermon Preached Before the King at White-Hall, the Eight of May.*

1604…Jerusalems Peace (London, 1604), sigs. C2v–C3. Elsewhere, Hooke compares Elizabeth and James to Castor and Pollux (sig C1v) and to David and Solomon (sig. C3v). I am grateful to Peter McCullough for calling this material to my attention.

13. Graham Parry, *The Golden Age Restor'd: The Culture of the Stuart Court, 1603–42* (New York: St. Martin's Press, 1981), 1.
14. Nichols, I: 338.
15. See David Riggs, *Ben Jonson: A Life* (Cambridge: Harvard University Press, 1989), 11–12.
16. On Elizabethan uses of this legend, see S. K. Heninger, Jr., "The Tudor Myth of Troy-novant," *South Atlantic Quarterly* 61 (1962): 378–87, and Hugh A. MacDougall, *Racial Myth in English History: Trojans, Teutons, and Anglo-Saxons* (Hanover: New England University Press, 1982), 7–27.
17. Roberta F. Brinkley, *Arthurian Legend in the Seventeenth Century* (1932; rpt. New York: Octagon, 1967), 1–25.
18. Haller, *The Elect Nation: The Meaning and Relevance of Foxe's Book of Martyrs* (New York: Harper & Row, 1961), 224.
19. Foxe, *Actes and Monuments…the sixth time newly imprinted, with certaine additions thereunto annexed* (London, 1610), 1,952a. All subsequent quotations from Foxe's narrative will be taken from this edition, and citations will be given parenthetically by page and column.
20. The known details concerning this manuscript's circulation are summarized in Bacon, *Works*, VI: 283–84. I quote Bacon's memoir (as translated from the Latin by James Spedding) from this volume. Subsequent quotations will be cited parenthetically by page number.
21. Adams, "Spain or the Netherlands? The Dilemmas of Early Stuart Foreign Policy" in *Before the English Civil War: Essays on Early Stuart Politics and Government*, Howard Tomlinson, ed. (London: Macmillan, 1983), 90.
22. Nichols, II: 50. See also Simon Adams, "Spain or the Netherlands," and R. Malcolm Smuts, *Court Culture*, 23–26.
23. As quoted in G. P. V. Akrigg *Jacobean Pageant, or the Court of King James I* (1962; rpt. New York: Atheneum, 1974), 73.
24. Woolf, "Two Elizabeths?," 174.
25. Bacon, *Works*, VI: 283–84.
26. H. R. Trevor-Roper, *Queen Elizabeth's First Historian: William Camden and the Beginning of English 'Civil History'* (London: Jonathan Cape, 1971).
27. For more detailed accounts of Camden's production of the *Annales* see Trevor-Roper, *Queen Elizabeth's First Historian*; Wallace T. MacCaffrey's introduction to his edition of Camden's *The History of the Most Renowned and Victorious Princess Elizabeth late Queen of England: Selected Chapters* (Chicago: University of Chicago Press, 1970), and D. R. Woolf, *The Idea of History in Early Stuart England: Erudition, Ideology, and 'The Light of Truth' From the Accession of James I to the Civil War* (Toronto: University of Toronto Press, 1990), 117–21.
28. Compare Christopher Haigh (*The Reign of Elizabeth I* [Athens: University

of Georgia Press, 1985], 9): "the virtues and successes of Elizabeth were ... defined by the flaws and omissions of James, and Camden wrote a commentary on the rule of James in the guise of a history of the rule of Elizabeth."

29. I quote Camden's text from its earliest English translation: *The Historie of the Life and Reigne of the Most Renowmed [sic] and Victorious Princesse Elizabeth, Late Quene of England*, R. Norden, trans. (London, 1630), 83. Subsequent citations will be given parenthetically by page number.

30. Camden describes a statute "concerning the possessions of Archbishops and Bishops, *That they should not give, graunt or Leasse out the livings of the church ... to others then to the Queene, and her successours, reserving the old rents*. But that exception *for the Queene*, proved gainefull to her Courtiours that abused her bounty, and to the Bishops that sought their owne profit, but to the Church very hurtfull, untill such time as King *James* in the beginning of his Raigne tooke it away, to the great good of the church" (27).

31. Woolf, *The Idea of History*, 122.

32. See John N. King, "Queen Elizabeth I," 70–72.

33. Smuts, *Court Culture*, 16–18.

34. Stuart M. Kurland and Lee Bliss both read Cranmer's vision as admonitory and didactic, encouraging James to live up to the terms of the prophesy. Kurland juxtaposes the prophesy with the play's depiction of Henry VIII, in which he sees criticism of the real James ("*Henry VIII* and James I: Shakespeare and Jacobean Politics," *Shakespeare Studies* 19 [1987]: 203–17). Bliss argues, in "The Wheel of Fortune and the Maiden Phoenix of Shakespeare's *King Henry the Eighth*" (*ELH* 42 [1975]: 20), that Cranmer's prophesy "fulfills the didactic function of panegyric in the Renaissance: idealized portraits...heighten the subject's exemplary traits in order to incite emulation."

35. Barbara K. Lewalski's recent *Writing Women in Jacobean England* (Cambridge: Harvard University Press, 1993) describes this process of encomiastic translation, noting that at least one text – Hugh Holland's *Pancharis* (1603) – was originally intended for Elizabeth but was addressed to Anne upon the former's death (18).

36. Daniel, *Works*, III: 188. Subsequent citations from this masque will be given parenthetically by page number.

37. Anne and her ladies were also dressed in costumes from the late queen's wardrobe: "their attire was alike, loose mantles and petticoats, but of different colors, the stuffs embroidered satins and cloth of gold and silver, for which they were beholden to Queen Elizabeth's wardrobe" (*Dudley Carleton to John Chamberlain 1603–1624*, Maurice Lee Jr., ed. [New Brunswick: Rutgers University Press, 1972], 55). Some of the late queen's clothing was also altered and sent to Berwick in 1603 so that Anne could wear it on her inaugural journey south. See *CSP Ven*, x (1603–07), 64, and also Ethel Carleton Williams, *Anne of Denmark; Wife of James VI of Scotland: James I of England* (London: Longman, 1970), 74.

38. Lewalski describes a number of other ways in which Anne and her ladies stage their resistance to James in this entertainment. See *Writing Women*, 29–30.

39. Lewalski's reading of Jonson's *Masque of Blackness* parallels my discussion here. She finds the framing power of James (Albion) challenged within the masque's fiction by the transformative power of Aethiopia, a moon goddess reminiscent of Queen Elizabeth as Cynthia. Anne, freighted in this account with the affect surrounding Elizabeth, challenges the central, organizing power of her husband's authoritative gaze (*Writing Women*, 31–33).

40. J. Leeds Barroll, "The Court of the First Stuart Queen," in *The Mental World of the Jacobean Court*, Linda Levy Peck, ed. (Cambridge: Cambridge University Press, 1991), 191–208. See also Lewalski, *Writing Women*, 18–43.

41. The peculiar phenomenon of Prince Henry's brief, dramatic presence in England has been the subject of a good deal of scholarship. The fullest treatments are Roy Strong's *Henry, Prince of Wales, and England's Lost Renaissance* (New York: Thames and Hudson, 1986), which traces the life and cultural influence of the prince, and Jerry Wayne Williamson's *The Myth of the Conqueror: Prince Henry Stuart; A Study of 17th Century Personation* (New York: AMS Press, 1978), which concentrates on the intense myth-making that surrounded the prince from birth to death. See also Elkin Calhoun Wilson's *Prince Henry and English Literature* (Ithaca: Cornell University Press, 1946), and two pieces by David M. Bergeron: "Prince Henry and English Civic Pageantry" *Tennessee Studies in Literature* 13 (1968): 109–16, and *Shakespeare's Romances and the Royal Family* (Lawrence: Kansas University Press, 1985), 50–60.

42. George Marcelline, *The Triumphs of King James* (London, 1610), sig. A2. See also Robert Fletcher's *The Nine English Worthies* (1606), Henry Peacham's *Minerva Britanna or a Garden of Heroical Devices* (London, 1612), sig. D4^V, 8–12, and Michael Drayton's "Paean Triumphal" (*Works*, I: 480–84).

43. Daniel, *Works*, III: 303.

44. On the Elizabethan theme in *Tethys Festival* see Strong, *Henry, Prince of Wales*, 156–57.

45. On Elizabethan chivalry see Richard C. McCoy, *The Rights of Knighthood: The Literature and Politics of Elizabethan Chivalry* (Berkeley: University of California Press, 1989), and Arthur B. Ferguson, *The Chivalric Tradition in Renaissance England* (Cranbury: Associated University Presses, 1986).

46. Strong, *Henry, Prince of Wales*, 67.

47. As quoted in ibid., 8.

48. Ibid., 75–60; Williamson, *The Myth of the Conqueror*, 50–54.

49. Williamson, *The Myth of the Conqueror*, 58–60. Anticipating arrest, Ralegh had signed his estate over to his son Wat. The papers were subsequently disallowed on technicalities and the estate reverted to the crown. Henry managed to stall the gift to Carr, but the property was finally given to the royal favorite after the prince's death.

50. Strong, *Henry, Prince of Wales*, 223–24; Parry, *The Golden Age Restor'd*, 64–94. On the association between the applied, practical sciences and imperial ambition at St. James's see Strong, 212–19, Lesley B. Cormack, "Twisting the Lion's Tail: Practice and Theory at the Court of Henry Prince of Wales" in *Patronage and Institutions: Science, Technology, and Medicine at the European Court, 1500–1700*, Bruce T. Moran, ed. (Rochester: Boydell Press, 1991), 67–83, and Christopher Hill, *Intellectual Origins of the English Revolution* (Oxford: Clarendon Press, 1965), 213–19.

51. Hill, *Intellectual Origins*, 213–214. Williamson describes the elegiac outpouring for Henry as a phenomenon modelled on the widespread elegiac response to the earlier loss of Sidney in *The Myth of the Conqueror*, 172.

52. Strong, *Henry, Prince of Wales*, 70.

53. Drayton, *Works*, V: 378, lines 117–20.

54. Strong, *Henry, Prince of Wales*, 157.

55. Drayton, *Works*, IV: 337–38, lines 341–53. John Selden is more diplomatic than Drayton in his notes appended to the end of the canto, listing "our present Soveraigne" among the royal defenders of "the true ancient faith" (IV: 358).

56. For an account of Meliadus's challenge see Nichols, II: 266–67. Wilson describes the ceremony between the challenge and the barriers in *Prince Henry and English Literature*, 78–79.

57. My text here is from Stephen Orgel, ed., *Ben Jonson: The Complete Masques* (New Haven: Yale University Press, 1969). This is from line 67. Subsequent citations will be given parenthetically by line number.

58. Norman Council's "Ben Jonson, Inigo Jones, and the Transformation of Tudor Chivalry" (*ELH* 47 [1980]: 259–75) describes Jonson's rejection of Arthurian values as evidence of his sense that chivalry and humanism were no longer compatible and that chivalric values were no longer feasible. John Peacock's "Jonson and Jones Collaborate on *Prince Henry's Barriers*" (*Word & Image* 3 [1987]: 172–94) compares Jonson's dismantling of his Arthurian sources with the hybrid of Arthurian and classical elements in Jones's settings. Williamson (*The Myth of the Conqueror*, 90–95) locates Jonson among a number of authors who he describes as trying to counter the martial myth-making that surrounded the prince. Strong (*Henry, Prince of Wales*, 141–51) detects in Jonson's text an inability to reconcile the demands of his two patrons, the prince and the king.

59. Strong, *Henry, Prince of Wales*, 144.

60. Stephen Orgel and Roy Strong, *Inigo Jones: The Theater of the Stuart Court*, 2 vols. (Berkeley: University of California Press, 1973), I: 159.

61. For the former, see Strong, *Henry, Prince of Wales*, 155. On the latter, see Stephen Orgel, *The Illusion of Power* (Berkeley: University of California Press, 1975), 67. It is also possible that the assassination of Henri IV of France, which changed the tenor of European affairs and made Prince Henry the focus of international Protestant hopes, may have caused James to shy away from so martial a public display in 1611.

62. Williamson, *The Myth of the Conqueror*, 95–102. There is a boisterous anti-masque of satyrs in *Oberon*, but it is treated in a manner consonant with the masque's emphasis on persuasive love: rather than being vanquished or transformed, the satyrs are awed and subsumed (Orgel, *The Jonsonian Masque* [Cambridge: Harvard University Press, 1965], 84). Chapman's *Conspiracy of Charles, Duke of Byron* (1608) is also poised between the prince's interest in Elizabethan material and more moderate politics. Unfortunately, Chapman's use of contemporary French history angered the French ambassador in England, and the published play has been cut: all that remains of Glorianna in Act 4 is Crequi's secondhand account of Byron's journey (see E. K. Chambers, *The Elizabethan Stage*, 4 vols. [Oxford: Oxford University Press, 1923], III: 257–58).

63. Reports of James's jealous opposition to the popularity of his son have been overemphasized. James himself used the popularity of his son as a negotiating tool in his financial dealings with parliament on more than one occasion (Strong, *Henry, Prince of Wales*, 25–26; see also Williamson, *The Myth of the Conqueror*, 39–40, 62–63).

64. On the emergence of an oppositional group of nostalgic Spenserian poets after 1612 see David Norbrook, *Poetry and Politics in the English Renaissance* (London: Routledge, 1984), 202–14.

65. On the proliferation of religious texts for the London citizenry see Louis B. Wright, *Middle Class Culture in Elizabethan England* (Chapel Hill: University of North Carolina Press, 1935), 228–96. Wright observes that "the zest for collections of pious aphorisms, books of prayers and religious guidance, printed sermons, adaptations of the Psalms, and moralized allegories was limited only by the ability of the printers to pour out such works" (228).

66. Dekker and Heywood have long been considered paradigmatic, non-aristocratic citizen playwrights. See "Dekker, Heywood and the Citizen Morality" in L. C. Knights, *Drama and Society in the Age of Jonson* (1937; rpt. New York: W. W. Norton & Co., 1968), 228–55, and Kathleen E. McLuskie, *Dekker and Heywood: Professional Dramatists* (New York: St. Martin's Press, 1994).

67. See Arthur Melville Clark, *Thomas Heywood: Playwright and Miscellanist* (Oxford: Basil Blackwell, 1931), 32–44, and the introduction to Madeline Doran's edition of the second part of Heywood's *If You Know Not Me You Know Nobody* (Oxford: Malone Society Reprints, 1935), xii–xix. Doran edited both parts of Heywood's play for the Malone Society in 1935; subsequent references to these plays will use these editions and will be given parenthetically by line number.

68. David M. Bergeron, *English Civic Pageantry 1558–1624*, (Columbia: University of South Carolina Press, 1971), 20–21.

69. The speech is reproduced in J. E. Neale, *Elizabeth I and Her Parliaments 1584–1601* (1958; rpt. New York: W. W. Norton & Co., 1966), 388–91.

70. Ibid., 391–93; see also C. V. Wedgwood, *Oliver Cromwell and the Elizabethan Inheritance* (London: Jonathan Cape, 1970).

71. John Stow, *The Survey of London*, 2 vols., Charles Lethbridge Kingsford, ed. (Oxford: Clarendon Press, 1908), 1: 192–93.
72. The basic outlines of the relationship between the queen and the Merchant Adventures was established by George Unwin in *Studies in Economic History: The Collected Papers of George Unwin*, R. H. Tawney, ed. (London: Macmillan and Co., 1927), 133–220.
73. On William Cecil's London clientage, for example, see Ian W. Archer, *The Pursuit of Stability: New Views on History and Society in Early Modern Europe* (Cambridge: Cambridge University Press, 1991) 34, 38.
74. Hexter, *Reappraisals in History: New Views on History and Society in Early Modern Europe* (1961; 2nd edn. Chicago: University of Chicago Press, 1979), 103.
75. Barbara J. Baines, *Thomas Heywood* (Boston: Twayne, 1984), 29–31. Heywood continued to re-use Foxe's account of Elizabeth's troubles in various forms throughout his career. See also Georgianna Ziegler, "England's Savior: Elizabeth I in the Writings of Thomas Heywood," *Renaissance Papers 1980*: 29–37.
76. *CSP Ven*, x (1603–7), 513.
77. Lever's poem is reproduced in the third volume of the *Miscellanies of the Fuller Worthies Library*, 4 vols., Alexander B. Grossart, ed. (1872; rpt. New York: AMS Press, 1970). I quote here from page 688; subsequent quotations will be given parenthetically by page number.
78. Louis Adrian Montrose, "The Elizabethan Subject and the Spenserian Text,' in *Literary Theory/Renaissance Texts*, Patricia Parker and David Quint, eds. (Baltimore: The Johns Hopkins University Press, 1986), 303.
79. *The Poems of James VI of Scotland*, 2 vols., James Craigie, ed. (Edinburgh: William Blackwood & Son, 1955–58), 1: 66.
80. Gordon, "*Heymenaei*: Ben Johnson's Masque of Union," in *The Renaissance Imagination: Essays and Lectures by D. J. Gordon*, Stephen Orgel, ed. (Berkeley: University of California Press, 1975), 184. See also Jonathan Goldberg, *James I and the Politics of Literature* (Baltimore: The John Hopkins University Press, 1983), 17–27.
81. Compare McLuskie, who emphasizes the oppositional charge carried by Protestant imperial sentiments in the early Jacobean works of Dekker and Heywood (*Dekker and Heywood*, 41–53).
82. Patterson, *Censorship and Interpretation: The Conditions of Writing and Reading in Early Modern England* (Madison: University of Wisconsin Press, 1984).
83. *The Dramatic Works of Thomas Dekker*, 4 vols., Fredson Bowers, ed. (Cambridge: Cambridge University Press, 1953–61), II: 497. Subsequent citations will refer to this edition and will be given parenthetically.
84. *The Poems of James VI of Scotland*, 1: 79.
85. As D. J. Gordon has shown, Dekker's opposition to Ben Jonson's brand of Jacobean esoterica dates back to their uneasy collaboration on James royal entry in 1604. See *The Renaissance Imagination*, 11–14.
86. For a more general account of the commonplace association between

Elizabeth's impregnable body and England's inviolable enclosure see Peter Stallybrass, "Patriarchal Territories: The Body Enclosed" in *Rewriting the Renaissance: The Discourse of Sexual Difference in Early Modern Europe* (Chicago: University of Chicago Press, 1986), 123–42.

87. On the networks of mythographic arcana underlying Jacobean masques and other expressions of Jacobean culture see the various essays in D. J. Gordon's *The Renaissance Imagination*. On the relation between these arcana and James's style, see Goldberg, *James I and the Politics of Literature*, 55–112.

88. Orgel and Strong, *Inigo Jones: The Theater of the Stuart Court*, 1: 6.

89. Frederick O. Waage, *Thomas Dekker's Pamphlets, 1603–9, and Jacobean Popular Literature*, 2 vols. (Salzburg: Institut für Englische Sprache und Literatur, Universität Salzberg, 1977), 1: 22–23. Bulkeley's assimilation of the Gunpowder Plot to the Foxean tradition (in the 1610 edition, quoted above) reinforces this reading.

90. Arthur Melville Clark, *Thomas Heywood*, 50–57.

91. Heywood, *Troia Britanica: or, Great Britaines Troy* (London, 1609), canto 1, stanza 8, lines 7–8. Subsequent citations will be given parenthetically by canto, stanza, and line.

92. On the former, Wright observes that the London audience was always "ready to approve sentiments expressing the subject's obligations of loyalty" in his *Middle-Class Culture*, 622. On mercantile expansion see B. E. Supple, *Commercial Crisis and Change 1600–1642; A Study in the Instability of a Mercantile Economy* (Cambridge: Cambridge University Press, 1959), 28–32.

93. Paul N. Siegel, *Shakespearean Tragedy and the Elizabethan Compromise* (New York: New York University Press, 1957), 37.

94. Ashton, *The Crown and the Money Market 1603–1640* (Oxford: Clarendon Press, 1960), 114–18.

95. Ibid., 121–22.

96. I quote from John Gouws, ed., *The Prose Works of Fulke Greville, Lord Brooke* (Oxford: Clarendon Press, 1986), 98, 103. Subsequent citations given parenthetically.

97. Rebholz, *The Life of Fulke Greville First Lord Brooke* (Oxford: Clarendon Press, 1971), 215. Rebholz discusses the *Dedication* in some depth on pp. 205–15.

98. Williams, *Marxism and Literature*, 123.

99. H. R. Trevor-Roper, "Oliver Cromwell and his Parliaments" in his *Religion, the Reformation and Social Change* (London: MacMillan, 1967), 345–91. Wedgwood, *Oliver Cromwell and the Elizabethan Inheritance*, 20; See also J. E. Neale, "November 17th."

6 ROYAL STYLE AND THE CIVIC ELITE IN EARLY JACOBEAN LONDON

1. A. L. Beier distinguishes between these groupings in "Engine of Manufacture: the Trades of London" in *London 1500–1700: The Making of*

the Metropolis, A. L. Beier and Roger Finlay, eds. (London: Longman, 1986), 141–67.

2. Ian Archer, *The Pursuit of Stability: Social Relations in Elizabethan London* (Cambridge: Cambridge University Press, 1991), 58–99.

3. See F. J. Fisher, "London as a Center for Conspicuous Consumption in the Sixteenth and Seventeenth Centuries" reprinted in *London and the English Economy*, P. J. Corfield and N. B. Harte, eds. (London: The Hambledon Press, 1990), 105–18; Lawrence Stone, *The Crisis of the Aristocracy* (Oxford: Clarendon Press, 1965), 385–403; Ann Jennalie Cook, *The Privileged Playgoers of Shakespeare's London* (Princeton: Princeton University Press, 1981). Though Cook's statistics and assumptions have been criticized in the second appendix to Martin Butler's *Theater and Crisis 1632–1642* ([Cambridge: Cambridge University Press, 1984], 293–306), her work demonstrates the distortions involved in treating London playgoers as a homogeneous group.

4. Archer, *The Pursuit of Stability*, 39–49. See also Frank Freeman Foster, *The Politics of Stability: A Portrait of the Rulers of Elizabethan London* (London: Royal Historical Society, 1977).

5. Lawrence Stone, "The Residential Development of the West End of London in the Seventeenth Century," in *After the Reformation: Essays in Honor of J. H. Hexter*, Barbara C. Malament, ed. (Philadelphia: University of Pennsylvania Press, 1980), 167–212. See also Emrys Jones, "London in the Early Seventeenth Century: An Ecological Approach," *The London Journal* 6 (1980): 123–33.

6. Lang, "Social Origins and Social Aspirations of Jacobean London Merchants," *Economic History Review*, 2nd series, 27 (1974): 47. See also Archer, *The Pursuit of Stability*, 50–55.

7. For an account of early Stuart London's governmental constitution see Valerie Pearl, *London and the Outbreak of the Puritan Revolution: City Government and National Politics, 1625–43* (Oxford: Oxford University Press, 1961), 45–69.

8. See Archer, *The Pursuit of Stability*, 74–75.

9. Pearl, "Social Policy in Early Modern London," in *History and Imagination: Essays in Honour of H. R. Trevor-Roper*, H. Lloyd-Jones, Valerie Pearl, and Blair Worden, eds. (London: Duckworth, 1981), 115–31.

10. Archer, *The Pursuit of Stability*, 50–51.

11. Laura Stevenson O'Connell, "The Elizabethan Bourgeois Hero-Tale: Aspects of an Adolescent Social Consciousness," in *After the Reformation*, Barbara C. Malament, ed., 267–90.

12. The Whittington of legend is the subject of a lost play written in 1605; in a ballad of the same year he lends money to the king and then burns the promissory notes, refusing to be repaid (*The Roxburghe Ballads*, 9 vols., W. Chappell and J. W. Ebsworth, eds. [1869–97; rpt. New York: AMS Press, 1966], VII, pt. 1, pp. 585–86). Information concerning the ballad's entry into the Stationers' Register can be found in Hyder E. Rollins, *An Analytical Index to the Ballad-Entries (1557–1709) in the Registers of the Company of*

Stationers of London (Chapel Hill: University of North Carolina Press, 1924), 243.

13. Stow, *The Survey of London*, 2 vols., Charles Lethbridge Kingsford, ed. (Oxford: Clarendon Press, 1908), II: 200–201.

14. See my discussion of Elizabeth's London persona in chapter 5 above.

15. Louis B. Wright describes the London audience as "ready to approve sentiments expressing the subject's obligations of loyalty" in his *Middle-Class Culture in Elizabethan England* (Chapel Hill: University of North Carolina Press, 1935), 622.

16. Robert Ashton, *The City and the Court 1603–1643* (Cambridge: Cambridge University Press, 1979), 70–82.

17. Samuel R. Gardiner, *History of England from the Accession of James I. to the Outbreak of the Civil War, 1603–1642*, 10 vols. (London, 1883–4), II: 1–15.

18. See Lawrence Stone, "Inigo Jones and the New Exchange," *The Archaeological Journal* 114 (1957): 107.

19. O'Connell, "The Elizabethan Bourgeois Hero-Tale," 269.

20. *The Works of Thomas Deloney*, Francis Oscar Mann, ed. (Oxford: Clarendon Press, 1912), 38.

21. See Bernard Capp, "Popular Literature" in *Popular Culture In Seventeenth-Century England*, Barry Reay, ed. (London: Croom Helm, 1985), 209–11, and Margaret Spufford, *Small Books and Pleasant Histories: Popular Fiction and Its Readership in Seventeenth-Century England* (Athens: University of Georgia Press, 1981), 222–24.

22. Siegel, *Shakespearean Tragedy and the Elizabethan Compromise* (New York: New York University Press, 1957).

23. Arthur Wilson (in *The History of Great Britain, Being the Life and Reign of King James I* [London: 1653], 12–13) observed that where Elizabeth had "with a well-pleased affection met her peoples Acclamation," James "endured the days brunt with *Patience*, being assured he should never have another."

24. Goldberg, *James I and the Politics of Literature: Jonson, Shakespeare, Donne, and Their Contemporaries* (Baltimore: The Johns Hopkins University Press, 1983), 31.

25. Nichols, I: 414.

26. *CSP Ven* x (1603–7), 513.

27. As quoted in Charles M. Clode, *The Early History of the Guild of Merchant Taylors of the Fraternity of St. John the Baptist, London, with Notice of the Lives of Some of its Eminent Members*, pt. 1 (London, 1888), 277.

28. No detailed account of the visit remains, but it is noted in Nichols, II: 132–34.

29. Clode, *Early History*, 280. Clode describes in detail both the preparation and the event itself: pp. 275–318.

30. See Thomas Platter's *Travels in England*, Clare Williams, trans. and ed. (London: Jonathan Cape, 1937), 193–95.

31. Quotations from this debate, including those to follow, are from Clode, *Early History*, 284.

32. Ibid.

33. Munday, *A Brief Chronicle* (London: 1611), sig. A5–A5^V. Subsequent citations will be given parenthetically by signature.

34. *The Non-Dramatic Works of Thomas Dekker*, 5 vols., Alexander B. Grosart, ed. (1884–6; rept. New York: Russell & Russell, 1963), IV: 28, 37. Subsequent citations will be given parenthetically.

35. See *A Calendar of Dramatic Records in the Books of the Livery Companies of London*, Jean Robertson and D. J. Gordon, eds., published by the Malone Society as *Collections* III (1954), 175–76.

36. As with a great deal of his *Brief Chronicle*, Munday reuses this material in his continuation of Stow's *Survey of London* (London, 1618).

37. David Bergeron's *English Civic Pageantry* (Columbia: University of South Carolina Press, 1971), 125–241, provides an authoritative survey of the form's development. Other accounts include Theodore B. Leinwand, "London Triumphing: The Jacobean Lord Mayor's Show," *Clio* 11 (1982), 137–53; Gail Kern Paster, "The Idea of London in Masque and Pageant," in *Pageantry in the Shakespearean Theater*, David Bergeron, ed. (Athens: University of Georgia Press, 1985), 48–64; and M. C. Bradbrook, "The Politics of Pageantry: Social Implications in Jacobean London," in *Poetry and Drama 1570–1700: Essays in Honour of Harold F. Brooks* (London: Methuen, 1981), 60–75.

38. Bradbrook, "The Politics of Pageantry," 64.

39. Knowles, "The Spectacle of the Realm: Civic Consciousness, Rhetoric and Ritual in Early Modern London," *Theatre and Government Under the Early Stuarts*, J. R. Mulryne and Margaret Shewring, eds. (Cambridge: Cambridge University Press, 1993), 157.

40. Leinwand, "London Triumphing," 137.

41. Plague forced cancellation of the mayoral pageants of 1592–94, and there is no record of performances in 1596 or 1599. Company records allude to pageants in the remaining years, but we do not have descriptions of their plots or devices.

42. Bergeron, *English Civic Pageantry*, 134–37. See also Jennifer Harrison, "Lord Mayor's Day in the 1590s," *History Today* 42 (January, 1992): 37–43.

43. *Pageants and Entertainments of Anthony Munday: A Critical Edition*, David M. Bergeron, ed. (New York: Garland, 1985), lines 277–81. Subsequent citations from Munday's pageants will be given parenthetically by line number.

44. Bergeron points out a number of Munday's borrowings from Dekker's text of the entry pageant: ibid., 32–34.

45. Ibid., 31–32.

46. The Merchant Taylors' accounts record payments for the lost pageant of 1610 for the making of nine pendants for kings seated on a rock on the Thames, as well as to an actor who played Merlin. Extrapolating from these payments, and from the Merchant Taylors' interest in their Company's privileged relationship to court and crown, one imagines that the show would have been of interest here. See the Malone Society *Collections* III (1954): 78–79.

47. On the importance of such oaths see Knowles, "The Spectacle of the Realm," 163–66.
48. Bergeron, ed., *Pageants and Entertainments of Anthony Munday*, 49.
49. *The Dramatic Works of Thomas Dekker*, 4 vols., Fredson Bowers, ed. (Cambridge: Cambridge University Press, 1953–61), III: 225. Subsequent citations from this pageant will be given parenthetically by line number.
50. It would be possible to read this as an example of veiled political commentary, since Neptune often stood for the king within the fictions of masques such as Samuel Daniel's *Tethy's Festival* (1610).
51. Bergeron, *English Civic Pageantry*, 170.
52. I quote from *The Works of Thomas Middleton*, 8 vols., A. H. Bullen, ed. (London, 1885–6), VII: 229. Subsequent citations will be given parenthetically by page number.
53. See Paster, "The Idea of London," 57.
54. David Bergeron, *English Civic Pageantry*, 179.
55. Bullen, ed., *The Works of Thomas Middleton*, II: 246n.
56. Wickham, *Early English Stages 1300 to 1660*, 3 vols. (New York: Columbia University Press, 1959–), II, pt. 1, p. 237.
57. Jonson, *The Complete Masques*, Stephen Orgel, ed. (New Haven: Yale University Press, 1969), line 225. Subsequent citations from Jonson's masques will be given parenthetically by line number. Susan Wells discusses Middleton's use of masque imagery in "Jacobean City Comedy and the Ideology of the City," *ELH* 48 (1981): 44–45.
58. Sergei Lobanov-Rostovsky sees the pageants of 1612–13 as a departure from the mimetic formulae of mayoral pageants unwelcome to the Companies themselves: "*The Triumphes of Golde*: Economic Authority in the Jacobean Lord Mayor's Show," *ELH* 60 (1993): 879–98.
59. Wickham, *Early English Stages*, II, pt. 1, p. 237.
60. Knights *Drama and Society in the Age of Jonson* (1937; rpt. New York: W. W. Norton & Co., 1968).
61. Recent examples include Walter Cohen, *Drama of a Nation: Public Theater in Renaissance England and Spain* (Ithaca: Cornell University Press, 1985), 282–301, and Lawrence Venuti, *Our Halcyon Days: English Prerevolutionary Texts and Postmodern Culture* (Madison: University of Wisconsin Press, 1989), 110–36. Susan Wells eschews Knights's vocabulary, but situates city comedy within long-range economic and ideological changes. See "Jacobean City Comedy and the Ideology of the City," 837–60.
62. City comedy as a subgenre was popularized by Brian Gibbons's *Jacobean City Comedy: A Study of Satiric Plays by Jonson, Marston and Middleton* (Cambridge: Harvard University Press, 1968). Recent studies include Alexander Leggatt, *Citizen Comedy in the Age of Shakespeare* (Toronto: University of Toronto Press, 1973), and Theodore Leinwand, *The City Staged: Jacobean Comedy 1603–1613* (Madison: University of Wisconsin Press, 1986). Douglas Bruster argues that its definition has been too rigid and exclusionary. See his *Drama and Market in the Age of Shakespeare* (Cambridge: Cambridge University Press, 1992), 29–46.

63. Unwin, *The Gilds and Companies of London* (London: Methuen & Co., 1909), 323.

64. Johnson, *The Pleasant Conceits of Old Hobson the Merry Londoner, Full of Humorous Discourses and Witty Meriments* (London, 1607), sig. A2.

65. Bowers, ed. *The Dramatic Works of Thomas Dekker*, 1: 1.4.15. Subsequent citations will be given parenthetically by act, scene, and line.

66. This reference to London's Bethlehem hospital shows that the depictions of city life are animated by Dekker's London despite the play's Milanese setting.

67. Bullen, ed., *The Works of Thomas Middleton*, 1: 3.4.6–7. Subsequent citations will be given parenthetically by act, scene, and line.

68. The association between lands and women is made explicit in an exchange between Quomodo and his assistant Shortyard: Quomodo announces "I've seen what I desire"; Shortyard responds "A woman?"; Quomodo: "No, land" (1.1.106). For a discussion of the intersection of gender and market see Karen Newman, "City Talk: Women and Commodification in Jonson's *Epicoene*," *ELH* 56 (1989): 503–18.

69. A. L. and M. L. Kistner have argued for the play's conservatism in "Heirs and Identity: The Bases of Social Order in *Michaelmas Term*," *Modern Language Studies* 16 (1986): 61–71. Margot Heinemann cautions against seeing the play as evidence of Middleton's support of gentry over citizenry in her *Puritanism and Theater: Thomas Middleton and Oppositional Drama Under the Early Stuarts* (Cambridge: Cambridge University Press, 1980), 90–93. For a reading of the play responsive to ambivalences in the depiction of civic and gentle status, see Paul Yachnin, "Social Competition in Middleton's *Michaelmas Term*," *Explorations in Renaissance Culture* 13 (1987): 87–99.

70. J. Cooke, *Green's Tu Quoque or, The Cittie Gallant*, Alan J. Berman, ed. (New York: Garland, 1984), lines 133–34. Subsequent citations will be given parenthetically.

71. Bruster, *Drama and Market in the Age of Shakespeare*, 37. Bruster argues against the position – articulated in Steven Mullaney's *The Place of the Stage: License, Play, and Power in Renaissance England* (Chicago: University of Chicago Press, 1988) – that the theatres existed on the margins of London proper, at once banished to the marginal space of the liberties and able to express destabilizing ideologies. Bruster maintains that "to posit a relatively stable and unchanging London against which the Liberties and certain plays seem rebelliously marginal is to underestimate the fluidity of existence and exchange in the early modern city" (10), an argument supported by the fact that in 1613 a proposal to build a theatre north of the Thames was blocked by a petition from the watermen, whose livelihood depended on the custom of theatre audiences needing to cross the river. In addition to weakening the inevitability of the metaphorical association between liberties and playhouses, this underscores the theatre's complicated involvement with London's varied economic structures. See Unwin, *Gilds and Companies*, 311–12.

72. Lawrence Stone (*The Crisis of the Aristocracy* [Oxford: Clarendon Press, 1965], 71–82) estimates that at Elizabeth's death there were roughly 550 knights in England. By December 1604 James and his agents had created 1,161 new knights.

73. Ashton, *The City and the Court*, 100. See also R. H. Tawney, *Business and Politics Under James I: Lionel Cranfield as Merchant and Minister* (Cambridge: Cambridge University Press, 1958). The alliance was smoothed by a decade of mercantile prosperity: see B. E. Supple, *Commercial Crisis and Change 1600–1642; A Study in the Instability of a Mercantile Economy* (Cambridge: Cambridge University Press, 1959), 28–32.

74. Gardiner, *History*, II: 232–49; Supple, *Commercial Crisis and Change*, 33–51; Robert Ashton, *The Crown and the Money market, 1603–1640* (Oxford, Clarendon Press, 1960), 121–22.

75. On Jonson's masque see Leah S. Marcus, *The Politics of Mirth: Jonson, Herrick, Milton, Marvell, and the Defense of Old Holiday Pastimes* (Chicago: University of Chicago Press, 1986), 76–85.

EPILOGUE: WARRANT AND OBEDIENCE IN *BARTHOLOMEW FAIR*

1. Heffner Jr., "Unifying Symbols in the Comedy of Ben Jonson," *English Stage Comedy*, W. K. Wimsatt, ed. (New York: Columbia University Press, 1955), 89.

2. On the play's interest in the practice of licensing see Richard A. Burt, "'Licensed By Authority': Ben Jonson and the Politics of Early Stuart Theater," *ELH* 54 (1987): 529–60.

3. H&S, VI: 9.

4. Aubrey, *Brief Lives*, 2 vols., Andrew Clark, ed. (Oxford: Clarendon Press, 1898), II: 14. I am not convinced by Keith Sturgess's contention that *Bartholomew Fair* is a play intended primarily for court performance (*Jacobean Private Theater* [London: Routledge, 1987], 137–89).

5. The text that accompanies Jonson's dedication to James is taken from Horace's epistle to Augustus, an epistle prompted – as Suetonius describes – by Augustus himself. See the Loeb Classical Library edition of *Suetonius*, 2 vols., J. C. Rolfe trans. (1914; rev. edn. London: William Heinemann, 1928–30), II: 486–89. Jonson's dedicatory motto contains Horace's criticism of contemporary Roman drama, and its audience: "si foret in terris, rideret *Democritus* . . . nam / spectaret populum ludis attentiùs ipsis, / ut sibi praebentem, mimo spectacula plura. / scriptores autem narrare putaret assello / fabellam surdo" ("Were Democritus still on earth, he would laugh . . . for he would gaze more intently on the people than on the play itself, as giving him more by far worth looking at. But for the authors – he would suppose that they were telling their tale to a deaf ass." I use the Loeb edition of *Horace: Satires, Epistles and Ars Poetica*, H. Rushton Fairclough trans. (1926: rev. edn. Cambridge: Harvard University Press, 1961), 413.

Horace's epistle juxtaposes this theatre audience – which cannot recognize talent – with the superior perception and munificence of Augustus: "Virgil and Varius, those poets whom you love, discredit not your judgement of them nor the gifts which, to the giver's great renown, they have received" (245–47). Thus, Jonson's dedication points toward a distinction between James and the play's Hope theatre audience, suggesting that the latter was unable to recognize the play's merit. But Horace's epistle distinguishes between the hapless writer of comedy – always reliant on a crowd's approval (180–81) – and those writers who "prefer to put themselves in a reader's hands" (214–15) more directly by forgoing the public stage. Though this distinction is of a piece with Jonson's own antitheatricalism, and though Jonson himself was a pioneer in putting his own plays "in a reader's hands," this epistle makes an odd introduction to a comedy written for the stage. For where Horace distinguishes sharply between poetry fit for a monarch and poetry for the undiscerning masses in the public theatre, Jonson's dedication insists that his public play is not only meaningful but meaningful for James.

6. Marcus discusses these similarities in *The Politics of Mirth: Jonson, Herrick Milton, Marvell, and the Defense of Old Holiday Pastimes* (Chicago: University of Chicago Press, 1986), 55. See also C. G. Thayer, *Ben Jonson: Studies in the Plays* (Norman: University of Oklahoma Press, 1963), 144–45.

7. H&S, VI: 5.6.111–13. Subsequent citations will refer to this edition and will be given parenthetically.

8. *Political Works*, 308–09. See Gillian Manning, "An Echo of King James in Jonson's *Bartholomew Fair*," *Notes and Queries* 36 ns (1989): 342–44.

9. Marcus, *The Politics of Mirth*, 38–63.

10. See W. J. Jones, "The Crown and the Courts in England 1603–1625," in *The Reign of James VI and I*, Alan G. R. Smith, ed. (London: Macmillan, 1973), 177–94. Jones argues that "notions that the king was 'opposed' by judges or common lawyers lack credibility" (177), and adds that even Sir Edward Coke, the most notorious Jacobean spokesman for the sovereignty of common law, "never conceived himself to be a critic of Crown or prerogative" (192). It is worth noting as well that the traditional Court of Pyepowders, over which Overdo is to preside, had extremely limited jurisdiction: it was authorized to hear only those cases occurring in the physical site of the fair for its duration. Moreover, it was to hear only commercial cases. It could hear charges of slander against wares, but not against people. This is hardly the kind of court that would be likely to represent prerogative squabbles with the crown. See Henry Morley, *Memoirs of Bartholomew Fair* (London, 1859), 96–100, and John Pettingall, "Of The Courts of Pypowder," in *Archaeologia: or Miscellaneous Tracts Relating to Antiquity*, 2nd ed., vol. 1 (London: printed for the Society of Antiquaries of London, 1779), 191–204.

11. David McPherson, "The Origins of Overdo: A Study in Jonsonian Invention," *Modern Language Quarterly* 37 (1976): 221–33.

12. Ibid., 223–24.
13. Johnson, *Looke on me London* (London, 1613), sig. A3.
14. McPherson, "The Origins of Overdo," 227–28.
15. James F. Larkin and Paul L. Hughes, eds., *Stuart Royal Proclamations, Volume I: Royal Proclamations of King James, 1603–1625* (Oxford: Clarendon Press, 1973), 46. See also Morley, *Memoirs of Bartholomew Fair*, 136.
16. Brian Gibbons has described Overdo's disguise as a parody of the disguised duke plot popular during the first years of James's reign (*Jacobean City Comedy* [Cambridge: Harvard University Press, 1968], 179–91).
17. Middleton's mayoral pageant was of course notable for its courtly extravagance and style (see chapter 6), itself taking cues fro the king's masques. This may have contributed to Jonson's sense that the performances of delegated authority take their cues from king and court.
18. See the discussion of panegyric fashion in chapter 1.
19. Licensing and the alienation of authority are the subjects of Burt's "'Licensed By Authority.'"
20. Heffner Jr., "Unifying Symbols," 90. Jonas Barish has suggested that Trouble-all is Jonson's edgy self-satire: "In the lunatic Troubleall ... Jonson travesties the craving for sanctions, the longing for official endorsement, that has haunted him since his earliest plays." See his "Feasting and Judging in Jonsonian comedy," *Renaissance Drama* ns 5 (1972): 28.
21. Marcus, *The Politics of Mirth*, 56.
22. Goldberg, *James I and the Politics of Literature: Jonson, Shakespeare, Donne, and their Contemporaries* (Baltimore: The Johns Hopkins University Press, 1983), 217.
23. Eugene M. Waith, in his edition of the play (New Haven: Yale University Press, 1963) attributes the line to Grace Wellborn instead of Quarlous.
24. Richard Levin has noted that the play is given structure by the successive humbling of these three hypocrites. See *The Multiple Plot in English Renaissance Drama* (Chicago: University of Chicago Press, 1971), 202–14.
25. Burt, "'Licensed By Authority'."
26. Quoted in David Harris Willson, *King James VI & I* (1959; rpt. New York: Oxford University Press, 1967), 225.
27. I borrow the term "Laureate" as a shorthand describing a public mode of poetic self-presentation from Richard Helgerson's *Self-Crowned Laureates: Spenser, Jonson, Milton, and the Literary System* (Berkeley: University of California Press, 1983).
28. The play's "Induction" stages Jonson's own desire to control the circulation of interpretations of his play, and to establish by contract what Michael Bristol has called "discursive sovereignty over the 'matter' or text of the theatrical event" (*Carnival and Theater: Plebeian Culture and the Structure of Authority in Renaissance England* [New York: Methuen, 1985], 119). But even Jonson's own desire for stable textual meaning is played here as a joke. See Joseph Loewenstein's "The Script in the Marketplace," *Representations* 12 (1985), 101–14.

29. Peter Stallybrass and Allon White, *The Politics and Poetics of Transgression* (Ithaca: Cornell University Press, 1986), 66. See also Michael McCanles, "Festival in Jonsonian Comedy," *Renaissance Drama* ns 8 (1977): 203–19, and Jonathan Haynes, "Festivity and the Dramatic Economy of Jonson's *Bartholomew Fair*," *ELH* 51 (1984): 645–68.

30 Jonas Barish, in his *Ben Jonson and the Language of Prose Comedy* ([1960; rpt. New York: W. W. Norton and Co., 1970], 189), notes that "*Bartholomew Fair* ... cuts a deep cross-section through almost the whole social hierarchy, and dissects out the fibers of weird jargon that compose its linguistic tissue ... [It] collects onto the stage a loose aggregate of social types, ranging from two gentlemen through the various strata of the citizenry represented by a proctor and his wife, a Puritan elder, and a city magistrate, to the polyglot swarm of swindlers who inhabit the Fair and prey on its visitors."

31. Bakhtin discusses heteroglossia – the internal differentiation within contextualized language – in *The Dialogic Imagination*, Michael Holquist, ed., Caryl Emerson and Michael Holquist, trans. (Austin: University of Texas Press, 1981). Paula Carin Blank notes that "Renaissance authors invoke linguistic difference in protest to a court standard – the 'rules' that governed matters of language, literature, or policy" in her "Broken English: The Uses of Dialect in Renaissance English Literature," unpublished Ph.D. thesis, Harvard University, 1991, 247. Heteroglossia is used to signify social and political heterogeneity.

32. See chapters 1 and 6 especially here.

Index

Adams, Simon 60–61, 258n22
addled parliament 2
Adelman, Janet 132, 133, 252n28, 254nn45–50,
  255nn63, 64, 68, 256nn72, 84, 85
Aers, David 42–43
Akrigg, G. P. V. 233n1, 258n23
Alpers, Paul 54
Anne of Denmark, Queen (wife of James)
  55–56
  and Elizabethan legacy 74, 154, 165–66, 184,
  240n21, 259n37
  independence from James 98, 166
  as patron 73–75, 98, 166
Archer, Ian W. 363n73, 265nn2, 4, 6, 8, 10
Aristotle 256n77
Armstrong, Archie 124
Armstrong, W. A. 248n77
Ashton, Robert 185, 216, 266n16
Aston, Sir Roger 90
Aubrey, John 218
Axton, Marie 252n31
Ayres, Philip 104–04

Babington, Thomas, Lord Macauley 233n34
Bacon, Sir Francis 92, 93, 100, 113
  Advancement of Learning 29–30, 32, 38, 41
  "In Felicem Memoriam Elizabethae"
  159–64
Baines, Barbara J. 263n75
Bakhtin, Mikhail 227, 273n31
Barber, C. L. 116, 254n52
Barish, Jonas 247n53, 272n20, 273n30
Barroll, J. Leeds 148, 232n29, 260n40
Barton, Anne 257n2
Bates, John 190
Beaumont, Francis 60
Bedford, Countess of, *see* Harrington, Lucy
Beier, A. L. 264n1
Bel-Védere 23, 235n25
Bergeron, David M. 236n42, 260n41, 262n68,
  267nn37, 42, 44, 45, 268nn51, 54

Bevington, David 10, 248n76
Blank, Paula Carin 273n30
Bliss, Lee 66, 259n34
Blount, Charles, Earl of Devonshire 245n19
Bodenham, John 23
Bodin, Jean: *The Six Bookes of a Commonweale* 119
Bolton, Edmund 246n38
Book of Bounty 249n3
Bordieu, Pierre 234n11
Botero, Giovanni 200
bounty 115–49
  as an ideal of monarchy 11, 115–24, 230n13
  and corruption 149
  Elizabeth and 124
  James and 115, 116, 119, 121, 123–24
Bradbrook, M. C. 199, 267n37
Braden, Gordon 86
Bradford, Alan 246n38, 247n56
Bradley, A. C. 136–37
Brady, Jennifer 236n46
Brink, Jean R. 242n53
Brinkley, Roberta F. 258n17
Bristol, Michael 241n44, 272n28
Britain's Bourse 190–91
Brooke, Sir Henry, Lord Cobham 247n54
Brown, Meg Lota 237n60
Browne, William 80
Bruster, Douglas 215, 268n62
Buc, Sir George: *Daphnis Polystephanos* 240n29
Buckingham, Duke of, *see* Villiers, George
Bulkeley, Edward 158–59, 264n89
Bullen, A. H. 268n55
Bullough, Geoffrey 248n71
Burt, Richard 226, 270n2, 272n19
Bushnell, Rebecca 112, 144–45, 249n81
Butler, Martin 241n36, 243n66, 246n34, 265n3
Butter, Nathanael 173
Bynum, Caroline Walker 119

Cabinet Counsel, The 83
Cain, Thomas H. 233n8

Camden, William: *Annales Rerum Anglicarum et Hibernicarum Regnante Elizabetha* 162–64, 177
Campbell, Sir Thomas 201–03
Capp, Bernard 266n21
Carew, Sir George 162
Carew, Thomas 250n9
Carey, John 145, 237nn56, 60
Carleton, Dudley 245n20, 259n37
Carr, Robert, Earl of Somerset 3, 167, 186
Caxton, William 182
Cecil, Robert, Earl of Salisbury 7, 37–39, 85–90, 107, 190–91, 249n3
Cecil, William, Lord Burghley 175
Chamberlain, John 28, 64, 245n20, 259n37
Chambers, E. K. 247n50, 262n62
Chapman, George 60, 86
  Conspiracy of Charles, Duke of Byron 262n62
  Eastward Ho (w/ Marston and Jonson) 90
Charles I, King 51, 113, 117, 124, 163
Charleton, H. B. 244n13
Chaucer, Geoffrey 29
Chaudhuri, Sukanta 238n11, 241n45, 243n65
Chettle, Henry: *Englandes Mourning Garment* 17, 58–59
Children of the Queen's Revels 86, 98
Chrimes, S. B. 244n2
city comedy 210, 211–15
Clare, Janet 98
Clark, Arthur Melville 262n67, 264n90
Clark, Stuart 255n67
Clode, Charles 266n27, 29, 31, 32
Clothworkers Company 194
Cockayne William 2–3, 216
Cohen, Walter 268n61
Coke, Sir Edward 271n10
Colie, Rosalie 254n52
Comes, Natalis 63
Cook, Ann Jennalie 265n3
Cooke, Joshua: *Greene's Tu Quoque* 212, 214–15
Cormack, Lesley B. 261n50
Cotton, Sir Robert 162, 236n52
Council, Norman 261n58
counsel 11, 83–114
  Elizabeth and 91
  Jacobean crisis of 83–84, 88–93
  traditional importance of 83–84
court culture 8–9, 15–16, 38–39, 49
Craig, Alexander 156
Craigie, James 234nn15, 20, 21
Crane, Mary Thomas 245n28
Craven, Sir William 203
Cromwell, Oliver 187
Cuddy, Neil 91, 245nn22, 23
Cullen, Patrick 238n6

Curtius, Ernst Robert 29

Daniel, Samuel 67, 98
  Civile Wars 16, 25
  Panegyric Congratulatory 25–26, 156
  Philotas 11, 78, 85–93, 106, 111, 114
  The Queenes Arcadia 10, 73–80
  Tethys' Festival 166–67, 171, 268n50
  A Vision of the Twelve Goddesses 165, 171
Davies, Sir John – "The Kinges Welcome" 30–33, 35, 37, 49
Davis, Natalie Zemon 251n25
Davis, Walter 78
Day, John: *The Isle of Gulls* 98, 242n50
Dekker, Thomas
  The Dead Tearme 197–98
  The Honest Whore, pt. 1 212, 214–15
  The Magnificent Entertainment Given to King James 157, 201, 205
  The Shoemakers' Holiday 191–93
  Troia-Nova Triumphans 205–08, 210
  The Whore of Babylon 171, 173, 179–84
Deloney, Thomas: *Jack of Newbury* 191, 193, 205
Devereux, Robert, 2nd Earl of Essex 85–89, 99, 107, 160, 167, 183, 245n19
Devereux, Robert, 3rd Earl of Essex 3
disguised duke plays 95, 246n44, 271–72n16
Doelman, James 235n31
Dollimore, Jonathan 135, 232n31, 248n74
Donne, John 9, 223
  ambivalence about court 40–47
  and Jacobean modes of address 39–49
  Pseudo-Martyr 40–41, 44, 45
  "The Sunne Rising" 45–47
  Verse Epistles 42–45, 47–48
Doran, Madeline 262n67
Drake, Sir Francis 183
Draper, John 252n31, 255n60
Drayton, Michael 9, 28–29, 37, 80
  "Ballad of Agincourt" 168
  Eclogues of 10, 67–75, 78–80
  "Paeon Triumphal" 260n42
  Poly-Olbion 168–69
  "To The Majestie of King James" 156
Dudley, Robert, Earl of Leicester 167
Dugdale, Gilbert: *The Time Triumphant* 192–93
Dutton, Richard 244n12, 245n19, 247nn46, 51, 54, 252n31, 256n89

Edward III, King 194
Eedes, Richard 142
Elizabeth I, Queen of England
  coronation of 172–74, 192, 208
  dedications to 24
  funeral of 155

"Golden Speech" 174
and Lady Macbeth 137
maternality and bounty 124, 133
and militarism 157–58, 160–63, 165–72, 176, 178, 183, 186
modes of praise for 16–17, 54–55, 61, 68, 257n7
nostalgia for 12, 61, 68, 71–73, 76, 153–87
persona in London 12, 154, 172–84, 189–90, 192–93, 195, 196, 200, 209–10
poetry of 233n4
and politics of access 90–91
stateliness of 195
Elton, William 254n52
England's Helicon 241n45
Englands Parnassus 235n25
Erickson, Peter 127, 254n47, 255n63
Erskine, Sir Thomas 91
Essex revolt
and Jacobean court factions 85, 89, 106–07
treated in drama 85–89, 99, 248n65
Essex, Earl of, *see* Devereux, Robert
Evans, Robert C. 236n49, 248n63

Fairfax, Edward 241–42n46
Faringdon, Nicholas 204
Ferguson, Arthur B. 244n4, 260n45
Ferry, Anne 239n13
Fields, Nathaniel 60
Finkelpearl, Philip 63, 232n29, 241n37, 247n48
Fish, Stanley 38, 41
Fisher, F. J. 265n3
Fitz-Alwine, Henry 204
Fletcher, Giles 80
Fletcher, John
Henry VIII (w/ Shakespeare) 164–65
The Faithful Shepherdess 10, 59–67
Fletcher, Phineas 29, 32, 58, 80
Fletcher, Robert: *The Nine English Worthies* 260n42
Form of Apology and Satisfaction 89
Foster, Frank Freeman 265n4
Foucault, Michel 3–6, 32, 230n7, 231n18
Foxe, John: *Actes and Monuments* 158–59, 161–62, 176–77, 179–80
Francis I, King of France 121
Freeman, Rosemary 250n9
French, Marilyn 254n50
Freud, Sigmund 251n24
Frye, Susan 230n1
Fulwell, Ulpian: *Ars Adulandi* 94
Fumerton, Patricia 250n13, 253n41

Garber, Marjorie 255n69
Gardiner, Samuel R. 266n17

Gardiner, Steven 177
Garnier, Robert 86
Geertz, Clifford 233n2
Gibbons, Brian 268n62, 272n16
Godyere, Henry: *The Mirrour of Majestie* 74, 119–22, 130
Gohlke, Madelon 254n47
Goldberg, Jonathan 4–6, 15, 19, 32–33, 40, 48, 52, 79, 92–94, 121, 139, 192, 223, 234n12, 236n43, 237n56, 238n69, 254nn61, 65, 263n80, 264n87
Goldsmiths Company 198, 203–05
Goodman, Godfrey 94, 153–55
Goodwin, Sir Francis 7
Gordon, D. J. 178, 250n9, 263n85, 264n87
Gorges, Arthur 167
Gower, John 29, 83
Gowrie conspiracy 183
Graham, Victor E. 251n26
Greenblatt, Stephen 7–8, 230n9, 231n16
Greene, Roland 239n14
Greene, Thomas: *A Poets Vision, and A Princes Glorie* 26–32, 35
Greene, Thomas 38
Greg, W. W. 238–39n11, 242–43n59
Gresham, Thomas 173, 175–76, 189
Greville, Fulke, Lord Brooke 86
Caelica 239n17
A Dedication to Sir Philip Sidney 185–87
Mustapha 11, 106–111, 114
Groom of the Stool 91
Grundy, Joan 80, 243n65
Guarini, Giovanni Battista - *Il Pastor Fido* 67, 76, 242n59
Guillén, Claudio 80
Gunpowder Plot 158–59, 161, 182–83, 226

Haigh, Christopher 258–59n28
Hall, Joseph: *The King's Prophecie* 235n31
Haller, William 158
Halpern, Richard 125, 129, 252n30, 253nn42, 44
Harbert, William: *Prophesie of Cadwallader* 29, 32, 49
Hardin, Richard 241n44
Hardison, O. B., Jr. 235n29
Harington, Sir John 37, 40, 52
Harrington, Lucy, Countess of Bedford 42–45, 242n57
Harrison, Jennifer 267n42
Hawkins, Michael 255n61
Hay, Sir James 90, 119
Haynes, Jonathan 273n29
Heffner, Ray Jr. 218, 223, 227
Heinemann, Margot 269n69

Helgerson, Richard 19–21, 36, 54, 234n65, 272n27
Heninger, S. K. Jr. 258n16
Henri III, King of France 158
Henri IV, King of France 158, 261n61
Henry V, King of England 166, 168, 170
Henry VII 156, 197
Henry VIII 171, 191, 230n1
Henry, Prince of Wales 55, 124, 197–98
  death of 2, 172
  and Elizabethan Legacy 12, 154, 166–72, 184–85
Herbert, Sir Philip, Earl of Montgomery 89–90
Hexter, J. H. 175
Heywood, Thomas
  If You Know Not Me, You Know Nobody
  (pt. 1) 173, 176–77
  (pt. 2) 173–75, 177, 189
  Troia Britanica 182–84
Hill, Christopher 261nn50, 51
Hilliard, Nicholas 124
Hirst, Derek 249n3
Holinshed, Raphael: *Chronicles* 136, 139, 141
Holland, Hugh: *Pancharis* 259n35
Holles, Sir John 167
Holliday, Sir Leonard 200
Holstun, James 231nn11, 17, 19
Homily Against Disobedience and Willful Rebellion 112
Hooke, Henry 156–57
Horace 270–71n5
Howard, Lady Catharine, Countess of Salisbury 47
Howard, Lady Frances 3
Howard, Henry, Earl of Northampton 7, 107, 247n54
Huet, Marie Hélène 256n78
Hunter, G. K. 244n4

Ironmongers Company 201–03

Jaggard, William 205
James I and VI, King of England and Scotland
  and *arcana imperii* 75, 91, 93–95, 104, 179–81
  attitudes toward drama 7, 148
  attitudes toward Elizabeth I 155–56
  and *Bartholomew Fair* 12, 219–29
  Basilikon Doron 18, 19, 24, 25, 34, 91, 112, 236n43
  bedchamber of 89–91
  and Bible translation 234n22
  contrast w/ Elizabeth I 1, 9–12, 17–18, 24, 49, 51, 90–92, 115, 123–24, 153, 157–65,
    168–72, 177–87, 190, 192–93, 195, 209–10
  and counsel 83–86, 88–93, 103–07, 111–14
  Counterblaste to Tobacco 74, 219
  Daemonologie 24
  dedications to 24
  relations w/ Parliament 2, 7, 89, 94–95, 156–57, 186, 219
  Essays of A Prentise 18–24, 31, 75, 178
  entry into London 34, 157, 159, 172, 192, 201, 205
  figured in *The Fawne* 95, 98
  figured in *King Lear* 124–25
  figured in *Mustapha* 107, 110
  figured in pastoral 51–52, 58–59, 63–64
  first speech in Parliament 94–95, 156–57
  gift-giving and bounty 115, 119–20, 123–24, 164, 249n3
  and Gunpowder Plot propaganda 158–59, 161, 182–83, 226
  and Hampton Court Conference 178
  and Henry's popularity 172
  historical reputation of 48, 115, 232–33n34
  interest in de Thou's *Historiae* 162–63
  and knighthoods 216
  and Law Courts 190, 220
  modes of praise for 24–36, 69, 156–59
  paralleled to Tiberius 93–94, 103–04
  Poetical Exercises 19, 235n25
  poetry of 9, 18–24, 51–53
  public relations problems 3, 7, 73, 79–80, 153–55, 163–64, 172, 184–87, 193, 196–99, 216–17, 226–27
  and puritans 218
  and recreation 64
  relations w/ London 183–84, 192–210, 215–17
  reunification of Britain 125, 156–57, 162–63, 200
  as *Rex Pacificus* 157, 160–61, 164–65, 168, 178–79, 182–83, 185–86, 200
  Scottish entourage and favorites 89–91, 115, 125, 153, 186, 249n3
  Trew Law of Free Monarchies 24, 112, 130, 250n11
  uses of Elizabethan legacy 154–57
  ventriloquized 7
  and witchcraft 137–38

Jardine, Lisa 239n16
John, King of England 204–05
Johnson, Richard
  Looke On Me London 220–21, 227
  The Pleasant Conceits of Old Hobson 211
Jones, Ann Rosalind 8
Jones, Emrys 265n5

Jones, Inigo 169, 171, 181, 261n58
Jones, W. J. 271n10
Jonson, Ben 9, 48–49, 60, 86, 181, 194, 235n25
  Althorpe Entertainment 52, 55–57, 60, 67, 73, 77
  Bartholomew Fair 12, 218–27
  Christmas, His Masque 216
  Discoveries 106
  Eastward Ho (w/ Chapman and Marston) 90
  Epigrammes 35–39
  Hymenaei 178, 208
  and James entry into London 34, 157, 263n85
  Masque of Beauty 208
  Masque of Blackness 208, 260n39
  Oberon 171–72
  Pan's Anniversary 243n66
  "Panegyre" 33–35, 38
  Sejanus 11, 98–106, 109, 111, 114
  Speeches at Prince Henry's Barriers 169–71
  strategies of address 32–39, 48–49, 104–06, 225–27, 270–71n5

Kahn, Coppélia 115–16, 123, 130, 143–44, 253–54n45, 254n47
Kamholtz, Jonathan Z. 236n45
Kastner, L. F. 244n13
Kenyon, J. P. 231n22
Kimbrough, Robert 251n20
King, John N. 257n2, 259n32
Kirk, Florence Ada 240n30
Kistner, A. L. 269n69
Kistner, M. L. 269n69
Knights, L. C. 210, 262n66
Knolles, Richard 119
Knowles, James 199, 267n47
Kress, Gunther 42–43
Kurland, Stuart M. 245n30, 259n34

Lake, Peter 231n19
Lang, R. G. 188–89
Lanyer, Aemilia: *Salve Deus Rex Judeorum* 242n54
Laqueur, Thomas 143, 256nn76–78
Lee, Sir Henry 167
Lee, Maurice Jr. 231n20, 232n34
Leech, Clifford 63
Leggatt, Alexander 268n62
Leicester, Earl of, *see* Dudley, Robert
Leigh, William: *Queen Elizabeth, Paraleld* 173
Leinwand, Theodore B. 199, 211, 231n24, 232n26, 252n29, 267n37, 268n62
Lentricchia, Frank 230n9
Lepanto, battle of 183
Lever, Christopher: *Queen Elizabeth's Tears* 173, 177, 180

Lever, J. W. 248n61
Levin, Richard 272n24
Levine, Jay Arnold 237n62
Levy, F. J. 83, 85
Lewalski, Barbara K. 41–42, 259n35, 260nn38–40
Lobanov-Rostovsky, Sergei 268n58
Loewenstein, Joseph 272n28
London
  as *camera regia* 200, 204
  civic pride 12, 175–76, 189–90, 192, 194–217
  Corporation of 175, 185
  elite of 175–76, 188–91, 193–96, 198–211, 215–17
  heterogeneity of 188
  nostalgia for Elizabeth in 11–12, 154, 172–85, 187
  plague in 221, 267n41
  relations with king and court 12, 184–85, 187–217
Lord Mayors' pageants 12, 199–210
Lydgate, John 29

Macauley, *see* Babington, Thomas
MacCaffrey, Wallace 55, 258n27
McCanles, Michael 237n54, 272n29
McCoy, Richard 260n45
McCullough, Peter 257–58n112
MacDougall, Hugh A. 258n16
McEachern, Claire 253n36
Macherey, Pierre 50–52, 57, 60, 67, 69, 79
Machin, Lewes: "Eclogue of Menalcas and Daphnis" 243n60
Mack, Phyllis 251n25
McLuskie, Kathleen E. 262n66, 263n81
McMullan, Gordon 241n39
McPherson, David 220–21, 235n25, 271n11, 272nn12, 14
Manning, Gillian 271n8
Mantuan 80
Marcelline, George: *The Triumphs of King James* 260n42
Marcus, Leah 57–58, 94, 137, 220, 223, 230n1, 231n16, 241n33, 252–53n31, 253nn32, 34, 42, 254n51, 270n75, 271n6
Marlowe, Christopher: *Edward II* 112
Marotti, Arthur 41, 43–44, 238n69, 239n17
Marston, John
  Antonio and Mellida 84, 142
  Eastward Ho (w/ Chapman and Jonson) 90
  The Fawne 93–98, 114
  The Malcontent 95
Martial 36–37
Mary Stuart, Queen of Scots 138, 155, 162–63, 183

Mary Tudor, Queen 159, 161, 173, 189–90, 230n1

Maurer, Margaret 237nn60, 62

Maus, Katharine Eisaman 106, 239n13

May, Stephen W. 235n24

Merchant Adventurers 175

Merchant Taylors Company 12, 193–98, 200–01, 206–07, 211, 267n46

Meyer, Barbara Hochstetler 251n19

Michel, Laurence 88

Middleton, Sir Thomas 207, 220–21

Middleton, Thomas
  Michaelmas Term 212–15
  The Phoenix 95
  The Triumphs of Truth 207–08, 210

Millard, Barbara C. 254–55n58

Molin, Nicolo 177, 193

Monmouth, Geoffrey of 157–58

Montrose, Louis Adrian 5, 17, 53, 239n18, 252n27, 263n78

More, Sir Thomas: *Utopia* 85

Moretti, Franco 114, 232n32

Morley, Henry 271n10, 272n14

Muir, Kenneth 252n30, 256n73

Mullaney, Steven 255n61, 269n71

Munday, Anthony
  A Brief Chronicle, of the Successe of Times 196–99
  Camp-bell 201–03
  Chruso-thriambos 203–05
  The Triumphes of Re-United Britannia 200–01, 207, 208

Munden, R. C. 7

Neale, J. E. 252n2, 266nn69, 70, 264n99

Neville, Sir Henry 161

new historicism 3–8

Newdigate, Bernard H. 242n52, 257n11

Newman, Karen 269n68

Norbrook, David 45, 231n17, 237n56, 243n65, 255n61, 262n64

O'Connell, Laura Stevenson 265n11, 266n19

Orgel, Stephen 181, 261n61, 261–62n62

Ornstein, Robert 84, 105

Overbury, Sir Thomas 3

panegyric: theories of 25–26, 41–42, 92–93

Parry, Graham 236n42, 258n13, 261n50

Parry, William 161, 179

Paster, Gail Kern 267n37, 268n53

pastoral 9–10, 50–80
  Elizabethan popularity of 53
  Elizabethan uses of 53–59, 63, 68, 74–75, 78–79, 239nn16, 18
  and Jacobean plain style 57, 69, 241–42n46

Jacobean political ideas in 51–53, 57–59, 64–66, 71–73, 77–78, 240n29
  social commentary in 53–55, 70–71, 73, 75–76, 78–80
  tradition 238n6
  uses of inwardness in 53–59, 62–63, 69–70

Patterson, Annabel 40, 53, 104, 178, 247nn52–53, 252nn28, 29, 252–53n31, 253nn32, 34, 256n88

Paul, Henry N. 255n60

Peacham, Sir Henry: *Minerva Britanna* 250n4, 260n42

Peacock, John 261n58

Pearl, Valerie 189, 265n27

Peck, Linda Levy 149, 247n49, 249nn2, 4, 251n18

Peele, George: *Descensus Astraeae* 200

Pemberton, Sir James 203–04

Pembroke, Countess of, see Sidney, Mary

Peterson, Robert 200

Pett, Phineas 167

Pettingall, John 271n10

Platter, Thomas 266n30

Pocock, J. G. A. 74, 244nn3, 4, 245n31

Popham, Lord Chief Justice 7

Puttenham, George: *The Arte of English Poesie* 16, 27, 55, 75

Ralegh, Sir Walter 83, 88, 167, 247n54

Ralegh, Wat 260n49

Rebholz, Ronald 107, 186, 248nn66–69, 72

Rees, Joan 235n29, 242nn57, 59

Richard, I, King 204–04

Richards, Nathanael 247n56

Riggs, David 240n21, 247n50

Ripa, Cesare: *Iconologia* 116–18, 250n10

Rollins, Hyder E. 265n12

Rosenberg, Marvin 136, 254nn54, 55

Rosenmeyer, Thomas G. 238n6

Royall Passage of Her Majesty From the Tower to White-Hall 172

Rubens, Peter Paul 117–18, 250n12

Russell, Conrad 244n11, 249n2

Saint Bartholomew's Day massacre 158

Salisbury, Earl of, *see* Cecil, Robert

Salmon, J. H. M. 247n55

Saunders, J. W. 257n10

Scaramelli, Giovanni Carlo 83–84, 90, 155

Schmidgal, Gary 230n2

Schwarz, Marc L. 232n34

Seldon, John 261n55

Shakespeare, William 67
  As You Like It 76, 78
  comic heroines of 61

Henry V 256n73
Henry VIII (w/ Fletcher) 164–65
and James I 11, 115–16, 123–25, 137–39,
147–49
King Lear 11, 123–38, 140, 146, 148–49
Macbeth 11, 123, 137–49
Measure For Measure 23, 95
A Midsummer Night's Dream 65
Richard II 112
Timon of Athens 115–16, 121–23, 244n9
Winter's Tale 77, 91–92
Sharpe, Kevin 231n19, 232n34, 233n4, 234n22,
236n52
Sharpham, Edward: *The Fleer* 95
Shuger, Debora Kuller 250n11
Sidney, Mary, Countess of Pembroke 86
Sidney, Sir Philip 29, 36, 67, 71, 167–68,
185–87
Old Arcadia 53, 54, 242n50
Siegel, Paul N. 192, 264n93
Sinfield, Alan 255n61, 256n86
Smuts, R. Malcolm 243n63, 257n2, 258n22,
259n33
Somerset, Earl of, see Carr, Robert
Sorocold, Thomas: *Supplications of Saints* 173
"Sorrowes Joy", 58, 235n34
Spanish Armada, defeat of 160, 173, 176, 179,
180, 182, 183
Speculum Principis tradition in drama 105, 112
Spedding, James 258n20
Spencer, Sir Robert 56
Spenser, Edmund 29, 36, 67
The Fairie Queene 56, 171, 240–41n32, 241n35,
254n57
The Shepheardes Calendar 17, 53, 54, 67, 242n48
Spenserian poets 80, 262n64
Spikes, Judith Doolin 257n2
Spufford, Margaret 266n21
Stallybrass, Peter 263–64n86, 273n29
Stone, Lawrence 251n17, 265nn3, 5, 266n18,
270n72
Stow, John: *The Survey of London* 175, 189–91,
205, 211, 267n36
Strathman, Ernest A. 244n5
Strong, Roy 167–68, 170, 181, 233–34n10,
260nn41, 44, 46–48, 261nn50, 54, 58–61,
262n63
Sturgess, Keith 270n4
Suetonius 270–71n5
Supple, B. E. 230n3, 264n92, 270n73
Swinnerton, Sir John 205–06

Tacitus 93, 103, 106, 144, 246n59
Tasso, Torquato 242n59
Tawney, R. H. 270n73

Taylor, Gary 252n30, 253n32
Tennenhouse, Leonard 230n2, 246n44, 255n63
Thayer, C. G. 271n6
Thompson, E. P. 5, 6, 231n18
Thou, Jacques-Auguste de: *Historiae Sui
Temporis* 162–63
Tilley, Morris Palmer 246n40
Tragedie of Claudius Tiberius Nero 111
Trevelyan, G. M. 249n1
Trevor-Roper, H. R. 187, 258nn26, 27
Tricomi, Albert 88, 103–04, 109, 246n44,
247n46, 248n75
True Chronicle Historie of King Leir 127–36
*True Narration of the Entertainment of his Royal
Majestie* 30
Tylus, Jane 242n49
tyranny and legitimacy 111–14

Underdown, David 240n48
Unwin, George 211, 263n72, 269n71

Venuti, Lawrence 268n61
Villiers, George, Duke of Buckingham 51, 89
Virgil 53, 238n6, 242n51

Waage, Frederick O. 264n89
Waddington, Raymond B. 251n20
Waith, Eugene M. 272n23
Watts, Sir John 194–97
Wedgwood, C. V. 187, 250n12, 262n70
Weeks, Jeffrey 3
Weldon, Anthony 93–94, 257n1
Wells, Susan 268nn57, 61
Wheeler, Richard 249n7, 254n52
Whetstone, George: *A Mirour for Magistrates of
Cyties* 221
Whigham, Frank 39
White, Allon 273n29
White, Hayden 5
Whittier, Gayle 254n47, 255n58
Whittington, Dick 189, 265n12
Wickham, Glynne 208, 209, 252n28
Williams, Ethel Carleton 259n37
Williams, Franklin B. 235n26
Williams, George Walton 255n60
Williams, Raymond 10–11, 52, 154, 186,
232n33
Williamson, Jerry Wayne 260nn41, 48, 49,
261nn51, 58, 262nn62, 63
Wills, Garry 255n60
Willson, David Harris 249n1, 272n26
Wilson, Arthur 93–94, 192, 266n23
Wilson, Elkin Calhoun 252n27, 260n41,
261n56
Wiltenburg, Robert 239n49

Wilton group 86, 106
Wither, George 80
Witherspoon, Alexander M. 244n13
Wittreich, Joseph 254n52
Woolf, D. R. 163, 257n3, 258nn24, 27
Wormald, Jenny 94, 232n34, 245n25
Wright, Louis B. 262n65, 264n92, 266n15

Wright, Pam 245n24

Yachnin, Paul 269n69
Yates, Frances 257nn2, 7
Yoch, James 61, 63

Ziegler, Georgianna 263n75